There are powerful word images in these pages you may not have heard from evangelicals in a while—Christian community development; a gospel that is both vertical and horizontal; a foreign mission field on our urban doorstep; wholistic ministry.

Other word pictures will be more familiar and less frightening—Jewish evangelism; ministry in the jails and to urban youth.

May God bless the reader as he discovers and rediscovers the challenge behind all these words and through grace transforms image into reality, word into deed.

Dr. Harvie M. Conn
Professor of Missions Emeritus
Westminster Theological Seminary

A Heart for the City is one of the most important books I have read on urban ministry. Each chapter is written by leaders and practitioners from every major field of the urban church. This volume provides vision, inspiration, philosophy, and practical advice for fulfilling the Great Commission in contemporary urban America.

Dr. Lyle W. Dorsett
Professor of Evangelism
Wheaton College and Graduate School

A Heart for the City is a harvesting of the richest insights of some of the nation's most effective contemporary urban ministry practitioners. Writing from hard-learned personal experience, these frontline veterans share important truths that are foundational for any who would venture into the urban frontier.

Dr. Robert D. Lupton, Executive Director
FCS Urban Ministries

This anthology on urban ministry will be of value to everyone with a heart for the urgent needs of our inner cities. Drawing on the legacy of D. L. Moody and the Moody Bible Institute which he founded, A Heart for the City issues a call for conservative Christians to reclaim our cities for God. The selections provide the theoretical, educational, and practical ministry to guide us in this endeavor. May it be used to motivate and equip God's people to more effective ministry in our urban centers.

Dr. Keith Phillips
President
World Impact, Inc.

D1449142

Urban ministry workers can never get enough of materials which blend the practical with the reflective, and this book provides a welcome addition to the literature. With its Chicago-Moody Bible Institute focus, the book's heart practically beats in the reader's hands. Dr. John Fuder and the writers have written a book which we'll all want to add to our shelf of texts to reach for when questions arise.

Dr. Judith Lingenfelter
Associate Professor of Intercultural Studies
Biola University
School of Intercultural Studies

God has a heart for the city, but often the church does not. Read this book and your heart for the urban mission frontier will grow.

Dr. Roger S. Greenway
Professor of World Missiology
Calvin Theological Seminary

For years I have yearned for a practical, "transferable," and at the same time, biblical guide to urban ministry. A Heart for the City is the answer to that prayer. The authors are not armchair theorists . . . they are servants of the Lord who share with us out of compassionate hearts for the city and successful models of ministry as examples of the transforming power of Christ for hurting people. This book will equip you to do the same.

Dr. Crawford W. Lorritts Jr.
Author, Speaker
Associate U.S. Director
Campus Crusade for Christ

A HEART FOR THE CITY

effective ministries to the urban community

JOHN FUDER
GENERAL EDITOR

MOODY PUBLISHERS
CHICAGO

To the urban churches and ministries in Chicago
that are equally worthy of these pages,
but whose stories exceed its capacity;

and to many other Moody alumni faithfully serving
in this city and metropolitan areas around the world

—this book is respectfully dedicated,
with the prayer that your lives and programs
will always reflect
the challenging balance
of exegeting Scripture and culture alike.

ABOUT THE AUTHOR

JOHN FUDER (Ph.D., Biola University) is currently a professor at The Moody Bible Institute's Graduate School in the heart of Chicago. He spent twelve years with City Team Ministries in San Jose, California, and two years with Impact Ministries in Chicago. For his doctoral research he worked with people on Skid Row in Los Angeles.

Dr. Fuder lives in Chicago's Edgewater community with his wife, Nel, and their three children.

CONTENTS

ABOUT THE
CONTRIBUTORS

Michael N. Allen is an Assistant Pastor at Moody Memorial Church, in the areas of discipleship and urban outreach. Born in Jamaica, his family immigrated to the United States when he was a boy. Michael has an extensive background in Evangelism Explosion and completed the M.Div. in Urban Ministry at Trinity International University. He and his Brazilian wife, Marla, have a son and a daughter and live in Rogers Park, on the North Side of Chicago.

Brian Bakke is a lifelong resident of the Uptown neighborhood on the North Side of Chicago. Since 1987 he has been on the staff of Uptown Baptist Church, where he is Director of Community Ministries and New Flight Art Ministry. Brian serves as an overseer of the church's homeless, street, and compassion ministries. He also coordinates a summer basketball evangelism league that brings together area churches to witness of Christ with at-risk youth and gang members. Brian and his wife, Lisa, have been married since 1991.

Raymond J. Bakke is Executive Director of International Urban Associates, a network of church and mission leaders seeking to empower God's people in the largest cities of the world. Ray pastored inner city churches in Seattle and Chicago for more than twenty years and is a co-founder of the Seminary Consortium for Urban Pastoral Education. He served as Senior Associate for Large Cities with the Lausanne Com-

mittee for World Evangelism for seventeen years. He has written numerous books and articles on urban ministry and taught at several
seminaries. He is currently Professor of Global Urban Ministry at Eastern Baptist Theological Seminary in Philadelphia. Ray lives with his
wife, Corean, on the North Side of Chicago.

Raouf Boulos, originally from Egypt, is the Founder and Director of
the Arabic Ministries Department at the Pacific Garden Mission, where
he has served nine years. He earned an MABS from the Moody Bible
Institute, where he teaches on Islam in the extension studies department. He and his wife, Denise, have two sons and live on the North
Side of Chicago.

David C. Brown founded Gospel Outreach in 1987 after serving for
more than twenty years with Sunshine Gospel Ministries. In addition
to serving as Gospel Outreach's director in the Robert Taylor homes,
he also leads the children's ministries at Glen Ellyn Evangelical
Covenant Church in Glen Ellyn, Illinois. David is a Moody graduate
and completed the M.A. in Urban Ministries from Trinity International
University. He and his wife, Ann, have two sons.

Sunday Bwanhot is an ECWA missionary partnering with SIM USA
and ministering to African immigrants on the North Side of Chicago.
Sunday and his wife, Grace, came to America with a rich ministry
background of more than a decade with the Evangelical Church of
West Africa. He completed an M.A. in Theology from ECWA Theological Seminary in Jos, Nigeria. The Bwanhots began Goodnews Evangelical Church in the Uptown community and have committed to a
second four-year term in Chicago. They have three boys and live in the
Rogers Park community on the North Side.

Noel Castellanos is the Founding Pastor of LaVillita (Little Village)
Community Church on the West Side of Chicago and the Chairman of
the Board of the LaVillita Christian Development Corporation. He is
also the Vice President of the Christian Community Development Association (CCDA). His passion is the training of Hispanic leaders on a
national scale. He also serves as the President of the Latino Leadership
Network and consults for the DeVos Urban Leadership Initiative. He
and his wife, Marianne, have two sons and a daughter and live in the
LaVillita community.

William Paul Dillon is the Founder and has been Executive Director of Inner City Impact for more than twenty-five years. His family has been an integral part of urban ministry in Chicago for three generations. Bill has written a book on support fund-raising and does fund-raising and management consulting through Resource Management Consultants. He is a graduate of Moody and Elmhurst College and earned his M.B.A. from Murray State University. He and his wife, Sandy, have three children.

Chad Erlenborn has ministered among refugees on three different continents over the past six years. The majority of his ministry was with World Relief Chicago. A graduate of Bethel College, where he met his wife, Christine, Chad is currently working toward a M.Div. from Trinity International University.

James Ford Jr. has been the pastor of South Shore Baptist Church for seventeen years and is the President and Founder of Impact Ministries. He is a Moody graduate and adjunct professor, and his weekly messages from the pulpit are aired over WMBI and across the country. He is currently working on his Master's degree from Trinity International University. He is married to Leslie. They have three sons and live in the South Shore community on Chicago's South Side.

John E. Fuder has been teaching at Moody Graduate School for the past five years. He spent twelve years with City Team Ministries in San Jose, California, and two years with Impact Ministries in Chicago. In between he received a Ph.D. from Biola University and did his doctoral research in Skid Row in Los Angeles. He lives in the Edgewater community on the North Side of Chicago with his wife, Nel, and their three children.

Wayne L. Gordon is the founder and has been pastor of Lawndale Community Church and its related ministries of healthcare and development on the West Side of Chicago for more than twenty years. "Coach" Gordon also helped to formulate the Christian Community Development Association. The Lawndale story has been told in a recent book written by Wayne, and the church received a "Point of Light" award from President Bush in 1989. Wayne is currently working on a D.Min. at Eastern Baptist Theological Seminary in Philadelphia. He and his wife, Anne, are raising their three children in the Lawndale community.

Brad Grammer founded and led Face-to-Face Ministries, an outreach of Breakthrough Urban Ministries in Chicago, for five years. His ministry included evangelistic outreach in the gay bars on the North Side and to men struggling with homosexuality and/or AIDS incarcerated at the Cook County Jail in Chicago. Brad moved to Indianapolis to become director of Hope & New Life Ministry in 1998. He and his wife, Laura, have two children.

Marc Henkel has been a partner with Milton Massie for a decade in the ministry of racial reconciliation. Marc came to the Agape Community Center in 1989. Marc and his wife, Sandy, both graduated from Wheaton College, and Marc is currently a M.A.Min. student in the Moody Graduate School. His family lives in the Roseland community, on the South Side of Chicago, where the Agape Community Center is located.

Mark Jobe is Pastor of New Life Community Church, which began twelve years ago and has four satellite congregations, in both English and Spanish. This young, multiethnic church has more than seventy home groups meeting throughout the city and suburbs. Mark earned a M.A.Min. from the Moody Bible Institute, and he and his wife, Dee, have three children.

Glen A. Kehrein was the Founder of Circle Urban Ministries and has been the Executive Director for more than twenty-five years. Glen is a graduate of Moody and Wheaton College, and was also the first of two Americans to receive the Doctor of Peacemaking degree granted by Westminster College in 1997. Glen has co-authored a Moody Publishers book, with Raleigh Washington, on racial reconciliation, and he continues to travel and speak extensively on that subject. He and his wife, Lonni, have raised their son and two daughters in the Austin community on the West Side of Chicago.

Lonni Kehrein is the Administrator of Circle-Rock Preparatory School. She has spent the past twenty-six years in the Austin community on Chicago's West Side, with her husband Glen, developing the outreach ministries of Circle Urban Ministries and Rock of our Salvation Evangelical Free Church. A graduate of the Chicago Musical College of Roosevelt University, Lonni is certified in Music and Special Education. The Kehreins have three children.

Russ Knight is the President of the Chicago Urban Reconciliation Enterprise. A Moody graduate, he served almost eighteen years with Youth for Christ in the Chicagoland area. He has contributed to several books and articles and is a past president of the National Black Evangelical Association. He and his wife, Bethany, have three children and live on the South Side of Chicago.

Phil Kwiatkowski is Vice President of Ministries at the Pacific Garden Mission in Chicago, where he has served in various roles since his graduation from Moody more than ten years ago. He has also been the interim pastor at the Belmont Bible Church in Downers Grove, Illinois, for the past two years. Phil and his wife, Ann, have two boys and two girls and live in a western suburb of Chicago.

Tom Locke has been working at Moody for the past six years as the Supervisor of Men's Ministries for the Practical Christian Ministries Department. He served with Youth for Christ for eight years as Outreach Coordinator and as a committed friend to young people involved in gangs. He is a graduate of Moody and lives with his wife, Lisa, and their daughter in a southern suburb of Chicago.

Tom Maluga is the Senior Pastor at Uptown Baptist Church, a position he has held for the past four years. Prior to coming to Chicago he pastored a church in inner city Dallas for ten years, after completing his Th.M. at Dallas Theological Seminary. Tom is married to Carol, and they have two sons and a daughter. They live on the North Side of Chicago.

Len Maselli has been a chaplain with the Good News Jail and Prison Ministry for the past seven years. He began serving at the Cook County Juvenile Detention Center as a Moody undergraduate student on a Practical Christian Ministry assignment. Len evangelizes, disciples, and counsels incarcerated youth ages ten to seventeen and coordinates volunteers from local churches who participate in the services and Bible studies. He and his wife, Debbie, have three boys and live in the western suburbs of Chicago.

Milton Massie has been a partner with Marc Henkel in the ministry of racial reconciliation for a decade. Milton has been involved at the Agape Community Center, which is Campus Crusade for Christ's urban ministry in Chicago, since 1980, and has been the director since 1992. He graduated from Chicago State University, and he and his wife, Cynthia, have two children. They live in the Roseland community, on the South Side of Chicago, where the Agape Community Center is located.

Connie L. Mead is the President and CEO of New Moms, Inc., a position she has held for the past five years. She is a graduate of Bethel College in Indiana and earned her M.B.A. from Loyola University in Chicago. After sixteen years in corporate America, including founding her own business, Connie followed her heart's passion of working with the disadvantaged, accepting God's call to serve with New Moms on the Northwest Side of Chicago. She and her husband, Bob, have a son and a daughter.

Dwight Perry is Professor of Pastoral Studies at the Moody Bible Institute. He has been a pastor and has worked with the Baptist General Conference, first as National Coordinator of Black Ministries and then as Associate Director of Home Missions. He earned a D.Min. from Covington Theological Seminary and a Ph.D. from Trinity International University, in whose M.A. urban ministries program he teaches as an adjunct professor. He and his wife, Cynthia, have four children.

Michael Rydelnik is Professor of Jewish Studies at the Moody Bible Institute, as well as a graduate of that school. The son of Holocaust survivors, he was raised in an Orthodox Jewish home in Brooklyn, New York. He has been ministering to the Jewish community ever since trusting Jesus the Messiah as a high schoool freshman. He was the founding pastor of Olive Tree Congregation in Long Island, New York, and also served for ten years in the leadership of Chosen People Ministries. He earned his B.A. from Azusa Pacific University, his Th.M. from Dallas Theological Seminary, and his D.Miss. from Trinity International University. He and his wife, Eva, have two sons.

Robert C. Smith is an Assistant Professor at the Moody Bible Institute. He has pastored churches in New York and Chicago for more than seventeen years and also served for seven years with the Conservative Baptist Home Mission Society. He is currently working on his Ph.D. in education from Trinity International University. He and his wife, Belinda, have three children.

Joseph M. Stowell is President of the Moody Bible Institute in Chicago. Dr. Stowell is heard on the radio broadcast "Proclaim!" daily. He has written many books. He received his B.A. from Cedarville College, his

Th.M. from Dallas Theological Seminary, and his D.D. from Master's College. He and his wife, Martie, have three children.

Arloa Sutter is the Executive Director of Breakthrough Urban Ministries in Chicago. In 1992, Arloa opened a storefront room owned by the First Evangelical Free Church on Chicago's North Side and began serving coffee and a hot lunch to the street people who were coming to the church for help. She formed a board of directors from the church and community and founded Breakthrough to more effectively meet the needs of the homeless guests. Arloa is a graduate of Moody and has an M.A. in Urban Mission from Lincoln Christian Seminary. She has two daughters.

Dana Thomas leads a ministry committed to bringing the gospel to the public housing projects in Chicago. Dana was born and raised in the inner city of Chicago and is the Executive Director of Sunshine Gospel Ministries in Cabrini-Green. He has been a pastor and is currently involved in planting a church in Dolton, Illinois. He is working on his M.A. in Urban Ministries from Trinity International University and is married to Bridget, with three children.

Michael Tsang serves at the Chinese Christian Union Church (CCUC) in Chicago's Chinatown. Michael was born in Hong Kong and has pastored churches in the Philippines and in Texas prior to assuming the senior pastorate at CCUC three years ago. He has an M.A. from Wheaton College and a D.Min. from Dallas Theological Seminary. He and his wife, Christina, have three children.

David Wu also serves at the Pui Tak Center, the church-based community center established by the Chinese Christian Union Church (CCUC). David is a second-generation Chinese-American and has attended CCUC all his life. He has served as the Executive Director of the Pui Tak Center since it was founded in 1995. He is a Wheaton College graduate and has a Master's degree from the University of North Carolina. He and his wife, Jane, and their son live in Chinatown.

FOREWORD

The astonishing fact of our time is that for the first time in the history of the world, the majority of the world's nearly six billion people live in cities. The greater Chicago metro area is home to 8.4 million people—almost exactly the net population growth of planet Earth *every single month.* Can you imagine 100 million people, or twelve new metropolitan Chicagos, fueling all the other changes on six continents each year?

Imagine a world in motion. We are living at the time of the greatest migration in human history. The Southern Hemisphere is coming north; East is moving west; and many are coming to cities like Chicago on six continents. The 1990 census showed that 51 percent of Americans lived in thirty-nine places, which, like Chicago, have more than one million people. Today about forty (a tithe?) of the world's 400 million-plus cities are in the United States.

A major missiological question for our time, then, is: How can the lessons God is teaching the churches inside the United States' forty world-class cities leverage or influence world missions and evangelism in the four hundred largest cities on this planet where the majority of unreached or unevangelized people now live? The strategic follow-up question is: Why do you suppose our Lord has placed the Moody Bible Institute in the heart of a world-class city laboratory and teaching center and prepared this school since 1886, if not to be an R&D (research and development) unit? The school is uniquely located to prepare a new kind of church leadership for the urban world of the third millennium and until He calls for us.

To many Americans, urbanization is a worrisome thing. Yet believers who read Psalm 24:1 know "the earth is the Lord's" (NASB), and according to Psalm 107:1–8, He often leads desperately needy people to cities. The church has had the Great Commission for nearly two thousand years and has been faithfully going to the ends of the earth to teach, baptize, and disciple all peoples. But, just as it was getting expensive to send us there, God seems to be sending all the people groups to us at their own expense. It is the great bargain in world mission today! The fifty-two nations of the British Empire live in London, the forty-six nations of the Francophone Empire live in Paris, and peoples from 120 nations live in one New York City community.[1] The frontier of mission has shifted to the cities. The greatest number of unreached people is no longer *geographically* distant but rather *culturally* distant. The world is next door in nearly every large- or medium-sized city. More than ever before, the local church can be the global church.

Mission work has always had its frightening side. In the past, missionaries confronted cobras and pythons; today those may be the names of the street gangs in the neighborhood. Incredibly, in the past, and against all odds, missionaries invented written languages, built schools, studied diseases, developed and funded hospitals, and created transportation and communication systems.

Today's cities need no less. The reality in many cities is that many of these systems have broken down. Sin has multiplied and destroyed families and communities. Urban ministries today must do at "home," in our cities, what foreign missions did abroad yesterday, and for the same reasons. Evil principalities and powers have taken over many parts of cities where the church either never existed or fled for various reasons.

Jesus is still the message and the model for urban ministry. "The Word became flesh" (John 1:14 NASB) in Galilee and calls the church to "occupy till I come" (Luke 19:13 KJV). There is no easy, painless, or inexpensive way to do this in the city today, where social pluralism abounds and nearly all ministry is cross-cultural. Urban ministry calls us beyond our comfort zone and often takes us to uncharted territory. Yet ministry in the city is absolutely critical. D. L. Moody said it well: "Water runs down hill, and the highest hills are the great cities. If we can stir them, we shall stir the whole country."[2]

Lyman Abbot said, "What shall we do with our great cities? What will our great cities do with us? These are the two problems which confront every thoughtful American. For the question does not concern the city alone. The whole country is affected, if indeed its character and history are not determined, by the condition of its cities."[3]

The good news is that, perhaps to the surprise of many, the Bible has much to say about ministry in the city. The biblical story begins in a garden, but climaxes in the city. More than 140 cities are mentioned in the Scriptures, some hundreds of times altogether. God would have redeemed even Sodom, mentioned fifty-one times as the Bible's epitome of an evil city, had there been ten warm-bodied believers in it. You see, biblically there is a relationship between the presence of godly people and the preservation of wicked places.

We find principles and models for urban ministry throughout both Testaments, including texts in Deuteronomy, Isaiah, and Jeremiah, and through persons like Nehemiah, Jonah, Jesus, and Paul. In fact, the word *city* or *cities* occurs some 1,250 times in the Bible.[4] We who take biblical doctrine seriously must not ignore such a pervasive biblical theme.

The "old, old story of Jesus and His love" is extraordinarily relevant to today's urban dwellers. As an example, let me tell you the Christmas story as we find it in the Bible.

It is about an Asian-born baby named Jesus, who was born in a borrowed barn and eventually buried in a borrowed grave. He became an intercontinental migrant to urban Egypt. One half of the world's babies are born in Asia, where Jesus was born. Half of the world's 30 million refugees are Africans today, and Jesus became a refugee in Africa. Oh yes, a whole village-full of baby boys died for Jesus there in Bethlehem before He could die for them on the cross—just as crack babies, fetal alcohol, and HIV kids still die in our cities because of the sins of adults.

So if anybody knows what it is like to be a homeless, intercontinental migrant or to suffer the pain of dying kids, it is my Jesus. He came "unto his own" (John 1:11 KJV); He has been where we are and has faced many of the same struggles that we face today in our modern cities.

Today more than ever, the church is called to be salt and light in the difficult places of our world, to take the gospel "up" to the powerful and "down" to the powerless with equal integrity. If a Bible school in the heart of a great city cannot show us how to do that, where then shall we go to learn ministry for the twenty-first-century urban world?

The chapters of this book represent a diagonal cut across the body of Christ in the city and what Christ is teaching us. It is not the complete text of everything God's people are doing in the city, but Dr. John Fuder has assembled a wonderful group, many of whom have Moody Bible Institute in common and all of whom work with ministries in Chicago. We meet again in these pages. Most of us are graduates of the Institute; others have strong relationships with Moody. Personally, my wife Corean and I both graduated forty years ago, in 1959. Later, Corean taught music and worship at Moody for sixteen years. Our kids grew up playing in the old gym. (One of them joins us in this book and returns to the Institute periodically to lecture as an artist and athlete in urban ministry.) As it has been for many, MBI was my bridge from rural to urban and to a surprising life of ministry in far more than two hundred cities around the world. Welcome to the urban world: To God be the glory!

RAY BAKKE

PREFACE

Martie and I live and work in the city of Chicago. We did not come to Chicago because we loved the city or the needs of its masses. We came to Chicago because God had called us to serve Him at the Moody Bible Institute. The city was incidental. Over the last twelve years at Moody much of that has changed.

Living in the city has confronted us with a reality that had been a vague notion at best. All of our lives we have both been around big cities. Martie grew up on the outskirts of Cleveland and I just outside of New York. In fact, the first message I ever preached was preached at a New York City rescue mission. But outside of brief forays into the city to visit the restaurants, enjoy major-league sports, or walk the major shopping streets, most of our lives have been in the anesthetized environment of the suburbs. But now, through twelve years of inescapable exposure to the dramatic and often drastic needs of the city, we have become convinced that one of the most strategic frontiers for the gospel is no further away than the closest urban area.

My heart has been touched for the needs of cities primarily through my exposure to our graduates who are doing an outstanding work for Christ in some of Chicago's most despairing neighborhoods. Glen Kehrein, Arloa Sutter, James Ford, Bill Dillon (whose stories unfold on these pages), and a host of others have been used of God to make me deeply aware of the fact that Christ really is the only answer. I have been impacted as well by the biblical reality that God has a great concern and a driving compassion for the disenfranchised and the oppressed.

It is for this reason that I am delighted that Moody Publishers can offer this book that combines the experience of seasoned veterans who have the smell of the streets fresh on their clothes—people like Glen, Arloa, James, and Bill—and the sage wisdom of some of the best urban strategists.

I have come to believe that we have a great opportunity in our day. It is to show a watching world that Christ can do what tax dollars, social theory, and political systems have failed to do . . . grant release to the poor and dignity and healing to the oppressed. All over America secular politics and philanthropy are beginning to recognize "faith-based ministries" as the most effective solution to our cities' most illusive problems. From inner city churches and city rescue missions to redevelopment projects, youth programs, and recovery programs, the gospel thrives in the darkness and dilemmas of our cities. The better we do at urban ministry, the more Christ will be known as the marvelous liberator that He truly is.

Most of you who profit from the material in this book will most likely be those who are already committed to urban ministry. You are our heroes. Our prayer is that you will be encouraged and strengthened anew in your resolve.

To the few who are somewhat detached from urban outreach yet interested enough to pick this book up, my prayer is that your heart will be touched in a life-changing way. I have often wondered what would and/or could happen if followers of Christ in the collar communities, where most of the resources lie, would get a burden for the cause of Christ. We are very good at sending money and people to far-off lands while leaving the needs of the gospel neglected within driving distance.

And, by the way, a special word of thanks to Ray Bakke whose help in the formation of this book has been indispensable. We are pleased and proud that he is a Moody grad. Thanks as well to those who took time from a schedule that already had no vacancies to add a chapter from their life and experience.

JOSEPH M. STOWELL

ACKNOWLEDGMENTS

It has been a privilege to serve as the General Editor for Moody Publishers's *A Heart for the City*. It truly has been a labor of love. The idea for the book was born during Moody's annual Founder's Week Conference in February of 1998, which had the theme "Compassion for the City." Many of the contributors spoke at that gathering. I am delighted that we can prerelease the book at the Christian Community Development Association's annual conference, held this year on our campus and at Moody Memorial Church. I cannot think of a more appropriate audience.

Much appreciation goes to Dr. Joseph Stowell for his help in articulating the vision for the book, and to Greg Thornton and Jim Bell at Moody Publishers for making it a reality. Special thanks to Bill Soderberg and Cheryl Dunlop for their editorial assistance and patience in answering my endless stream of questions and pleas for help.

I would also like to express my love and respect for Dr. "Bud" Hopkins, Dean of our Graduate School. Without his believing in me, I would not be teaching at Moody.

I would be remiss not to acknowledge my profound gratefulness to one of our graduate students and my former faculty assistant, Nathan Richey, for his tireless work on the computer. Nathan, I could not have done it without you. Finally, to those who graciously endorsed this book—your writings, teaching, and encouragement over the years have affected my life in more ways than you will ever know. Thanks, from the bottom of my heart.

But the real heroes of this project are the contributors—men and women whose lives and ministries I have seen firsthand and respect greatly. You model the title of these essays, and I look forward to using this urban anthology as a textbook in our new M.A. Urban Ministries program in the Moody Graduate School. Your enthusiasm for this project has been a delight, and your commitment to sacrifice to meet deadlines is to be commended. May your tribe increase.

To you, the reader, it is my fervent prayer that the passion for the city and its people expressed in these chapters will more deeply fuel your own involvement in the urban community. May the models portrayed and the principles expressed on these pages be used to stimulate your own efforts to "seek the peace and prosperity of the city" (Jer. 29:7). In it all may God be glorified, His church strengthened, and a growing, needy urban world impacted by the gospel—in word and deed alike.

JOHN E. FUDER

part one

CONTEXT AND HISTORY

chapter one

CHICAGO'S PLACE IN WORLD EVANGELIZATION

WHERE GEOGRAPHY AND HISTORY CONVERGED

RAY BAKKE

Introduction: The City of Chicago

It is widely believed that the name "Chicago" is a corruption of an old Indian word for "bad smell." In its early days, the Indian trails converged at the brackish lowlands and skunk cabbage patches where the river meandered into Lake Michigan. This was the place of portage to the Des Plaines and Illinois River systems, which made it strategic for the British, French, and Americans. Fort Dearborn was founded on the high ground south, where the Tribune Tower now stands. In 1925 historian Herbert Asbury wrote, "*Chickagou* or *Checagou* . . . a bad smell, a symbolism which is kept alive by the politicians and the stockyards."[1]

Illinois, like the rest of the Midwest, was settling from south to north, for the earliest settlers came through the Cumberland Gap and up the Mississippi and Ohio River systems. To this day, everything in Illinois outside the Chicago area is called "downstate."

In 1825 the Erie Canal opened, connecting the Hudson River and Lake Erie. That started the race between what historians called the "lake cities"—Cleveland, Detroit, Milwaukee, and Chicago—and the "river cities"—St. Louis, Louisville, Cincinnati, and Pittsburgh. Founded in 1837, Chicago came onto the scene as a scrappy town set down in the midst of the middle west prairies. From the start it was raucous, entrepreneurial, and, above all, European.[2]

To the north lay the cheap ore for steel that could be floated down the lakes; to the south lay huge coalfields that could be inexpensively railroaded north. All was in place for the "cheap labor" from Europe to find a productive spot to settle. The "push factors" that led people to leave their homelands included famine, religious persecution, and political oppression in Europe. The "pull factors" that drew people to Chicago included the Civil War, the rail expansion providing passage around the lakes to the West Coast, the industrial revolution taking root across the U.S., and the political will to make it work.

Although as late as the 1840s St. Louis, Alton, and even Navoo (the temporary Mormon city) rivaled Chicago as the capital of the American inland empire, Chicago soon surfaced as the pre-eminent Midwestern city. Between 1860 and 1900, Chicago grew at an average rate of thirty thousand each year. In fifty years it went from being a "wild onion patch" to being the "second city" of the Western Hemisphere. The sheer scope of that growth was unprecedented in history.[3]

It is hardly accidental that the founding of the University of Chicago coincided with the establishment of the academic discipline of sociology. The burgeoning city of Chicago was ripe with social issues to be studied, and University of Chicago scholars—Park, Burgess, and Wirth, among others—guaranteed that Chicago would be used as the laboratory for urban research on all subjects.[4]

THE IMMIGRATION ERA:
EUROPE ARRIVES (1837–1918)

The famous potato famine in Ireland compelled thousands of Irish to leave their country after 1837 to look for work to sustain them. Many came to the U.S. to help carve out the 4,400 miles of canals dug between 1800 and 1850 in the race with the railroads. The Illinois–Michigan canal, the stockyards, and industry provided low threshold entry for the Irish into the Chicago area.

The Irish, who settled primarily in the West and South Loop (Bridgeport) neighborhoods, were largely rural in background. However, their national identity had been forged by centuries of conflict with Britain. To survive, the Irish had learned two valuable political skills: the English language and ethnic networking/political coalition-building. That is why, against all odds, the Irish eventually captured three major urban leadership roles: police officers, pastors, and politicians (the so-called "urban trinity").[5]

Very quickly the Irish learned political leveraging to affect political change in their ancestral land, Ireland. Long before American Jews organized for the establishment and success of Israel, the American Irish organized Hibernian societies in 1925 to work for the liberation of Ireland from Britain. The Irish then became part of the mainstream society in Chicago and other U.S. cities.[6]

In the early 1800s Germany did not exist as a unified political entity. Instead, a patchwork society of some three hundred duchies, principalities, and free cities occupied Middle Europe. Culturally the region was unified by the publication of Luther's Bible in the German language after 1524. The desire to unify politically was felt both in the north and south regions. The Prussian militarist north and the culturally driven South Germans contrived to form a national ("professors") parliament in Frankfurt in 1840, but it collapsed in the European revolutionary climate of 1848. Thereafter, the movement toward unification proceeded rapidly. The impetus was not democratic; rather, the militaristic drive of the Prussians from the north into the southern regions provoked the exodus of large numbers of Protestant Germans from the Baden-Württemberg Southwest and equally large numbers from Catholic Bavaria in the Southeast. At least 250,000 Germans came to Chicago during those years. Cincinnati and Milwaukee also attracted multitudes of German immigrants, changing the social, political, and religious fabric of these cities in ways most Americans never really understood.[7]

A Tale of Two Cities

The earliest Chicago was constructed almost entirely of wood. The Great Fire of 1871 ended that era! As Chicago rebuilt, the city spilled over Western Avenue (originally the western boundary of Chicago) with the brick and factory look that exists today. The "two cities" that emerged were the "WASP" lakefront district (White, Anglo-Saxon, Protestant; but which might better be called "Wealthy, Alienated, Separated, and Protected") and the river wards, which Michael Novak described with the tongue-in-cheek term PIGS—Poles, Italians, Greeks, and Slovaks.[8]

Visitors over the years have disparaged the architectural and social makeup of the riverward districts of Chicago. People who visit Williamsburg, Virginia, usually understand that the immigrants who built that city modeled it after the places they left in England. Likewise, Chicago was built to look like the old river cities of Central Europe. The Rhine, Rhone, Po, and Danube river cultures flourished everywhere outside the Loop and the lakefront. Outsiders, including most evangelical pastors, often didn't understand this dynamic. Unlike missionaries, they almost never learned the languages or cultures around them. Protestant evangelism most often nibbled at the edges of ancient Catholic and Orthodox cultures, mostly ministering to the dispossessed and socially alienated among them—a ministry that expanded with the advent of World War I.[9]

Italians in Chicago

As with Germany, there was no unified nation of Italy during the nineteenth century prior to 1870. Italians who came to Philadelphia and Chicago did not come from the northern renaissance cities of Milan, Florence, Genoa, or Venice, but rather from the Apennine mountain and Sicilian regions. These were the *contadini,* or village Italians, with profoundly local cultures who practiced what some have described as "folk Catholicism." They settled southwest of the Loop on Taylor Street, and at one time had the largest parish church in the world—Holy Family on Roosevelt Road with 73,000 members coming to about thirty-seven services a week.[10]

Polish Chicago

After the influx of Jews, Scandinavians, and Bohemians, the Poles were the last major group of nineteenth-century European immigrants to come to Chicago, the majority arriving between 1890 and 1914. They were also the largest group of immigrants. The Chicago area is now home to more than 800,000 Poles (actual numbers vary depending on how wide an area is included in the count). To put this in perspective, Chicago has more *Poles* than Seattle or San Francisco has *people.* Chicago functions culturally, politically, financially, and religiously for Poland like New York functions for Israel.

During the nineteenth century Poland did not exist as an independent state. Its regions were partitioned and ruled by the three neighboring states: Prussia to the west, Russia to the east, and Austria to the south. For a century Polonia was an idea kept alive in church basements.[11]

The Polish pastors set out to build Poland in Chicago across the river, west of where Moody Bible Institute now stands, into the Nobel Square communities. St. Stanislaus Koska Catholic Church, the mother church of the Poles, had forty thousand communicants in 1895, but one thousand families broke off and founded Holy Trinity, just south of Division Street. Unlike the mother church, whose sanctuary faced east so worshipers could face Poland as they prayed for it, the daughter church's doors faced east so these more upper-class Poles could depart and work for the liberation of Poland.[12]

DWIGHT LYMAN MOODY (1837–99)
AND THE HAYMARKET RIOT OF 1886

D. L. Moody was the prototypical American evangelist in the line from Charles Finney to Billy Graham. A recognized giant, he tended to defy categories, and he "colored outside the lines" of traditional evangelicalism. A century after his death in 1899, he can be seen as the father of modern evangelicalism, and to a degree as a grandfather of the ecumenical movement stemming from his Northfield Conferences after 1883 that led to the Edinburgh Mission Conference of 1910.[13]

After early years in Boston, he arrived in a raucous, disease-ridden Chicago in 1856, just in time for the financial panic of 1857. It wasn't long before he joined the YMCA movement and started his amazing Sunday school ministry that drew more than 1,500 kids. Moody watched Chicago institutions and most possessions burn in the Great Fire of October 1871. Shortly thereafter he became the world-renowned evangelist of many cities on both sides of the Atlantic.

After the Great Fire, Ashland Avenue became a cauldron of worker union organizing even as the Protestant industrialists of the Lakefront counties cranked up some of the world's most powerful industrial empires. The city had risen like a phoenix from the ashes of the fire. Chicago became "The City of Big Shoulders" and "Hog Butcher of the World." The ethnic newcomers, however, were known in the media as "the masses" or, even worse, as "scum."

While Chicago rebuilt as a city, the church and mission activities expanded exponentially in the final quarter of the nineteenth century. The YMCA, Salvation Army, and rescue ministries are too numerous to mention here.[14]

As early as 1873, D. L. Moody and Emma Dryer had discussed starting a Bible training school in Chicago to meet the growing need for ministry leaders. The idea remained undeveloped, however, until the Haymarket riot of 1886 heightened the urgency for such an institution.

On a warm May evening in 1886, police and the working class clashed near Haymarket Square, where labor and community leaders had been rallying in protest of police brutality against strikers and other injustices. When 176 armed policemen converged on the dwindling crowd of about 200 people (there had been as many as 2,500 observers earlier in the evening), someone lobbed a dynamite bomb at the police. This was the first time in U.S. history that such a bomb had been used for violent purposes. The bomb and the gunfire that ensued killed seven police officers and four workers and injured scores of others.[15] Chicago's lakefront was in fear and panic. This was a class war, not a race war, between ideologies, religions, and cultures.

Three months after the riot, Emma Dryer received an initial grant from Fourth Presbyterian Church to found what we know as the Moody Bible Institute to "train gap men who would stand between the church and the masses."[16] D. L. Moody had moved back to Northfield, Massachusetts, a year after the fire, and by this time had begun his national and international evangelistic ministries. He returned periodically to bless the school until his death in November of 1899.

So Moody Bible Institute was founded in the aftermath of an urban riot to be salt and light in the city and to offer specialized training for lay and professional ministry. In fact, R. A. Torrey, MBI's second president, continued in this tradition by serving on public slum clearance committees in Chicago, as reported by William Stead in his classic World's Fair—era book, *If Christ Came to Chicago,* published in 1894.[17]

CHICAGO ETHNICS RESPOND TO WAR

The 1893 World's Fair put Chicago on the world stage for good, but the class and race conflicts increased in the decades leading to World War I. The most recent European immigrants, the Poles, received the brunt of the animosity. Even the *Chicago Tribune* slandered them. The "Polish joke" is the vestigial remains of that lingering hatred. By and large, Poles stayed to themselves and out of politics.

When World War I broke out, the Poles decided what they would do to earn acceptance as Americans: Huge numbers of them traveled back to France by ship and train to fight on the front lines in American uniforms. Surely this would win over American opinion. To their horror, they discovered the Germans had conscripted large numbers of Poles to fight against them in the trenches. The American Poles were fighting their brothers, cousins, and uncles. The war became a Polish holocaust.

In front of Chicago's St. Hyacinth Church on Wolfram Avenue stands a huge obelisk honoring the 499 men of its parish who served in World War I, listing the names of those who died in battle. According to Professor Charles Shannabruch of Notre Dame, at least 40 percent of the U.S. soldiers in World War I were ethnic urban Catholics, earning their right to be American citizens by fighting on European soil.[18]

Most ethnic groups have a holocaust in their history that marks their collective psyche and leaves abiding scars. The pain in the Jewish community for atrocities committed against it during this century is well-known. But African-Americans, Armenians, Poles, Arabs, Greeks,

Palestinians, indigenous peoples in this country, and many other ethnic groups are shaped as well by histories of oppression and persecution. What kept these communities alive in the midst of hardship was their faith and kinship with one another. Unfortunately, American evangelicals, who tend to be individualistic and nuclear-family oriented about their life and faith, have often been very insensitive to such peoples and have minimized the significance of the churches, synagogues, and mosques to their communities.

Furthermore, while the Irish, Italians, Poles, and many Germans were all "Roman Catholic" in their faith, there were significant differences between their styles of spirituality and the ways their parishes functioned. Again, evangelicals have not always caught these nuances in their respective neighborhoods.

MIGRANT CHICAGO: 1914–60

After World War I, Americans hankered for a "return to normalcy," and by 1925 they had closed many doors to immigration. During this time, however, there was a substantial movement of people from the South to the North. Demographers agree that more people came north to the cities during the twentieth century than went west during the nineteenth century, contrary to our "frontier" thinking.

Mexicans were brought to Chicago by Protestants and other groups "to help break up the unions." This kind of "divide and conquer" strategy, a common experience among the city's ethnic groups, certainly did not promote healthy and peaceful neighborhoods.

Meanwhile, the cotton industry became mechanized in the South, and as sharecropping ended for many, throngs of black and white southerners were prompted to move north to live and work in the city built by, and now run by, European immigrants. By 1947 John L. Lewis was organizing the deep coal miners in the twelve-state Appalachian range from Binghamton, New York, to Birmingham, Alabama. However, when the northern cities began switching from coal to gas (from Appalachian fuel to southern and western oil), declining markets, strip mines, and increased usage of machinery put thousands on the roads heading north. It was said in the sixties: "The only kind of bussing George Wallace never opposed was putting the poor on Greyhounds and shipping them north."[19]

And what did these miners, sugarcane workers, and sharecroppers find in Chicago? A European city in the midst of yet another industrial shift, where the old factories in the city were closing and reopening in the suburbs, the Sun Belt, or overseas countries. Chicago lost up to

500,000 jobs in the 1960s, and few of the new migrant laborers had the job skills to compete in the shrinking-pie economy.

Although blacks had been in Chicago since the beginning with flourishing neighborhoods, churches, businesses, and robust culture, structural racism confronted the growing black community in ways from which other migrating peoples were exempted. For example, post–World War II public housing policy sent whites to the suburbs with VA mortgages and 90 percent federally funded expressways to support them. Blacks, on the other hand, got public housing apartments and services mediated by outsiders to the community. Often, that locked them into ghettoized neighborhoods.[20]

The long delayed civil rights revolution led by Dr. King and the anti–Vietnam war movement converged in the Chicago riots of 1968, a watershed era for ministries in Chicago and elsewhere. Frankly, to the practiced eye of many of us who pastored churches or ran mission agencies in Chicago at that time, it seemed we lost both the war in Vietnam and the "war" in the inner cities of America for similar reasons. In Vietnam, when ground combat began to cost too many human lives, the U.S. military pulled out the ground troops and relied on air raids and other technologically driven strategies. Here at home, public and church officials tried to run programs and services for the city from the safety of the suburbs, substituting technology and technique for building relationships in the neighborhood. This kind of half-hearted battle rarely works, of course. While data on the period are still being analyzed, many of its strategies are being reconsidered today. Housing projects are being demolished, perhaps bringing problems of other kinds as communities are broken apart, and new philosophies and strategies are emerging at government levels as well as in the church and nonprofit sectors.

Many have questioned the effectiveness of the millions of dollars that have been poured into urban neighborhoods with seemingly few results. During the mid-seventies I participated in a study group that looked at the economic realities of a Chicago inner city neighborhood with this question in mind: What is happening to the money being spent in this community? What we found was that the money targeted for inner city communities does not remain in those communities. The poor are targeted for services; the money itself goes to the professional service providers.[21] The economic benefits of the institutions operating in the community (hospitals, banks, schools, businesses, government services, and even the church) were going outside the community to the suburbs and prosperous neighborhoods that were "homebase" to the institutions and service providers.

THE ESCAPING URBAN DOLLAR

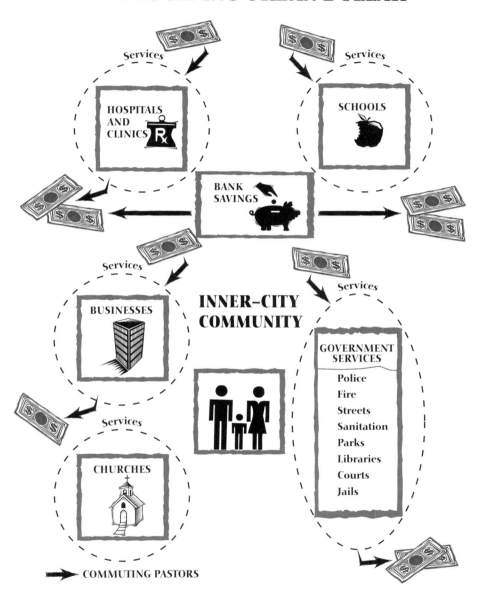

I've concluded that poverty is not so much the absence of money as the absence of power.[22] Neither Republicans nor Democrats seem willing to admit this, for one group advocates shrinking the budget while the other calls for more funding. But without the corresponding changes that empower these communities to attract real money and not just services, little long-term change happens.

Many churches and mission programs have imitated the public sector's model. Doing little or nothing to change the system, their pattern of ministry is to have funders give them the money to provide services. Again, even though their motives may be wonderful and their work may even result in some personal spiritual conversions, these ministries often become codependent with the very people they purport to serve.

By contrast, the many ministries you will read about in this book have addressed these problems and operate with wonderful spiritual integrity in ways that empower the poor.

INTERNATIONAL CHICAGO SINCE THE 1960s

Between 1964 and 1965 the United States Congress passed three monumental pieces of legislation that dramatically changed Chicago, other cities, and the nation as a whole: the Civil Rights Act, the Voting Rights Act, and the Immigration Law. The last was least understood, but is having a most lasting impact on the metroscape we call Chicago.

Before 1965, most Asians, Africans, or Latins could not migrate here. We had biased the laws on behalf of northern European immigrants. That changed, and our formerly European city is now being pushed in Asian, African, and Latin directions. The consequences are phenomenal for ministry in the city. The nations of the earth are now in the neighborhoods of our cities. The poor and the lost are coming together here, and ministries must reach out with the gospel and with strategies that build healthy persons and communities.

Broadly speaking, urban ministry is developing five specializations in Chicago today beyond the traditional functions of the gospel ministry and pastoral care:

- Ministries with at-risk persons from cradle to grave, with a huge and growing population of street children, battered women, and addicted peoples in an aging nation
- Ministries focused on the retrieval of at-risk neighborhoods, including church-based economic development

- Multiethnic and multilingual churches with around-the-clock language ministries
- Lay witnesses in the marketplace with affinity-group evangelism in the arts, theater, sports, business, and academics
- Specialized congregations that keep all the traditional functions of biblical ministry, but adapt the *forms* creatively to meet their special contexts

We used to define cities as unique places, using sociological categories like population size, density, heterogeneity. No longer. Urban ministries have been influenced by social psychologists and communications theorists who define cities by roles, functions, or processes rather than places.

Today, for example, we see suburbs not as the escape from the city, but as the extension of it. Cities are the "catch basins of the nations" in a global economic era. The frontiers of mission are no longer across the ocean, but across the street as well.

We have also learned that although most ministries in Chicago are still very traditional, many new models and strategies are needed. Pastoring the traumatized in broken-down communities or pastoring the AIDS or crack-addicted populations is not a science, but rather an art. We now study urban ministry *not* just because it is so different from rural, small town, or suburban ministry. Rather, we are learning what ministry will be in all these places within a decade or two. Put another way, Chicago's ministries are the "R&D" unit for the whole church. Chicago has been prophetic about the future of the nation, along with New York, Los Angeles, and other urban centers in new patterns of life and work for millions of people.

The city that brought us D. L. Moody and the Olive Branch and Pacific Garden rescue missions and launched Billy Sunday, Paul Rader, the Gospel Tabernacle movements, Torrey Johnson, and Billy Graham —along with social reformers Jane Addams and Saul Alinsky—continues to affect the world. The Christian Community Development Association launched here a decade ago by John Perkins and Wayne Gordon in Lawndale and Glen and Lonni Kehrein's Circle Urban Ministries in Austin are just two of the ministries that are transforming Chicago's neighborhoods and affecting urban mission throughout the nation.

Conclusion: Prospects for the Future

O ur God has given the church yet one more opportunity to reach the world's nations here in Chicago. It is absolutely critical that the Moody Bible Institute continue to be a launching pad for ministry in this internationally integrated urban world of the twenty-first century. D. L. Moody came to the World's Fair of 1893 and ministered vigorously there, and he continued his ministry throughout this city until he died one hundred years ago. This Institute was created in 1886, in the midst of a riot-prone city, to proclaim the gospel and train "gap" or "bridge" people who would stand between the churches and the masses. What a glorious call and illustrious century it has been. Our Lord, the Divine Choreographer, has set the stage by creating a world-class laboratory and has kept Moody in the midst of it "for such a time as this." God help us to accept our call.

Reflection Questions

1. Why should urban pastors or missionaries study the history of their city or specific neighborhood? How can we go about such a study?

2. If most of the world's "far-off" peoples have migrated into our local city and neighborhoods, what might be some implications for the local church's evangelism, worship, pastoral care, and mission?

3. We know historically how God used the Babylonian exile to teach the Jews the need for synagogues (as portable teaching centers) and the Alexandria Jews the need to translate the Hebrew Bible into Greek. We also know how that influenced the spread of the gospel after Pentecost throughout the Roman world. What do you think God is teaching Christian Japanese in Chicago, Chinese in San Francisco, Koreans in New York, Cubans in Miami, or various nationalities in your city that may influence the evangelization of those countries in the next century?

part two

BIBLICAL AND PHILOSOPHICAL FOUNDATIONS

chapter two

CALLED TO CHRIST, CALLED TO COMPASSION

PUTTING FAITH INTO ACTION

JOSEPH STOWELL

Introduction: Between Two Worlds

John Grisham's novel *Street Lawyer* opens with a partner in a posh law firm stepping confidently into the elevator of a high-rise office building to travel up to his lavish suite of offices. As he pushes the button for his floor, a smelly, ragged street person steps onto the elevator with him. The doors close, locking the two men inside the small space. The attorney, in his pinstriped suit, exhibits all the trappings of success —in stark contrast to the disadvantaged street person, who seemingly stands dazed and disinterested. The defeated look on his face reveals his lot in life. The aroma of his streetness fills the close air of the elevator. As the elevator begins its ascent, the disparity and tension between two separate worlds grabs the reader's attention.

The same sort of tension is obvious in my world. In Chicago, where Moody Bible Institute is located, you don't have to go very far to run into the unfortunate, the down-and-out, and the defeated. Poor people, street people, and other disadvantaged folks stand on virtually every corner. Even a quick walk to the office or the train offers regular encounters with a world that is radically foreign to mine. It's easy to step around these people, ignoring their plight as we console ourselves with the thought that there is really nothing we can do to make a difference . . . or, worse yet, the thought that if they wanted to they could smarten up and make a life for themselves like everyone else.

Recently while walking to work I passed a StreetWise vendor. If you are not from Chicago, you may not know about this program designed to help some of our homeless people raise a little money by selling a small newspaper on the streets for a dollar apiece. It was a bitterly cold January morning and I had already stopped by Starbucks and paid more than a buck for a measly cup of coffee. Feeling noble, I struggled to find my wallet, reached in, and took out a dollar.

As I did, she said to me, "Do you really want the paper, or can I keep it to sell to someone else?" "Keep the paper," I replied. "That's fine." Then I added, "How are you today?" She looked at me and said, "I'm cold. I'm so cold." I turned to go, and told her matter-of-factly, "I hope the sun comes out, it warms up, and you have a good day."

I continued on my way to Moody, with the cup of coffee warming my hand. About a half block toward the office the conversation finally registered in my mind, along with the words of James 2:15–16: "Suppose a brother or sister is without clothes and daily food. If one of you says to him, 'Go, I wish you well; keep warm and well fed,' but does nothing about his physical needs, what good is it?" I wrestled for a moment with what I should do, but I was late, so I kept walking.

I have regretted that decision ever since I made it. For weeks I prayed that the Lord would let me see her again. To this day I would do anything to give her a cup of hot coffee in Christ's name.

Sadly, my actions that day were not uncommon. Each Sunday morning, many of us gather in comfortable churches, tucked safely away in middle-class neighborhoods, all dressed up and ready to worship God. We might never say the words out loud, but we act as though our God is the God of clean people, the God of the wealthy, the God of the middle and upper classes.

But one quick glance at the heart of God in the Old Testament and the actions of Christ in the New Testament and we see that God has a special interest in the disadvantaged and the oppressed. In fact, it is biblically clear that when God sees the disadvantaged that His response is one of active compassion. A lack of interest in the needs of those who are lost in the underground of our class structures only confirms that our hearts do not reside where the heart of God gets busy. This distance from God's interests most likely is unintentional for most of us. Yet that does not qualify for a legitimate excuse. When we distance ourselves from the disadvantaged, we distance ourselves from the approval of God and the source of His blessing (notice Isaiah 58), regardless of how good or well conformed we are to other expectations He has for us.

SEEING BEYOND THE EXTERNALS

Have you ever been around a perfectionist? Someone who not only thinks he is perfect, but wants everything else to be perfect?

I am amazed that God, who *is* perfect, could come into my world and walk alongside people like me—purveyors of imperfection—and demonstrate compassion toward us. I would expect God to be irritated with my inconsistency and frustrated by my imperfections. I would expect Him to be angry with my frequent failures. But surprisingly, Scripture teaches that God is a God of compassion. He is touched by our infirmities, and He acts on those feelings to provide grace and mercy and to help us in our times of need.

Compassion is all about connecting with the helpless condition of a hurting world. I find it interesting that as Jesus encountered the multitudes, He consistently responded with compassion. Matthew 9:36–38 captures one of these moments when Jesus expressed His compassion for the masses:

> *Seeing the people, He felt compassion for them, because they were distressed and dispirited like sheep without a shepherd. Then He said to His disciples, "The harvest is plentiful, but the workers are few. Therefore beseech the Lord of the harvest to send out workers into His harvest."* (NASB)

Notice the sequencing of the text. The NIV says, "When he *saw* the crowds . . ." What do you see when you encounter crowds? Crowds can be rude and noisy. You can get lost in a crowd. Crowds violate your space and intrude on your solitude. Crowds make us irritable. But the text says that when Christ encountered a crowd, He was moved with compassion. How can that be?

Matthew tells us that Jesus was moved with compassion *because* He saw more deeply than we see; He saw beyond external appearances to the hearts of the people. He saw that they were distressed and dispirited. In the original language, these two words are very graphic descriptions of despondency. The word *distressed* literally means "to be flayed open, to be in hopeless despair." *Dispirited*, or downcast, means "to be thrown down, to be at the end of yourself."

In Greek, these words appear in a grammatical construction known as the *perfect passive participle*. The perfect tense tells us that this distress is the result of a past action that has an ongoing impact— much like throwing a rock into a pond sends waves out to the shore. It reflects a past action with continuing results. The passive mood suggests that these people had been impacted by something outside of themselves. Combining the powerful words with the grammatical structure, we can conclude that they suffered from circumstances that they were not able to contain or conquer. When Jesus saw their plight, He was moved to compassion.

Matthew added a graphic metaphor comparing the crowds to sheep that are without a shepherd. Because we do not live in an agrarian society, we may miss the powerful significance of this comparison. If a shepherd does not lead a flock of sheep from one pasture to another, they will eat a pasture dry, then stay there until they die of starvation. If sheep ever get lost, they will never find their way home by themselves. If you have ever seen lambs, you know how vulnerable they are. Without a shepherd to protect them from predators, they do not stand a chance.

When Jesus looked at the multitudes, He saw that they were unprotected, unsustained, and unguided—like sheep without a shepherd. And, this inner view drove His heart beyond sympathy to an active compassion.

When we walk down the streets of our cities, when we drive through the neglected, despairing, destitute neighborhoods, when we see crowds of people, how do we respond? How deeply do we see? Are we moved to compassion or revulsion?

If Jesus Christ were walking with us today, He would ask, "Do you see it? Do you see the need, the depths of despair, the pain?" When you look at a crowd, do you see the bustling noisy irritation of it all, or can you see the real needs that move in the lives of those who comprise the faceless multitudes?

TRADING CONDEMNATION FOR COMPASSION

One of the reasons we have such a hard time feeling compassion, such difficulty seeing beyond the externals, is that our lives are guarded by carnal instincts. One of our instincts is our propensity to condemn people rather than feel compassion. As a rule, we are far too quick to condemn hurting people.

"Why doesn't he get a job?"

"Doesn't she care what she looks like?"

"How can he abuse his body that way?"

"If she had been a better wife, he wouldn't have left her."

In Luke chapter 15, we find Jesus at the center of a crowd filled with tax collectors and sinners. If you were a first-century Israelite, you would speak those words with the proper measure of scorn: *tax collectors* and *sinners*. These were the most repulsive people in the land of Israel. Tax collectors were unscrupulous men who had sold out to the occupying Roman Empire. Not only did they collect the exorbitant taxes levied by the Romans, but also they lined their pockets by assessing additional taxes on their fellow Jews. Sinners were Jews who lived their lives in open rebellion against God. These were the worst kinds of people you could imagine; yet there was Jesus at the center of the crowd.

The religious leaders of the day could not believe it. They stood at the outskirts of the crowd, murmuring and grumbling: "Look, He claims to be God, yet He spends time with *those* people." Rather than compassion, they were filled with condemnation. Rather than seeing the problems of the people, they saw the people as the problem. They felt revulsion at the way these people lived and behaved.

A few years ago, there was a terrible late-night accident in Kentucky involving a church bus bringing a bunch of teenagers home from an activity. All their parents were waiting in the church parking lot for the bus that was already an hour or two late. Out on the interstate, as the bus came over a hill, a pickup truck in the wrong lane hit it head-on. The collision sent the bus veering into a ditch, where it burst into flames. Nearly every child on the bus died that night.

I think of the scene in that parking lot, where those parents who would never see their children alive again waited, and my heart is filled with sorrow. When I heard about the accident, I found myself saying, "I wonder if the pickup driver was drunk." Sure enough, a couple of days later, the newspapers reported that his blood-alcohol level was well above the legal limit. In my heart, I muttered, "I hope they've got one great prosecutor in that county."

Today, I am ashamed of that response. I wonder if when that pickup driver stands before God he will say, "No one ever cared for my soul. They just wanted my hide, that's all. No one cared for my soul."

As tragic as that collision was for the families of the lost, there were other issues at stake that night—one of them was the pickup driver's eternity. Did anybody care? Did anybody pray for him? Was there even a flash of compassion among Christians across the country for that man's soul? Or did we all take great delight in condemning him?

One thing is clear about the Lord Jesus: He had compassion on sinners. Even those that seemingly deserved condemnation had His compassion. From the woman taken in adultery to the thief on the cross, the Lord emphasized compassion over condemnation.

REPLACING CURIOSITY WITH ACTION

Another carnal instinct, seemingly much more innocent but equally lethal, is curiosity. In John chapter 9, when Jesus and His disciples walked past a beggar born blind, the text says the disciples stopped Jesus and asked, "Lord, tell us who sinned that this man would be born blind? Was it his parents, or did he sin in his mother's womb?" Rather then eliciting compassion, the man's affliction became the object of the disciples' theological curiosity.

When someone you know has walked into a tragic, despairing moment, have you ever caught yourself saying to your friends, "Maybe God is chastening him," "Maybe he is a horrible father; maybe that's why this is happening," or "I do not think she would be suffering like this if she were a better person"?

Instead of coming alongside the suffering to offer our support, we get caught up in the desire to know the details of the sin. Have you ever heard anyone open a prayer meeting by saying, "I wouldn't share this normally, but just so you can all pray more intelligently, let me fill you in on all the details"?

In response to the question about the blind beggar, Jesus refused to indulge the disciples' curiosity. He said, "This happened so that the work of God might be displayed in his life" (v. 3). In a moment of compassionate power, Jesus touched the man's eyes, and he could see! And God was glorified.

Before my wife and I moved downtown to be closer to Moody, I used to commute to work from the suburbs. Every once in awhile, on a traffic report, they would tell me that the Eisenhower Expressway was like a parking lot. To avoid delays, I had several alternate routes worked out, most of which took me through some of the seedier neighborhoods in Chicago. As I drove those streets to avoid the gridlock on the expressway, I would see prostitutes standing on corners, boarded-up buildings, windows with iron bars, and scores of people standing on street corners with seemingly no purpose. Every once in a while, I witnessed a drug exchange. Since that was not my usual world, I was curious. How much better it would have been to have moved beyond my curiosity to compassion.

Thank God, many students who have come to Moody Bible Institute have seen the underside of the city and refused to be merely curious. They've moved beyond condemnation and curiosity and instead have become instruments of God's compassion among the disadvantaged. Arloa Sutter came to Moody from a farm in Iowa. She never went back. Seeing the need, she was driven by a kind of divine compassion to reach the disadvantaged in the neighborhood. This Mother Teresa of Chicago has spawned effective ministries in gay bars, among gang members, and a particularly noteworthy work among the homeless that has been recognized by the mayor of Chicago as a model work. Compassion drove her to leave the tending of her father's lambs to the tending of lambs dramatically separated from her heavenly Father.

Glen Kehrein came to Moody as a country boy from the north woods of Wisconsin. While he was here, he became so gripped by the needs of the city that he began Circle Urban Ministries, which has made its mark on the West Side of Chicago. Among the many great accomplishments under his leadership at CUM are medical relief, redevelopment, and many who have come to Christ. A school is perhaps Glen's most significant ministry. Seeing that one of the great needs in the city is for education, Glen started a Christian school where parents can send their young children for a quality education. As the children have blossomed and come to know Christ, their parents have begun to ask questions. "What are you doing with my kids? I can't believe the improvement I'm seeing!" Glen responds by saying, "Well, let me tell you about Jesus Christ, and how He can change a life, a home, a street, and a neighborhood."

Several months ago, Glen took me on a tour of the new school his group has recently founded. He told me that if these children were not coming to his school, Circle Urban Ministries would probably never reach them. The parents can't afford to send their kids to private school, most of the kids don't have fathers living at home, and the families are beyond the reach of most ministries. These are the truly needy families in our neighborhoods. Looking in the children's faces and hearing them recite Scripture, I could not help but think that this is what Christ meant when He said "even to the least of these."

BRIDGING THE CULTURAL CHASM

Another carnal instinct that stands between other people and us is the cultural chasm. In John chapter 4, Jesus and His disciples were traveling from Judea to Galilee, which took them through the region of Samaria. I think Jesus arranged this journey through Samaria for the disciples' sake, because if you know anything about Jewish history, you know that a Jew would never travel through Samaria if it could be avoided. Despite the deep ethnic, religious, and political chasm between the Jews and the Samaritans, Jesus went there because an immoral woman needed to have her hurting, empty heart filled with the living water of the Messiah. He bridged the cultural chasm and set an example for us all.

Each of us must ask ourselves, "Am I able to set aside my prejudices and offer living water to a hurting soul from another ethnic, religious, or political culture?" Think about it for a minute, because even in our churches there are prejudices and criticisms. So what's your view of people from a different race or a different culture? Do your carnal instincts clog your compassion and render you unfit for the Master's use? Are you prone to condemn like the Pharisees? Do you tend to be curious like the disciples? Are you perfectly satisfied to live in your own little cultural box and never see the worth and dignity of others who are outside of your circle? Until we repent of these carnal instincts, the compassion of God cannot flow through us to touch a hurting world.

CULTIVATING COMPASSION

If we are going to move beyond condemnation, a critical curiosity, and our prejudice, we must let the mind and heart of Jesus touch us. The church has largely ignored the inner city, moving out to the more comfortable suburbs. But in doing so it has left an entire group of people without the gospel, yet God has never been satisfied with a gospel that reaches only the safe, the clean, and the whole. He wants us to cultivate compassion and reverse the flight of churches out of the inner cities.

Four principles drawn from the ninth and tenth chapters of Matthew's gospel will lead us from appropriate repentance to a godly response. The first principle is to *go where the need is.* In Matthew 9:35, we are told that Jesus "went through all the towns and villages," teaching and healing. Not only was He encountering the multitudes, He was coming into close contact with them. Perhaps our compassion has been short-circuited because we have not been willing to connect with the real needs of people. The word translated "compassion" in this text (v. 36) comes from the Greek word *splagchnizomai,* which is the deepest word for compassion in New Testament Greek.

Jesus walked the streets and rubbed elbows with real people. He was not afraid to get close enough to see the need. We can follow Christ's example by finding ourselves where the needy are. When we get outside of our safe little worlds, down to where real needs are, we will find that compassion is a normal heartfelt response to pain and despair. Compassion is about connecting with real needs.

The second principle is that *compassion is a response rather than a reaction.* The biblical concept of compassion is not to be confused with our modern-day notion of sympathy. *Splagchnizomai* is a compassion that is moved to action. Sympathy merely *feels* sorry. Biblical compassion always *acts* on that sorrow. It is not a reaction; it is a response.

In Matthew 9:38, Jesus told His disciples to pray that the Lord of the harvest would send workers into the field. Then, in chapter 10, He split the disciples into teams of two and sent them out into the surrounding villages, telling them to preach the kingdom, preach the gospel, and heal the sick. He promised to supply them with power and authority over evil spirits. Christ commissioned His followers to personally engage needs. They went to teach, heal, and, when necessary, do battle with demons. As we get close enough to see the real needs of people, Christ will commission our hearts to respond by *doing* something to meet those needs. Biblical compassion is an active response to real needs.

The third principle for cultivating compassion is to recognize that *biblical compassion is a commitment, not a convenience.* As you read through Matthew chapter 10, you'll see that Jesus warned the disciples that some people would ignore them, and others would work against them. As we seek to express the compassion of our hearts to hurting people, we will often be faced with circumstances that are bewildering, dangerous, and challenging beyond our ability to cope. We will need to pray and perhaps fast in order to get the work done. Compassion is a tough, risky business. It requires commitment.

If you choose to minister to people dying of AIDS, some people will say you are soft on sin. If you choose to minister to drunks and drug addicts, some will criticize you for hanging out with sinners. You'll run the risk of self-pity when you see others who prosper in soft and affluent settings. Active compassion is costly. It takes a special kind of commitment to hit the streets, to go to a mission, or to join an inner city ministry. Yet Jesus modeled such commitment. He invested three years in a ministry that was driven and defined by compassion, then He sent His disciples out to carry on His heart's passion. And just as He commissioned the disciples to minister in ancient Palestine, He commissions us to reach the hurting people of our generation.

The fourth principle is that *compassion takes people all the way to Christ.* In Matthew 9:35, we see that Jesus not only felt compassion for the people and healed them, He also preached the gospel of the kingdom. The most compassionate thing we can do is to reconnect a lost soul to the eternal God. We can fill a person's stomach and meet their other physical and emotional needs, but only Jesus Christ can take a hurting life and make it whole.

THE MARK OF FAITH

Scripture clearly teaches that if we truly desire to express genuine love for Christ, we will express authentic love to the poor, the disadvantaged, and the oppressed. In Matthew 25:34–40, Jesus laid out this principle in bold relief:

> Then the King will say to those on His right, "Come, you who are blessed of My Father, inherit the kingdom prepared for you from the foundation of the world. For I was hungry, and you gave Me something to eat; I was thirsty, and you gave Me something to drink; I was a stranger, and you invited Me in; naked, and you clothed Me; I was sick, and you visited Me; I was in prison, and you came to Me." Then the righteous will answer Him, saying, "Lord, when did we see You hungry, and feed You, or thirsty, and give You something to drink? And when did we see You a stranger, and invite You in, or naked, and clothe You? And when did we see You sick, or in prison, and come to You?" The King will answer and say to them, "Truly I say to you, to the extent that you did it to one of these brothers of Mine, even the least of them, you did it to Me." (NASB)

While Ephesians 2:8–9 clarifies that we are not saved by our works but by the grace of God exercised through the gift of faith, verse 10 adds that we have been redeemed and created in God's image *for the purpose of glorifying Him through the good works of our lives.* James also teaches us that authentic faith produces good works.

What Christ is saying in the text from Matthew is that one of the leading evidences of a truly righteous life is service to the disadvantaged. In fact He makes it clear that when we touch the oppressed with our love, we have touched Christ with our love.

Leo Tolstoy, the brilliant nineteenth-century novelist who penned the classic *War and Peace,* also wrote volumes of short stories. One of his lesser-known works, titled "Where Love Is, God Is,"[1] tells the story of a Russian shoemaker who lived a very difficult and disappointing life. His wife died early, and his children forsook him. In the depths of his bitterness, a visitor to his home showed him the forgiveness of God. As a result, his life was radically transformed.

As Tolstoy unfolds the story, the shoemaker is reading Luke 7, where the immoral woman came to see Jesus at Simon the Pharisee's house. Simon has been rude to Jesus and has held Him at arm's length. Martin the shoemaker sees the connection:

> "That Pharisee must have been like me. I've only ever worried about myself, thinking of the next cup of tea, keeping warm and cozy. I've never shown anyone hospitality. Simon only worried about himself and couldn't have cared less about his guest. And who was his guest? Why, it was Christ Himself. Now would I have behaved like that if Christ had come here?"
>
> Martin laid his head in both arms and dozed off almost before he knew it. "Martin!" He suddenly heard as though someone were whispering in his ear. Martin started and sleepily asked, "Who's there?" turned around and

glanced at the door and no one was there. He laid his head down again to sleep and heard quite distinctly, "Martin, Martin, look out into the street to-morrow for I will come."

The next morning, Martin got up before dawn, said his prayers then lit the stove, warmed up some cabbage soup and porridge, lit the samovar, put his apron on and sat down to work by the window. As he sat there, he could not forget what had happened the night before. He was in two minds about it, thinking first that he had imagined everything and then persuading himself that he had heard a voice. "Well," he decided, "I think I really did hear one."

Martin went and sat at his window, but he concentrated more on what was happening outside than on his work. Whenever anyone would come past in unfamiliar boots, he would crouch in such a way that he could clearly see the person's face as well as his feet. A house porter went by with a brand new left boot only. Then a water carrier. Then an old soldier from Nicholas I's time, wearing old, patched felt boots, with a shovel in his hand, appeared outside the window. Martin recognized him from the boots: the man's name was Stepanych and a neighboring tradesman gave him food and lodging out of charity. His job was to help the house porter, and he began clearing the snow outside of Martin's window. Martin looked at him and resumed work. "I must be going soft in the head!" Martin exclaimed, laughing at himself. "It's only old Stepanych clearing away the snow, and I immediately conclude that it's Christ who's come to visit me. Silly old fogy!"

However, after about a dozen more stitches, Martin again felt the urge to look out the window. This time he saw that Stepanych had propped the shovel against the wall and he could not quite see whether he was warming himself or simply resting. He was obviously a poor, broken-down man, who just did not have the strength to clear the snow away. Martin thought he might offer him a cup of tea, especially as the samovar happened to be on the boil. Martin stuck his awl in the piece of leather, put the samovar on the table, made the tea and tapped on the window. Stepanych turned round and came over. Martin beckoned him to come inside and went to open the door. "Come in and warm yourself," he said. "You must be frozen stiff."

"God bless you! My bones are aching," Stepanych replied. Then he came in, shook off the snow and started tottering as he wiped his feet so as not to dirty the floor. "Don't bother about that," Martin said. "I'll clean up after-wards. It's all in a day's work! Come through and sit down. Now, have some tea." Martin filled two glasses, offering one to his guest and emptying his own saucer and blowing into it. When Stepanych had emptied his glass, he turned it upside down, put the remains of his sugar on it and thanked his host. But he obviously wanted some more. "Drink up," Martin said, refilling his guest's glass and his own. As he drank the tea, Martin kept looking out into the street.

"Are you expecting someone?" his guest asked. "Am I expecting some-one? Well, I feel too ashamed to tell you. As it happens I'm both expecting and not expecting. The fact is, there are some words I cannot get out of my head. Whether I imagined I heard them, I can't really say. You see, my friend, last night I was reading the Gospels, about our dear Lord Christ and how He suffered and walked this earth. I'm sure you must have heard all about it."

"Yes, I've heard about it," Stepanych replied, "but I'm an ignorant man, can't read or write."

"Well, I was reading about how He walked this earth and how He went to the house of a Pharisee who did not make Him welcome. Well, as I read further, I thought to myself how badly Christ the Father was treated. Supposing Christ had come to my house—or to someone like me—what wouldn't I have done to give Him a proper welcome! But that Simon would not receive Him into his house. That's what I was thinking when I fell asleep. And in my sleep I heard someone calling my name. Then I lifted my head and thought I could hear someone whispering, 'Expect me, for I shall come and see thee tomorrow.' Twice I heard that voice whisper. Well, as you can imagine, those words have affected me deeply. I know I'm being silly, but I'm really expecting our heavenly Father!"

Stepanych silently shook his head, emptied his glass and laid it on its side. But Martin stood it up and refilled it. "Here, drink some more. And I was thinking about the time when our Lord was upon the earth, despising no one and mixing mostly with ordinary folk. Yes, He always went with the humble and chose His disciples mainly from folks like us, from ordinary sinners and working people."

Stepanych left and Martin went back to sewing, making shoes and keeping watching out the window. Soon a woman in a springtime dress, with tattered boots, freezing in the cold, clutching a baby to her bosom, stood outside. He invited her in. Later, an old woman came by with a little boy who only had an apple. Seeing this poor, disadvantaged woman trying to rear her boy with nothing at all, Martin invited her in. After they left, Martin went back to his work, and Tolstoy concludes the story:

Martin turned around and saw what appeared to be people in the dark corner, but he could not make out who they were. A voice whispered in his ear, "Martin, Martin! Don't you know me?" "Who is it?" Martin asked. "It is I," the voice said. "Behold it is I!" And out of the dark corner stepped Stepanych. He smiled and then he was gone, melting away like a small cloud. "It is I," repeated the voice. And out of the dark corner stepped the woman with the baby. She smiled, and so did the child, and they too vanished. "It is I!" said the voice. And out stepped the old woman and the boy with the apple. Both smiled, and then they too disappeared. And Martin's heart was filled with joy. He . . . looked at the page where the Bible had fallen open. At the top he read, "For I was hungered, and ye gave me meat: I was thirsty, and ye gave me drink: I was a stranger, and ye took me in. . . ." And lower down, "Inasmuch as ye have done it unto one of the least of these my brethren, ye have done it unto me" (Matthew 25). And Martin understood that his dream had come true, that his Savior had visited him that day, and that he had welcomed Him into his house.

Tolstoy understood that when you touch the disadvantaged with your love, you touch Christ with your love.

Conclusion:
Touching Others with the Love of Christ

When I was a boy, I remember watching my dad sign the bottom of letters he had written. Over in the corner of the page, he always wrote the reference for Isaiah 58:10–11. These verses contain a powerful statement detailing what God thinks about the oppressed and the disadvantaged.

In this text, Israel was complaining about doing everything right but still not feeling close to God. They didn't sense His presence. They went through a whole list of things they had done for Him, including their daily devotionals, and God responded by saying that if they really wanted to know why they never felt close to Him, it was because they were missing something:

> *Is not this the kind of fasting I have chosen: to loose the chains of injustice and untie the cords of the yoke, to set the oppressed free and break every yoke? Is it not to share your food with the hungry and to provide the poor wanderer with shelter—when you see the naked, to clothe him, and not to turn away from your own flesh and blood? Then your light will break forth like the dawn, and your healing will quickly appear; then your righteousness will go before you, and the glory of the Lord will be your rear guard. . . . If you spend yourselves in behalf of the hungry and satisfy the needs of the oppressed, then your light will rise in the darkness, and your night will become like the noonday. The Lord will guide you always; he will satisfy your needs in a sun-scorched land and will strengthen your frame. You will be like a well-watered garden, like a spring whose waters never fail. (Isa. 58:6–11)*

The Lord told Israel that they were missing the point of what touches Him. For all their devotion and fasting, they had failed to minister God's love to the disadvantaged in their midst. I am reminded of Jesus' response when John the Baptist sent a group of His disciples to check out Christ's credentials. It is fascinating that rather than dazzling John's men with a spectacular review of His finest qualities, Jesus offered a simple response: "Go back and report to John what you hear and see. The blind receive sight, the lame walk, those who have leprosy are cured, the deaf hear, the dead are raised, and the good news is preached to the poor. Blessed is the man who does not fall away on account of me" (Matt. 11:4–6).

Then, in Luke 4:18–19, when Christ taught in the synagogue, He read from the prophet Isaiah to proclaim His own identity as the Messiah: "The Spirit of the Lord is on me, because he has anointed me to preach good news to the poor. He has sent me to proclaim freedom for the prisoners and recovery of sight for the blind, to release the oppressed, to proclaim the year of the Lord's favor."

Our acts of love for the disadvantaged authenticate the genuineness of our faith. When we touch the disadvantaged with our love, we touch Jesus Christ.

Reflection Questions

1. What is the "spiritual temperature" of your heart toward "the least of these"? Are there calluses keeping you from reaching out to them?

2. What steps can you personally take to "trade condemnation for compassion"? Can you identify some tangible ways in your own life to replace curiosity with action toward the poor?

3. Are there "cultural chasms" keeping you from loving the unlovely? If so, are you willing to bridge those gaps by "cultivating compassion" within your sphere of influence? How will you do so?

chapter three

A CASE FOR WHOLISTIC* URBAN MINISTRY

THE CITY, EVANGELICALS, AND THE SOCIAL GOSPEL

GLEN KEHREIN

Introduction: Understanding the City

When I first came to Chicago from a small town in Wisconsin, I found it a confusing place. It seemed just a jumble of chaotic humanity —people thrown together by chance. My assessment could not have been more wrong. For more than twenty-five years I have been a student of the city—trying to listen to her and understand why she is like she is and acts the way she acts. How did she begin, grow, mature? I have learned that no neighborhood or community is a product of chance. Each city has its own unique history of forces and counter forces that have shaped the city and all of her neighborhoods. Effective urban ministry requires a comprehensive understanding of the city and neighborhood to which God has called you.

Urban neighborhoods are not unrelated bits of geography that happen by chance. Some neighborhoods—like some biblical texts— seem to make sense at first glance, but there is usually much more to them than meets the untrained eye. The large-scale drama of a city affects its neighborhoods and should confront congregations with ministry opportunities. If the pastor does not understand the larger urban

---

* Commonly the word "holistic" is used in the context of alternative medicine or New Age mysticism. That is why we intentionally use this spelling.

picture, his daily experiences and local situation can overwhelm him. If he does not understand his community, how can his church effectively reach out?[1]

Urban ministry has a history as well. The religious life in a city contributes to its well-being—or maybe even its decay. But I have learned that many churches, ministries, and even training institutions have little understanding of their city or even their own neighborhood. Yet we observe the decay and wonder why—and we wonder why nothing is being done to stop it.

GROWTH OF THE CITIES

America's inner cities have always been the repositories of human need. When Jesus told His disciples that the poor would always exist, He could have added, "and they will move to the city." The poor have always found their way to the city. When Lady Liberty bid to the world, "Send us your tired, your poor, your huddled masses yearning to breath free," they did come. Poor and uneducated immigrants fled oppression, starvation, and often their unsavory past in Europe and came to America. Many settled in the cities. The old and dilapidated portions of town usually served as a "port of entry," offering cheap slum housing and nearby employment.[2] One such community, the Back of the Yards on Chicago's Near Southwest Side, has been described by Upton Sinclair in his classic muckraking book, *The Jungle*. Poor immigrants labored long hours in the massive meatpacking industry that Carl Sandburg referred to when giving Chicago one of its nicknames: Hog Butcher for the World.

Reformers and missionaries alike found mission opportunities in the slums crowded with urban poor. Jane Adams defined the modern social work movement while William Booth of the Salvation Army and Dwight L. Moody defined the urban missionary.

Demographic Shift

By the middle part of the twentieth century the major northern industrial cities experienced radical and rapid change. Major social, economic, and demographic forces converged to change the face of the inner city community for every generation that followed.

For several generations the urban slum had been a transitional point of entry. The European immigrant, just off the boat, moved into cheap housing, established himself and his family, practiced a trade, and built a future, usually by purchasing a home in his ethnic enclave. By the second generation, upward mobility had proven that America was indeed the land of opportunity. No longer was the "old neighborhood" with its small dwellings and crowded streets adequate for the socially advancing new generation. The second and third generations, aided by mobility of the automobile, no longer wanted or needed to live in the old neighborhood. Economic growth following World War II fueled the engine of upward mobility. A completely new community emerged called the suburb, which sprang up to supply the housing demand and new lifestyle. The promise of a better life provided an alluring pull, but that alone did not account for suburban sprawl. There was a "push" as well.[3]

Although competition and turf conflict between immigrant groups was ever existent, most had learned the art of shared living.[4] Northern industrial cities like New York, Philadelphia, Detroit, and Chicago were carved into distinct ethnic communities that shared the land much like the old countries shared the European continent. But that was to change following WWII. The newly arriving group was not immigrants from Europe but migrants from the South. Although Poles could tolerate the Irish as neighbors and Germans the Italians, none of the ethnic groups would tolerate the new emigrants—the transplanted southern African-Americans. A new demographic phenomenon developed: white flight.

> *But everyone I knew who once lived here is long gone. It was as if a neutron bomb fell on this neighborhood in the late 1960s. The buildings and the trees and the parks were left standing, but the people, the white community—my community —disappeared, and a new group of people, a black community, moved in . . .[5]*

As mechanization of the agricultural South made unskilled labor expendable, the industrial North craved factory workers. Blacks responded in unparalleled numbers.

> *The black migration was one of the largest and most rapid mass internal movements of people in history—perhaps the greatest not caused by the immediate threat of execution or starvation. In sheer numbers it outranks the migration of any other ethnic group—Italians, Irish, Jews or Poles—to this country.[6]*

In twenty short years, five million African-Americans "followed the drinking gourd" to the land of freedom in the North.

The established ethnic communities responded as if this were an invasion of hostile forces. But the tide was unstoppable and the need for housing severe. At first the cities attempted to contain the new residents in public housing projects. Cities like Chicago built the infamous Cabrini-Green housing project on the Near North Side and the massive Robert Taylor Homes on the South Side, which both eventually became almost exclusively African-American. But the projects could not contain the demand. Soon blacks began to look for housing in the same "port of entry" communities as did the immigrants before them. And white flight was on.

The slums of the major cities now became ghettos as well. Just as Jim Crow laws defined segregation in the South, racial steering and a common racial containment philosophy of real estate brokers segregated the North. Blacks were restricted to living in ghettos that, in turn, became slums when the middle class fled, taking industry and jobs with them.[7]

Never before had the country seen the deteriorating social conditions of these new, ever-expanding ghetto/slums. Now a new kind of slum dweller was emerging. The promise of economic opportunity proved elusive to the common person. Many of the immigrants were poorly educated and found educational opportunities almost as restricted in the North as in the South. Jobs began to disappear as the Rust Belt lost industry to the South and overseas competition. Welfare rolls ballooned and a new class of people emerged: the permanent underclass. With them came a pessimistic prediction of social stagnation.[8]

Historical Summary of the Church's Response

Evangelicals neglected the urban centers as a mission field for two major reasons.

1. Growth of the suburbs, flight from the cities. Most modern cities became increasingly minority and poor. Both the geographical distance and the class/race differential created separate and isolated communities who had little contact. Yet this alone cannot account for the lack of missionary activity in the cities. These barriers were minor compared to the same barriers facing foreign missions. The continent of Africa and the country of China, as examples, presented these hurdles and more (language, travel, danger of all types, health risks, enormous financial costs, etc.). Yet missionary societies and organizations overcame all of these obstacles to recruit large numbers of missionaries eager to spread the news to peoples and cultures radically different than themselves. That is why I believe the second reason better explains the retreat from urban missions and gives keen understanding to the proper urban mission strategy of today.

2. Resistance to the social gospel and liberalism. The missionary

approach overseas clearly embraces the "earn the right to be heard" philosophy by addressing physical needs. Health care, sanitation, education, and many forms of development went hand in hand with church planting and evangelism in third world countries. But by the mid-twentieth century evangelicals actively warned the church about social ministry as the slide toward liberalism. Social action was pitted against evangelism and seen in direct opposition to orthodoxy. Saving souls through evangelism alone was the only valid form of ministry. Although there might be some room for feeding a hungry stomach, it was only valid ministry if preceded by a sermon. Conservative training institutions prepared pastors and missionaries for the suburbs, rural churches, and foreign field, but not the inner city.

The only acceptable method of reaching the unchurched city dweller was the evangelistic crusade in the tradition of evangelists like D. L. Moody, Paul Rader, and Billy Sunday. These had a long urban history. However the new inner city residents of the 1940s, '50s, and '60s were not, in large part, attracted to attend, or, worse, were discouraged by racial segregation. This left the mostly white, middle-class evangelical community largely without a strategy or even perhaps a motivation to reach into the teaming inner cities. Simply stated, the cities of America were not seen as a mission field and, as such, were neglected.

In 1970, I was living in an inner city community on the near northwest side of Chicago and working as a volunteer in a small inner city youth program. The once Scandinavian community and local church had been an evangelical stronghold that gave birth to The Evangelical Alliance Mission (T.E.A.M.). But now the community was rapidly becoming Hispanic. A fellow recent Moody graduate was temporarily living in the housing owned by the church while completing preparation for an overseas mission assignment. On a street corner my friend challenged me, "Kehrein, when are you going to get yourself together and get on the mission field?" My friend, very sincere and well-meaning, could not see the mission field that was literally at his doorstep.

Theological Shift

During this period significant philosophical and theological shifts were taking place within the Christian community that had first begun during the "Enlightenment Period" of the 1800s.[9]

The Enlightenment championed scientific methodology, where everything—including the Bible—was subject to rational, empirical analysis. In this environment, the discipline of biblical criticism grew up. It was also the context in which Charles Darwin concluded the world wasn't created in six days but was the product of millions of years of evolution.[10] The "modernists" began to liberalize Christianity by embracing this metaphysical view of life and theology. The miracles of Scripture, including the deity of Christ and redemptive atonement, needed to go the way of the flat earth theory.[11] With the redemptive work of God irrelevant, the gospel needed redefinition. Walter Rauschenbusch's classic work, *A Theology of the Social Gospel*,[12] did just that. Rauschenbusch, America's most prominent social gospel theologian, emphasized the corporate nature of Christian commitment at the sacrifice of individual salvation.

In short, the social gospel parsed Scripture strictly along a social path. The gospel was a force for social change. To "love your neighbor" or "offer a cup of cold water" became the essence of the gospel. Conducting matters of social justice or service was, in fact, preaching the gospel. Repentance and redemptive cleansing were dismissed as religious myths along with all stories or acts of the supernatural found in Scripture.[13]

So Christianity divided into two large theological camps: evangelicalism/fundamentalism and liberalism/neo-orthodoxy.[14]

As defenders of orthodoxy, evangelicals clarified their traditional doctrines such as the deity of Christ, the divine inspiration of Scripture, and so on. One distinct battleground became the meaning of the gospel. It was here that the dichotomy clearly found expression. Liberals asserted the gospel's horizontal (social) dimension and evangelicals its vertical (spiritual) dimension. Many evangelicals could not find social justice in Scripture. David Knox listed the arguments given by those who resisted social activism:

> *The teaching and actions of Jesus nowhere show a concern for "social justice." The reason is that the call for social justice springs from envy rather than from compassion. The notion of equality is not set before us by God in Holy Scripture as something to be striven for. Equality was the catchword of the French Revolution, which was anti-Christian in its motivation.*[15]

Each camp was clearly in diametrical conflict with the other.[16]

Traditional Christian institutions, including universities and seminaries such as Yale, Harvard, and the University of Chicago, "went liberal" with the social gospel as a main theological tenet. Conservative

Christianity created its own teaching institutions such as Moody Bible Institute (1886), Evangelical Theological College (1924—later Dallas Theological Seminary), and Westminster Theological Seminary (1929).[17] Teaching against the social gospel and all forms of liberalism was commonplace.

The schism had tragic impact because each side held half the loaf. Historically, evangelicals had been strong social activists, believing Scripture mandates certain moral behavior from believers. The Scriptures had been the moral compass of the nation. Eliminating the slave trade, operation of the Underground Railroad, and eventually the abolition of slavery had strong evangelical roots. Donald Dayton's *Discovering Our Evangelical Heritage* reminds us of the reformist social activism in many evangelical denominations.[18] Care for the poor had resulted in the establishment of charity hospitals, orphanages, and rescue missions. In the late nineteenth century, D. L. Moody's Sunday schools taught reading, writing, and religion to the children of the slums who were exploited as child laborers the other six days of the week.

But the social gospel battle caused evangelicals to retreat from social concerns and ministry. Concern for the poor was equated with the "social gospel" and declared to be the slippery slope toward liberalism. "Look at what happened to the YMCA!" soon became an evangelical warning. Social activity and evangelism were put at odds with each other.

By the 1950s this was a major theme of concern in evangelicalism, making the separation of the vertical (spiritual) from the horizontal (social action) complete. With a few notable exceptions such as rescue missions and the Salvation Army, evangelicals could rarely be found in urban ministry to the poor. The evangelical neglect of the poor was further exacerbated by the flight to the suburbs (described earlier). The larger white evangelical community was becoming increasingly suburban (and rural) and had little in common with the new urban, largely minority, poor. The increasing urban culture of welfare, violence, and drugs broadened the gap and deepened the alienation.

As a student at Moody in the 1960s I first heard the debate: "What comes first, telling a poor person about Christ or feeding him?" The rationale for the "salvation first" approach went something like this: "What good is it to feed a person who is on his way to hell? It is like arranging deck chairs on a sinking ship."

This approach reflects the delineation between vertical and horizontal ministry—the long-term result of the social gospel schism. But the schism created more than just dorm-room debate for theology students. The evangelical church withdrew dramatically from the human need side of ministry in reaction to the social gospel liberalism. Social concern increasingly became a liberal/Democratic agenda while evangelicals increasingly were becoming conservative/Republican. Although overseas missionary activity grew rapidly in the twentieth century—and even included human relief and development activity (i.e., through organizations such as World Vision, Compassion International, World Relief, etc.)—urban ministry that attempted to do the same things at home raised suspicion from evangelicals.

Building upon the momentum of the New Deal of President Roosevelt, social programs for the poor moved firmly into the hands of the government and the liberal church. As the social needs of the cities grew during the 1940s, '50s, and '60s, evangelicals developed very few mission efforts to reach the urban poor. It would have been quite unusual to find even one urban missionary on the roster of a conservative church that supported twenty or thirty foreign missionaries.

Even urban church planting was very limited. Suburban sprawl created ample opportunity for church growth. Additionally, the homogeneous church growth and the homogenous unit principle articulated by Donald McGavran[19] and Peter Wagner[20] supplied a practical rationale that encouraged and justified the development of culturally isolated churches, though that was arguably not their intent. As members moved to the suburbs, urban churches dwindled; as urban presence declined, urban concern waned. At the same time suburban church growth intensified. As years passed few Christian institutions remained committed to the city. Chicago, by way of example, lost three evangelical seminaries to the suburbs. Moody Bible Institute became the rare example of an institution that intentionally chose to remain in the city.

EVANGELICAL PIONEERS, BABY BOOMERS, AND THE WHOLE GOSPEL

Anyone born early enough to remember the Great Depression was forever affected by that experience. The same could be true for the evangelicals who remember the modernist/fundamentalist conflict. But the reaction of burying Mason jars filled with silver coins in the backyard and viewing charity as liberalism has faded as the years passed. A new generation began to invest in the stock market, and a new generation also began to invest in the spiritual lives of inner city residents. They saw the fallacy of dichotomizing the spiritual from the physical: "Humans were created to be whole persons, with physical, mental and spiritual dimensions. Deprivation in any of these dimensions has a deadening effect on the others, since all parts are interrelated and interactive. . . . The soul without a body is a ghost; the body without the soul is a corpse."[21]

In the 1980s, liberal politicians began to lose heart over the impotence of the war on poverty. "We declared war on poverty, and poverty won!" seemed to be a universal concession. Liberal pastors and theologians likewise experienced disillusionment. Mainline churches began losing members by the droves, and few inner city parishes showed any major growth or accomplishments in spite of major financial and human investment. It seemed that the city was losing religious investment on all fronts.

But there was a quiet, nearly imperceptible, noncoordinated movement of evangelical ministry back into the city. An early pioneering example was David Wilkerson. While a rural transplant, Pastor Wilkerson found himself in a foreign land called New York City. Street gangs comprised of violent inner city urchins rocked Wilkerson's world. The traditional church structure was not going to penetrate this community of need. The much-acclaimed Teen Challenge ministry emerged as a parachurch ministry strategy to present the gospel to the unchurched gang member and drug abuser. It was a new ministry paradigm.

Around the same time, and in a most unlikely place, another model of ministry to the poor was awakening. John Perkins's amazing life has been well documented.[22] John's ministry activity and philosophy was born out of Mississippi's poverty and racial struggle and has grown to become a model for Christian inner healing, reconciliation, and community development. Many of the emerging evangelical baby boomers, myself included, found the teaching and testimony of John Perkins to be articulating real answers to our urban ministry struggles. Dr. Perkins was the first person in my memory to articulate the "whole gospel" and "wholistic ministry" in a comprehensive approach that has come to be known as Christian Community Development. When I began working in the inner city in the early 1970s it seemed that a count of biblically based, community based urban ministries (other than rescue missions) left ample fingers to spare on one hand. In the last thirty years God has raised up hundreds of urban ministries across the country committed to wholistic ministry to the poor.

Hundreds of ministries and several thousand people gather each year in the annual conference of the Christian Community Development Association. Each of these ministries has a commitment to the "whole gospel" and "wholistic ministry" to the poor.

The Whole Gospel

Inserting the modifier "whole" before gospel is merely a call to return to the gospel taught by Jesus and a rejection of the dichotomy that divides spiritual and physical needs. Human physical needs, while temporal, still caught Jesus' attention. Healing the sick and feeding the hungry were genuine expressions of His love, not "attention-getters" to build a crowd. In fact, when teaching about the reality of our faith, Jesus said that genuine faith could be recognized by its fruit, rather than its doctrine. How will our fruit prove genuine? How will our love prove sincere? How will we be judged? When the "expert in the law" challenged Jesus in Luke 10, it was the horizontal dimension of "loving your neighbor as yourself" that made the lawyer uncomfortable. Hence the question, "Who is my neighbor?" was an attempt to find a loophole in the personal responsibility that Jesus (and the Law) called for. The story of the Good Samaritan is a parable of living out love on the horizontal plane. Personal salvation without social response is to "love the Lord our God" but to neglect loving our neighbors as ourselves. In truth, Jesus taught, one cannot truly love God without showing love to others.

To deny the social ramifications of the gospel is to create what Ron Sider calls "one sided Christianity."[23] We say, in effect, that the cross has only a vertical timber without the horizontal cross member.

When evangelicals left the city both physically and spiritually, this turf was conceded to the government and liberal church and, I believe, removed "salt and light" from the city. With few wholistic ministries present, our enemy devoured the inner cities.

Dwight L. Moody provides a good historical illustration of urban ministry before the modernist/fundamentalist split. Moody's ministry began with the children of the slums of Chicago. Exploited by industry before child labor laws existed, these children received no formal education and were destined for a life of poverty. Moody's Sunday schools taught basic academics and the Bible.[24] His concern for human suffering always accompanied his zest for soul winning. "Moody had no patience with those who preached bliss in heaven while doing nought about misery on earth."[25] Most famous for his evangelistic crusades, Moody also was a leader in the Young Men's Christian Association (YMCA) movement, established in Chicago as a result of the 1857–58 great revival.[26] The YMCA was designed to evangelize and offer wholesome activity to the young men tempted by drink, gambling, and all sorts of illicit activity. Moody exemplified a minister of the "whole gospel."

But this example also validates the apprehension of evangelicals and illustrates a powerful lesson to every ministry to the poor. Tragically, there is little, if any, "Christian" mission left in the YMCA. When our ministry, Circle Urban Ministries, began on Chicago's West Side, we heard a common warning, "Be careful or you will become just like the YMCA." By that they meant our social passion for the poor would overwhelm our spiritual passion for souls. It was, and remains, a very good admonition that we have never forgotten. But if the once-evangelistic YMCA abandoned its Christian mission, our response must not be to abandon our social concern. This knee-jerk reaction should cause an equal concern about the effectiveness of a one-sided gospel. "As the body without the spirit is dead, so faith without deeds is dead" (James 2:26).

Felt–Need Neglect

Perhaps evangelicalism's neglect of the whole gospel can be understood by the felt-need concept. The prosperity of America from the Second World War did not pass evangelical Christians by. We have enjoyed the unparalleled economic advancement along with all other Americans who have joined the ranks of the middle class. Our churches that once started orphanages for our children, charity hospitals for the sick, and rescue missions for the "down-and-out" no longer feel this need within our ranks. For the most part our churches' members are economically secure in communities that provide what services are necessary (Little League, 4H, etc.). Now the church needs only to focus on the spiritual needs of the flock. Increasingly, the poor have become nameless, faceless statistics. "The poor" are no longer our next-door neighbors, nor do they sit in the pew beside us. A need is going unmet.

The social gap coupled with the geographical gap (i.e., poor in the city and evangelicals in the suburbs) requires us to rethink how urban ministry to the poor must be carried out. How do we extrapolate the whole gospel into urban "wholistic ministry"?

Simply stated, wholistic ministry is applying the whole gospel into a context of need. In this modern age, given the context of need in our inner cities, given the separation by class culture that exists, given our history—what would Jesus have us do?

Rejection, Redemption, and Reconciliation

Scripture teaches that deteriorating social conditions result when people reject God. As urban ministers—by which I mean every person called to serve God in the city, not just clergy—we cannot lose the spiritual perspective described in Ephesians 6:12: "For our struggle is not against flesh and blood, but against the rulers, against the authorities, against the powers of this dark world and against the spiritual forces of evil in the heavenly realms." The social gospel obscured the spiritual dimension. We cannot forget that our battle is against the strongholds of Satan. But God has not left us defenseless: "For though we live in the world, we do not wage war as the world does. The weapons we fight with are not the weapons of the world. On the contrary, they have divine power to demolish strongholds" (2 Cor. 10:3).

Signing up for that war begins with redemption. The Cross redeems us from sin and places within us the power of God's Spirit. All Christians believe this. But redemption is not the end. It is a means to the end. The end is reconciliation, the ultimate purpose of the gospel. To be redeemed from sin (the state of alienation from God) is to be suddenly and miraculously reconciled to God. Redemption—that is Christ's atoning work on the cross—pays the debt caused by our sin and makes reconciliation possible. Grace (i.e., forgiveness) makes it a free gift. God's love is what motivated His grace to us while we were yet sinners. When we accept God's gift we are reconciled to God; the old is gone, the new has come. But our new status carries with it new responsibilities: We are now to be God's ambassadors of reconciliation.[27]

> All this is from God, who reconciled us to himself through Christ and gave us the ministry of reconciliation: that God was reconciling the world to himself in Christ, not counting men's sins against them. And he has committed to us the message of reconciliation. We are therefore Christ's ambassadors, as though God were making his appeal through us. We implore you on Christ's behalf: Be reconciled to God. (2 Cor. 5:17–20)

This is God's plan.

But, of course, Satan, prowling around roaring like a hungry lion, has a plan too (1 Pet. 5:8). It is the opposite of God's plan. Satan's plan is to alienate, to separate, and to divide us from God and from each other. He will use any means—sin of all types—to do just that.

An inescapable fact is that a disproportionate number of racial minorities are poor, live in ghetto and slum conditions in our major cities and on Indian reservations, and are now labeled the "permanent underclass." Our legacy of racial injustice has created a present culture of racial and social alienation. Current racial tension is a cultural stranglehold that society has not been able to break. Why is the grip so strong? It has been thirty years since civil rights legislation, but racial conflict lies just below the surface in many social settings. Why? Because the real issue is a spiritual one. Paul tells us in Ephesians 6:12 that the real battle hides behind the physical manifestations.

When I first started working in the inner city, I could not understand the anger of poor people. Maybe I expected the poor to be like the Cratchit family in Charles Dickens's classic novel *A Christmas Carol*. In spite of the injustice, greed, and abuse this family endured at the hands of Mr. Scrooge, they remained happy. Little Tim faced a life with a serious handicap only because his family could not afford an operation. Yet he seemed the happiest of all.

As morally instructive as this timeless classic may be, I have found its portrayal of a poor family hopelessly romantic. Poverty often is a source of alienation. Inequity breeds anger. Destructive survival behavior becomes a mentality and lifestyle that sucks families into ever-downward whirlpools of negative behavior.

As Christians we must view this condition with the "mind of Christ." Satan's plan is highly effective. It must be confronted by the gospel of reconciliation that brings people into right relationship with God and each other.

But the church needs reconciliation as well. Satan's "fiery darts" have effectively separated the church along racial lines and marginalized its effectiveness in the area of race relations. When society looks to the church for answers, only to see racial separation greater on Sunday morning than any other day, the power of the gospel is compromised. This great inconsistency does more than make us look bad. It robs us of the spiritual power to break the bondage. On the other hand, when "brothers live together in unity" (Ps. 133:1), spiritual impact is transformational.

Jesus continually instructed His disciples in the importance of unity (as in John 17) and Paul followed suit, continually exhorting the early church to reconciliation and unity (Gal. 3:28).

Wholistic ministry starts from a reconciliation understanding of salvation: to love God with all your heart and love your neighbor as yourself (Luke 10:25–37). Jesus' illustration, which we commonly call the Good Samaritan, crossed lines of culture and class.

Relocation and Restoration

To study the life and activity of Jesus is to understand God's approach to bring us the gospel. This should be our pattern. The only reason we can understand God's love at all is because of the incarnation of that love. God did not appear on one occasion to dramatically declare His love through miraculous manifestation and then depart. Rather He "relocated" from glory, became as we are, and lived with all manner of temptation just as we do. We call this incarnational love. It began with relocation.

We are well into our third decade of ministering the whole gospel at Circle Urban Ministries, but it all began with this truth. In the early 1970s my wife and I, along with a small group of friends, moved into a racially changing neighborhood on Chicago's West Side. We relocated into this "community of need" because we knew God was calling us to do just that. This is arguably the most contentious of topics when strategies of urban ministries are discussed. "But do I really need to live 'in there'?" is the challenge. "Can't God use me if I live in a safer community?" Often the dangers of the inner city and the vulnerability of a worker's children are brought up as counteracting issues. These are justifiable concerns. However, how are these concerns any different for a missionary going overseas, where relocation is a "given"? Does our theology of God's control evaporate in "bad neighborhoods"? I wonder if Jesus, up in heaven just before the first Christmas, said to the Father, "But do I really have to go down there, with them?"

After a quarter of a century of living in the community of our ministry, rearing three children, and making it home, I cannot think of a more important decision. In regard to relocation we do not even have to ask "What would Jesus do?" We know what Jesus did. In relocating, Jesus experienced life as we do.

Living in the community does the same for urban ministers. We experience many of the same struggles as our neighbors and gain a more "whole" sense of their struggles. The common bond that is formed can exist no other way. Our ministry must grow from a sensitivity that can only be gained experientially.

Do all urban ministers—even all effective ones—live in their community? No, certainly they do not. But I believe it is a compromise that limits effectiveness. We should ask ourselves why God would have us live anywhere else and then listen to His answers rather than be swayed to live elsewhere by our own desires and concerns. Instead, those desires and concerns will be felt needs we have in common with our neighbors that can produce effective wholistic ministry.

After accepting Christ and choosing my wife, living in the community was the best decision I ever made!

Living in the neighborhood gives a perspective on how to reach out to the community. Walking past abandoned buildings and watching their inevitable demolition moved me to begin a housing rehabilitation ministry. Observing the struggles our children had in the public schools moved us to begin a high quality Christian school. The doctors of our medical clinic delivered our children and serve all our medical needs. If I lived elsewhere, I wonder if having a vital local church in the community would have the same kind of priority. Probably not.

But maybe the best reason to live in the community is that it breaks one's heart. I've seen neighbors' children join gangs and die violent deaths. When a young man who grew up with your son gets shot, he is more than a face on the television tube or a name in the newspaper. It steels your resolve to build a more effective youth program so that it will not happen again. When the girl down the street, who used to come for sleepovers with your daughter, gets pregnant at sixteen, it makes you want to weep—to weep just like Jesus wept over those who were "like sheep without a shepherd" (Matt. 9:36).

In high school my son lived to play football. He made the varsity football team in his sophomore year in a public high school on Chicago's North Side. By the end of the summer after his graduation, two of his teammates were already dead. One he had played ball with since "pee-wee" leagues. I regularly look at their faces on the team picture that hangs in the dining room of our house and think about what inner city children face. It breaks my heart, and it breaks God's heart.

But living in the community should not just acclimate us to the environment; ministering the whole gospel will give us a vision of restoration. And when a community of believers relocates into a deteriorated neighborhood, God begins to stir within them a vision of restoration. Bob Lupton calls this "achieving neighbors" in a chapter about relocation:

> Perhaps the greatest need of under-resourced communities is for achieving neighbor-leaders. Achieving neighbors can do much to break the isolation of poor neighborhoods and reconnect them with the life-giving systems that are the common grace of the city and larger society. Achieving neighbors bring living, personal modes of hope back into a disheartened environment. Achieving neighbors bring resources and skills into a depleted neighborhood, along with fresh energy to deploy them.[28]

This restoration vision is both spiritual and physical. One of the most exciting examples of this in our ministry is the Transformation Crusade Home, a discipleship home for men who have been enslaved to drugs and alcohol.

Once the users and abusers of the community, these men are now restoring the community through their work and testimony. After working all day in some kind of physical labor in the neighborhood or in our ministry, they knock off at 3:00 P.M. and go into the streets to witness about the love of Jesus. Often they talk to the same people who sold drugs to them (or bought them from them). This is wholistic ministry that comes full circle!

The restoring power of the gospel knows no limits. Sometimes it seems like almost everything in our community is broken. The housing stock, medical services, schools, families, whatever—you name it and it needs restoration. But such crying needs present tremendous opportunities for ministry. Circle Urban Ministries has acquired more than twenty buildings, most of which were vacant and vandalized. Those buildings have been restored and served to house a church, a school, a youth recreation center, a food pantry, a homeless shelter, a children's tutoring program, four hundred units of family housing, an adult literacy program, a medical clinic, a discipleship home, Bible classes, volunteer housing, a legal aid clinic, and more.

We have seen that God restores to Himself lives of individuals and entire communities by the power of the whole gospel. We have seen that God has been faithful to His promise: "Seek the peace and prosperity of the city. . . . Pray to the Lord for it, because if it prospers, you too will prosper" (Jer. 29:7).

Conclusion: The Future of the City

Conventional wisdom offers little hope for the city. The failure of social experiments of the 1960s and '70s have given rise to a cynical void. Even though Christians once retreated from the mission field of the cities, there is now a movement of God's Spirit and His people back to city missions. But penetrating the inner city with the good news of the gospel will require that we preach and live the whole gospel. If we can do this, the spiritual fruit will be great. Wholistic urban ministries that are emerging in nearly every city illustrate God's unmistakable blessing. Out of the darkness these candles burn brighter and brighter and offer undeniable evidence to the reality of the gospel and God's love for the people of the city.

When Horace Greeley poignantly urged this country toward the vast Western plains by writing, "Go west, young man, go west!" a generation of pioneers responded to the material opportunities. Today, in a kind of "back to the future" poignancy, God is calling the church to send urban pioneers back into the cities to seek spiritual opportunities and to spread the whole gospel to the vast spiritual wastelands of our inner cities. May many respond as did that servant of old, Isaiah: "Then I heard the voice of the Lord saying, 'Whom shall I send? And who will go for us?' And I said, 'Here am I. Send me!'" (Isa. 6:8).

Reflection Questions

1. What is your level of understanding of the city? How can you increase that understanding?

2. Do you see any latent evidence of the social gospel split in the mission giving of your church? Do you think there is a neglect of missions in "our own backyard"?

3. Do you agree that the evangelical church is neglecting the inner cities? Why? What is your evidence?

4. What effective wholistic ministries are you familiar with? How have you been involved with them? How could you get your church interested in wholistic ministry?

5. If you were called to urban ministry, where would you live, and why? What issues would it raise?

chapter four

A PHILOSOPHY OF URBAN MINISTRY
THE PRINCIPLES OF CHRISTIAN COMMUNITY DEVELOPMENT

WAYNE L. GORDON

Introduction: Our Deteriorating Cities

Nehemiah begins with a lament over the city of Jerusalem: "Those who survived the exile and are back in the province are in *great trouble and disgrace. The wall of Jerusalem is broken down, and its gates have been burned with fire*" (Neh. 1:3b, italics added). This describes the situation in parts of most American cities today. They have been neglected and allowed to deteriorate for almost forty years. The church of Jesus Christ has, at best, sat back and watched this happen, yet in many areas it has contributed to the problem. The words "great trouble and disgrace" ring true for us in the church today.

The question arises as to what our response as Christians will be to the troubles of the poor and the inner cities today. The desperate conditions that face the poor call for a revolution in our attempts at a solution. Through years of experience among the poor, many of us have come to see that these desperate problems cannot be solved without strong commitment and risky actions on the part of ordinary Christians with heroic faith.

CHRISTIAN COMMUNITY DEVELOPMENT
Many philosophies have been suggested to solve the problems, but

most fall short of any lasting change. The most creative long-term solutions to the problems of the poor are coming from grassroots and
church-based efforts. God's work is being done through people who
see themselves as the replacements, the agents, for Jesus here on earth,
in their own neighborhoods and communities.

This philosophy is known as Christian community development,
which was not developed in a classroom, nor formulated by people
foreign to the poor community. These are biblical, practical principles
evolved from years of living and working among the poor. John
Perkins in Mississippi first developed this philosophy.[1] John and Vera
Mae Perkins moved back to their homeland of Mississippi from California in 1960 to help alleviate poverty and oppression. Through their
work and ministry, Christian community development was conceived.
CCD has a proven track record with more than six hundred models
around the country making great progress in difficult communities.[2]

Christian community development has eight essential components
that have evolved over the last forty years. The first three are based on
John Perkins's Three Rs of community development: Relocation, Reconciliation, and Redistribution.[3] The rest have been developed by
many Christians working together to find ways to rebuild poor neighborhoods. The following is a brief description of the eight key components to Christian community development.

Relocation: Living Among the Poor[4]

Living out the gospel means desiring for your neighbor and your
neighbor's family that which you desire for yourself and your family.
Living out the gospel means bettering the quality of other people's lives
spiritually, physically, socially, and emotionally as you better your own.
Living out the gospel means sharing in the suffering and pain of others.

How did Jesus love? "The Word became flesh, and dwelt among
us, and we saw His glory, glory as of the only begotten from the Father,
full of grace and truth" (John 1:14 NASB). Jesus relocated. He became
one of us. He did not commute back and forth to heaven. Similarly,
the most effective messenger of the gospel to the poor will also live
among the poor to whom God has called the person. A key word to
understand relocation is incarnational ministry.

By relocating, we will understand most clearly the real problems
facing the poor; then we may begin to look for real solutions. For example, if our children are a part of that community, we will do whatever we can to make sure that the children of our community get a good
education. Relocation transforms "you, them, and theirs" to "we, us,
and ours." Effective ministries plant and build communities of believ-

ers that have a personal stake in the development of their neighborhoods.

Relocation is community-based in the very essence of the word. Three kinds of people live and minister in the community. First, people like myself, "Relocators," were not born in the Lawndale community of Chicago, but obeyed the call of God and moved into the neighborhood. Second are the "Returners." These are the people born and raised in their community who then left for a better life. Usually they return from college or the military. They are no longer trapped by the surrounding poverty of their neighborhood. Yet they choose to return and live in the community they once tried to escape. Lastly are the "Remainers." Some of these could have fled the problems of the inner city but chose to stay and be part of the solution to the problems surrounding them.

In 1975 I moved into the neighborhood of North Lawndale on Chicago's West Side. This community was typical of most inner city neighborhoods with a high crime rate, inferior education, ravaged by lack of services and white flight. There is no question that relocation is the linchpin of Christian community development. All the other principles draw upon it for meaning. After twenty-three years of my wife Anne and I raising our three children, Angela, Andrew and Austin, in Lawndale, I can say that it works. But beyond that, we are all better people and have been taught far more than we have taught and been given more than we have given.[5]

Reconciliation: People to God, People to People

Reconciliation is at the heart of the gospel. Jesus said that the essence of Christianity could be summed up in two inseparable commandments: Love God and love your neighbor (Matt. 22:37–39; Mark 12:30–31; Luke 10:27). First, Christian community development is concerned with reconciling people to God and bringing them into a church fellowship where they can be discipled in their faith.

Evangelism is very much a part of Christian community development. We recognize that the answer is not just a job or a nice place to live but a true relationship with Jesus Christ. It is essential that the Good News of Jesus Christ is proclaimed and that individuals place their faith in Christ for salvation. Christian discipleship is very much a part of this philosophy also.

The gospel, rightly understood, is wholistic. It responds to people as whole people; it does not single out spiritual or physical needs and just speak to those. Christian community development begins with people transformed by the love of God, who then respond to God's call to share the gospel with others through evangelism, social action, economic development, and justice.

It is well documented that the most segregated time of the week is Sunday morning during church services. American churches rarely are integrated, which weakens the gospel message. We pray in the model prayer that our Lord taught us: "Thy kingdom come, Thy will be done on earth as it is in heaven." Our churches should reflect heaven on earth. Yet we all know that heaven will be the most integrated place ever. People of every nation and every tongue will worship Christ together.

The question is, Can a gospel that reconciles people to God without reconciling people to people be the true gospel of Jesus Christ? Our love for Christ should break down every racial, ethnic, and economic barrier. As Christians come together to solve the problems of their community, the great challenge will be to partner and witness together across these barriers. Christian community development recognizes that the task of loving the poor is shared by the entire body of Christ: black, white, brown, and yellow; rich and poor; male and female; urban and suburban; educated and uneducated. The Bible transcends culture and race, but we in the church are still having a hard time with these essentials.

Christian community development is very intentional about reconciliation and works hard to bring people of all races and cultures into the one worshiping body of Christ. This comes not so much through a program but through a commitment to living together in the same neighborhood. This is why relocation is so important. You can see how each of the other principles builds upon it. Glen Kehrein and Raleigh Washington's book *Breaking Down Walls* is a great resource to help in racial reconciliation,[6] along with Spencer Perkins and Chris Rice's book *More Than Equals*.[7]

Redistribution: Bringing Our Resources into the Community

When the body of Christ is visibly present and living among the poor (relocation), and when we are loving our neighbor and our neighbor's family the way we love ourselves and our own family (reconciliation), the result is redistribution. If we as God's people with resources are living in the poor community and are a part of it, our skills and our resources will be applied to the problems of that community. Bringing our lives, our skills, our education, and our resources and putting them to work to empower people in a community of need is redistribution. Christian community development ministries find creative avenues to create jobs, schools, health centers, home ownership, and other enterprises of long-term development.

Many communities lack some of the most basic resources for survival. In Lawndale, when we first began to study our community and find opportunities for ministry, we found that health care was sorely lacking. We discovered that the physician-to-population ratio was seven times the national crisis level. For all intents and purposes the people did not have access to good, affordable health care. Dr. Art Jones and his wife Linda moved into Lawndale to open a health center. Today more than twenty other physicians have joined Art, seeing more than 75,000 patients per year. The health care needs of our neighborhood are being met in the name of Jesus. The motto of Lawndale Christian Health Center is "Quality, Affordable Healthcare in an Atmosphere of Christian Love."

We also did not have a sit-down family restaurant to take our families to dinner. The Malnati family of Chicago partnered with Lawndale Community Church to open a Lou Malnati's pizzeria in Lawndale. Marc and Rick Malnati are Christians who wanted to help others. They have not relocated themselves, but they have relocated a business to serve our community.[8] This provides a place of hope and affirms the people of our neighborhood. Lou Malnati's is an example of economic development and true partnership of Christians.

These and others are examples of redistribution at its best, helping people help themselves. We as Christians must deal with the huge divide between the haves and the have-nots of society. Redistribution is a starting point in the Bible for justice and love.

LEADERSHIP DEVELOPMENT[9]

The primary goal of redistribution is to restore the stabilizing glue and fill the vacuum of moral, spiritual, and economic leadership that is so prevalent in poor communities. This is most effectively done by raising up Christian leaders from the community of need who will remain in the community. Most Christian community development ministries put a strong accent on youth development, winning youth to Christ as early as kindergarten and following them all the way through college with spiritual and educational nurture. Another ministry creates opportunities for leadership upon return to their community—but many do not return. At the core of this vacuum of leadership in inner city communities has been a philosophy of getting out. For many, success is being able to move out of communities like North Lawndale. Many believe that the only hope is to help a few people leave the neighborhood so that they can escape the problems of inner city communities. This core value of escapism has caused a major drain on the community.

When I first moved to Lawndale, I did not know another college graduate who was living in the community. For the first two or three years, my philosophy of leadership development was finding empowered leaders outside of the community with the hope of their moving into Lawndale. After being unsuccessful in convincing anyone to move to Lawndale (except my wife Anne) and join in our work, out of frustration I had a life-changing talk with Tom Skinner. I told Tom that I was having a difficult time finding black leadership to join me in Lawndale. His answer was profound and challenging. He looked me in the eye and said, "Wayne, there are leaders that will lead here in Lawndale, but you're looking in the wrong place. The leaders are already in Lawndale. It is your job to develop them so that they can lead in the future." It was Tom Skinner's philosophy that we should raise up leadership from among the poor to lead the poor. After our discussion on this, he then looked at me with great intensity and said, "There's just one problem, Wayne—it'll take you fifteen years to raise up a new generation of black Christian leadership for Lawndale. Will you stay fifteen years to accomplish this task?" Obviously, I responded with an enthusiastic yes.

This discussion with Tom Skinner set me and the ministry of Lawndale Community Church on the quest to raise up a new generation of black Christian leadership for North Lawndale. I began by trying to help as many young people as I could to get into college. Our beginning attempts were mostly unsuccessful. Of the first ten young people we sent off to college, not one graduated. We began to learn from our mistakes, as everyone does, and we now have an entire ministry revolving around preparing students to be successful in college. Today, a student from Lawndale Community Church who is in college can expect a visit from a staff member while on campus, care packages, monthly letters with updates of our ministry, an adoptive family that prays for and writes the student, as well as several other activities. One of our pastors oversees our college ministry, striving to help students continue on and be successful in college.

Leadership development has probably been one of the most effective ministries at Lawndale Community Church. As of today, we have helped more than one hundred young people graduate from college, with more than half returning to live and work in Lawndale. We are blessed with people like Richard and Stephanie Townsell who graduated from Northwestern University and then returned to Lawndale where Richard heads up the multimillion-dollar development arm of Lawndale Community Church, Lawndale Christian Development Corporation. After college Lance and Cindy Greene moved back to Lawndale, and today Lance serves in a full-time ministry capacity as the coach and youth leader of our Kaboomer track team. Both Richard and Lance are great examples of continuing the leadership philosophy as they are raising up new leaders for the next generation.

I remember with great fondness a celebration a few years ago at Lawndale Community Church to mark Anne's and my ministry of more than twenty years in Lawndale. The church went all out with flowers, plaques, great tributes, good speakers, all the wonderful things that made Anne and me feel very loved. All our three children also felt loved.

As I was lying in bed that night thanking God for that special day, my mind began to picture people who were out in the congregation while I was preaching. I began to count the young couples who were sitting in our congregation that morning whom I had discipled and whose weddings I had performed. As I pictured each couple, I realized that eight of them were going to have babies. Joy filled my heart as I realized that these eight new lives were going to grow up in a neighborhood that was much different than what their parents grew up in. It was going to be a neighborhood where there was community, and they would have relationships with one another. They are the third generation that will be the leaders of Lawndale. It was with great joy and satisfaction and tremendous fulfillment of purpose that I fell asleep that night thinking about what God had done.

Leadership development is possible only when there is longevity of ministry. All too often we are guilty of trying to have "quick fixes" in our neighborhood.[10] Leadership development is of the highest priority in Christian community development. Each ministry must have a dynamic youth ministry that is reaching young people with the good news of Jesus Christ and then discipling them in their faith. It will take at least fifteen years to accomplish, so plan to stay put in your neighborhoods.

The Felt–Need Concept

The great question is, "How do we affirm the dignity of people, motivate them, and help them take responsibility for their own lives?" By beginning with the people's needs we establish a relationship and a trust, which then enables us to move to deeper issues of development. Two major strands of community development are prevalent today, the first being a needs-based development. This is where development is based on the great needs in poor communities. The other is asset-based community development that focuses on the assets of a community and builds upon them.

The felt-need concept of Christian community development strives to use the best of both of these philosophies. First, it gathers the community and discovers the talents, abilities, and skills in the neighborhood—those assets that often are passed over. It then realistically finds out through a series of neighborhood meetings and discussions what are some of the areas that people in the community would like to see improved. The areas of focus are not chosen by some outside group or a demographic study. Instead, the community itself decides what area it would like to improve.

After a community has decided where it wants to focus some of its attention, it is then directed to the means that the residents themselves can use to bring this about. What qualities, talents, and abilities do the community have that can help solve these problems? The community itself, not some government program or outside group, finds the solution to the problem.

It is essential for the leadership to help the community to focus on their strengths and abilities to make a difference. The philosophy of Christian community development believes that the people with the problem often have the best solutions and opportunities to solve those problems.

One danger of the felt-need concept is a preoccupation with the problems and needs in a community. The felt-need concept is only a tool for the very beginning of development to listen to the people and give them hope for life-changing solutions. Quickly, this should then move to seeing the great potential that is in their community.

Church-Based

Nothing other than the community of God's people is capable of affirming the dignity of the poor and enabling them to meet their own needs. It is practically impossible to do effective wholistic ministry apart from the local church. A nurturing community of faith can best provide the thrusts of evangelism, discipleship, spiritual accountability, and relationships by which disciples grow in their walk with God. One problem today has been that churches are not involved in developing their communities. Often, the church has been an unfriendly neighbor in communities across our country. Churches are guilty of being open only on Sunday mornings and Wednesday nights and being almost irrelevant to the needs of the people around them. Because of this, many parachurch organizations have started to do the work of loving their neighbor that the church had neglected. Christian community development sees the church as taking action toward the development of its community.

It is the responsibility of the church to evangelize, disciple, and nurture people in the kingdom. Yet it is also the responsibility of the church to love its neighbor and its neighborhood. Churches should be seen as lovers of their communities and very neighborhood-friendly. It is out of the church body that ideas and programs should emerge.

This has certainly been the story of Lawndale Community Church. Our ministry began with high school students and a few adults desiring to live out this commandment of our Lord Jesus Christ. Through the people of Lawndale Community Church, Lawndale Christian Health Center was spawned in 1984. The people of Lawndale Community Church wanted to have a health center that would meet health care needs in an affordable manner for the people of Lawndale. Almost every ministry and program that is a part of the Lawndale Ministries grew out of Lawndale Community Church.

The church is also the source of energy and sustaining power for community development. Mary Nelson of Bethel New Life on Chicago's West Side says that the church is "the gas, the glue and the guts of Christian community development."[11] It is the greatest community-organizing tool that a group can have. Picture several hundred people gathering each week for worship and inspiration. They then are equipped to go out into the community and to make a difference.

This concept is certainly not new in the black community. Most of the substantial community efforts in housing and economic development have been spawned by the black church. The church has built shopping centers and senior housing units, developed, and literally changed communities. As natural as it has been for the black church, it continues to be foreign to the traditional white church. Often, white denominations and church groups still oppose the church being involved in community development.

Last, probably the greatest sustaining power of community development is the community building of a local church. Because Christian community is based on relocation and people living in the community, having a local church to worship together is essential. This is true for staff members as well as people who are more on the receiving end of ministry. How exciting it is to see doctors at Lawndale Christian Health Center worshiping and sitting next to their patients on Sunday morning. This is community building at its very best. The church helps people to understand that each of us has gifts and talents and we must use those for the greater good of the community. A worshiping church breaks down many of the barriers, including racial, educational, and cultural ones, that often separate us in our communities.

Wholistic Approach

Many of us get very passionate and involved in one area of need and think if we solve this particular problem that all the other things will work out. As Christians, of course, this area is a personal relationship with Jesus Christ. Evangelism and discipleship are the most vital element to Christian community development. When I first moved to Lawndale, I focused most of my attention on these two essentials. I was under the impression that if somebody made a personal commitment to Jesus Christ, then the rest of the problems in his or her life would be solved. I found this not always to be the case.

One of the first young men whom I helped to become a Christian was struggling with his grades at Farragut High School. He was a member of the football team I coached at the school, and we were concerned as to whether or not he would be eligible to play. After he became a Christian, I noticed that his grades did not improve. Upon further exploration, I discovered that the young man could not read. I set up a one-on-one tutoring program to teach him how to read. Another young man who was involved in Bible studies was living in a twenty-five-unit apartment building that had no heat though it was the middle of winter. During this time, he made a commitment to Jesus Christ. A few weeks later I found that the heat still had not been turned on in his apartment building. His becoming a Christian did not change the hardened heart of the landlord who was responsible for paying the gas bill. We organized a tenant meeting and set up an escrow account for them to pay their rent into until the landlord paid the gas bill.

These are just two examples that guide us into understanding the importance of a wholistic approach. There is never a simplistic answer to the problems in poor communities. Often people will say that the problem is spiritual, social, or educational. Of course these are problems, but only part of the larger problem. Solving the housing problem does not solve the emotional struggles a person has. Christian community development has a wholistic approach to ministry that deals with the spiritual, social, economic, political, cultural, emotional, physical, moral or justice issues, educational, and family life of each person.

Of course, the wholistic approach is difficult because a person's life has so many aspects. That is why there is no better way of helping a person than having that person plugged into a local church. A church that is committed to Christian community development sees not only the soul of a person as significant, but also his whole of life on earth. It is caring for a person, not only eternally, but also as he lives on this earth.

We must network with other churches and organizations in our communities, not thinking that we have to solve every problem ourselves. If your neighborhood has a good health center in it, support that one; do not start one. When a park district is strong with wonderful programs, you may not need to build a gym; instead, volunteer and adopt the park district as your recreational program. In order to accomplish the wholistic aspect of ministry, we must be networkers. Christian community development builds coalitions in communities so that we might work together to solve the problems.

Empowerment

Everyone is talking about empowerment, but who is really doing it? Empowering people as we meet their needs is an important element to Christian community development. How do we make sure that people are able to help themselves after we have helped them? Often Christian ministry, particularly in poor communities, creates dependency. We are no better than the federal government welfare program; it just happens to be done in the name of Christ. The Bible teaches us that is not the way to do it.

In the Old Testament, we see empowerment as an important aspect to God's care for the poor. In Deuteronomy 24:19–22 and Leviticus 19:10, God instituted the gleaning system. When farmers harvested their crops they were only allowed to go through the field one time. What was left behind or dropped on the ground was available for any widow, foreigner, orphan, or poor person to come and harvest. This program empowered people.

Three principles come out of God's welfare system in the Old Testament. First, there must be an opportunity for people to get their needs met. In Deuteronomy and Leviticus, this was a field with food in it. Second, the person who had a need must be willing to work to meet it. The widow, foreigner, orphan, or poor person must go into the field and pick up the crops that had fallen to the ground or the ones that were still on the tree. This, then, involved work on the part of the poor. Of course, this is also seen in 2 Thessalonians 3:10, which says, "If you don't work, you don't eat" (my paraphrase). Third, we find that when these first two principles are working, help then affirms the person's dignity. All people have inherited dignity by being created in the image of God (Gen. 1:26–27). Often, however, charity demeans people and strips them of their dignity.

Here at Lawndale, we try to do two things as a staff to empower people. We always ask a person whom we are helping, "What is it that you need to do so that you won't need our help one year from now?"

This puts it in a time frame that is doable. The person then needs to identify areas where he needs help: possibly getting some training, getting a better job, changing a housing situation, getting off drugs, or something else that would help him so that he would be standing on his own a year in the future. After the person has decided what needs to be done, we help him to design a plan of action to accomplish those goals. These, of course, are not the leader's ideas, but those of the person with the problem. Christian community development believes that the people with the problem have the best chance of solving the problem. They know the solution, but they often need help in implementation and the resources to do so.

We also work under the understanding that we should never do something for a person that he could do himself. Doing it for him not only strips him of his dignity, but it creates dependency on others. We must often use tough love and tell the person, "No, we will not help you" when we know that he could do it himself. We may need to encourage and inspire him to do this, but we should not do for him what he can do for himself. Sometimes we need tough love to help people hit bottom so that they can then be raised up.

Our ministries must be empowering ministries that do not demean and demoralize people as we help them. We also need to be very careful in how we write about the stories of the people that we have helped. I like to ask myself the question, "Would I want somebody to read this about myself that I'm writing about this person?" When I wrote *Real Hope in Chicago*[12] a couple of years ago, every story I told was approved by the person it was about. This was a great learning experience for all of us as we worked hard together. It made writing the book a team-building experience instead of exploitation of the poor.

Christian community development empowers people to be all that God has created them to be.

OUR TRACK RECORD

Christian community development has been effective in many phases of ministry. In Mendenhall, Mississippi, we see home-grown leaders such as Dolphus and Rosie Weary, Artis and Carolyn Fletcher, and many other young people return to their community to begin a health center, businesses, a Christian school, a law office, a church, and a pastor development program that is nurturing black church leadership throughout the state of Mississippi. These programs in turn led to economic development, creating jobs and opportunities for many others in Mendenhall.[13]

Bob and Peggy Lupton went to Atlanta and became burdened by the plight of young black boys. Out of that burden came FCS (Family Consultation Service) Urban Ministries, which is pioneering in the "re-neighboring" of the deteriorating Summerhill community, site of the 1996 Olympics.[14] A young white Moody Bible Institute graduate named Glen Kehrein relocated into the Austin neighborhood of Chicago and started Circle Urban Ministries. A black pastor, Raleigh Washington, joined him.[15] Ted and Shelly Travis moved into the Five Points neighborhood of Denver, Colorado. Now this is a Neighborhood Ministries and Jubilee Community Church. Other ministries have been started in cities like Detroit, Denver, Baltimore, Seattle, and dozens of others.[16]

With these men and women and many others attempting to live out the reconciling love of God among the poor, we recognized our need to encourage and learn from each other. In 1989 the Christian Community Development Association (CCDA) was born. CCDA is now more than six hundred member organizations in more than two hundred cities and forty states.[17] These churches and ministries are showing that it is possible that the church can live out the love of God in the world; that black and white and yellow and brown, rich and poor together, can be reconciled; and that we can make a difference, that we can rescue the ghettos and barrios of this nation.

In hundreds of communities and cities across the world, these defining principles of Christian community development are proving that grassroots, community-based ministries led by people who have made the community their own are the most effective agents for healing of the poor.

Conclusion:
The Measure of Our Success

Everywhere I have been across the nation where churches are practicing these principles of Christian community development, I find success. Success is not defined by huge numbers of people and million-dollar budgets, but in the changed lives of people who are now living for Jesus Christ. Their quality of life has been improved and they are able to function in a positive way in their community.

One of John Perkins's favorite poems tells us what Christian community development is really all about. If we will go and practice these things with the Lord's enabling, we will have success in our efforts:

Go to the people
Live among them
Learn from them
Love them
Start with what they know
Build on what they have:
But of the best leaders
When their task is done
The people will remark
"We have done it ourselves."[18]
                    —Author unknown

Reflection Questions

1. Are you willing to live and serve the Lord in a community of need? Why or why not? What are the advantages/disadvantages of doing so?

2. It takes fifteen years to develop indigenous leadership in an urban setting. What are the implications of this fact for church planting and church development strategies in an urban context?

3. What does this mean for you personally, if God calls you to a church planting and Christian leadership development ministry in the city?

4. Why is there such a need for racial reconciliation in our world today?

chapter five

PROMOTING RACIAL RECONCILIATION IN THE CITY

THE AGAPE COMMUNITY CENTER AND INTERRACIAL FRIENDSHIP

MILTON MASSIE AND MARC HENKEL

Introduction: What God Has Done

How heroic is your faith? Is it strong enough to pry open the doorway of your heart to let in those who are not your family, clan or ethnic group? Or is it only strong enough to do what comes naturally and accommodate those who are enough like you?

—Spencer Perkins[1]

In beginning a piece on racial reconciliation, we are flooded with conflicting questions as to where to start. We express this first of all because we realize that we are not experts on racial reconciliation. We would go so far as to say that no one or two people can claim to be the experts in this area. Yet, for the sake of bringing glory to God and contributing to the healing of the body of Christ, and then prayerfully to reach the world more effectively, it is our goal in this effort to tell the reality of what God has done in our lives and ministry as we have intentionally pursued racial reconciliation. We thank the Lord Jesus Christ first of all for the privilege and honor to serve Him and the body of Christ in this way. Then we again acknowledge the numerous mentors, experts, and examples of brothers and sisters who have addressed this issue and from whom we have learned how and what to do to promote racial reconciliation within our lives, families, and ministry.

MARC'S STORY

Growing up in the northwest suburbs of Chicago, I, like many others who grew up in a suburban context, did not know many people from different ethnic groups. My world was primarily homogeneous. I thought that everything was pretty cool between the different races, but that a few people still had problems accepting others from a different background. Little did I know that everyone, to some degree or another, has some baggage to deal with, some more than others. I did not realize that, although I thought I was reconciled with everyone, I still had biases toward people who were more like me. In my heart I showed favoritism toward them. I found out at college that this was not just my problem, but one of the main shortcomings of the church as a whole and mankind throughout the world.

God made it possible for me to attend Wheaton College, a Christian liberal arts college in the western suburbs of Chicago. After a year there, I figured that the town of Wheaton was very much like the suburbs that I grew up in, except even better, because more Christians inhabited the town. As I became more sensitive to the needs of the inner city and of people from different ethnic backgrounds while tutoring in Cabrini-Green, a housing project near downtown Chicago, I began to wonder if there were many African-Americans living in Wheaton. To my surprise I found out that there was a significant number. I thought this to be kind of odd, because by that time I had been to at least five churches in Wheaton and had seen very few people of color. I discovered that there were two churches in the part of town where many of the African-Americans lived, and I decided to attend one of the churches to see what it was like. I had a great time worshiping on several Sunday mornings at the church, but I saw very few white people in attendance.

This reality in Wheaton, which is well-known for its many Christian residents and numerous churches and mission organizations, confused me. Why did these believers of different color not have fellowship? Surely the message of Ephesians 2:14 applies to all people groups, not just Greeks and Jews, for it says that "He [Jesus] himself is our peace, who has made the two one and has destroyed the barrier, the dividing wall of hostility." Surely it is not God's desire for His people to exist in a "separate but equal" society. Why is it that eleven o'clock on Sunday morning is the most segregated hour of the week? These questions make my brain stagger, and I have not yet fully recovered.

In my short ten-plus years of learning about racial reconciliation, I have found only one solution. The solution is to take the initiative, in the power of the Holy Spirit, to build quality cross-cultural friendships that are intentional, Christ-centered, and honest. One illustration always sticks with me to remind me of the power of Christ to break down the dividing barriers, and it happened during my first years in ministry at the Agape Community Center. The Agape Center is the Chicago inner city ministry of Campus Crusade for Christ. At the center we seek to make disciples of the people in the community through wholistic programs such as tutoring, recreation, martial arts, twelve-step programs, and Bible studies.

One summer Milton and I were doing some follow-up visits in the neighborhood. As we walked down 112th Place, we saw two muscular African-Americans sitting outside, drinking, and playing their music loudly. Since I was a newcomer in the community, I was intimidated by their presence. As we approached, one of them said, "What's a white guy doing in our neighborhood?"

Milton turned around, pulled out a Christian tract, and replied, "We're telling people about Jesus."

The man shot back quickly, "Oh yeah, well, you can't show me in the Bible where Jesus was white." We told the two men that Jesus was not really white or black. He was Jewish, and his skin color was probably somewhere in between. After about two seconds of shock, one of the men put his arm around me and said, "Well, I'm not really prejudiced. I've just been drinking a little. I *love* white people!" God has the power to turn people's perspectives around, but we need to take the initiative in love to present the truth, and be willing to be different.

Have Things Really Changed in the Past Few Years?

Racial reconciliation is a term that was seldom heard ten years ago. Largely through the work of John Perkins and the Christian Community Development Association,[2] it is being discussed more. Interracial speaking teams, like the late Spencer Perkins and Chris Rice of Voice of Calvary Ministries, and Raleigh Washington and Glen Kehrein of Rock Church and Circle Urban Ministries in Chicago, have made huge inroads to bridging the gap between the races. When Milton and I first started talking to college students who came to the Agape Center in the early 1990s, racial reconciliation was a new topic to most of the students. Now most college students we speak to have already been introduced to the issue to some extent.

Most often, however, what they have really heard about is not racial reconciliation, but "cultural sensitivity," which is another term for learning to tolerate people who are different from ourselves. Although it is true that college campuses and America as a whole are becoming more culturally sensitive, it is not true that real racial reconciliation is taking place. I am grateful for the steps that America is making toward racial reconciliation, but we still have a long way to go.

Nationally, racial residential segregation has declined. Last year, the *Chicago Tribune* printed the results of a report done by Reynolds Farley of the University of Michigan. "Of the 232 communities (metropolitan areas) Farley studied, segregation declined in 191 during the 1980's, he found."[3] More and more, communities, businesses, and government agencies are seeing a greater mixture of races than they have seen in the past.

At the same time, although there may be more integration than ever before, white people are too often not willing to give up their control. Dateline NBC aired a special report, "Why Can't We Live Together?" in June of 1997.[4] It was about the changing racial makeup of Matteson, Illinois, a suburb of Chicago. The community started out with the vast majority of the home owners being white. In the past few years the community has become increasingly mixed, half-black and half-white. The real estate agencies were finding that now only one white family for every twenty black families expressed interest in buying a home in Matteson. Now that whites no longer make up the majority, they are starting to leave the community by the dozens. Cultural sensitivity and integration will not bring long-term change unless accompanied by racial reconciliation.

Another study done in Chicago by the Metropolitan Chicago Information Center says that blacks and whites are feeling more comfortable with each other. "Among Chicago whites the perception of comfort is up 18 percent" and "among Chicago blacks the perception of comfort is up 4 percent" since 1992. The survey also said that the number of Chicago whites who "report that they 'frequently' try to find opportunities to meet black people is up 26 percent," and that the number of Chicago blacks who "report that they 'frequently' try to find opportunities to meet white people is up 12 percent" since 1992.[5]

These statistics denote that some progress is being made, but still 54 percent of whites and 43 percent of blacks could not say that they felt comfortable with each other. Although encouraging, the total of those blacks and whites who actually seek out opportunities to meet other races "frequently" is less than 50 percent.[6] Some are willing to be intentional in building friendships cross-culturally, but even when we work in the same buildings and live in the same neighborhoods, many Americans are not pursuing cross-cultural friendships. Racial reconciliation cannot take place except through friendships. So, again, we see that true racial reconciliation is not taking place.

Realistically, we cannot expect America to embrace racial reconciliation when the church, to whom the mandate has been given, has been so slow to embrace it. For many years the white church has been silent on issues regarding justice and equality with other races. This is another area where, slowly but surely, things are beginning to change. Jim Wallis of *Sojourners Magazine* wrote, "A deep conviction and growing passion about racial reconciliation is taking root in the very unexpected soil of the white, conservative Christian world."[7] He went on to tell how Don Argue, the president of the National Association of Evangelicals, willingly "confessed the sin of racism by white evangelicals, asked forgiveness, and committed the NAE to forge new multiracial relationships to change evangelical institutions."[8] Wallis also mentioned that Promise Keepers has become committed to racial reconciliation and promoting cross-cultural friendships.

Even though these long overdue changes have begun, there is still a long way to go. Is racial reconciliation just another fad, or is the church willing to back up its talk with its walk? Jim Wallis mentioned a black evangelical leader who is skeptical. He wonders if those "who still hold the trump cards will ever be willing to give them up" and begin to share the financial rewards and decision-making power with qualified minorities.[9] During the Fifth Annual Wheaton Theology Conference at Wheaton College, Eugene Rivers, the pastor of Azusa Christian Community in Boston, said, "I don't care how many stadiums you fill with men hugging each other and crying. If our idea of reconciliation is divorced from a commitment to truth and justice, we're shuckin' and jivin' and livin' a lie."[10] Whether or not Christians are serious enough about racial reconciliation to go beyond lip service still remains to be seen. Americans as a whole, and Christians in general, have learned more about tolerating our differences, but most are nowhere near being racially reconciled.

The City of Chicago and the Roseland Community

When we look at the city of Chicago, we see a sober picture. Chicago has always been a city with racial problems, and it continues to struggle with racial issues. While protesting housing segregation in Chicago in August of 1966, Dr. Martin Luther King Jr. said, "I have seen many demonstrations in the South, but I have never seen anything so hostile and so hateful as I've seen here today."[11] Dr. King, and others at the time, categorized Chicago as the most segregated city in the nation.

Today in Chicago, not much has changed. It still holds the title as the most segregated city in the nation. In the report done by Reynolds Farley, quoted earlier, Chicago was ranked as the third most segregated city behind Gary, Indiana, and Detroit, Michigan.[12] But as Pierre de Vise pointed out three weeks later in the *Chicago Tribune,* Farley's report looked at metropolitan areas as opposed to the actual people within the city limits. "Hence, Chicago's reputed status over the last 25 years as the nation's most segregated large city is not challenged."[13]

This segregation is not just a black/white issue. It extends to almost all ethnic neighborhoods. As you drive through Chicago, it is possible to stay on one street and cross into many different "villages." There are a few exceptions on the North Side, but on the whole, many different worlds are located in this one city. Often, crossing the boundary street that divides two communities is like crossing a war zone for different residents. This can be seen in going from South Lawndale, a Latino neighborhood, to North Lawndale, an African-American neighborhood. We have friends whose lives were threatened just because they were on the "wrong side" of the street.

The racial tension that exists in the Roseland community that Milton and I live and work in can be felt just about anywhere we go in the community. In the early 1960s this community was predominantly white. With the passing of the "Fair Housing Act" in 1968, the neighborhood changed racially almost overnight. To this day, many white people still feel angry about "having to give up their community" and talk negatively about those who live there now. On the other side, I have seen a few instances where a black person has not been happy to see whites in the neighborhood and has even said some insulting things to them.

Much of the problem in the Roseland community stems back to the sin of favoritism shown by Roseland's first settlers. The first group of people ever to live in this area were from the Netherlands. For the most part, they were Christians and they came for religious purposes. As Chicago began to grow and more immigrants began moving into the community, they developed a new word for these "outsiders." They called them "vremde,"[14] a word that had connotations of unacceptance, mistrust, and sometimes hatred. Many people from different European countries moved to Roseland, but in the 1960s, a "vremde" that was worst of all moved in: the African-Americans. I believe that if the Christians who first lived in the Roseland community had taken a stand against racial injustice and learned to "love their neighbor," racism would not be half the problem it is today in our community. Just imagine what would have happened if America's founding fathers were committed to racial reconciliation instead of to manifest destiny.

MILT'S STORY

In the 1960s and '70s, Roseland, a former Dutch community, was going through turmoil. At that time I lived north of Roseland in the high-rise projects known as the Robert Taylor Homes. Having lived there for some six or seven years, my parents were ready to move their family of five to a better neighborhood. They had their eyes on Roseland. Real estate companies were selling *hope* to the blacks and *fear* to the whites. They made money hand over fist by telling blacks that the neighborhood was quiet, the schools were top of the class, and there were plenty of businesses. For a working-class family, this was the realization of the American Dream: a place to work, worship, and raise one's family in a safe environment. That is all any person in America wants.

However, when we moved here we were met with fear, standoffishness, and a cool communication that we were not welcome. I vividly remember our moving onto our block as one of the few black families in the predominantly white neighborhood. It was October of 1969, when I was a month into my seventh-grade school year. The culture shock of going from an all-black neighborhood to a predominantly white neighborhood was quite an adjustment for all of us.

Within two years Roseland went from being mostly white to practically all black. "White flight" was at full throttle. In my first year of junior high, I was chased home nearly every day by little white boys who effectively delivered the message to me and my family that they did not want blacks in *their* community. By the time I graduated from eighth grade, blacks were in the majority. Now we were the ones chasing the little white boys and their families out of the community.

Much of my experience with racial tension and issues of this type were based in the "separate but equal" mind-set. From high school until my experiences with Campus Crusade for Christ in college, I had limited and only superficial involvement with whites. It was not until I received Jesus Christ and began to read the Scriptures that I realized any kind of need for reconciliation.

In fact, being intentional about racial reconciliation only became real to me as I involved myself with Campus Crusade and began to read the works of John Perkins and those who had made a similar journey along the path of racial unity.

My relationship with Campus Crusade has been bittersweet in this area. It has been sweet in that I have developed lifelong relationships with white brothers and sisters who have been courageous, humble, tenacious, and teachable in order for us to even begin building relationships. These brothers and sisters have gone beyond color to character. We operate as much as possible in the spirit of love and unity.

It has been bitter as well because there is still such a long, long way to go. This is true in my experience both with the white and the black church. As a result, I have accepted the call of God on my life to be misunderstood.

Simply put, as long as I am on staff with a white, middle-class organization, I will be explaining to blacks "why Campus Crusade" and not their denomination or some other African-American organization. It also means that I will continually be a sounding board and translator for whites who are journeying through the process of biblical unity. However, this is what the call to this process involves. It will take a lot of God's grace and trust in His example of being intentional in spite of being misunderstood.

I believe this is best illustrated in Jesus' example with the woman at the well (John 4:4–42). We can observe and learn a wealth of lessons from this account of Jesus' life: being intentional, full of grace, willing to be misunderstood, and committed to "making disciples of all nations." The story shows Jesus' intentionality in crossing race, gender, class, and cultural barriers in His conversation with the Samaritan woman. As a Jewish rabbi, Jesus was not supposed to be talking to a woman, especially one with a bad reputation, or a Samaritan. However, His willingness to ignore the cultural taboos of that time resulted in the salvation of many believers in that town. This is the primary basis for my commitment to racial reconciliation.

My second motivation for being involved in racial reconciliation is the illustration of God's institution of marriage. Anyone who is committed to the biblical standard for a godly marriage knows how challenging it can be learning to be married to someone who is the opposite gender and who has a different personality. There are few greater challenges. Everyone who has been married for some length of time and reading this should be shouting "Amen!" The same dynamics necessary to experience a godly marriage relationship are necessary for biblical unity to take place. Some of those dynamics are grace, being intentional, willingness to accept and celebrate differences, practicing unconditional love, having thick skin, acceptance, not being afraid of failure, releasing bitterness and resentment, believing the truth or the best about each other, tenacity, recognizing who the real enemy is, being supportive of each other, and plenty of forgiveness.

Borrowing from my enjoyment of *Star Trek,* no two "species" could be more different than males and females! However, our biological drive and emotional motivation will move us to learn *everything* it takes to speak the language of Man or of Woman. We would even employ the use of a "universal translator" if it were possible. The point is, in order to experience unity in marriage, those who are committed to this holy institution will "make every effort" in order to succeed.

I believe that in order for true biblical love and unity to exist in the body of Christ across racial, gender, social, and denominational lines, those willing and committed to the process of racial reconciliation will sacrificially invest their lives and "make every effort." It is the minimum we can give in order to obey the Great Commandment and to fulfill the Great Commission. After all, Jesus gave the maximum in order that the world might be reconciled to Himself. He initiated reconciliation even though He did not cause the breach. He accepted the charge of guilty though He was guiltless. We are commanded to follow in His footsteps if we are truly His. Unconditional love was His motivation, and the salvation of the world was His goal. Our motivation and goal can be nothing more and certainly should be nothing less.

Biblical Basis and Philosophy of Ministry

Why should I as a believer of African-American descent invest my life in the process of racial reconciliation? Actually, I believe that the more critical question is why should any believer be involved in the process of racial reconciliation? I believe the answer lies in what Jesus said in Matthew 22:37–40 as He avoided yet another attempt of the religious leaders of His day to entrap Him in their petty squabbles. He told them that the two greatest commandments were to "love the Lord your God" and "love your neighbor." He told them that "all the Law and the Prophets hang on these two commandments." I do not believe that the answer is complete without looking at what Jesus said in Matthew 28:18–20. There we have the all too familiar Great Commission. Jesus said, in verse 19, to "make disciples of all nations." The phrase "make disciples" is an imperative or a command. The root word for "nations" is *ethnos* or ethnicity. In other words, we are commanded to make disciples of people from every nation. However, we will not obey the command to "make disciples of all nationalities" if we are not obeying the commands to love God and love our neighbor.

Therefore, I believe that the answer to the question of why a believer should invest his or her life in the process of racial reconciliation is that it is evidence of obedience to the greatest commandment and it is foundational to fulfilling the Great Commission.

I believe that there are a few other issues to consider when deciding upon an effective motivation for involving oneself in the process of biblical unity. One is tied to the first reason mentioned earlier. That is, true and biblical unity in the body of Christ across racial barriers could result in one of the most effective witnesses to win the lost for Christ that the world has ever seen.

Jesus taught the disciples that His love for us is the motivation for us to love one another. Furthermore, He taught that we prove that we are His disciples by demonstrating love for one another (John 13:34–35). In the epistle of 1 John (3:11, 23; 4:7, 11, 12), the apostle John further admonished us to prove our discipleship status and live out love for one another. I am positive that this love was not to be limited to those of our individual race. If our witness to the world is going to break through the disbelief that the lost have toward our God, then one effective means is to involve ourselves in the process of biblical unity and reconciliation.

The other issue that comes to mind in regard to racial reconciliation in the body of Christ is that of spiritual warfare. I truly believe that the division in the body of Christ is one of the most effective strategies Satan has created for hindering God's plan for the world to be saved. I believe this is no more clearly realized than in the current chasm that exists among believers of *all* racial, class, gender, economic, and denominational backgrounds.

Because our society has become more global in its exchange of information, carrying out business, and awareness of the needs of the world, it is imperative that the body of Christ get serious and proactive about destroying the unnecessary barriers that keep us apart. In order to reach the increasingly diverse ethnic populations that are present in the large urban centers of the United States and the world, Christians of *every* ethnic group must begin to put off the destructive deeds of division and participate in the process of healing across racial lines. Our motivation must be biblical love, and our goal must be the salvation of the lost. Ultimately we must desire to obey and please our worthy God whom we all call "Abba" Father.

The final issue that motivates me to be involved in the process of racial reconciliation is that I see the "signs" and "birth pains" of the anticipated return of our Lord Jesus Christ. As I observe the world, racism is not just a white man's problem, an American problem, or a problem that exists only between whites and blacks. Matthew 24:7 is being fulfilled, for truly nations *(ethnos)* are fighting against nations on a global scale. We are not talking about political states. We are talking race against race worldwide. The stage is being set for the return of our Lord. How will He find you when He returns? Will He find you hating your brother because of his skin color or cultural background? Or will He find you operating in biblical love for the sake of obedience to the greatest commandment and fulfillment of the Great Commission? I pray that He finds me faithful in His will and service for Him as His son and servant. It is time to discontinue our participation in Satan's plan to hinder the salvation of the lost, and it is time we blew the smoke from in front of our eyes to see who the real enemy is. Once we accept that we are called to be allies, we will begin to make a difference in the war for the souls of the lost.

The Practical Application of Biblical Truth

The biblical mandate of racial reconciliation must become more than just intellectual truth; it must be fleshed out in our everyday lives. Before Milton and I sought to teach these principles to others, we first made it our goal to apply them to our own relationship. Our friendship has been an intentional one from the very beginning. In the early years, we spent many hours getting to know each other. I can remember the first few years at the Center when I was still single, spending at least an hour every day during lunch with Milton telling stories, sharing dreams, working through difficulties, and developing a close friendship. When I got married in 1993, I immediately knew who I would ask to be the best man in my wedding. Milton is not just a work associate, but he has affected my life more than any other man I know.

Not only are we intentional about our friendship, but our families are committed to each other as well. In 1994, both of our families were looking for a home in the Roseland community. All four of us had been inspired by the Antioch community of Calvary Fellowship in Jackson, Mississippi. Several families from different racial backgrounds committed themselves for twelve years to live together in the same house and share everything. The late Spencer Perkins and Chris Rice had been a part of this community and talked about their experiences in their book, *More Than Equals*.[15] We searched for more than a year together for a house big enough or several empty plots of land on which to build a house. God never opened a door for that, but even as neighbors (a few blocks away), we are committed to having a close friendship with each other.

Every summer we also take part of our vacation together as families and go camping. This provides us an opportunity to get to know each other in a more relaxed, non-ministry setting outside of the inner city—except for a few times we have encountered bears at our campsite.

Lately, one of the most important things Milton and I have done to build our friendship has been to meet on Friday mornings at 6:00 A.M.

to tell how we are doing and to pray. These times have been some of the most refreshing over this past year.

Communicating This Truth to Others

As our friendship has deepened, we have sought ways to promote racial reconciliation on our staff team, to those in our community, and to college students who come to the Agape Center each year during the spring and summer.

Once, when Milton and I had just gotten back from a conference on racial reconciliation, several members of our staff team mentioned to us that they did not consider our staff team to be racially reconciled. Although our team is quite well integrated between black and white, they realized that our friendships, for the most part, were more superficial. We decided to implement the Vanilla, Chocolate, and Fudge Ripple meetings described by Raleigh Washington and Glen Kehrein in their book, *Breaking Down Walls*.[16] Once a quarter, we split our staff team up racially and have separate meetings, called the "Vanilla" meeting and the "Chocolate" meeting. In those times, we tell honestly how we are feeling about our relationships with those of the other race, and we often answer pre-written questions individually. Then we come together for our "Fudge Ripple" meeting and discuss our findings with each other. These have helped our friendships begin to go to deeper levels by addressing experiences and feelings in an honest and safe environment.

The Agape Center is also a great laboratory for building racial reconciliation into the lives of the youth in the community. Since we often have mainly white groups from the outside who volunteer with us during the year, we thought it was important to teach the youth about this very important topic. At least once a year we focus our Bible lesson with the teens on racial reconciliation. The white college students from outside the community and the African-American teens in the community are able to dialogue about their experiences and feelings. Some of the youth had to deal with their friends' criticism of them attending the "white" community center. Over the years, they have come to appreciate the long-term relationships they have with white people, especially the staff.

Even before they become teenagers, we teach the children about the importance of racial reconciliation. One time we used a practical experiential learning activity with the children at our after-school ministry. As they came in the door they were each handed a little colored square of paper. Some were given a blue one, and others received a green one. As they walked through the Center, they began to realize that special rules applied to those who had the blue square. "Blues" could have their choice of snack and sit at a nice table, but the "Greens" didn't have a choice and had to stand while they ate their snack. We told them the reason was that the Blue kids always seemed to be a bit nicer and more obedient than the Greens. Halfway through, we told them that we had made a mistake; it was the Greens who deserved the special treatment and not the Blues. For the remainder of the day, this new group was the one who was favored. The Greens got to go to the gym to play after they did their homework, but the Blues had to do extra worksheets, because their grades weren't as good as the Greens.

At the end of the day we had a debriefing time. The children told how they felt when they were on the different sides. Many of them were very frustrated, and a few even cried. Some of the children admitted they treated people on the other side differently during the game just because they had a different colored square. They also told how this translated to their relationship with the white volunteers. The enthusiastic discussion time went on for at least forty-five minutes until it was time to go home. They will never forget the lesson that they learned that day about racism.

Not only are the community youth affected by these lessons on racial reconciliation, but the college students who volunteer with us are challenged as well. During our spring break project we devote one evening to training and teaching them about racial reconciliation, and during the summer project, they spend a full day on the topic. The rest of their time in the community is the practical working out of what they learned during that training time. Many of them walk away incredibly changed. We challenge them to take what they learn to their own college campus and commit to building cross-cultural friendships. Some come back and tell stories of what God has done on their campus, and others decide to go into full-time urban ministry because of the friendships they have developed and the things they have learned.

We would both like to tell you a few things *we* have learned in the process of our intentional friendship.

MARC'S TRANSFERABLE PRINCIPLES FOR WHITES

In my ten years of friendship with Milton, I have learned a great deal about relating to people from different ethnic backgrounds. I could write many more, but I have chosen the top six principles.

1. *Become a learner of other cultures, especially the cultures of those that God has put around you.* When I first moved to the Roseland com-

munity, I must admit that I was ignorant about African-American history. One of the first things I did was apply myself to learn all I could about it. I wanted to know more about the experiences of their ancestors so that I could better appreciate African-Americans and understand a little more how they thought and felt. To do this I asked African-Americans to recommend books to me. But book knowledge is not enough, so I also immersed myself in the community to spend time learning the environment that was so new to me. I moved into the community, and I joined a volleyball league at the local Park District, where I was the only white player. I spent time, often with Milton, walking around the community getting to know new people. Attending an African-American church has also helped, because I have learned different styles of worship.

2. *Be intentional about building friendships cross-culturally, and look for ways to turn those friendships into "yokefellows."* Good cross-cultural friendships do not happen naturally, because most people do not go out of their way to learn about those who are different. We like things that are comfortable, but we have not been called to live comfortably; rather, we have been called to love our neighbors. Make sure when you do this that friendship does not take place only in your world. Be willing to be a minority on their turf. This will go a long way in communicating your seriousness about building a real friendship. Once you have stepped out to develop a friendship with someone from a different background, seek ways to deepen that friendship, to become yokefellows. Chris Rice and Spencer Perkins have described the difference between friendships and yokefellows.

- Friendships can happen with very little effort; yokefellows are intentional.
- Friendships are built for the benefit of the friends; yokefellows come together for the benefit of the kingdom.
- Friends are drawn together by their common interests; yokefellows are drawn together by a common mission.
- Friends like each other; yokefellows respect each other.
- Friendships are based on compatible personalities; the yokefellow bond is based on gifts that are needed to realize the goal.
- Friendships are fueled by emotion; yokefellows are linked by commitment.
- Friends separated by a fight may never speak to each other again; yokefellows will cheer each other on until their goal is reached.[17]

3. *Become interested in the hobbies of others and not just your own.* Milton's favorite hobby is *Star Trek,* whereas mine is baseball. For the first few years of our friendship, I teased Milton about his interest in *Star Trek,* and he occasionally teased me about the White Sox. One time I went a little too far, and the Lord convicted me that I was hurting Milton with my comments. From then on, we have stopped teasing each other, but have learned to appreciate our different hobbies. I would not consider myself a "Trekkie," but I have attended one of Milton's "Star Trek Fests." Milton has not become an avid baseball fan, but he has joined me on a few outings to Comiskey Park, bringing along a good book to read, of course.

4. *Acknowledge the reality of racism and the subtle or overt ways we have participated in it.* Take time to scroll through your memory of the past and bring up past occurrences when you may have offended people of another race. Confess your sin to God, and, if needed, share your story and confession with a trusted friend. This may help alleviate some unresolved tension in your heart toward people of color. Confessing the sins of your forefathers may be another needed step in the process of racial reconciliation. Sure, you may have not participated outright in the racism of the 1960s or slavery, but you have probably benefited economically from it. Seek ways to reconcile the errors of the past and make the playing field level for all races at your job and church.

5. *Place yourself in situations in which you are able to submit to black leadership.* I am grateful that when I came to the Agape Center there were two strong African-American male leaders I could learn from. Milton became my discipler, and I have learned more about life and ministry from Milton than anyone else I have known in the past ten years. I have learned that the Lord has me here to help build up indigenous leaders in the community, not to climb the "corporate ladder" to become the director of the Agape Center. There have been times when it has been hard, and when I have wrestled with my identity and motivation for ministry. Jesus became "downwardly mobile" when He came to earth. He came to serve and not to be served. Can I expect anything different for my life if I am His follower?

6. *Be sensitive and loving.* Some people will reject you, but if you are sincere, sensitive, and loving, many will be open. Once at the Agape Center I was busy getting some college students ready for an outreach, when the doorbell rang. A homeless man was at the door. The college students had just finished breakfast, and there was a little left over, so I invited him in for some food. As we sat and ate, he felt comfortable to tell me about his past. He told about an incident when he was in the

army and wanted to fly airplanes. At that time, African-Americans did not fly planes; they were just allowed to do menial tasks. After about twenty minutes of conversation a tear came to his eye. He thanked me for listening to his story. He said he had never had a white person treat him nicely like I had done that day. You never know who God will lead across your path, but remember to be loving and sensitive.

MILTON'S TRANSFERABLE
PRINCIPLES FOR PEOPLE OF COLOR

Why would I or any believer of color, particularly of African-American descent, want to involve himself in racial reconciliation? I believe that as a person of African-American descent I bring an inestimable amount of value to the process. In Marc's transferable principles, he mentioned things he has learned that have helped him in the process of our relationship. Three of them apply to people of every culture: being intentional about building cross-cultural relationships, being interested in learning about the other person, and being sensitive and loving. I have also learned a lot about these three principles. I have learned about three others that apply specifically to people of color.

1. *People of color must take on the immeasurable challenge of releasing our bitterness for historic and present-day racism.* This will help the process of healing. This sounds like, and actually is, an ideal. However, all of what the Bible teaches is ideal apart from believers choosing to be obedient. Because racial reconciliation (biblical unity) is difficult, should we continue to remain in a state of a body divided? Where does such rationalization end? Biblical principles of obedience are difficult at times, but God still requires them of us. We must choose, as people of color, to tenaciously commit ourselves to the long-haul process of being reconciled.

2. *People of color must be willing to accept the call of being misunderstood.* Other African-Americans often ask me why I am involved with a predominantly white organization like Campus Crusade for Christ. My answer is that I believe this is God's call on my life to be obedient to the Great Commandment and to help fulfill the Great Commission. Many people also do not understand why so many of my friends are white. I have learned from others who are more experienced in this process that we must look beyond a person's color and get to know his character. However, I am convinced that being misunderstood is part of the discipleship process in following Jesus Christ. Frankly, I am more concerned about pleasing Him than I am about pleasing man.

3. *Remember that people of color can have attitudes of racism too.* I was once in discussion with a pastor from England, who happened to

be Irish. I asked him to explain to me what the war between the Protestants of England and the Catholics of Ireland is all about. He told me that it is a six-hundred-year-old war over land. I asked, "Why are these people fighting? They are the same color." He replied, "How do you explain the tribal wars in Africa, the attitudes of Japan against other Asian nations, or the battle between the Serbs and the Croatians?" He concluded that the problem is sin, not skin. Racism is a matter of the heart, and is not confined to people in positions of power.

Conclusion: Accepting the Job

We have explained how racial reconciliation is, for the most part, being ignored by the body of Christ, and why it is essential that we begin to put the biblical mandate into practice. God has called us to love our neighbors; not just the neighbors who are most like us, but *all* of our neighbors. Becoming involved in racial reconciliation is part of obeying the Great Commandment and fulfilling the Great Commission. Neither is an option for believers.

We acknowledge that if any believer is going to get involved in the process of racial reconciliation, he must accept it as a messy job. I (Milton) remember when my children were infants and the time came, as it often did, to change their diapers. The process was not the most appealing. There was the smell of the product in the diapers, the obvious need of the party wanting to be cleaned up, and the reluctance of the party who had the initiative to do the clean up (me or my wife, Cynthia). Nonetheless, it had to be done. I realize that the word picture is quite graphic. Yet I believe it somewhat describes the nature of racial reconciliation in the body of Christ. There is a historic and present-day reality of a messy and even repugnant job in front of us, and most of us are reluctant and even unwilling to accept our responsibility in the cleanup process.

Our prayer for the body of Christ is that we begin to take seriously the sin of partiality as explained in James 2, repent of our racism, and begin to intentionally reach out and build friendships with people of a different color. As we begin to do this, the world will see something unique and begin to wonder if Jehovah is really as powerful and awesome as we claim He is. Then, perhaps, God will be able to bring revival to our cities.

Reflection Questions

1. Which Scripture verses about racial reconciliation that were given in this chapter stand out to you the most, and why?

2. Is your community, school, or church more homogeneous, integrated, or racially reconciled? What evidence would you give to support your claim?

3. What do you perceive to be the major roadblocks toward seeing racial reconciliation becoming a reality in our lifetime?

4. Which steps from the transferable principles that Marc and Milton gave could you apply to where you are?

Bibliography

Alcorn, Randy. *Dominion*. Sisters, Ore.: Multnomah, 1996.

Berk, Stephen. *A Time to Heal*. Grand Rapids: Baker, 1997.

Dawson, John. *Healing America's Wounds*. Ventura, Calif.: Regal, 1994.

Ellis, Carl. *Malcolm: The Man Behind the X*. Chattanooga, Tenn.: Accord Books, 1993.

Evans, Dr. Anthony. *Are Blacks Spiritually Inferior to Whites?* Wenonah, N.J.: Renaissance Productions, 1992.

_____. *Let's Get to Know Each Other: What White Christians Should Know About Black Christians*. Nashville, Tenn.: Nelson, 1995.

Face to Face: Seeking Racial Reconciliation - video. Madison, Wisc.: InterVarsity Christian Fellowship, 1990.

Keener, Craig and Glenn Usry. *Defending Black Faith: Answers to Tough Questions About African-American Christianity*. Downers Grove, Ill.: InterVarsity Press, 1997.

Marsh, Charles. *God's Long Summer: Stories of Faith and Civil Rights*. Princeton, N.J.: Princeton Univ., 1997.

McKissic, William Dwight. *Beyond Roots: In Search of Blacks in the Bible*. Wenonah, N.J.: Renaissance Productions, 1990.

Okholm, Dennis L. *The Gospel in Black and White: Theological Resources for Racial Reconciliation*. Downers Grove, Ill.: InterVarsity, 1997.

Perkins, John. *Restoring At-Risk Communities: Doing It Together and Doing It Right*. Grand Rapids: Baker, 1995.

_____. *With Justice for All.* Ventura, Calif.: Regal, 1982.

Perkins, John, and Thomas A. Tarrants III with David Wimbish. *He's My Brother: Former Racial Foes Offer Strategy for Reconciliation.* Grand Rapids: Chosen, 1994.

Perkins, Spencer, and Chris Rice. *More Than Equals: Racial Healing for the Sake of the Gospel.* Downers Grove, Ill.: InterVarsity, 1993.

Reconcilers Magazine. Jackson, Miss.: Reconcilers Fellowship.

Washington, Raleigh, and Glen Kehrein. *Breaking Down Walls: A Model for Reconciliation in an Age of Racial Strife.* Chicago: Moody, 1993.

Weary, Dolphus. *I Ain't Comin' Back.* Wheaton, Ill.: Tyndale, 1990.

part three

EDUCATION
AND TRAINING

chapter six

BECOMING
AN "INSIDER"

EARNING THE RIGHT TO
MINISTER TO STREET PEOPLE

JOHN E. FUDER

Introduction:
A Divine Appointment

Follow me. You can write a paper about this one!" Skip was right! Much of this chapter are his words come true. Wade, a Moody undergraduate student, met Skip in front of McDonald's three blocks from our campus. Skip was homeless. God had been burdening Wade's heart for the street community. He longed to respond compassionately to the persistent requests of panhandlers, and he began to pray for God to use him.

Wade had been graciously allowed to take leftovers from our student dining room, and he had his backpack full that night. When Skip asked him for money, Wade said he was a Moody student and had food that he wanted to give to people in genuine need. Skip responded, "Wait till you get a load of this" and led Wade to an area called Lower Wacker, about a half mile away.

A JOURNEY DOWN UNDER

"To many people, Lower Wacker Drive is downtown's dark and dangerous underbelly, a speedy shortcut tunnel through the Loop."[1] It follows the south branch of the Chicago River, from Lake Michigan to the Eisenhower Expressway. A subterranean, "hidden world of dumpsters, delivery trucks and loading docks," it has for years been a haven for the homeless.[2] "People have been living under Wacker Drive virtually since it opened in 1926. During the Great Depression, the street was home to thousands of jobless men who dubbed it 'Hoover Hotel,' after President Hoover, whom they blamed for their plight."[3] Those numbers have shrunk drastically in recent years to over 100,[4] and were whittled down to fewer than fifty in a sweep by the city in December of 1997.[5]

Skip led Wade that night into another world. He discovered "makeshift digs, ranging from a couple of blankets to an extensive array of mattresses, tables, chairs, and cardboard boxes."[6] But even more than their environment, it was the people who grabbed Wade's heart. "He took me around to meet several people (under Lower Wacker), just introduced me to them, 'This is Wade from Moody . . .' I passed out all the meals, but it broke my heart. There were so many people down there and I only had a few meals."[7]

So Wade went back to campus, recruited his friend Josh, and the two of them ministered faithfully under Lower Wacker and in the surrounding area for two semesters. Week by week they went out, while their wives, Katie and Jodie, interceded for them in prayer back in the dorm. "We found so many places [to minister], plus Skip was telling us where more guys were," Wade recounted.[8] These included an alley behind the Walgreen's on Michigan Avenue, a remote area off 18th Street near Chinatown, and a place called "the Bat Cave" by Navy Pier.

If It Wasn't for the Christians . . .

Wade and Josh shared the love of Jesus with some very needy guys named Gizmo, Black, and Maniac (also known as Grave Digger), among others. They continued to take food, as well as clothing donated by Josh's church. I tagged along with them at times and brought some graduate students with me. We had Bible study and prayer and sang choruses, accompanied by Wade on the guitar. As we sang, I gazed over the dilapidated dwellings, a collection of tired, smelly mattresses, tattered blankets, empty food containers, and piles of dirty clothes. My mind recalled a comment made by a young African-American boy in Watts, South Central Los Angeles, to Keith Phillips, president of World Impact, many years ago, "If He [Jesus] lived today, He'd come to Watts."[9] I felt the same way about Lower Wacker.

After the study I spoke with Billy, an on-again off-again veteran of Lower Wacker for more than twenty years. He said, "A lot of people come down here and bring food, but you guys bring manna. . . . They [Josh and Wade] keep coming back and befriend the guys—really care for them. . . . They're good guys. . . . If it wasn't for the Christians coming through, we'd be in trouble."[10] But if it was not for Skip, Wade and Josh may never have been escorted into the world of Lower Wacker. This was made all the more evident when "Congress recently approved funding for a $350 million rebuilding of Wacker Drive" that is scheduled to begin in 2001,[11] fenced off all access to Lower Wacker, and relocated the residents to local shelters.[12] Skip played the role of an "informant,"[13] a gatekeeper, one who ushered them into a subculture, enabling them to become "insiders." It would have been much more challenging for Wade and Josh to gain entrée without him.

The World of "Green Eyes"

My deepest immersion as an "insider" took place in the early 1990s as a part of my doctoral research at Biola University.[14] I set out to explore the world of the homeless, gangs, prostitutes, and undocumented immigrants in Skid Row in downtown Los Angeles. L.A. County has the dubious distinction of containing the largest homeless population in the nation. A study by Shelter Partnership, Inc. estimated that "more than 77,000 people were believed to be living on the streets in mid-1992."[15] Skid Row is home to more than half of that population.[16]

The informant who let me in to those subcultures was known on the street simply as Green Eyes. As I observed in my dissertation:

> For 2 1/2 years, this intriguing, caring, and amazingly resilient Black man in his late 40's was my passport into the potentially overwhelming and extremely needy world of homelessness, gangs, and prostitution. Despite over a dozen years of prior urban ministry experience with City Team Ministries, when it came to awareness of life on the streets, I was the rookie and he the seasoned veteran. I, the would-be teacher, was instead the naïve student, learning from him, my street-wise mentor and instructor as I chronicled his adventures and interactions, struggling with cocaine while living on sidewalks, in cardboard boxes, skid row hotels, and in jail. In it all he was my sounding board and protector; through it all he became my friend.[17]

I had been told by friends, members of the Cambria Christian Community ministering in that area, that Green Eyes was the gatekeeper to that community. He stayed in a "cardboard condo" a block from their center. I knocked ever so gently on top of his refrigerator box that first day we met. He poked out his head, and I explained that I was a graduate student and a missionary studying to be a teacher and that I wanted my students one day to better understand life on the streets. I then asked if he, Green Eyes, would be my teacher. He agreed enthusiastically, and without hesitation he scrambled out of his box and began to unfold his story. He never knew his real father, and his only brother was murdered. His stepdad died of cancer, and he had not seen his mother for years. He had a fifth-grade education and had done a total of eighteen years in juvenile detention, jail, and prison, including two years in "the hole" (solitary confinement), which he described simply as "hell." He had nowhere to go upon his release and landed in Skid Row, falling prey to cocaine and the harsh reality of life on the streets. He was jumped and beaten with a pipe so severely by a group of street people that his neck was broken and 70 percent of his right side paralyzed. He was hospitalized for more than a year and was still on a walker when we met. He scratched out an existence by panhandling and "dumpster diving" (scrounging for goods in garbage containers), attempting to sell or trade whatever treasures he discovered.

Meeting "the Neighbors"

Green Eyes relished his role as my tutor, and "school" was in session every Saturday morning for months. Each week he had someone else for me to meet "for the book" (dissertation). He introduced me to Funee Man, the seventeen-year-old Hispanic leader of the seventy-five-strong Bonnie Brae Criminals (BBC), one of the estimated six hundred to six hundred fifty gangs in Los Angeles County, comprising sixty to eighty thousand members.[18] Their average age is thirteen-and-a-half years old.[19] It is no overstatement to suggest that "Los Angeles is a city of gangs."[20]

The BBC "turfed" the area in which Green Eyes stayed. Funee was amazingly receptive to a "Wetto" (white boy) and introduced me to many of his "homies," such as Negro, Cholo, Boxer, Pelon, and Dundee, among others. He and these "officers" formed their gang when he was ten, choosing the name "Criminals" because they would "shoot or stab people who mess with them." Funee himself had gotten off on a technicality after a shooting incident with a sawed-off shotgun. While I was doing my research, Negro was arrested for shooting at a rival gang's car during a drive-by, and Pelon was "locked up" because he "shot a guy from 18th Street [a rival gang] in the head with a shotgun."

Green Eyes' world was also heavily populated by street women, involving a variety of lifestyles. This growing population of women has been estimated to make up as much as 20 percent of the homeless community.[21] Many, like "Sparky," were prostitutes, and several of them were bisexual. Most, such as Little Mousie, were addicted to "the pipe" (crack cocaine) or "chiba" (heroin) and are known as "strawberries" on the street, turning "tricks" for drugs. Some have an older "sugar daddy" (provider of drugs for sex). A few were the proverbial bag 4 ladies, like sixty-year-old Billie, who had been on the streets off and on for more than twenty-five years.

The Bridge People

Billie was staying with Red Dog, another significant gatekeeper, whom I met while looking for Green Eyes one day. He opened up for me that segment of the homeless community living under the bridges (freeway overpasses) and unknowingly suggested a taxonomy of homelessness (see table 1) as he eagerly described where he had lived and who he knew in various locales.

TABLE 1
A TAXONOMY OF THE HOMELESS[22]

Category	Description
Bridge People	Live under freeway overpasses
Bush People	Live in clusters of bushes near freeways
Street People	Live in boxes, alleys, abandoned cars, sidewalks
Highway People	Transient, hitchhiking or riding the rails from city to city

A fourteen-year veteran of the bridges, Red was one of the most coarse, carousing characters I have ever known. His weathered, pock-marked face and long, bushy red beard reflect the look of a survivor extraordinaire. He too had no father figure, his mother was dead, and his education fell short of junior high school. He had been in trouble with the law as a twelve-year-old boy and in and out of prison ever since. He had taken human life on more than one occasion. I went on "canning runs" (collecting aluminum cans) with Red, which was how he attempted to carve out a living. One of those escapades took us by a set of bridges under which he had lived for a number of years. Some of his old cronies were still there, and he introduced me to each one.

The ringleader of the bunch was Big Jim, who had called the free-way overpasses home for more than ten years. Like most of the guys under the bridges, alcohol was his downfall. "My mom was an alco-holic, so what do you expect, you know?" Jim said as he hoisted a forty-ouncer to his lips. "All the trouble I've ever been in is because of this right here" (pointing to the liquor bottle). He definitely had seen his fair share of trouble. His first stint in jail was as a fifteen-year-old. Seven felony counts followed in succeeding years. Jim explained, "I did eleven years all total. That ain't countin' all the jails I've been in and out of. I've been locked up probably half my life."

Jim first learned of the bridges from Dirty Jack, whom he met while panhandling on the freeway off-ramp. Red introduced me to Jack while we were descending the steep slope back down to the sidewalk from their encampment under the freeway. As Red was the roughest of the bunch, Jack was certainly the most pitiful. The sight of him broke my heart. Jack was barefooted, caked with dirt, and sat cross-legged on a filthy blanket propped up against the massive concrete freeway support beam only a few feet off the sidewalk. Garbage was strewn all around him. His long, lice-infested hair was matted down, and his body odor was incredible. Red kept his distance. Jack had tried to take his own life several years before by jumping off a building. He succeeded only in crippling himself. Thus his perch beside the post. He was the proverbial "leper outside the gate," due in part to his physical condition, but also because he "had bugs." He had been on the streets for more than twenty years.

Red introduced me to Lefty that day too. It was Lefty who told me that because of Jack's "pests" (lice), "we don't ever get near him." He and Big Jim were pals, and they had for all practical purposes shunned Jack. Lefty was also handicapped, having lost his right arm in an automobile accident at the hands of a drunken driver when he was six years old. That crash claimed the lives of his mother and brother. Tragically, the accident drove Lefty's father into alcoholism, from which he ultimately died. Lefty admitted to being "a drunk" himself since he was twelve. At the age of fifteen he ran away from his grandparents' home and joined the circus. An impulsive marriage during those years fell apart, and he tried to commit suicide with a .22 caliber rifle. He put the barrel to his head and pulled the trigger, but it would not fire. He reflected, "I know Someone up there was watching out for me and it wasn't my time to go yet!" On a whim he headed to California and ended up on skid row, where he had lived for the past twenty-five years.

The Bush People

Red also introduced me to Tommy, known on the streets as "the Beached Whale." Big Jim had commented, "He looks like a beached whale, just layin' and drinkin' up in the bushes. That's the reason he got that name." But I soon discovered that Tommy too had been banished from the bridges, as he was blatantly homosexual and an object of scorn to the others. Struggling with his sexuality as a child, Tommy immersed himself in the gay lifestyle. "For many years I thought I was a girl," he explained. "My family, their whole attitude is they could care less. . . . I'm just a faggot . . . and a drunk . . . my parents don't keep in touch with me because I'm a queer . . ." He too tried on more than one occasion to take his own life, once by slashing both wrists and the other time with a drug overdose after the death of his gay lover.

After the second attempt failed, his parents packed his suitcase, picked him up at the psychiatric hospital, and, in Tommy's words, "gave me a twenty-dollar bill and some blue chip stamps and said, 'You're on your own. It's your problem!' That's the last time I saw my family." More than twenty years had passed since that day, and he had learned to survive on the street by panhandling in Chinatown and dumpster diving for food outside a nearby restaurant. He chose Chinatown because he was also the occasional beneficiary of food from a "momma-son" who worked in one of the restaurants. He also claimed to be Buddhist mainly because "the Christian Bible condemns homosexuals!" What he liked best about Buddhism was that "they don't criticize my lifestyle."

One other engaging "bush person" I met through Red Dog was Louie, or the "Cat Man," because of his prowess for burglary. He stayed in a cluster of bushes tucked into the hillside overlooking the freeway. Louie looked the part of a stereotypical street person with his chest-long gray beard and ratty old hat. Abandoned by his mother when he was a five-year-old boy, he was taken in by his grandparents who regularly beat him and, in his words, "used me like a slave." Six years later his mother returned to reclaim him, this time with a new husband. "I went through hell with my stepfather, too," he recalled. "He was beatin' on me. . . . I had welts all over." After many years of abuse and later having quit school, Louie left home at fifteen.

After bouncing around from job to job, a failed marriage, and too many scrapes with the police, he headed west and the streets became his home. His means of income was "working a sign" on the freeway off ramp (see table 2 on the next page). He had difficulty writing, so I helped him draw the large bold letters on old pieces of cardboard: "HOMELESS. NEED FOOD OR MONEY. PLEASE HELP. GOD BLESS YOU." I went out, sign in hand, and sat beside him on an old milk crate at his spot along the ramp one morning. I still remember his gentle benediction whenever we parted ways, "God be with you, John."

A Window of Opportunity

Why this parade of people's lives from years past? Even the mere review of their stories reminds me once again of the tremendous window of opportunity I was given, not just for research, but for ministry. Green Eyes and Red Dog, as my "informants," gave me access to the gangs, prostitutes, bridge and bush people. They assisted me in becoming an "insider" to these intense, isolated subcultures in a way that would have been far more difficult and nearly impossible to do on my own. But most important, they enabled me to earn the right to present the gospel.

TABLE 2
A TAXONOMY OF FINANCIAL ACCRUAL
BY THE HOMELESS[23]

Category	Description
Working a Sign	Holding a cardboard sign
Canning	Collecting from dumpsters, etc.
Sale of Goods	Selling clothing, assorted merchandise
Panhandling	Extending one's hand, hat, etc. asking for money

Editor's Note: This chapter has highlighted the needs of the chronically homeless, those who have been on the streets for years and are quite removed (intentionally or otherwise) from the services of a shelter or mission. Later chapters in this volume will address the temporarily homeless (regardless of the cause) or longer-term homeless, who survive shelter to shelter.

Green Eyes responded, attended the Church on Brady with my family and me in East Los Angeles, and was in our home on several occasions. He spoke to a group of children from a local Christian school in Whittier, California, who had collected food and household items for him when we set up his apartment. He addressed the students from Biola University who were in Dr. Judy Lingenfelter's Urban Research and Ministry class and were immersed with me in the project. He was the guide and protector to that same group the night we spent on the streets. He went through the program at the Union Rescue Mission, spent a month in John Perkins's rehabilitation program in Pasadena, California, and occasionally attends Central City Community Church in downtown Los Angeles.

Funee Man, and many of his gang members, including Pelon, heard the plan of salvation. So did Little Mousie. We brought her to the women's rehabilitation program at the Los Angeles Mission. The students and I talked extensively with Red Dog and Billy. We had helped move them into an apartment and they had us over for a meal, to say thanks. We had "Thanksgiving Under the Bridge" for Big Jim, Lefty, the Cat Man, and the Beached Whale. I often read Scripture to Jim and Lefty, and I talked for hours with Louie. I prayed with them and for them all as I drove back and forth from Biola to Skid Row.

Their lifestyles and resistance to a typical church or rescue mission approach to evangelism made it all the more essential to tell them about Christ at every opportunity. I was back in California a year and a half ago for a conference and spent an afternoon on Skid Row. I had braced myself for what I might learn, but nonetheless it still hurt deeply. Green Eyes was back in a rehabilitation program, still struggling to be free from cocaine. Both Jack and Lefty were dead, and Tommy (the Beached Whale) was in a hospital dying from AIDS. Jose (Funee Man) and Jim were in prison. My informant was Louie. I found him under the very same bridge where I had last spoken with him and the others five years before when we moved to Chicago. We hugged, talked, and prayed together. I descended that old familiar slope back to my car and wiped away the tears as his familiar, parting words rang in my ear, "God be with you, John."

ON THE STREETS OF CHICAGO

Coming to teach at Moody, my heart's desire has been for students with a burden for the marginalized. Certainly Wade and Josh fit that mold, as do two of our graduate students, Rich and Noah. They have been faithfully ministering on the streets around campus these past two semesters as part of their internship, with their contacts taking them under Lower Wacker and into the Cabrini-Green housing projects as well. Rich summarized their vision and passion:

> *I look out my 10th floor window from my N. LaSalle apartment and I see an area of Chicago (Cabrini-Green) that is dying without Jesus. Sirens constantly go off at night. . . . People out there are involved in violence at dusk, at dawn, it doesn't matter. There's car-jackings, shooting in the streets, crack is being sold, and prostitution makes a living for many. Satan is running rampant out there. . . . I'm not a missionary overseas. I'm a missionary here on this side of Lake Michigan, in downtown Chicago . . . on N. LaSalle Boulevard, the home of Moody Bible Institute.[24]*

Rather than using an informant, Rich and Noah have become "insiders" on the streets by their persistent presence, bathed in prayer, and a keen sensitivity to the leading of the Holy Spirit. Noah commented:

> *Rich and I meet at the Dunkin' Donuts on the corner of Clark and Division. We generally begin by going to a bench and praying. . . . Then we go out to meet people. . . . At all times we attempt to be Spirit-led. . . . We simply speak to whomever God leads us to. Furthermore, we attempt to go wherever God asks us to go.[25]*

These contemporary "apostles to the city"[26] dress down for the streets, with hats reversed, baggy pants, and old shoes. "Prayed up," they make eye contact and look to engage people in conversation by asking basic questions like, "What's up? What's on your heart tonight?" Rich reflected, "I was able to, if you will, 'see the heart in their eyes' when they would answer. Some had eyes of repentance; some had eyes of confusion."

The guys told those they met that they had "Good news of Jesus Christ." Noah commented, "I often used my Bible as a sort of 'badge of authenticity.' I would pull it out of my pocket whenever I told some-one that I was out sharing the gospel." Rich added, "After weeks of ministry on the streets, and after running into the same people very of-ten, many of the homeless know why I'm out here." Noah concurred, "I believe we got into people's worlds simply through our persistent presence. The more people saw us, the more they saw we were for real. I believe that fact, more than any other, made them willing to associate with us."

They realized their ministry was primarily to "plant seeds." Rich concluded, "This was really 'cold turkey' encounters. Most people you meet on the streets aren't quite ready for salvation. You kinda meet those who are seeking." Undaunted nonetheless, he continued, "God brought them right to Noah and I. It was just a matter of making our-selves available for God . . . standing on the corner when it was cold, wind blowing, and a tired feeling from classes all week."

The guys found the streets to be a volatile, modern-day mission field to which many become ensnared. Rich summarized:

> The homeless person on the street was forever running from something, whether it was fear, sin, pain, cops, drug dealers, etc. . . . When I'm talking to them about the gospel, they're always looking around, as if someone is watching them. The truth is, most of the time, someone always is watching them, because they're ei-ther running from a gang member, or someone from whom they may owe money —for crack. Often, even they will tell you that they "gotta move on because there's a cop."

One such example is a young man named Shorty who runs with a lo-cal gang. When Rich and Noah first met him he replied, "Every white person I've met today is sharing the Lord with me!" They saw him often on the streets, once while he was looking for food in garbage cans. He wants to follow Jesus, but has difficulty giving up his lifestyle. Others in-clude Larry and Lloyd, both addicts, who were living under Lower Wack-er, and Rodney, who was living in a box after his release from prison. All have heard the gospel and some have responded, like Cookie, who trust-ed Christ in front of the Mark Twain Hotel, and Darrell, with whom the guys are studying the Bible at his Cabrini-Green apartment.

REFLECTIONS AND RECOMMENDATIONS

Becoming an insider involves a willingness to be a learner, to be instructed and informed by knowledgeable individuals who can swing open the doors to a particular subculture. It requires consistent, visible presence in a community of need. Examples of those who have filled that role have been highlighted extensively in this chapter. But for me, it has also included being taught by my students, by their zeal and compassion, obedience and action, prayer and proclamation. These qualities are truly timeless and transferable.

In Chicago, Los Angeles, and any other major city, the needs of those on the street vary minimally, yet persist consistently. What is in short supply, however, are consecrated, compassionate men and women who are willing to become "insiders" in order to penetrate such seething subcultures as the homeless, gang members, and prostitutes. The following principles are recommended to help you begin:

1. God Is Already at Work in the City

Wade reflected, "We were joining God in His work. It's His ministry. He is already doing it, that's what we've seen. He's already been working there. He's allowed us to enter into this, to experience His glory in touching lives. We're just along for the ride." Rich agrees, "God is strong and ever present; in fact, He's already out there waiting on me to join Him in His work."

2. Remember That You Are a Weak Vessel

Noah highlighted 2 Corinthians 12:9, "My grace is sufficient for you, for my power is made perfect in weakness." Josh summarized,

> One thing I learned is how weak I am. The Lord can use anyone He wants. He just chose us. It's a privilege. It's "not by might or power, but by [His] Spirit" (Zech. 4:6). He shows us how weak we are on our own. We're just tools. Jesus tells us [that when we minister] do it as a servant (John 13:1–15). There's no praise to us. We're just doing our duty. And the most valuable thing is how close you get to God through it.

3. Bathe Everything You Do in Prayer

Rich and Noah often spent time "prayer walking" the streets. They, along with Wade and other Moody students, consistently interceded on Monday nights for their respective ministries. Wade and Josh reported back their wives of God's protection or direction in specific conversations under Lower Wacker only to learn that God had been guiding them to pray along those very lines. Rich concluded, "There is power in prayer, no doubt."

4. Step Out in Obedience and Persist Faithfully

Wade and Josh concurred, "We were just obedient to God. We had no idea what God would do as we obeyed. All we did was take a step of faith." Noah realized the need to "go out even when we do not feel like it," acknowledging that "God is waiting to work everywhere and in everyone." He reminds us of Galatians 6:9, "Let us not become weary in doing good, for at the proper time we will reap a harvest if we do not give up."

5. Go as a Learner and Be Vulnerable

Noah commented:

> Oh, how much deeper are God's ways than ours! He is always able to work in everyone. We simply need to make ourselves vulnerable. . . . We must associate with the "lowliest of the low" (i.e., drug dealers). . . . I cannot allow my fears to stand in the way of being used by God. "It is not the healthy who need a doctor, but the sick" (Matt. 9:12).

Wade recalled, "You go down to minister, but you get ministered to so often. I've evangelized before but these guys (under Lower Wacker) would almost train me. I remember one guy looked me right in the eye and said, 'You have to warn them that they're going to face eternal damnation. . . . They have to be scared straight!'"

6. God Keeps Those Whom He Calls as Insiders

Josh testified, "A lot of people have asked me if we're afraid of the danger. What the Lord has kept speaking to me is, 'Josh, you're in My will right now and you're just as safe down in those streets as you are sitting on your couch in your apartment.'" Wade agreed, "When we go out, we always commit the evening to the Lord. . . . We know He's going to guide our steps. . . . I had such a confidence that they couldn't do anything to me because I was in the middle of God's will. . . . God was showing me that He is our rear guard."

7. We Must Revisit "Doing Church" on the Streets

Roger Greenway pointed out the need for "street pastors," not to preach necessarily, but to build relationships and demonstrate a caring, Christlike compassion. Street pastors with "big hearts, lots of street savvy, and a firm knowledge of God's Word" are still the need of the hour.[27] But our typical approach to "doing church" in the city must also be reconsidered. Noah prophetically exclaimed:

> *One very significant observation became apparent. It sheds light on our theology of the city. The problem is not that the nightclubs are open, but that the churches are closed [at night]. Not that the streets are "alive" but that our prayer life is "dead." Churches need to open their doors to the "dead and dying." Too many are "locked monuments." We need churches open, where the praises of God can be heard from the street. . . . [Churches] must be lighthouses in the darkness. They must guide those lost in Satan's "nighttime fog" toward their Maker/Redeemer.*

8. Compassion Is at the Core of Our Commitment

The late Henri Nouwen provided us with challenging thoughts on the meaning of compassion. He wrote:

> *Compassion asks us to go where it hurts, to enter into places of pain, to share in brokenness, fear, confusion and anguish. Compassion challenges us to cry out with those in misery, to mourn with those who are lonely, to weep with those in tears.*[28]

Jesus modeled compassion and calls us to the same (Matt. 9:36; Mark 6:34). Specifically, we are told to, "Go and learn what this means" to cultivate a lifestyle of compassion among sinful people (Matt. 9:13). I have seen this process at work in my own life and among the students at Moody, as well as in those involved in my dissertation research at Biola (see table 3).

I recall a Biola student's reflections on our experience with Green Eyes, et. al.:

> *I learned about true compassion. I learned to see people as individuals, humans just like me, and not just "those people." . . . I learned that God loves the city. Most of all I learned that God is teaching me to love the city and its people. . . . My heart breaks for the city. Often I wonder what one young person can contribute to the overwhelming need. . . . But I have to remind myself that God has been taking care of the city for a long time. All He asks is that I be available. He'll take care of the rest.*[29]

Noah realized the urgency of compassion in our lives and ministries. He suggested, "A doctor does not live in fear of the diseases he is testing. Instead, his compassion for human suffering drives him to treat illness. We believers must develop compassion for the spiritual ills of men so that we will be driven to offer Jesus as the cure!" Josh, too, saw God deepen his heart of compassion. He reflected:

> What really hit me as we visited a lot of dark corners in Chicago that the Lord led us to was that I just felt the love of God for them. So many cars drive by and regard "those people" on the streets as basically the trash that the dumpster people pick up. . . . But God sees them as precious treasures in the midst of the garbage. . . . Now I'll never see any man the same, or woman. God has given me such a heart to see how He truly loves them. I've been praying for Him to give me the ability to weep when I see people . . . just to soften my heart.

Conclusion: A Call for "Insiders"

Harvie Conn said, "It's not simply that the city needs us, we need the city."[30] We, the instructors and practitioners alike, must become the instructed and draw near the urban masses. Jesus said, "Take care of my sheep" (John 21:16). Sometimes we have to go out and find them before we can care for them. Countless "harassed and helpless" (Matt. 9:36) sheep wander the streets of our cities. God give us shepherds' hearts to draw them into His fold.

> Where cross the crowded ways of life,
> where sound the cries of race and clan,
> above the noise of selfish strife,
> we hear Thy voice, O Son of man!
> The cup of water giv'n for Thee
> still holds the freshness of Thy grace;
> yet long these multitudes to see
> the sweet compassion of Thy face.
> O Master, from the mountain side,
> make haste to heal these hearts of pain;
> among these restless throngs abide;
> O tread the city streets again;
> Till sons of men shall learn Thy love
> and follow where Thy feet have trod;
> till glorious, from Thy heav'n above,
> shall come the city of our God.[31]
>   —Franklin Mason North

Table 3

A COMPASSION CONTINUUM [32]

Matthew 9:13–"Go and learn what this means, 'I desire compassion . . !'"

Matthew 9:36–"Seeing the multitudes, He felt compassion for them . . ."

Pre-exposure	"Seeing"		"Feeling"		"Acting"
+ Enthusiasm		LEVEL 1	TRANSITION	LEVEL II*	COMPASSION
+ Teachability		Vulnerable	Discouraged	Acceptance	"TO SUFFER
+ Naïveté	EXPOSURE	Intimidated	Frustrated	Confession	WITH"
o Indifference	TO	Overwhelmed	Disillusioned	Commitment	Incarnation
– Overconfidence	URBAN	Anxious	Helpless	Conviction	Identification
– Prejudice	NEED	Hurt	Inadequate		Empowerment
– Fear		Angry			Servanthood
– Guilt					Brokenness
Stage 1	**Stage 2**		**Stage 3**		**Stage 4**

Key: + Positive, o Neutral, – Negative

* Denotes a cyclical pattern

Reflection Questions

1. What does it mean that God is already at work in even the darkest areas? Do you really believe that? Could it be that we miss seeing His handiwork by avoiding these places? Why are we so afraid?

2. What examples of "insiders" can you identify in Scripture? In what ways did God use them to enable His people to accomplish His purposes?

3. What nearby subculture or community of need could God use you to penetrate with the gospel? Who is an "insider" who could let you into that area? What practical steps can you take to make contact?

For Further Reading

Christensen, Michael J. *City Streets, City People.* Nashville: Abingdon, 1988.

Grant, George. *The Dispossessed: Homelessness in America.* Fort Worth, Tex.: Dominion, 1986.

Grigg, Viv. *Companion to the Poor.* Monrovia, Calif.: MARC, 1991.

_____. *Cry of the Urban Poor.* Monrovia, Calif.: MARC, 1992.

Hertenstein, Jane. *Orphan Girl: The Memoir of a Chicago Bag Lady.* Chicago: Cornerstone, 1998.

McClung, Floyd. *Living on the Devil's Doorstep.* Seattle: YWAM, 1988.

Pulinger, Jackie. *Chasing the Dragon.* Ann Arbor, Mich.: Servant, 1990.

Resener, Carl R., and Judy Hall. *Kids on the Street.* Nashville: Broadman, 1992.

Van Houten, Mark E. *God's Inner-city Address.* Grand Rapids: Zondervan, 1998.

_____. *Profane Evangelism.* Grand Rapids: Zondervan, 1989.

chapter seven

TRAINING COLLEGE STUDENTS FOR URBAN MINISTRY

PHILOSOPHICAL AND PRACTICAL CONSIDERATIONS

ROBERT C. SMITH

Introduction: College Students in Ministry

In the 1850s a group of college students got together in a haystack to pray for revival in the nation. They were concerned with what they saw as the lack of devotion and commitment to Jesus Christ demonstrated by the lives of their countrymen. History tells us that their prayers were answered and God poured out His Spirit on them. As a result of this revival many college students committed themselves to missions and ministries to the poor and disenfranchised, often in urban centers of the world.[1]

Over the decades college students have been at the forefront of missions and urban ministry, committing themselves to reaching the unreached in our cities. During their days at Bible college, Ray Bakke (Moody Bible Institute) and Wayne Gordon (Wheaton College) both discovered their calls to the city of Chicago. Even though I had grown up in the city, it was at Nyack College in New York that I sensed God's call to urban ministry. If the cities of the world are going to be reached with the message of the gospel, it will be necessary for the church to tap into the vast resources of college students, especially students within our Christian colleges, and prepare them for the task of effective urban ministry.

Therefore, the focus of this chapter will be on what Christian colleges and their faculty need to do to prepare the next generation of college students for urban ministry. The chapter will discuss what needs to be done to prepare the student cognitively for urban ministry. We will then show what types of nonformal educational experiences the college student needs to have to prepare him or her for urban ministry. Finally, the chapter will explain the role of the college professor as mentor and guide in the process of preparing the college student for urban ministry. The Bible tells us that one of the main reasons God gives the church spiritual leadership is "for the equipping of the saints for the work of service" (Eph. 4:12 NASB). If God has called Bible schools and Christian colleges to teach and prepare the next generation of urban ministers, we will need to prepare for this work.

THE GOAL OF OUR INSTRUCTION

It will be necessary to discuss from the very start what the students, the faculty, and the college see as their goals in the educational process. You may have heard of the story of the archer who never missed the center of the target; he shot the arrow into the side of the barn and then drew the target around it. With this methodology he never failed to hit the bull's-eye.

Many times we do not discuss the final outcomes of the educational process as they relate to preparing students for urban ministry. I had been involved in urban ministry for some eighteen years when I came to the Moody Bible Institute, from community development to evangelism. I had learned a lot of things about ministering in the city and serving the poor. When Moody hired me, I was being asked to pass these experiences and information on to the next generation of urban ministers. I began to ask myself what was the goal of my training for these students. As I thought about these goals, two passages of Scripture from the apostle Paul came to mind.

Paul wrote in Ephesians 4:12 that God gave us gifted individuals for the "equipping of the saints for the work of service," and in 1 Timothy 1:5 (NASB) he wrote that the "goal of our instruction is love from a pure heart and a good conscience and a sincere faith." These passages reveal a balance that is needed in educating the students for urban ministry. On one hand the college student needs to be taught how to *do* the service of urban ministry. The focus of this training will be task-orientated. It will have as its goal the preparation of the student to be able to function as an urban servant. The student learns how to present the gospel in the urban context, how to do community development, and how to minister to the poor and disenfranchised.

On the other hand, the college student also needs to be taught how to *be* an urban minister. Students need to be taught how to be servants who love the people of the city, clearly conscious about their call to the city, and with a strong dependence on God's divine resources. These goals are much more difficult to measure in the educational context. Character development is crucial for those going into urban ministry. In all my years of urban ministry I have not seen a person disqualified from service because he could not or did not know how to *do* urban ministry. Rather, most disqualified individuals had failed to *be* the man or woman God required for urban ministry tasks. These people left urban ministry because of moral failures or because of their inability to get along with their peers. They disqualified themselves because of their failure to use good judgment in key situations. These urban ministers were trained how to *do* urban ministry, but they failed to comprehend what it meant to *be* an urban minister. The goal, therefore, of the Christian college urban ministry program needs to be the preparation of the student with the knowledge and experiences to *do* and to *be* an urban minister.

PREPARING THE COLLEGE STUDENT COGNITIVELY FOR URBAN MINISTRY

If the goal of our training is to prepare the college student to *do* and *be* an urban minister, there will be some things that the student will need to *know* if he or she is to be effective in urban ministry. Colleges invest a lot of time in the development of what the student should know in order to graduate from their institution. What the student is required to know is seen in the courses and the hours of study needed for graduation. It is sometimes assumed that if a student spends a certain amount of hours in a fixed number of classes he will have the knowledge needed to do the job he has been trained for. Too often, though, the things the student needs to know take more time than the hours spent in those courses allow him to learn. Therefore, Christian college students need to glean specific information from several courses if they are going to get the cognitive information they need to be prepared for urban ministry.

Thinking Biblically and Theologically

The college student needs to acquire four key areas of cognitive knowledge if he is going to be effective in urban ministry. First, the student needs to learn to *think biblically and theologically* about urban ministry. Many people involved in urban ministry today did not attend Bible schools or Christian colleges. God prepared them for Himself on the streets and corners of urban centers throughout the world; they attended the "University of the Hood." These faithful servants at times have had to focus their attention on getting the job done, a difficult job with few resources. They have not had time to develop a biblical and theological basis of urban ministry. Therefore, the Christian college can provide a great asset to urban ministry by training its students to think biblically and theologically.

If Christian colleges are going to train urban ministry students to think biblically and theologically, they will need to begin with the Bible. This may seem a bit elementary, but it is not necessarily so. When I enrolled in Bible school in the early seventies, the school asked me what I wanted to study in college, what major I wanted to declare as my focus. I had not thought much about that but I knew I wanted to study the Bible. I was informed that the best major for those wanting to study the Bible would be theology. I said, "Groovy," and I became a theology major. The school enrolled me in Theology 101, and off I went to study the Bible.

Theology 101 was a systematic theology course. We studied Barth and Bultmann; we studied about neo-orthodoxy and existential theology and the like. In class we talked a lot *about* the Bible, but we did not do much reading *in* the Bible. We talked a lot *about* God, but spent little time talking *to* God. I was disappointed; I expected more from the Bible. This is the approach many Christian colleges take in training their students to think biblically and theologically, and it is an approach that does not serve the urban minister well.

The Christian college student preparing for urban ministry would better be served by starting off with a biblical theology course. "Systematic theology articulates the biblical outlook in a current doctrinal or philosophical system."[2] These "doctrinal and philosophical systems" come from the collecting, arranging, comparing, and defending of the facts concerning God and His Word.[3] According to Paul Enns, before a person can do the work of systematic theology he needs to do the work of biblical theology. "Biblical theology is preliminary to systematic theology; exegesis leads to biblical theology which in turn leads to systematic theology."[4]

The urban ministry student needs to study the Bible in a way that seeks to discover what the biblical writers, under divine guidance, believed, described, and taught about the city and its effects on one's relationship with God. This is by definition biblical theology,[5] and the college student needs to know how to think biblically if he is going to be able to communicate the Bible in the urban context. Too often the student leaves Bible school with a cut-and-paste approach to theology that attempts to fit the biblical text into predetermined theological categories, rather than allowing the biblical text to speak to his or her theological presuppositions.[6] Letting the Bible itself speak is especially important as the student begins to work among cultural groups that do not approach theology with the same systematic categories or paradigms. These cultural groups will see the work of theology somewhat differently than those who have been trained from a purely systematic approach.

To assist the Christian college student in developing a biblical theology of urban ministry, the student should be encouraged to do extensive reading in the area of biblical theology. Several books come to mind that could be recommended for the student's study: Ray Bakke's *A Theology As Big As the City* (Downers Grove, Ill.: InterVarsity, 1997), Charles Ryrie's *Biblical Theology of the New Testament* (Chicago: Moody, 1959), Paul Enns's *The Moody Handbook of Theology* (Chicago: Moody, 1989), and George Peters's *A Biblical Theology of Missions* (Chicago: Moody, 1972). These books can provide a foundation for the student who needs to think biblically about theology and its application to urban ministry. Then as the student reads through the Bible he or she can begin to systematize the passages into the necessary doctrinal or philosophical system.

Thinking Sociologically

Thinking biblically is only one aspect of what needs to happen to prepare the urban ministry student for service; the student also needs to know how to *think sociologically* about urban service. James and Lillian Breckenridge affirmed this when they wrote, "While, from an evangelical standpoint, theology has priority over all other disciplines . . . it is still necessary to study all of the social sciences."[7] We can learn from the Bible that all people are sinners (Rom. 3:23), but when we look at patterns of sin in a society we are doing sociology. "Sociology is one of the family of social sciences that seeks to explain patterns of human behavior. Specifically, sociology is the study of the groups and societies people create and how these, in turn, affect the people who create and maintain them."[8] The urban ministry student needs to learn how to study and explain the patterns urban dwellers develop as they interact together.

One of the key skills that the urban ministry student will need to learn is how to acquire and interpret demographic information. Bakke, when discussing the urban challenges, agreed that there is a need for demographic information. He wrote, "The challenge we face as we approach the twenty-first century is *demographic* or numerical."[9]

Students of urban ministry need to be taught how to collect and interpret the demographic data as they develop a strategic ministry plan. I have my students spend several days collecting demographic data about a target urban ministry area. They count and classify the types of housing in their target area, the types of cars the people drive, the types of stores the community shops in. The students also spend time in a local library studying census, crime, and economic reports. The students collect this data so that they can ascertain the sociological patterns, and from them they create ministry strategies and plans to reach that target ministry area.

Thinking sociologically about urban ministry can help the urban ministry student in four important ways.[10]

1. Thinking sociologically can help the urban ministry student become aware of the different ways that social patterns and arrangements shape the lives of the people they are serving. Many Christians are unaware of how social patterns and arrangements affect ministry effectiveness.
2. Thinking sociologically can help the urban ministry student challenge underlying conventional wisdom and popular ideas that may be wrong. Some Christians might believe that the reason a certain minority group has high unemployment is that they are lazy, when in fact they might be the recipients of racial discrimination. Thinking sociologically may help the student discover the truth of the problem.
3. Thinking sociologically can help the urban ministry student identify social problems the church has not yet recognized. Upon evaluating the demographic data, the student may identify that the community is aging. For such a church, expanding its children's ministry may be a poor strategy decision sociologically.
4. Thinking sociologically can help the urban ministry student design and evaluate alternative solutions for persistent ministry problems. The student may discover that the homeless people in his community need more than just housing; they need to be a part of families and communities, which are the important agents of socialization.

Thinking Anthropologically

Third, the college student going into urban ministry needs to be taught to *think anthropologically.* It is very important that the urban ministry student understand the cultural intricacies of the urban landscape. George Gmlech said, "The typical city contains a wide spectrum of subcultures based upon class, ethnicity, occupation, religion, and so forth."[11] The student who thinks anthropologically will attempt to discover cultural similarities, differences, and patterns he observes within the urban context. The student does this to find out the rituals, rules, traditions, norms, mores, and folkways as they relate and affect the urban context.[12]

So that my urban ministry students can learn to think anthropologically, I have them participate in an urban ethnographic fieldwork project. This project will provide the student an opportunity to "observe and describe the daily life, behaviors, and language of a group of people for long periods of time."[13] The city of Chicago provides us with a unique "lab" for ethnographic research among its more than twenty-nine different ethnic groups, not including the significant African-American population. Chicago is also a diverse economic community. Within walking distance from the Moody Bible Institute are some of the poorest (Cabrini-Green) and wealthiest (Gold Coast) people in the city. Therefore, we have almost ideal conditions for urban ethnographic research.

In their urban ethnographic fieldwork project, the students spend a whole semester observing and studying a particular racial, ethnic, or cultural group. Each week[14] the student observes a selected ethnic/cultural group as a participant-observer[15] and writes weekly fieldnotes. The students further interview individuals who can inform them about behaviors or patterns that seem unclear, adding that information to their fieldnotes. Each student then codes any patterns he or she may find in the fieldnotes, using them to write an ethnographic research paper. This ethnographic experience helps them think anthropologically about ministry in the city.

Thinking Multiculturally

Fourth, the urban ministry college student needs to be taught to *think multiculturally*. The American mosaic is continually becoming more multicultural. Jaime S. Wurzel is correct in writing "human existence is inherently and universally multicultural, even though through history, mankind has resisted recognizing it."[16]

By the year 2050, the "average" American, as projected by the U.S. Bureau of the Census, will look very different from the American of 1996. According to the U.S. Bureau of the Census, in 1996 the U.S. population was estimated at 265 million people. That number represented an estimated 194 million white (non-Latino) people (73 percent of the overall population), 32 million African-Americans/blacks (12 percent), 2 million various Native American peoples (1 percent), 9 million Asians/Pacific Islanders (3 percent), and 28 million Latinos (11 percent).[17]

The U.S. Bureau of the Census has conservatively projected that by the year 2050 these numbers will increase significantly. The total U.S. population will increase to 394 million people, a 49 percent overall increase in population, with the most significant increases among the nonwhite population. It has been projected that the white population will increase in number to 207 million people, but decrease in total percent to 53 percent of the overall population. African-Americans will increase to 54 million (14 percent). Native Americans will remain at 1 percent of the population, but their overall numbers will double to 3.5 million; Asians/Pacific Islanders will increase to 32 million (8 percent); and Latinos will grow to 97 million (24 percent).[18]

The U.S. Bureau of the Census further showed the significance of these changes when it stated:

> More than one-quarter (6.7 million) of the total foreign-born population in 1995 were born in Mexico. . . . California had the largest foreign-born population in 1995, over 7.7 million persons, or one-quarter of all California residents. New York ranked second in the number of foreign born with 3.0 million.[19]

William A. Henry III in his *Time* magazine article, "Beyond the Melting Pot," summed up the crux of the issue when he said:

> While there may remain towns or outpost where even a black family will be something of an oddity, where English and Irish and German surnames will predominate, where a traditional (some will wistfully say "real") American will still be seen on almost every street corner, they will be only the vestiges of an earlier nation. The former majority will learn, as a normal part of life, the meaning of the Latin slogan engraved on U.S. coins—E PLURIBUS UNUM, one formed from many.[20]

Therefore, if the college student is going to be prepared for urban ministry, he will need to know how to think multiculturally. Thinking multiculturally the student must "(1) become aware of one's own ethnocentric conditioning and (2) accept the fact that society is indeed multicultural."[21] To achieve these two dynamics the Christian college must place students in situations that challenge their ethnocentrism.[22] Many of my students come from rural towns or small suburban communities. They come to Moody because of a sense of God's call and desire to serve Him in the city, but many are unaware of the cultural baggage they bring to the urban setting. Through cultural awareness sensitivity training, field trips, multicultural dinners and concerts, etc., educational institutions need to push their students out of their "comfort zone" and help them begin to challenge their own ethnocentrism.

One spring break I took several of my students to New York City for an urban exposure trip. These trips are usually whirlwind tours of the city; we see several ministries in less than two weeks. During that time we ate Chinese food in Chinatown and West Indian food in Queens. We went to big churches and even larger ones, small churches and struggling congregations. We saw the very wealthy, the poor, and the homeless. After the trip the students told how their perceptions of New York City were challenged and how they were deeply affected.

Trips and multicultural sensitivity workshops are only the beginning of the process in helping students think multiculturally. Ultimately they will need more than a weekend excursion; many will need, as John Perkins said, to relocate among the poor in an area of need.[23] Perkins went on to say, "I'm not talking about a group of people renting a storefront through which to provide services to the community. I'm talking about some of us people voluntarily and decisively relocating ourselves."[24]

The idea of relocating urban ministry students among the poor will be discussed later, but suffice it to say if multiculturalism is going to become more than just the slogan for those who strive for political correctness, the Bible school or Christian college must help its students think more multiculturally.

PREPARING THE COLLEGE STUDENT EXPERIENTIALLY FOR URBAN MINISTRY

Not only do we need to prepare the college student cognitively for urban ministry, the student needs to be prepared experientially. Experiential learning has been a significant aspect of higher education for a long time. Since the mid-nineteenth century, scholars like John Dewey encouraged education to become more experiential in its approach. Dewey taught that "experiential learning meant a cycle of 'trying' and 'undergoing' by becoming aware of a problem, getting an idea, trying out a response, experiencing the consequences, and either confirming or modifying previous conceptions."[25] This philosophy of education can be seen in Christian higher education in the form of internships, work-study programs, laboratory classes, and field projects.[26] The belief in experiential learning is that the student learns in doing.

I hear my students asking, and justly at times, "How is what I'm learning today going to help me in my future ministry?" These students are asking how does this stuff work in the "real" world of ministry. This question could be answered if the learning process took place in some fieldwork experience outside the classroom.

To achieve this integration of learning in doing, the Christian college will want to do four important things. First, schools of urban ministry need to *be located in the inner city*. This may seem like a no-brainer for some, but many schools bypass it. You cannot train urban ministry students by shipping them in from the suburbs or beyond. Even though many fine books have been published on urban ministry, you cannot prepare students for urban ministry just by having them read books. Therefore, we need to relocate our schools of urban ministry into the inner city and among the poor, the disenfranchised, and the ethnically diverse.

This will be difficult, if not impossible, for those institutions that are located in rural or suburban communities. Many of these institutions started among the inner city poor, but later they relocated to the suburbs or rural communities. I would like to see these institutions recommit themselves to the inner city by relocating, but I know that is unlikely. Therefore, another option will need to be found to achieve this goal.

Christian colleges and Bible schools could cooperate more significantly to provide urban ministry training within the inner city context. For example, those within the same accreditation family could establish a more liberal student exchange policy so students can receive an urban learning experience in an inner city setting. The precedent for this has been established in schools' participation in overseas study programs. Many Bible schools and colleges are eager and willing to send their students to Israel, Europe, or other institutions throughout the world for a year or more. They believe that these experiences enhance the learning process. How much more should Christian institutions of higher education cooperate to release their students to the urban centers of the world with the purpose of providing them the experiences that will enhance their ministry preparation?

Second, once the student has relocated to the inner city to study, the student needs to be given a *significant amount of inner city fieldwork*. Just having the students study in the classroom in the inner city is not enough; the students need to get into the field. Bible schools and colleges need to see the inner city as a laboratory. As the laboratory is to the physical sciences, so is the city the training ground for urban ministry. Fieldwork projects, like demographic and ethnographic research, have to be an integral part of the urban educational program.

Third, Bible schools and Christian colleges need to provide an option for their *urban ministry students to live in the inner city* while doing their studies. Several schools provide this option: Bethel College in

Minneapolis has its Urban House, and Wheaton College has an inner city relationship with Emmaus Ministries in the Uptown community on Chicago's North Side. These programs provide the students with a yearlong opportunity to live and study in the inner city. Upper-class students at Moody Bible Institute can apply for permission to waive the undergraduate requirement to live on campus and instead live in an inner city neighborhood where they have already begun to minister. Some choose to do so, but we are currently exploring a more intentional off-campus urban housing plan for both our undergraduate and graduate students alike.

Ideally these "urban houses" would be closely connected with key urban ministries throughout the city, enabling the student an opportunity to focus his studies in a particular strategy of urban ministry. Too often students get to their last year of Bible school or college without a clear knowledge of where they should minister. Having the student live, study, and serve with an inner city ministry may provide the focus needed for career selection.

Bible schools and Christian colleges may think that the financial obligation to develop these urban houses prohibits their consideration. This is untrue. Not-for-profit educational institutions can secure buildings from the Department of Housing and Urban Development (HUD) for relatively little cost. Many of the "best buys" with HUD are located in the poorest communities, where strategic urban ministry is presently taking place. Many of these buildings need some rehabbing, but what better way to teach urban ministry majors community development and planning than by rehabbing a house? The rehabbing could even be done as a school-wide community service project to enlist the whole student body in an urban ministry effort.

The urban house can also provide a means of developing the type of learning community today's college students want. This generation has been significantly affected by postmodernism. Stanley Grenz, in his book on postmodernism, tells us that the postmodern individual needs community, and this community helps in the learning process. Grenz wrote, "The postmodern worldview operates with a community-based understanding of truth. It affirms that whatever we accept as truth and even the way we envision truth are dependent on the community in which we participate."[27] Of course, community does not change what is true and what is not, as secular postmodernists might be inclined to accept, but Christians have long believed that those we associate with affect our beliefs, thoughts, and actions.

In my early years of urban ministry, my wife and I lived in a large three-bedroom parsonage on the second floor of the church building.

We were newlyweds with no children, so we had lots of room. Throughout our ministry we were confronted with several people who needed housing. Two of these individuals were college classmates, and we also had a newlywed couple from Minnesota, a guy who just wanted to minister with us in New York City, and yet another who was a recovering drug addict. We lived, ministered, laughed, and cried together as we sought to find our place in the ministry. We were a community of urban learners, and there was nothing like it. We lived together, seeing each other's idiosyncrasies and challenging each other to deeper character development. We worshiped together and discussed what we sensed God was teaching us. We read John Perkins's *A Quiet Revolution* and then weeks later had dinner with Perkins in our home. We were able to discuss with him the application of his "3 Rs of community development" in our ministry location.[28] It was exhilarating, stimulating, and a dynamic learning environment. Students preparing for urban ministry should be offered the blessing of living and learning in community with other students as they serve together.

The only missing element in this plan to relocate the schools of urban ministry and their students into the inner city is the need for the relocation of the teacher as well. The role of the teacher in preparing the student for urban ministry will be discussed in the next section. The example, influence, and guidance of the teacher is a key component in the preparation of college students for urban ministry.

THE ROLE OF TEACHERS IN PREPARING STUDENTS FOR URBAN MINISTRY

If Bible schools and Christian colleges are going to prepare men and women for urban ministry, it will take a faculty that becomes more actively involved in the lives of the students. This may mean a change in the teacher's role and function in the training process. Many professors in Christian higher education have devoted themselves to teaching and research, seeing themselves as intellectual leaders for the students they have been entrusted with. This function of the professor as teacher and researcher fits with formal educational structures.[29] But this understanding of the professor may be a by-product of educational systems and structures where program design, materials, class time allotments, and procedures are dictated by forces outside the control of both the teacher and student.[30] These structures must change if we are going to adequately prepare the student for urban ministry.

First, if students are going to be prepared and trained for urban ministry, they will need teachers to fulfill the *role of mentor.* The mentoring process can be defined as "a relational experience in which one person empowers another by sharing God-given resources."[31] Based on this definition, the teachers of urban ministry will need to invest their time and themselves into the lives of their students. There are no shortcuts to the development and maintenance of mentoring relationships with college students.

For more then ten years my wife and I have been in a mentoring relationship with a college student, now a graduate student, named Kevin. Over the years he has lived with us, ministered with us, and been an extended part of our family. We have shared the joys and sorrows of his life and ministry. Our lives and his have been significantly blessed and enhanced by this long-term mentoring relationship. I do not believe that the things we have learned together about ministry, Christian character, time management, and faith could have been experienced without this mentoring relationship.

Some faculty may say this is impossible with the more than a hundred students they have each year. If ten years were spent with each it would take a lifetime to mentor the whole group. In reality, not every student will be willing or interested in entering this length and depth of mentoring relationship. Even Jesus developed a deeper relationship with the apostle John then He did with Peter, Andrew, and James. Jesus also had a deeper relationship with Peter, Andrew, James, and John than He did with the rest of the Twelve; and a deeper relationship with the Twelve than He did with the multitudes. Of the hundreds of students we encounter going into urban ministry, the professor of urban ministry needs to select a few in whom to invest more deeply.[32]

Second, the urban faculty member needs to be a *guide* who helps the urban ministry student connect field experience with cognitive information by overseeing the classroom experience. The urban ministry student will be involved in classroom instruction in a formal setting as well as various fieldwork experiences within the urban context. It is, therefore, the urban faculty member who connects the cognitive information with the fieldwork experience by guiding the student with a regularly scheduled session.

This enhanced role of the faculty as mentors and guides will also require a broadening of our concept of "faculty." For many institutions this will require a significant increase in the number of faculty members and the associated increase in funding to pay for such faculty. It may be asked, "Is it worth it?" I believe it is. But it will require us thinking beyond the constraints of the formal education paradigm.

Many institutions could expand the ranks of their faculty by recruiting adjunct faculty from those in urban ministry who have graduated from the "University of the Hood." Many of these faithful servants have years of experience that could be brought to the classroom, free-ing the "formal" faculty to participate in extensive mentoring. Other institutions could develop an educational department of mentoring, in conjunction with the department of student development, that would recruit and deploy urban ministers and faculty as mentors. Finally, in-stitutions could reevaluate and redeploy their faculty across educa-tional departments and disciplines to better use the faculty and free up time and resources to mentor students in urban ministry.

I tell my students that the solution to their problem may lie out-side the realm of their experience. We need creative ways of thinking and experimental programs for educational institutions to mentor their students with their existing faculty.

More than twenty years ago, when I was a student in Bible school, I took more than one hundred and forty credit hours of course work. I heard hours of lectures and wrote hundreds of pages in reports. I re-member many of the lectures, class discussions, and chapel messages, but what I remember most were informal and nonformal experiences with my professors. Those informal times in their homes and on field trips, the discussions, and the advice they offered is with me to this day. Maybe the old adage is true: Much more is caught than taught. It is a worthwhile endeavor to create an environment conducive to as-sisting the student in catching what is needed for *doing* urban ministry and *being* an urban minister.

Conclusion:
Changing Methods for a Changing World

We are living in a time of radical change, change that has affected and will continue to affect the church and institutions of Christian higher education. These changes require that we change how we pre-pare students for urban ministry. May we provide the cognitive, expe-riential, and faculty needs to deploy an army of workers, committed to urban revival, who will seek the peace and prosperity of the city. The Bible promises that "if it prospers, you too will prosper" (Jer. 29:7).

Reflection Questions

1. As you read through or study the Scriptures, consider keeping a journal or notebook where you write your reflections on passages that speak to urban life. What did these passages say then, and what are they saying to us today?

2. Spend some time volunteering at an inner city ministry. Record in a journal or notebook the sociological and anthropological patterns you observe among the people. Discuss these notes with individuals involved in that ministry to see if your perceptions are accurate. What patterns are similar to your situation? Which ones challenge your presuppositions?

3. Read the biography of a person who is from a race or culture different from your own. What steps can be taken to prepare yourself and those around you for increasing racial and cultural diversity? What is one thing you can do immediately to think and act more multi-culturally?

4. If you are an instructor of urban ministry, what changes in your schedule could you make to provide more time to mentor and guide an urban ministry student? Consider accountability with a colleague to facilitate consistency in a mentoring relationship.

Bibliography

Bakke, Raymond J. *A Theology As Big As the City.* Downers Grove, Ill.: InterVarsity, 1997.

Bassis, Michael S., Richard J. Gelles, and Ann Levine. *Sociology: An Introduction.* Upper Saddle River, N.J.: McGraw-Hill, 1991.

Breckenridge, James, and Lillian Breckenridge. *What Color Is Your God?* Wheaton, Ill.: Victor, 1995.

Cairns, Earle E. *Christianity Through the Centuries.* Grand Rapids: Zondervan, 1954.

Chiseri-Strater, Elizabeth, and Bonnie Stone Sunstein. *FieldWorking: Reading and Writing Research.* Upper Saddle River, N.J.: Prentice-Hall, 1997.

Dowley, Tim, ed. *Eerdman's Dictionary of Biblical Theology.* Grand Rapids: Eerdmans, 1977.

Elwell, Walter A. *Evangelical Dictionary of Biblical Theology* [CD-ROM]. Grand Rapids: Baker, 1996.

Enns, Paul. *The Moody Handbook of Theology.* Chicago: Moody, 1989.

Gmelch, George. "Introduction," edited by George Gmelch and Walter P. Zenner, 130–35. Prospect Heights, Ill.: Waveland, 1996.

Gmelch, George, and Walter P. Zenner. *Urban Life,* 3d ed. Prospect Heights, Ill.: Waveland, 1996.

Grenz, Stanley J. *A Primer on Postmodernism.* Grand Rapids: Eerdmans, 1996.

Groothuis, Douglas. *The Soul in Cyberspace* [CD-ROM]. Grand Rapids: Baker, 1997.

Kolb, David A. *Experiential Learning.* Englewood Cliffs, N.J.: Prentice-Hall, 1984.

Lewis, Linda H., and Carol J. Williams. "Experiential Learning: Past and Present." *New Directions for Adult and Continuing Education,* no. 62 (Summer 1994): 5–16.

Perkins, John. *A Quiet Revolution: The Christian Response to Human Need: A Strategy for Today.* Waco, Tex.: Word, 1976.

Spradley, James P., and David W. McCurdy. *Anthropology: The Cultural Perspective,* 2d ed. Prospect Heights, Ill.: Waveland, 1989.

Stanley, Paul D., and J. Robert Clinton. *Connecting: The Mentoring Relationships You Need to Succeed in Life.* Colorado Springs: NavPress, 1992.

Thomas, Alan M. *Beyond Education: A New Perspective on Society's Management of Learning.* San Francisco, Calif.: Jossey-Bass, 1991.

chapter eight

MINISTERIAL FORMATION IN THE AFRICAN–AMERICAN CHURCH

A HISTORY OF EDUCATION AND TRAINING

DWIGHT PERRY

Introduction: The Race Question

Andrew Hacker captured the essence of the problem this chapter seeks to address, namely the context from which alternative models of theological training for African-Americans need to be developed.

> Race has been an American obsession since the first Europeans sighted "savages" on these shores. In time, those original inhabitants would be subdued or slaughtered, and finally sequestered out of view. But race in America took on a deeper and more disturbing meaning with the importation of Africans as slaves.[1]

Joseph Barndt, in his book *Dismantling Racism*, echoed this sentiment when he said,

> Racism is an evil weed sown in the garden of humanity. It has grown wildly, entangling the healthy plants and covering the pathways, creating a great maze, a labyrinth with twists and turns that entrapped us all. Its deep roots are embedded and intertwined in the life and history of the United States. Whether it be the genocide of the Native American Indian or the enslavement of Africans from another land . . .[2]

He went on to state that "racism is nothing more than prejudice plus power."[3] The reality that this type of racism is alive and well even today in America should not be a surprise to anyone who takes the time to listen to the evening news or read the daily newspaper. What is disheartening is that not only does this characterize much of what we see in the world, but that it has also been able to infiltrate the one entity that should be showing the world what it truly means to live—the church.

Billy Graham said that the one area in which he wishes he could have seen more progress during his more than fifty years of ministry is race relations. In a series of meetings on racial reconciliation in 1991 and 1994, the National Black Evangelical Association (NBEA) and the National Association of Evangelicals (NAE) committed themselves and their representative constituencies to combat racism within the confines of the church. The problem of racism has even spilled over into the area of theological education. J. O. McCloud, who focuses on ethnics in theological education, said, "There is a unique challenge facing theological education and theological schools today. The challenge is to provide relevant responses to the increasing diversity within the Christian community in North America and in the U.S. in particular."[4]

He went on to state that there have been five major barriers to seeing effective strategies for theological education for African-Americans become a reality:

1. The perception that racial ethnics have nothing to contribute to theological education. Many historians continue to perpetuate the fallacy that people of color and specifically African-Americans have contributed very little if anything to the field of theological education. Years of experience by African-Americans in a variety of situations are simply not added into the theological equation in terms of relevancy or perceived viability.
2. The perception by the majority community that blacks are only good enough to teach their own. This perception is reinforced even in the way many evangelical organizations are structured. For example, when one is looking for someone to direct the ministry initiatives to African-Americans or to Hispanics within the context of most denomination and/or parachurch agencies, the selection of a person of color is immediately given high priority. Rarely, however, does a person of color occupy offices outside of these designations.
3. Inadequate commitment to doing whatever is necessary to diversify one's workplace, especially within the leadership realm.

In many settings, diversity is given intellectual assent; unfortunately, when it comes down to hiring practices within the organization, it somehow loses its impetus.

4. Psychological—the feeling that the inclusion of people of color and specifically African-Americans would be some type of threat organizationally. The thought of having to learn how to accommodate and affirm another culture's way of doing things is, for some in the majority community, an unsettling thought.

5. Spiritual and Theological Barrier—exegetically, African-Americans, because of their experience, interpret the Scriptures from a different point of view. The issue of justice, the rights of the poor, as well as one's view of God as a liberator will be of primary importance to most African-Americans.

The problem of the lack of formal theological training among African-Americans is further compounded by the duality of mission of theological schools, that of scholarship versus ministerial training. For the past two hundred years, this tension has been a major area of concern for the theological community. It has escalated over the last several years, amplified by the fact that within a U.S. context, those who are involved in the training of prospective candidates for ministry have had classical theological training and tend to emphasize scholastics versus applied ministry practice.

This is a very relevant issue for those who minister in the black community for two reasons: (1) Due to the orientation of the typical evangelical seminary toward the classical theological disciplines, many of the questions being asked, even though important, have very little relevance to the community that one is being equipped to serve. (2) Teaching in a way that does not seem relevant to blacks continues to reinforce the theological chasm that currently exists between those in the black community. Most have received little formal theological training within the conservative evangelical settings such as Moody Bible Institute,[5] but a few have had formal theological training. Many leaders in minority communities are doing the best they can with what they have but are woefully underprepared and are not able to minister the Scriptures in a way that produces life-transformational change and not just the continued reinforcement of one's tradition.

Foundational to understanding this issue is the reality that within the African-American community the whole issue of call and access to ministry is totally contrary to what is typically observed in white settings. For example, an African-American comes to know Christ, senses God's call to minister, acknowledges that call before others through what is known as a "trial sermon," becomes ordained, enters ministry, and then somewhere down the line might go back to school in order to receive some type of formal theological training. The process of ministry accessibility is totally opposite in most situations in the white community. Here, a person senses God's call, goes off to seminary or Bible college, and then, after graduating from seminary or Bible college, gets ordained and moves into full-time vocational ministry.

This chapter seeks to address the question of ministerial formation within the African-American church. It will look at this question from the perspective of the historical context out of which ministerial formation has evolved in both the black and white communities. It will examine the impact of racism on the theological development of African-American leaders, the need for alternative models of theological training, and some specific educational implications as a result of this study.

THE CONTRAST IN HISTORICAL CONTEXT

Historically, there has been a difference in the way that European-American ministers and African-American ministers are trained for ministry. The primary difference has been in the use of formal versus nonformal training systems.

Ministerial Formation in the European–American Context

The major issue in curriculum design is the impact of ethnocentrism. All of us, whether we realize it or not, look at life through the grid of culture and the question "How does it make sense to me?" The issue of worldview comes into play at this point, seeing that one cannot help but look at life through one's own perspective.

Ethnocentrism not only affects how one views one's current situation but also one's history, because the grid of one's worldview is always going to affect how history is recorded and how one communicates the reality of his experience to others. Thus, when people of color are not portrayed in the curriculum mix as having any significance, their absence gives the impression that they must be of no consequence.

Seminaries as schools set apart for the education of clergy did not occur until the Council of Trent in 1563. Prior to this time, ministerial formation was primarily done by religious orders, monasteries, and cathedral schools. The primary focus of this training was spirituality and character development.[6] In the twelfth century, there began to be a shift in focus away from character development and spirituality to scholasticism being the primary emphasis. This rise in scholasticism coincided with the rise of the university's putting emphasis on the mastery of curriculum.[7] This eventually evolved into a fourfold curriculum model that has at its core philosophical theology, biblical studies, historical theology, and practical theology. This created what Edward Farley calls the "clerical paradigm" or the underlying premise that a scholastically focused theology was necessary for the training and development of clergy.[8] This underlying premise has reinforced the classical core of study of most of today's theological seminaries within the North American context.

Critical to the development of today's focus was the founding of the University of Berlin in 1809. Berlin was described as a place where professors and students were "free to seek truth."[9] Berlin was unique in that it was here that the scientific method of inquiry gained its most prominent platform. Friedrich Schleiermacher, who is considered to be the father of this classical paradigm of theological education, was a professor at the time at the university. When faced with the expulsion of theology as a discipline within the university, he sought to recast theology as a science. Philosophical theology became the core of the curriculum, with historical theology being capsulized as that part of the theological discipline that takes a look at God's presence with His people, and practical theology as that which gives order to the church. Schleiermacher's classical design positioned theological education in a slightly different slant than had been done up to this point overall. The focus of theological education had begun to shift subtly from ministerial training being primarily spiritual and character development. It now began to swing significantly toward theology as a cognitive discipline of rational inquiry as the critical foundational piece to the development of clergy for ministry.[10]

As seminaries were being formed in North America, the German model of education was not the only model to influence their development. The English model of education had retained the idea of *paideia.* Its focus was on character and spiritual formation. This process of developing the culture of the soul as the primary outcome of theological education worked its way out in what became known as "reading divinity."[11] A prospective ministerial candidate would sit under the tutelage of an experienced pastor, college president, or professor and would literally be taken, in the context of this one-on-one relationship, through a rigorous, systematic study of Scripture. The student might even live with the mentor in order to be exposed as much and as close as possible to the mentor's theology and life.

This process did not have any type of prescribed time limitation, but the process culminated in ordination. What made this process so unique was not only the one-on-one personal interaction between the student and the mentor, but also the fact that the student had to apply what he was learning within his particular ministry context. Eventually, however, this system of theological development faltered, at least in the broader white context. It became increasingly difficult for the denomination to monitor what was being taught by the mentors to these prospective clergy. The denominations were concerned that one of their future clergy would be sent to a mentor who did not think as they did. This was coupled with the growing tendency to see the teacher more and more not as someone who is primarily responsible for the instruction of people, but as a professor who is responsible for a particular area of study.

More and more, Schleiermacher's German model became the predominant model of theological education in America as we moved from the nineteenth to the twentieth century. This tendency was also a reflection of the trend within education in general to place more emphasis on the area of accreditation and quantification of educational learning experiences. The late 1800s to the early 1900s saw the development of accrediting agencies and commissions developed at both the secondary and the university level. These were put in place to evaluate the quality and effectiveness of the instruction that was being offered. Increased specialization became more and more of an issue in both secular and theological studies at the turn of the century. This trend continues even to this day with the proliferation of degrees. The various disciplines reflect this emphasis on specialization.

Ministerial Formation in the African–American Church

While this trend was taking place, primarily within the white church in America, the black church was not only alive, but thriving under the leadership of those whose formal training within a seminary context was nonexistent. Much like the African priest, who recited the history of the clan, the black preacher from the days of slavery had served his people well as their benevolent father, wise guide, prophet, intercessor, and liberator.[12] He was the holder of the oral tradition of the community, the holder of the story that linked an oppressed people in a land that was not their own to their past in a land from which they should never have been taken.

Even though he typically lacked formal theological training, the black preacher did have the privilege of learning under the tutelage of an older minister who eventually recommended the young minister for his first church. Similar to the process of "reading divinity" that was discussed earlier in this chapter, the black preacher's theological education was heavily dependent on his preacher/mentor. The relationship between the aspiring black preacher and the older mentor also became the key to his ability to gain access to his first ministry assignment, since a person's credentials to minister were related more to whom he knew in the denomination and how well he could "preach."[13] This nonformal system of training is still the predominant means of credentialing used today, as the majority of black ministers in the pulpit of the land today have very little, if any, formal theological training.

Despite this pressing reality, the black preacher was extremely effective. With limited resources, very little training, and continued oppression, he led an oppressed and downtrodden people not only out of the bonds of slavery, but also through the racial oppression of Jim Crow, the disappointment of the Great Migration, and the struggle for equal rights under the law.

The focus of the black church began to shift as it became more urbanized, especially as it entered the twentieth century. It shifted from a primarily religious entity to an institution that was more politically and socially motivated. Theology and the African-American's view of God were still primary; however, unlike the white church, the outworkings of this were primarily in the social and political arenas. This was in response to the context of oppression and misery in which the African-American continued to be found.

This period is portrayed as a shift away from the church's spiritual roots to a more social/political action focus. This is, of course, true in the sense that there was a continued and definite focus on the church's role in the community. The black church and thus the black preacher were perceived by black people as the only place where they could gain some semblance of empowerment, thus the black preacher needed to address the social and political issues of the times.

This does not mean that no one in the black community received formal theological training. As a matter of fact, schools such as Wilberforce University and Payne Theological Seminary were established with the express purpose of developing a trained clergy. However, those who have had the opportunity for such training are in the minority.

This is even more pronounced when one looks at the numbers of those who have had the opportunity to matriculate through the predominantly white conservative evangelical seminaries and Bible colleges of our land. Over the past ten years, only 1 percent of the students attending such schools as Moody Bible Institute, Trinity Evangelical Divinity School, and Gordon Conwell Seminary have been African-American.[14] This statistic is abysmal, especially from those who supposedly have the right theology. Obviously they have a grossly underrepresented constituency.

Part of the reason for this abysmal showing is the perception by some who have attended such schools that not only are they not user-friendly environments, but that they are downright "hostile," in a covert way, to African-Americans who choose to attend. There are a number of reasons for this perception, ranging from the subtle inferences of a curriculum that looks at the history of the church and lists primarily European and/or European-Americans as significant contributors, to the area of systematic theology that uses terminology such as "black" to represent evil and "white" to represent good. In addition, practical theology communicates, either outwardly or by implication, the perception that some of the cultural expressions of African-American faith are incorrect because they do not line up with the expectations of the majority community. The lack of minority faculty as role models and administrators[15] also contributes to this perception of an unfriendly, if not hostile environment. The educational implications section of this chapter will seek to address some of these concerns.

Not only is there a considerable gap between theologically trained and untrained black clergy, but also the gap between a trained clergy and level of education of the constituency has become more of an issue over the past twenty years. More and more African-Americans have some level of training on either the undergraduate and/or graduate level. And they are increasingly expecting those who serve them, including their preachers, to have a corresponding level of education.

EDUCATIONAL IMPLICATIONS

1. Black leaders, if they pursue some type of training, will typically pursue it later in life. This is directly related to the issue of the process of call. Culturally, the predominant experience of the black pastor is that one's call is consummated before one embraces some type of formal educational experience. This fact by itself will push back the entry point for many black ministers.

2. Black leaders are not able to take advantage in as large numbers of many of the traditional residency-based seminary programs, because they have additional responsibilities along with their ministry, such as outside jobs (many black pastors are bi-vocational and must support themselves through some type of outside employment), family, debt, and so on. In all fairness, this problem is not only confronting theological education for the black church, but the church in general. The traditional seminary student right out of college is becoming increasingly rare. More and more older students are going

to seminary. Some are hindered earlier by cost, the inability to relocate, and family commitments. The successful seminary of the future will offer multiple options or entry points for its training or it will be squeezed out of the market.

3. The likelihood of not seeing the need for further theological training will continue to be prevalent in certain segments of the black community. Ministers who have a successful ministry but who have not matriculated through a formal Masters of Divinity program at an accredited seminary will continue in the foreseeable future to be in the majority in the black community. Since the primary vehicle for ministerial employment for the majority of black ministers is not tied into any type of formal theological training but to how well one can "preach," the doors of opportunity for pastoral service will be just as open, if not more so, to the nonseminary graduate. The reality of seeing a number of very successful church models in the black community led by those with little or no formal training will also decrease the initiative to continue on or become involved in more formal stages of theological study.

4. The development of a more inclusive curriculum is critical if more and more African-Americans are going to be drawn to more formal models of theological training, especially within conservative, evangelical settings. Curriculum that only reflects the values and vision of one group will not be able to attract, retain, and develop prospective ministerial candidates from the black community.

   McCormick Seminary's African-American leadership program has been formed in conjunction with McCormick Seminary. It is designed for black pastors who already are in ministry and who desperately desire a theological experience that does not pull them out of their context but contextualizes their experience in the context of the classroom. The black studies programs at Fuller Theological Seminary, Colgate Rochester Divinity, and Vanderbilt School of Theology are examples of programs within predominantly majority community settings that have taken the time to develop a more inclusive curriculum that does not simply reinforce majority community norms and values for ministry.

5. Affirmation given by ministerial credentialing needs to directly relate to ministry context. No longer can we continue to perpetuate the fallacy held by many in the more formal settings of theological education that the fourfold classical curriculum is able to train every person for ministry, regardless of context. When determining "whether someone is qualified or not" we must include an in-depth analysis of the context in which one will minister.

6. Training must include the creation of a community that reflects those whom we are trying to reach. The issue of diversity is not a sociological issue; it is a theological issue (Eph. 2:11–22; Gal. 3:28; James 2:1–13). If we are to represent the body of Christ and reflect His body there is no more appropriate place than that place of nurturing and development for tomorrow's leaders—the seminary—to reflect such diversity.

Conclusion: Our Challenge

The issue of theological education in the black church and community is critical. As more and more statistics continue to come out that verify the desperate needs of those in the black community, whether relating to the skyrocketing percentage of dysfunctional broken homes, increased drug usage, HIV statistics that show the spread of the disease far greater in the black community than in the broader culture, or continued economic deprivation, the question one must ask is, Where is the church? Where is that bulwark of stability that has been the center of our community for literally hundreds of years but that now in many places is becoming increasingly marginalized? The corresponding question is, Where is the black religious leader, that change agent who is being used by God to bring deliverance to God's people?

As evangelicals we cannot continue to reach out more effectively to our brother and sister across the world than to our neighbor across the street. Both the black and white church need to acknowledge their joint responsibility to equip and empower individuals who, like Joshua, can truly help us as a people experience the spiritual promised land of the goodness of God's Word. The religious heritage of the black church and thus the black preacher is rich and substantial. Its ability to interface effectively, in a relevant way, and be equipped to meet the challenges of the twenty-first century will be directly related to the commitment to develop in the days and years ahead the type of quality catalytical leaders it has come to know and rely upon.

Reflection Questions

1. What are implications for conservative training institutions in relationship to the difference in the nature of the call for African-American ministers in contrast with those from the majority community?

2. What is institutional racism? Why is it important that both white and black Christians understand not only what institutional racism is, but how it manifests itself within many of our conservative evangelical structures?

3. What impact, if any, has the historical exclusion of African-Americans from the broader framework of society had on the conservative evangelical church?

Bibliography

Daniel Aleshire, Interview by Barbara Hopson, 7 February 1992.

The Aims and Purposes of Evangelical Theological Education by the Lilly Foundation.

Arnez, Nancy L. "Equity and Access in the Instructional Material Arena." *Journal of Black Studies* 23(4). 500–514. Sage Publications, 1993.

Barndt, Joseph. *Dismantling Racism.* Minneapolis: Augsburg, 1992.

Breckenridge, James and Lillian. *What Color Is Your God?* Wheaton: Victor, 1995.

Cannell, Linda. *Theological Education: Retrospect and Prospect.* Trinity Evangelical Divinity School, 1995.

Earl, Riggins R. *To You Who Teach in the Black Church.* Nashville: National Baptist Publishing Board, 1972.

Evans, Anthony T. *Are Blacks Spiritually Inferior to Whites?* Wenonah: Renaissance Productions, 1992.

Evans, James H. "I Rose and Found My Voice." *Journal of Theological Education.* Spring 1995.

Ferris, Robert W. *Renewal in Theological Education: Strategies for Change.* Wheaton, Ill.: Billy Graham Center, 1990.

Fletcher, John C. "Theological Seminaries in the Future." *Journal of Theological Education.* Autumn 1984.

Gilpin, W. Clark. "The Seminary Ideal in American Protestant Ministerial Education." *Journal of Theological Education.* Spring 1984.

Glenn, Norval D. and Erin Gotard. "The Religion of Blacks in the United States: Some Recent Trends and Current Characteristics." *American Journal of Sociology,* 83(2). 1977, 443–53.

Hacker, Andrew. *Two Nations Black and White, Separate, Hostile, Unequal.* New York: Scribner, 1992.

Hargrove, Barbara Watts. "Modernity and Its Disadvantaged: The Cultural Context of Theological Education." *Journal of Theological Education.* Autumn 1983.

Harris, James H. *Pastoral Theology: A Black Church Perspective.* Minneapolis: Augsburg, 1991.

Hughes, Michael and David H. Demo. "Self Perceptions of Black Americans: Self Esteem and Personal Efficacy." *American Journal of Sociology* 95(1). July 1989, 132–39.

Knowles, Malcolm S. *The Modern Practice of Adult Education.* New York: Cambridge, 1980.

McCall, Emmanuel. *Black Church Life Styles: Rediscovering the Black Christian Experience.* Nashville: Broadman, 1986.

McCloud, J. O. "Theological Education and Racial/Ethnic Leadership." *Journal of Theological Education.* Autumn 1992.

Molnar, Alex. "Racism in America: A Continuing Dilemma." *Educational Leadership* 47(2). October 1989, 71–75.

Perry, Dwight. "Educational Precepts for Valued Ministerial Attributes and Practices." Trinity Evangelical Divinity School, 1998.

_____. "Two Churches: Separate But Unequal." Trinity Evangelical Divinity School, 1994.

_____. "Institutional Racism Within Conservative Evangelical Settings: The Discongruence of Right Theology yet Wrong Sociology." Trinity Evangelical Divinity School, 1992.

_____. "Case Study on the Pastoral Studies Department of the Moody Bible Institute." Trinity Evangelical Divinity School, 1995.

_____. "Insight Paper on Non-Formal Education." Trinity Evangelical Divinity School, 1995.

_____. "A Literature Review on the Critical Need of Theological Education Within the African American Community." Trinity Evangelical Divinity School, 1995.

Reed, Jeff. "Church Based or Church Housed." Second Annual BILD Conference, 1991.

Rooks, Charles Shelby. "Vision, Reality and Challenge: Black Americans and North American Theological Education, 1959–83." *Journal of Theological Education.* Autumn 1983.

Rose, Amy. "Non-Traditional Higher Education." *Encyclopedia of Educational Research.* 10. 906–8.

Suchocki, Marjorie. "Theological Foundations for Ethnic and Gender Diversity in Faculties or Excellence and the Motley Crew." *Journal of Theological Education.* Spring 1990.

Terry, Robert. *For Whites Only.* Grand Rapids: Eerdmans, 1974.

Volz, Carl A. "Seminaries: the Love of Learning or the Desire for God." *Dialog* 28(2), 103–7.

Ward, Ted. "Non-Traditional Models of Education." Evangelical Mission Quarterly. 9(1). Fall 1972.

Ward, Ted. "The Quest for Orderly and Responsible Assessment of Nonformal Education for Ministry." Trinity Evangelical Divinity School, Summer 1995.

chapter nine

THE ROLE OF PREACHING IN THE AFRICAN–AMERICAN CHURCH

A HISTORY OF DIALOGICAL PREACHING

JAMES FORD JR.

Introduction: Knowing the Destination

The famous jurist Oliver Wendell Holmes once boarded a train but was unable to find his ticket. After watching him fumble through his pockets with growing dismay, the conductor said politely, "That's alright, Mr. Holmes. I'm sure you have your ticket somewhere. If you don't find it before you've gotten off, just mail it in to the railroad. We'll certainly trust you to do that." Looking the conductor straight in the eye, Holmes replied, "Young man, that isn't my problem at all. I don't care about giving my ticket to the railroad; I just want to find out where . . . I'm going!"

Just as the key to Holmes's reaching his destination was centered on the instructions found on his lost ticket, so is the need for and the centrality of the preached Word within the life of the black church. It is a reality, even to this day, that the one voice to which more African-American people in America are exposed, week in and week out, is the African-American preacher. One cannot examine the issue of growth and development of the African-American church without looking at the relevance and importance of preaching in the African-American church.

Preaching—good preaching—is vital to the traditions and to the satisfactions of
the Black church. It is the spiritual élan vital around which the Black church is
organized and from which it draws the peculiar nourishment by means of which
it flourishes and sustains a determined and long-suffering people. Preaching is
also an art and Black preaching is a unique art peculiar to the Black Church.[1]

Dialogical preaching is inseparable from the African-American church and is the focus of this chapter. I have decided to address this very important topic from five perspectives:

(1) the definition of dialogical discourse
(2) the history of dialogical discourse within the African-American experience
(3) the design of dialogical discourse
(4) the distortions of dialogical discourse
(5) the need for integration of the dialogical style of preaching into the grid of expository preaching

THE DEFINITION OF DIALOGICAL DISCOURSE

The root of the word *dialogue* is taken from two Greek words: *dia,* which means "to divide," and *logos,* a noun meaning "word." Dialogical preaching is the external, unsolicited action and exchange that occurs between the preacher and those in the pews during the delivery of a discourse or sermon. This exchange is based on the sermon's theological, practical, or emotional relevance that involves the people in the preaching process. Dialogical preaching is more than a mode of communication; it is a vehicle that transforms the preaching process into a time of celebration. "Celebration is the culmination of the sermonic design where a moment is created in which the remembrance of a redemptive past and/or the conviction of a liberated future transforms the events immediately experienced."[2] In other words, dialogical preaching, in its very essence, touches the heart of the congregation's lives. The discourse is theological in nature in that it is based upon biblical truth, but it is biblical truth communicated in simplicity coupled with a rhetorical flair.

For example, the truth of the immensity of God is defined theologically "as that perfection of the Divine Being by which He transcends all spatial limitation and yet is present in every point of space with His whole being."[3] But the African-American preacher would communicate that truth in the following manner,

> God is so high—you can't get over Him.
> He's so low, you can't get under Him.
> So wide, you can't get around Him.
> But He's a right now God.
> He's a doctor in the sickroom.
> He's a lawyer in the courtroom.
> He's my Lily in the valley. My bright and Morning Star.
> He's my wheel in the middle of the wheel.

The phrase "wheel in the middle of the wheel" is used by the African-American preacher to refer to intimacy with God based on Ezekiel 1:16. The simplicity of the truth coupled with its rhetorical flair elicits a response from the congregation.

The discourse is also emotional in nature. It has sense appeal based on intonation of voice, choice of words, dramatic presentation, vivid images, and contextualization. Frank Thomas appropriately commented on this aspect of the discourse when he stated, "If we want people to experience rather than solely intellectualize the good news, then we must construct sermons to help people see, taste, hear, touch, and feel the gospel."[4]

Consider the following excerpt from a sermon that I preached, which illustrates the aforementioned quote.

> *Jesus promised never to leave you nor forsake you. In fact, every direction you look Christ is there for you (Hebrews 13:5).*
> *When you look back—you see Christ dying on the cross for you (Romans 5:8).*
> *When you look up—you see Christ praying for you (Hebrews 7:25).*
> *When you look in—you see Christ in you, the hope of glory (Colossians 1:27).*
> *When you look beside—you see Christ with you—He said I will never leave you nor forsake you (Hebrews 13:5).*
> *When you look ahead—you see Christ coming for you (1 Thessalonians 4:11–18).*
> *When you look under—you see Christ—on Christ the solid Rock I stand, all other ground is sinking sand.*
> *He'll be what you need Him to be.*
> *To the woman who had the issue of blood He became a hematologist—a blood specialist (Matthew 9:20).*
> *To the man born blind He became an optometrist—an eye doctor (John 9:1–25).*
> *To the child that was sick unto death He became a pediatrician—a children's doctor (Luke 9:42).*
> *To the man with leprosy He became a dermatologist—a skin doctor (Luke 5:12–13).*
> *To the lame man He became a podiatrist—a foot doctor (Matthew 21:14).*
> *Jesus' disciples were troubled because He told them in John 14 that He was going away. He took off His preacher's robe and put on His psychologist's smock and counseled them—"let not your heart be troubled." He is with you and will become who you need Him to be.*

This particular discourse elicited an emotional response that culminated in "shouting." Shouting generally occurs near or at the end of a dialogical sermon. The congregation responds with unrestricted praise to God because the message has intersected with their lives by touching their hearts, enlightening their minds, and increasing their hope.

Dialogical discourse is not exclusive to African-American preaching. Its roots are found in the Jewish synagogue model, used during Jesus' day. This model includes interaction and involvement of the audience with the one who is making the presentation. In fact, it can be seen in several Old Testament passages, such as Nehemiah 8:1–7:

> And all the people gathered themselves together as one man into the street that was before the water gate; and they spake unto Ezra the scribe to bring the book of the law of Moses, which the Lord had commanded to Israel. And Ezra the priest brought the law before the congregation both of men and women, and all that could hear with understanding, upon the first day of the seventh month. And he read therein before the street that was before the water gate from the morning until midday, before the men and the women, and those that could understand; and the ears of all the people were attentive unto the book of the law. And Ezra the scribe stood upon a pulpit of wood, which they had made for the purpose; and beside him stood Mattithiah, and Shema, and Anaiah, and Urijah, and Hilkiah, and Maaseiah, on his right hand; and on his left hand, Pedaiah, and Mishael, and Malchiah, and Hashum, and Hashbadana, Zechariah, and Meshullam. And Ezra opened the book in the sight of all the people; (for he was above all the people;) and when he opened it, all the people stood up: And Ezra blessed the Lord, the great God. And all the people answered, Amen, Amen, with lifting up their hands: and they bowed their heads, and worshipped the Lord with their faces to the ground. Also Jeshua, and Bani, and Sherebiah, Jamin, Akkub, Shabbethai, Hodijah, Maaseiah, Kelita, Azariah, Jozabad, Hanan, Pelaiah, and the Levites, caused the people to understand the law: and the people stood in their place. (KJV)

The people responded to the reading of the Scripture with amens and exuberant body language.

This is in contrast to a monological style of preaching, which puts the presenter in the role of a one-way disseminator of information. The monological style of preaching is the primary methodology that is taught in most evangelical seminaries and Bible schools today.

THE HISTORY OF DIALOGICAL DISCOURSE

African-Americans have a rich oral tradition. In America, as well as in Africa, heritage, traditions, and rituals have been primarily passed down orally, very similar to the process of the Jewish race passing down the oracles of God.

Paul told the Roman believers that the advantage the Jews had was that God had committed to them His oracles (Rom. 3:2). The word *oracles* refers to the content of the communication but more completely to its mode of communication. It is the passing on of information by word of mouth. African history was preserved primarily through oral tradition, which is a key reason that the Negro spirituals became so popular during slavery. "In Africa, storytelling is used to paint pictures of life. The whole culture, its history and its essence, is preserved through oral tradition and celebrative rituals."[5]

The spirituals allowed the predominantly illiterate masses of blacks to be able to hold onto and grasp for themselves the hope guaranteed in Scripture, that no matter what one's lot is here on earth, there is indeed a better place for those who trust in Christ. Putting the truth of Scripture to song allowed countless numbers of blacks the ability to comprehend spiritual truths.

> *The final method of cultural transference was the rise of the new African, the Black preacher. The new Christianized leader of African people provided the cohesion and cultural reference point that kept slaves in touch with the strengths of the past, the needs of the present and the hopes of the future.* **Since African religion was handed down from one generation to the next by oral tradition, it would be natural for the African culture to continue to be transferred through that vehicle.** *The Black preacher became the channel for this process to persist. They were the new African point men in America who maintained the key elements of the African past.*[6] *(emphasis added)*

This then laid the foundation for the beginning of dialogical preaching and was the root of what we have come to know as the "Dr. Watts" experience. A "Dr. Watts" is a call and response generally begun by the preacher immediately before the sermon. One of the most popular elements of a "Dr. Watts" is entitled "I love the Lord." In a slow, rhythmic, syncopated fashion the preacher begins the Dr. Watts by singing the following: I-I-I-I-I love the Lord, He heard my cry-y-y-y-y. The congregation responds in antiphonal fashion, repeating the line the preacher just articulated. Each line of the four-line song is sounded out by the preacher and echoed by the congregation. The Dr. Watts is an important precursor to the sermon and in most cases sets the stage for dialogical preaching.

Another reason dialogical preaching became so predominant in the black culture was that it could not be controlled or understood by whites. The various dialects and ways of expression allowed African-Americans some sense of control in relationship to their white masters. It provided many with a sense of both intimacy and identity. Intimacy was based upon a common cultural expression whose uniqueness enhanced identity. It also indicated the listener's level of comprehension by his or her ability to repeat what was being said.

Dialogical preaching continued to be the primary form of preaching in the black church up to and including the early 1900s. More and more African-Americans were leaving the South, but were still seeking to find roots to help them cope with the growing complexity of being black not only in white America but in urban America as well. During this time the church served as the primary bridge between the North and one's roots in the South. In fact, the black church was and is the most stable institution in the African-American community. It is the hub of spiritual, social, economic, and political activities.

> The Black church viewed itself as more than just a loose gathering of individuals. It saw itself as a community in which everyone was related. The communal mind set again owed its existence to the African world view. In Africa, tribal life was family life, and family life was also religious life. The Black church provided a context for the redefinition of the slave in terms of God rather than the society in which he now lived. In church he was perpetually reminded of who he was from the divine perspective. One who was considered a "boy" on the plantation became "Deacon Jones" on Sunday. An elderly woman who would be known as "girl" during the week by her mistress, would become "Mother Smith" in church. The church then was crucial for maintaining God's view of Black dignity and significance under the hand of God.[7]

The popularity of dialogical preaching continued for other reasons as well. It was less formal than the highly liturgical form of worship in the Roman Catholic and Lutheran churches to which some African-Americans were being exposed. Because it put less emphasis on the need for formal education, it was used by preachers who were not able to receive more training due to either ignorance or the racist policies of many evangelical seminaries. Also, its very style lent itself better to a context of high emotions, both in worship and in the expression of one's walk with God. To this day the major style of preaching in the African-American church is dialogical. The major difference, as opposed to even thirty or forty years ago, is that those of us in the baby-boom generation have been exposed to a great deal more opportunities and educational options than our forefathers. We are looking for a message that not only raises questions and challenges our spiritual being, but is more intellectually challenging.

THE DESIGN OF DIALOGICAL PREACHING

Given the abuses of this form of preaching, some might question its validity. However, there are three important reasons that dialogical preaching is a viable form of responding to the needs of African-Americans specifically, but also to those in the majority culture. They are:

1. The ability of dialogical preaching to relate deep theological truths in such a way that they are both understandable and memorable. One of the present-day masters of this is Dr. E. V. Hill, pastor of the Mt. Zion Missionary Baptist Church in Los Angeles, California. Dr. Hill has the unique ability to take some of the deeper theological truths of the faith and make them understandable and memorable through the use of story. Consider the following story regarding the resurrection of our Lord Jesus Christ.

> *Satan, Death, Hell, and the Grave had a committee meeting. Satan spoke first and told the others that he couldn't do anything to Jesus but get Him to the cross. Death chimed in and said, "Well, if you can get Him to the cross, I can sting Him, but I can't hold Him." Immediately the Grave responded, "Well, Satan, if you can get Him to the cross, and Death, if you can sting Him, I can hold Him, but I can't keep Him." About that time, Hell stuck out his chest and bellowed, "Satan if you get Him to the cross, Death, you sting Him, Grave, you hold Him, I can keep Him." So Jesus was hung, stung by Death, placed in the tomb (grave). And Peter says He descended into hell. But early Sunday morning—He rose! Death couldn't sting Him, the Grave couldn't hold Him, and Hell couldn't keep Him. He rose with all power in His hands and said, "I have the keys of death and hell."[8]*

2. The ability of dialogical preaching to be practical and relevant in its application. Because the story is taken from the context of life, the hearer is able to respond to the message as he or she sees how it relates to everyday experience. Dr. Tony Evans, pastor of Oak Cliff Bible Church in Dallas, Texas, is a master of making his messages relevant and practical through use of illustrations.

> *Saddam Hussein attacked Saudi Arabia, an ally of the United States. The United States wanted to come to their aid, so they built a coalition with the Allied Forces. Saddam Hussein's mama didn't raise a dummy. He wanted to split the coalition by drawing Israel into the war. He fig-*

*ured Arab brothers would stop fighting against him if Israel was in the
war. So Saddam began to bomb Israel. But enter the heroes of the war,
scud missiles, that intercepted the bombs in the air. The coalition held,
and Saddam Hussein was defeated. Well, there's another Saddam Hussein on the loose today. His name is Satan and he's destroying the lives of
men and women, but God's got His coalition called the church comprised
of black Christians, white Christians, Hispanic Christians, Asian Christians. Our job is to defeat Satan and "scud" him with our prayers.*[9]

3. The ability of dialogical preaching to gain a response from the
   hearer, namely because it hits the emotions of the hearer.
   Whether we like it or not, we are emotional beings who respond
   to life on a feeling level more than many of us are willing to admit.

Allow me to clarify the phrase "to tell a story" in describing dialogical preaching. This refers to the use of narration, allegories, and examples to communicate scriptural truth. As mentioned earlier, this
methodology did not originate in the African-American culture, but
finds its roots in Scripture. Jesus made extensive use of parables. The
word *parable* comes from two Greek words, *para,* which means "to
come alongside" and *bolè,* which means "to throw." A parable was a
teaching device using the known to teach the unknown by means of a
story. According to Warren Wiersbe, it had three aspects. "First Jesus
would show you a picture, so you could see life. Secondly, He would
show you a mirror so you could see yourself. Thirdly, He would show
you a window so you can see God."[10]

A man had two sons—a picture—see life. One son rebelled—a mirror
—see yourself. The father ran to receive him—a window—see God.

Jesus made extensive use of parables, and much of the Old Testament was written in the narrative form and employed allegories and
examples as well. In telling the story, nine key criteria must be observed:

1. Make sure that you, as the communicator, know the point of the
   story. It is very confusing for an audience when it is obvious that
   the preacher did not understand the real point of the story. The
   key to discovering the main point is the context of Scripture. I
   was taught in homiletics that a text without a context is a pre-
   text. Key to discovering context is two questions. First, what is
   the subject? Second, what is he saying about the subject?

2. Be descriptive and not prescriptive. Description is turning ears
   into eyes through narration. It is aimed at the imagination and

the heart, focuses in on the communication process, and is designed to get you to know something; whereas prescription is linear, logical, focuses in on content, and is designed to get you to do something.

3. Distinguish between allegory and narrative. If we confuse the two, then we run the danger of misinterpreting the story, looking for a deeper meaning than the literal comprehension of it. *When the plain sense makes sense, seek no other sense.*[11]

4. Relate the story to contemporary life. The story has no meaning or value unless it is seen as relevant. The account in Luke 12:16–21 of the man and his barns could be told like this:

> *A man looked at his ranch-style home, with his two-car garage, in Barrington Hills, Illinois, and was satisfied. He said, "I've got my 401(k). I drive a BMW. I'm eligible for early retirement. I think I'll buy a time-share in Florida and take it easy." But God . . .*

We need to help people see themselves in the story. One of the best ways to do this is to keep those of each age group in mind as you prepare the story. Ask yourself, "How does this relate to their life experience, and how can I best communicate this truth to them?"

5. Don't just tell—re-create. Make an effort to so tell the story that your audience feels a part of it. Frank Thomas read the book *The Color Purple*. Yet, when he saw the movie, it was like he had never read it. "When Celie put the razor to Mr's throat, even though I knew she doesn't cut him, yet my emotions overrode my mind and I just knew she'd do it. Steven Spielberg so skillfully touched my emotions that he ordered my experience even though my mind already knew the outcome."[12]

6. Enhance—don't embellish. We preachers have been said to exaggerate at times, but we never want to do that with the story. It must remain true to the biblical text.

7. Know the story thoroughly. The key to this is saturation. Immerse and rehearse are my bywords when it comes to retaining, maintaining, and attaining a cogent, concise, and clear presentation of the story. The better you know the story, the better you

are able to maintain eye contact. Eye contact improves your ability to communicate with your congregation. It enhances attention, generates a sense of the preacher's sincerity, and strengthens the validity of the story.

8. Use sensory language. You want them to respond to the depth and relevance of theological truth depicted through word pictures. Dr. S. M. Lockridge painted a beautiful picture of the existence of God through sensory language. "Nietzsche said God is dead! Well, if God is dead, then who killed Him? What coroner examined Him? (Pause) What funeral home had His body? (Pause) What paper carried His obituary? (Pause) Who preached His eulogy? And why wasn't I notified because I'm the next of kin. No, God's not dead! He's alive—I spoke to Him this morning."[13] Or consider this graphic description of the death of Christ as given by Dr. Gardner C. Taylor. "When our Lord Jesus died on Calvary, the sun bowed its head in shame and covered himself with his overcoat of darkness. The earth shuddered and shook in anticipation of the death of the Son of God. The stars refused to give their iridescent light as all heaven is silent."[14]

9. Speak in the first person. Use a homiletical approach rather than an exegetical one. Instead of saying "the apostle Paul loved the Lord" say "we are to love the Lord" or "you are to love the Lord" or "I am to love the Lord."

THE DISTORTIONS OF DIALOGICAL PREACHING

All of us have a frame of reference and a multitude of perceptions that can hinder us from looking at life objectively. As one trained in exposition and convinced of its extreme importance and viability for the life of the African-American church, I had the misconception that African-American preachers whose primary mode of delivery was dialogical were not really preaching. I only saw the abuses of this particular mode of delivery. Now I see the validity of this style, especially when it is combined with an expository framework. At the same time, it is important to recognize and guard against the following distortions that are often associated with dialogical preaching:

1. Rhetorical manipulations: the use of catchy phrases without any real substance or relationship to the text being preached. Phrases like "ain't He alright," "say yeah," are catch phrases designed to solicit a response for the sake of a response.

2. Voice intonation: the rhythmic singsong cadence commonly designated as "whooping." It should always be linked to solid biblical content. In other words, it should be inherently moving as well as movingly presented. "Whooping" without a relevant basis is similar to a preacher who wrote in his notes "point real weak here—yell like crazy."

3. Repetitious meanderings: repetition for reaction rather than re-inforcement. The phrase or statement elicited a spontaneous response, so the preacher uses it throughout the sermon. Hoping to get the same response, he repeats the phrase.

4. Frivolous gestures: movement meant to elicit a response apart from the text. A preacher in my hometown had the reputation of being a good preacher because of how he handled his hand-kerchief when he preached. An extreme situation, but one that illustrates the point nonetheless.

5. Solicitations: all through the sermon the preacher tells the con-gregation how and when to respond with phrases like, "say amen, somebody" and/or "say yeah!"

Real dialogical preaching, on the other hand, is fairly discernible and distinguishable from the aforementioned distortions. It occurs charac-teristically in response to the preacher's relating the Scripture to the life experiences of the congregation.

THE NEED TO INTEGRATE THE DIALOGICAL APPROACH WITH THE EXPOSITORY FOCUS

Dialogical preaching's primary focus is on the delivery of the ser-mon. Even though it has encouraged, inspired, and helped countless people, it is not sufficient as a preaching form *in and of itself*. This is be-cause some who use it do not use a systematically, well-defined ap-proach to a text of Scripture. They often fail to inductively examine Scripture from an exegetical point of view. (What does it say? What does it mean? How does it apply?)

At times some African-American preachers superimpose a thematic perspective on the text by focusing more on the story and how it is de-livered than on the truths of the text. This leads to an incorrect under-standing of Scripture and the tendency to do eisegesis (imposing my perspective on the text and not allowing it to drive my interpretation), rather than exegesis (taking the meaning of the sermon from the text).

From my point of view, expository preaching is the meat of the meal, while good dialogical preaching is the gravy and seasoning that makes the same piece of meat not only more desirable, but also more memorable. In fact, Dr. Richard Allen Farmer said, "A good meat will make its own gravy."[15] This in no means implies that African-American preachers who preach dialogically are not evangelical and theologically sound. The basic tenets of evangelism have been espoused by the black church since its inception.

> The Evangelical Theological Dictionary defines evangelicalism as "the movement in modern Christianity, transcending denominational and confessional boundaries, that emphasize conformity to the basic tenets of the faith and a missionary outreach of compassion and urgency." Theologically, there is stress on the sovereignty of God, the transcendent, personal and infinite Being who created and rules over heaven and earth. Furthermore, evangelicals regard Scripture as the divinely inspired record of God's revelation and the infallible, authoritative guide for faith and practice. In addition, the person and work of Christ as the perfect God-man who came to earth as God's means of providing salvation are seen as the center of the evangelical Christian message.[16]

A greater emphasis on the marriage of dialogical preaching and expository preaching is spreading through the black church because of what God is doing in the black evangelical movement in America. It is an effort to preserve dialogical preaching and enhance it with exposition.

No matter where one lands on this issue, the reality is that the most effective preacher will have the ability to not only provide a good meal every Sunday, but will also need to make it taste good as well. Paul told Timothy,

> I charge thee therefore before God, and the Lord Jesus Christ, who shall judge the quick and the dead at his appearing and his kingdom; Preach the word; be instant in season, out of season; reprove, rebuke, exhort with all longsuffering and doctrine. For the time will come when they will not endure sound doctrine; but after their own lusts shall they heap to themselves teachers, having itching ears; and they shall turn away their ears from the truth, and shall be turned unto fables. But watch thou in all things, endure afflictions, do the work of an evangelist, make full proof of thy ministry. (2 Tim. 4:1–5 KJV)

We live in a media-centered culture that is used to top quality communication on an everyday basis. Can we in the church of Jesus Christ afford to do anything less?

Conclusion:
The Strength of Dialogical Preaching

Dialogical preaching has been and is a very powerful mode of communication in the African-American church. It affirms the preacher and facilitates his ability to communicate God's Word because of its narrative form, imaginative rhetoric, colorful illustrations, and relationship to the listener's everyday lives. It involves the congregation and is relevant to them in three ways:

1. It is theologically relevant because it reduces profound thought to simple terms.
2. It is practically relevant because it relates to the congregation's everyday experiences.
3. It is emotionally relevant because I am encouraged to express how the discourse makes me feel. (This is much like people who attend sporting events and react to field goals, three-pointers, etc.)

Finally, dialogical preaching enlivens the Word of God, or more appropriately, allows the Word of God to keep its life. It is communicated with a contextualized dramatic flair that allows listeners to experience the text. The response of members of the congregation is usually an indicated confirmation of their comprehension of God's Word. Dialogical preaching can be a blessing in communicating God's Word to this present generation. It is a powerful mode of communication and the staple of the African-American church. It is the African-American preacher allowing the Bible to use him.

Reflection Questions

1. List your initial responses to dialogical preaching and evaluate them to determine whether they are cultural, biblical, or otherwise. In other words, what motivated your responses?

2. What steps can you take personally to gain a greater perception of dialogical preaching? How could you help create a deeper awareness of dialogical preaching within the larger body of Christ?

3. What benefits do you see in integrating dialogical preaching into other cultures, like the evangelical white community?

4. Do you see a need to facilitate a stronger marriage in our churches
   between dialogical and expository preaching? If so, how would you
   go about it?

part four

LOCAL
CHURCH
MODELS

chapter ten

MULTIPLYING CHURCHES TO TAKE CITIES FOR CHRIST

NEW LIFE FOR THE CITY THROUGH CHURCH PLANTING AND PRAYER

TOM MALUGA

Introduction: The Church in the City

The knock on the door broke into the conversation I was having with my associate. It was not unusual for people to bring their needs to the church all times of the day or night. Still, prudence demanded that a measure of caution be exercised. It was late at night after Bible study in an inner city church located in one of the highest crime areas of the city. Thus, before opening the door, I asked, "How can we help you?" Rather than answering, the person knocked again. Figuring that maybe I had not been heard, I repeated my question, but again the only response was a further knock. Now I was concerned. Perhaps it was the memory of another night after Bible study when I saw a man from our church come back inside bloody and battered, having been assaulted right outside that door.

Suddenly I remembered that the front door of the church had not yet been locked. My associate dialed 911 as I raced through the church, wondering if this seemingly sinister visitor would go to that door and make entry before I could lock it. Reaching that door I could feel someone pulling on the door just as I was turning the lock. This time I demanded that the person identify himself and his intentions. I heard a man's broken voice say, "I need God. . . . I need my life to change."

Hesitating a moment, I opened the door and met a man whose life had been devastated by his addiction to crack cocaine. He had already lost his wife and kids and was about to be evicted from his apartment. His kids had come to outreaches of the church, so when he hit bottom he thought of the church. I will never forget the look of joy in his tear-filled eyes as he prayed and invited Christ into his life that evening. In the weeks and months following that, Raymond was a changed man. He rarely missed church services and often brought his five children with him to the service. When we gave the award on Father's Day to the dad who had the most kids with him in church, Raymond won. And even more exciting was the way that Raymond stepped up to actively participate in the outreach ministries of the church.

The cities of our country are places where God is actively at work changing lives. This is happening through urban churches that have embraced God's call to the city and refused to follow the masses of churches that have fled to the relative comfort and security of the suburbs.

As more and more people move into our cities, the potential for kingdom impact grows greater and greater. Chicago, like most of the large cities of our country, continues to see a wave of immigration. This tide of immigration includes many coming from lands where mission work is illegal or very difficult. But in His providence, God has brought these people to us. This presents a divinely appointed opportunity for kingdom impact on a scale that staggers the imagination.

For this impact to be realized, we must see our cities as Jesus sees them. How does Jesus see our densely populated cities? Matthew 9:35–38 describes Jesus as moved with compassion for the multitudes because they lacked a shepherd to lead them out of their harassed and helpless condition. Jesus was moved deeply by the crowds He saw. But He did not just feel sorry for them. He saw their spiritual need. He told His followers that the only thing keeping this need from being met was a shortage of those who would invest themselves in this work. That potential is even greater today. And so is the need for those who will invest themselves in connecting modern city dwellers with the Good Shepherd.

Seeing cities today with the eyes of Jesus will move us with compassion because of the enormous needs. It will also move us with excitement because there is such dramatic potential. Imagine cities with a harvest of people being connected with the Good Shepherd through the starting of new churches. Watch as blighted neighborhoods become transformation zones. Smiles light up faces once shadowed by fear and despair. Hope replaces aimlessness, relationships are healed, and the actual appearance of buildings begins to change. A dynamic of transformation flows out of churches, progressively eliminating pockets of darkness in the community. People whose lives once seemed irreversibly broken are now the excited leaders of teams of change agents sent to start transformation zones in other city neighborhoods.

In this chapter we are going to look at some models and principles for transforming urban neighborhoods through starting and multiplying churches. Many of the same principles here can also be adapted for turning around urban churches that have been in decline.[1] The infusion of hope and life-changing power into diseased neighborhoods through church planting is a critical component of a strategy to realize the kingdom potential of our cities. We will also highlight the priority that prayer must take for us to be successful in our mission.

MODELS OF URBAN CHURCH PLANTING

The following are church models with multiplying and city-impacting ministries.

Uptown Baptist Church

Located on the North Side of Chicago in one of the city's most diverse neighborhoods (with more than eighty languages), Uptown Baptist Church is a model of effective church planting in the inner city. The founding pastor, Jim Queen, came into an area screaming with need and began to reach out with compassion. Churches in the suburbs and from across the country linked with Jim and helped to start ministries through which people were brought to Christ and became a part of the church. Steady growth was maintained by an unwavering commitment to the core values upon which the church was started. Today Uptown Baptist continues as a growing, thriving church with a myriad ministries. But perhaps what is most noteworthy about Uptown Baptist Church is that it has served as a catalyst for other churches to be started in the urban context as well. A passion to multiply churches is part of the church's genetic code.

This commitment to multiplication can be seen in the mission and vision of the church. The mission of Uptown Baptist Church is to grow and develop followers of Jesus Christ who will impact our world as servant-leaders. The church's vision is to be a multicultural base for equipping and deploying urban leaders who will be change agents for God's kingdom in Chicago and in cities around the world.

Southside Tabernacle

Located on the South Side of Chicago in a predominantly African-American community, Southside Tabernacle serves as a model of another church that has multiplication in its genetic code. Pastor Spencer

Jones came to an established church, but he has been a catalyst for planting other churches, not only in Chicago but in cities across the country. His commitment to and passion for church planting, particularly in the inner city, is outstanding.

Tree of Life Missionary Baptist Church

For several years, Gary, Indiana, just outside of Chicago, was the murder capital of the United States. But in the midst of the violence and disintegration of the city, a seed of hope was sprouting. Tree of Life Missionary Baptist Church, planted by Pastor Cato Brooks, has developed into a vibrant congregation with numerous community-impacting ministries and an intentional strategy of birthing new churches.

Vickery Baptist Church

Vickery Baptist Church is located amidst a sea of apartment complexes that make it the densest area in the city of Dallas. Going to pastor this church right out of seminary, I found a church overwhelmed by the waves of changes in the surrounding community. Over the course of ten years, this church charted a new course that led to growth and the development of many need-based ministries among the community residents.

PRINCIPLES FOR URBAN CHURCH PLANTING

The Prayer Priority

The urban context demands that prayer be the priority for church growth and multiplication. Jesus called for His people (who collectively are God's present-day temple) to be a "house of prayer for all nations" (Mark 11:17 NKJV). In today's ethnically diverse urban communities, urban churches have a unique advantage for fulfilling this call. Churches that are houses of prayer are churches in which "every opportunity is prayer-birthed, every ministry is prayer-based, and every activity is prayer-bathed."[2]

God spoke through His spokesman Jeremiah, calling His people who were living in cities dominated by spiritual aberration to "seek the peace and prosperity of the city to which I have carried you into exile. *Pray to the Lord for it,* because if it prospers, you too will prosper" (Jer. 29:7, italics added). Rather than focus on escaping from the city, God's people were to positively affect the quality of life in the city. Unfortunately, this has not been the pattern that most Christians in this century have followed. Note also that the primary vehicle through which God's people were to affect the quality of life in the city was by praying for it.

One of the reasons that prayer is so critical for urban church growth and multiplication is the ferocious nature of spiritual warfare in the city. Strongholds of evil that sometimes have persisted for generations dominate life and do not yield easily. Many have gone into cities thinking to have great impact for God, only to withdraw in discouragement and defeat.

Jesus addressed this type of situation in Mark 9:14–29. The disciples of Jesus had failed to overcome evil when a father brought his demon-oppressed son to them. Their failure resulted in people doubting even the ability of Jesus to overcome evil (see vv. 22–24). When Jesus then cast the demon out, His disciples asked Him, "Why couldn't we?" Jesus' answer, "This kind can come out only by prayer" (vv. 28–29), demands our attention. We too have to ask ourselves why we fail to overcome evil. And we need to note that Jesus' answer tells us that *whole dimensions of experiencing God are only accessible to us through prayer.* A tremendous example of an urban church praying and overcoming evil is Brooklyn Tabernacle.[3] "The church must establish prayer as a primary strategy for community healing and renewal."[4] Prayer is the way we do battle with the forces of evil that dominate urban communities. Through prayer we conquer in the "air" before sending in ground troops.

One of the vital convictions for anybody ministering in the city is that God is already at work. Cities can be overwhelming and intimidating. When the apostle Paul was beginning the outreach in the city of Corinth that would result in a church being planted there, God spoke to him in a dream, encouraging him to continue his aggressive proclamation by telling him, "I have many people in this city" (Acts 18:9–11). Seeing so many people seeking for meaning in the wrong places in the city should not daunt us but challenge us to "open [our] eyes and look at the fields! They are ripe for harvest" (John 4:35). One of the passages that God has used to encourage and challenge me to see Him already at work in the city is Proverbs 1:20–21: "Wisdom calls aloud in the street, she raises her voice in the public squares; at the head of the noisy streets she cries out, in the gateways of the city she makes her speech." In the noisiest, busiest sections of the city, still God raises His voice. Prayer allows us to hear His voice and see His hand and join Him in what He is already doing.

Prayer is also essential if a church is truly going to be a multiplying church. In Acts 1–2 we see that prayer led to the birth of the church itself. We should then expect that prayer plays a vital role for birthing urban churches today. The book of Acts shows us two very different models of church planting, the Jerusalem Church Model and the Antioch Church Model.[5] (My assumption is that *churches*, not individuals, give birth to churches, though individuals may at times play a very prominent role.) The Jerusalem Church Model is that of a church that multiplies because of crisis (in this case, persecution) or outside forces on the church (see Acts 11:19–30). The Antioch Church Model is that of a church that multiples because the Spirit speaks to them as they pray (see Acts 13:1–3). The Antioch model is a *sending* church. Only praying churches can truly be sending churches.

Many churches around the world have started from prayer cell groups. This strategy relies on God's power demonstrated through answered prayer to draw people to faith in Christ. New believers are then brought together to form a new church.[6]

When Uptown Baptist Church started an outreach to Asian-Indians, prayer was specifically written into the job description as the top priority of the point person.[7] Following this was the gathering of a prayer core group for the ministry that would not only pray for this specific outreach but also for outreaches to Hindus worldwide.

Leadership Deployment

Prayer also plays a vital role in this next key principle. The need to begin an outreach to the Asian-Indian population of Chicago's North Side was discovered through prayerful observation of the multitude of Asian-Indians who needed the Good Shepherd. Compassion gave birth to the vision for starting a church to reach this population. The prospects of securing leadership to begin the outreach seemed dim, but this compelled the church to pray. While people prayed in Chicago, on the other side of the world, in India, God worked. He brought together two couples from the United States. One couple was from Uptown Baptist Church, and the other couple was preparing to return to the States to begin theological training in the Chicago area. During this encounter, the couple from Uptown Baptist drew a map for the other couple to get to the church. When, a few months later, the couple visited the church, God gave clear guidance that He was answering the prayer for harvest laborers through bringing this couple to the city and the church.

A powerful implication here must not be missed. When Jesus saw the potential in the multitudes and the need for people to invest themselves as His harvest agents in this mission, He made prayer the priority assignment for addressing this need. And the prayer was specifically devoted to the need for leaders.

Southside Tabernacle Church on the South Side of Chicago concentrates its church planting strategy on the recruitment and training of leaders. Pastor Jones systematically recruits potential church planters as a part of his regular schedule. Visiting at his denomination's schools, he serves as God's microphone for extending a call to serve God in the city. Those who respond are placed in a rigorous internship program in which their character and capabilities for urban church planting are evaluated.

In too many cases, students at our evangelical Bible colleges and seminaries are not adequately exposed to what God is doing in the city. They may not perceive the strategic importance of the city for God's kingdom agenda. Urban churches and pastors must take the initiative to help them do so. Not only must we call students to the city, but churches must be prepared for students to come and experience the city and see what God is doing there. In a number of cases students who have come to Uptown Baptist Church from Moody Bible Institute and Wheaton College (and other places as well) to do internships in one of our ministries have sensed God's call into urban ministry. Even with those students who will eventually go as God's representatives to other nations and cultures, a time of reaching out to people of that culture in the city can do more for preparing them for their mission than many years in school.

Though it is vital to draw from the pool of future leaders in training through colleges and seminaries, it is just as important to deploy leaders that we have developed ourselves in the urban church. Rather than seeing developing disciples simply as potential Sunday school leaders and ministry leaders, they must also be seen as potential church planters. Too often urban churches fall into the trap of trying to hang on to people rather than releasing them and sending them to open new works of God. For this to happen, churches have to move from an identity as a surviving church to that of a sending church.

Two passages in particular highlight the kind of leaders we need in the city today. In Mark 10:35–45 Jesus emphasized that leaders should follow His model of leading through serving. The city has so many power grabbers that coming as a servant is all the more important. In Ecclesiastes 7:19 we are told, "Wisdom makes one wise man more powerful than ten rulers in a city." When I take this verse seriously and then think of the power that political rulers wield in Chicago, I get really excited about how much potential we have to affect the city through developing wisdom. This also points up the need for these leaders to be people with a priority for prayer (as can be seen in passages like Prov. 8:34 and James 1:5.)

Jim Queen, the founding pastor of Uptown Baptist Church (and currently executive director of the Chicago Metropolitan Baptist Association), stresses the following gifts and character qualities as those most important for urban church planting: "Love for the people and community and prayer. . . . A supportive, understanding, and loving wife and family." Jim also emphasizes several convictions and disciplines that sustained him through the church birthing process: "A growing love of people in community. . . . Flexibility and understanding of needs of community. . . . Surrounding myself with gifted people and mentoring relationships with other urban pastors."[8] The wise aspiring urban church planter would do well to heed the counsel of a man who passed the test!

Pastor Spencer Jones of Southside Tabernacle Church highlighted the gifts and character qualities needed by an urban church planter this way:

> The ideal candidate is usually an individual called to inner city ministry, an aggressive self-starter, a person acquainted or familiar with the unique needs of inner city dwellers, and a person able to identify the needs and problems these people face. Inner City Ministry is not for the faint-hearted, the delicate, gentle-spirited person, not the person looking for an established work providing financial security. It is a labor of love and reward to those who will embrace it.[9]

Relationships in the Community

This third key principle for starting urban churches is modeled by the apostle Paul in starting the church in the city of Thessalonica. In his own words: "We loved you so much that we were delighted to share with you not only the gospel of God but our lives as well, because you had become so dear to us" (1 Thess. 2:8).

Relationships were the core of Jim Queen's approach in starting Uptown Baptist Church. Jim continues to emphasize the importance of developing relationships in the following strategy[10] he advocates for starting churches:

1. Walk in the neighborhood and observe. Ask yourself: Who is there?
2. Introduce yourself to the key institutional people. Tell them that you are there to help them (whether business people, apartment managers, politicians, etc. . . . this is related to our next principle: *community impact*).
3. Go back and revisit. Then, at some point, they will begin to call you.
4. You will be attracted to a part of the neighborhood because of your giftedness, but you do not want to get limited to just that arena (e.g., the school system).
5. Visit in the community so that through knowing the community

and meeting the people you will begin to define target groups. You will begin to use events to attract groups.

6. Start offering church—a place to come. You are never a church until you have church (worship and congregation together).
7. Keep going back to the visitation.
8. Begin to have contextualized worship—music the people can relate to so that they are hearing their own sound.

In revitalizing Vickery Baptist Church in an inner city area in Dallas, Texas, developing relationships was at the very core of rebuilding a connection between the church and the community. Both for this and the following principle, it is critical that a church have a vision for its immediate community. This could be called a *parish* church model. A *cathedral* church model emphasizes drawing from an extended radius. Although such an approach often helps to bring needed resources into the inner city church, care must be taken that the church not become disconnected from its community. In some cases of thriving churches in the inner city, the churches are inner city by location but not by nature. They may even run ministries or programs for the people of the community, but they do not really provide discipleship or "church" for the people of the community.

Community Impact Through Service

Community impact is a fourth critical principle for starting effective urban churches. It is particularly key in the inner city where "snake oil peddlers," whether preachers or politicians, have come in with big promises that left people poorer and more disillusioned. Community impact is making a positive difference (physically, emotionally, economically, socially, educationally, spiritually, and so forth) in the lives of people of a specific locale or a people group. Serving others is a biblical and powerful way of making a positive difference. The way that Jesus most often developed relationships with others was through serving them according to their needs.

This approach is strongly endorsed in the pages of Scripture. Consider that in John 13:12–17 Jesus called us to follow His model of servanthood, promising a blessing for those who do so. The apostle Paul in Philippians 2:5 called us to have the same attitude "as that of Christ Jesus." This attitude was clearly seen in the following verses (Phil. 2:6–8) as an attitude of humble, sacrificial servanthood. In highlighting the signs of a true disciple, Jesus in Matthew 25:31–46 pointed not to the miracle worker, but to the one who ministered to people's basic needs, such as providing food, clothing, or health care.

Many people don't reject Christianity or the church; they see it as irrelevant. Since being a servant is so contrary to the self-centered, control-obsessed ways of the world, it gives us credibility that we can't have any other way. Instead of being a mirror of the world, we become a miracle to the world! It also brings us into contact with the world. Too many churches and Christians are trying to shout to the world from a safe distance. As a result, a lot of them are only talking to themselves (which usually ends up as arguing with themselves!). Through service we become the "salt of the earth" and the "light of the world" that Jesus called us to be (Matt. 5:13–16).

In the urban community, serving others according to their needs is a potent form of leadership. Rather than being overcome by evil, we overcome evil with good (Rom. 12:21). This is the very definition of what it means to be a kingdom change agent! Because many urban communities tend to be clusters of people with little power and many needs, service provides an open door into the lives of people who need Christ. Because the needs are seemingly endless, so too are the ministries that can be developed to serve people. Some specific examples of ministries that have been used at Uptown Baptist Church or at Vickery Baptist Church in Dallas are included in the following list.

List of Ministries for Community Impact Through Service

1. The event or seasonal approach:
    **Fall Family Festival
    **Election Day Welcome Center
    **Block Parties
    **Health Fair
    **Job and Career Fair
    **Thanksgiving Food Outreach
    **Spring Blast (spring vacation Bible school)
    **Ethnic Celebrations (Cinco de Mayo, Fourth of July, Via Dolorosa)
    **Finders, Keepers: Finding and Keeping Love (Valentine's Day)
    **Back to School Pizza Party
    **School Supplies Aid
    **Summer Academy
    **Summer Outdoor Concert Series
    Benefits of this approach: Takes advantage of seasonal interests/ needs; can be an easy way for people to get involved in ministry in the church because the commitment is for a specific (and shorter) period of time.

2. Ongoing approaches:
   **After-school Programs
   **Tutoring/Literacy Ministry
   **Community Meal
   **Sewing Classes
   **Art Classes
   **Parenting Classes
   **Marriage Seminar
   **Divorce Recovery Group or Seminar
   **Support Groups (addictions, grief/loss, weight-reduction, etc.)
   **Food Pantry
   **Clothing/Furniture
   **Seniors' Activities (fitness, field trips, etc.)
   **Job Search Assistance/Training
   **Career/Job Specific Growth/Witness Groups (nurses, lawyers,
      FCAP[Fellowship of Christian Airline Personnel], Social Services)
   **Ministry to the mentally handicapped
   **Ministry to the physically handicapped
   **Day Care for low-income families
   **Single Parent Ministries
   **Operation Good Samaritan
   **Domestic Abuse Ministry
   **Spiritual Keys to Success
   **Citizenship/Refugee Assistance
   **English as a Second Language
   **Immunizations
   **Multifamily Housing Activities Coordinator
   **Block Club/Neighborhood Association
   **Housing Assistance (shelter, construction, finding housing, aid)
   **Financial Freedom (budget, debt-relief training)
   **Hospital/Jail Chaplaincy (also police, fire, sports, nursing
      homes, etc.)
   **Music Lessons/Community Choir
   **Miracle League
   **Murals/Arts/Drama
   **AIDS Ministry
   **Uptown Leadership Project—summer jobs for serious teens
      leading Bible clubs for kids
   **Fifth Quarter/Youth Movie Nights
   **Christian Women's Job Corp—mentoring and training in skills
      to get and keep jobs for women who have been on welfare
   Benefits of this approach: Better for developing relationships with
   people who are served.

The process for starting new ministries must be bathed in prayer. This process is shown in the flow chart below.[11]

COMMUNITY IMPACT

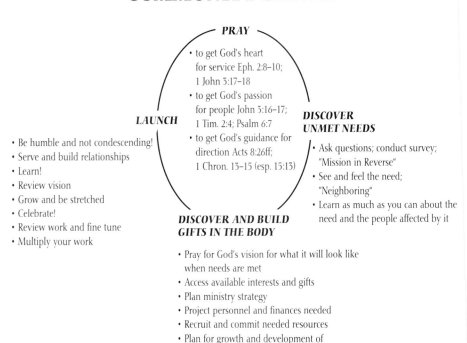

PRAY
- to get God's heart for service Eph. 2:8–10; 1 John 3:17–18
- to get God's passion for people John 3:16–17; 1 Tim. 2:4; Psalm 6:7
- to get God's guidance for direction Acts 8:26ff; 1 Chron. 13–15 (esp. 15:13)

DISCOVER UNMET NEEDS
- Ask questions; conduct survey; "Mission in Reverse"
- See and feel the need; "Neighboring"
- Learn as much as you can about the need and the people affected by it

DISCOVER AND BUILD GIFTS IN THE BODY
- Pray for God's vision for what it will look like when needs are met
- Access available interests and gifts
- Plan ministry strategy
- Project personnel and finances needed
- Recruit and commit needed resources
- Plan for growth and development of personnel and resources

LAUNCH
- Be humble and not condescending!
- Serve and build relationships
- Learn!
- Review vision
- Grow and be stretched
- Celebrate!
- Review work and fine tune
- Multiply your work

Amidst the many options for serving the community, start with the gifts already available in your core group that match needs in the community. At Uptown Baptist Church, when God brought Brian Bakke to the church to use his artistic gifts in ministry, many others with similar gifts were attracted to minister through art as well. How God used Brian's commitment, passion, and exceptional gifts is told in Brian's chapter.

When Uptown Baptist looked to begin outreach to the Asian-Indian population of Chicago, Hindus were specifically chosen as the target group. In order to reach Hindus, a way had to be found to build relationships with Hindus in the community. Because this population is mostly made up of people with the affluence to immigrate and because it tends to hide its needs, this was not easy. One way of discovering needs is through the use of surveys (which this ministry has used with the Asian-Indian university population in Chicago). But simply meeting people and getting to know them is perhaps the best way of exploring the needs that exist. Two needs surfaced in this community. First, new arrivals in the country need assistance in accessing services that are meant to help them. Second, there was a need to somehow help the victims of the domestic violence that is widespread but largely hidden among this people group. Amazingly God opened doors to meet needs in both these ways. An agency run by Hindus and Muslims to help Asian-Indian victims of domestic violence even invited our church to help provide services to its clients.

Once a church develops credibility in its community, the opportunities to serve the community are staggering. For instance, in Gary, Indiana (just outside Chicago), court judges regularly "sentence" young male offenders to receive mentoring at Tree of Life Missionary Baptist Church. Pastor Cato Brooks has affected the blighted community around the church with many services, including the development of housing for low-income families. Pastor Brooks also models a strong commitment to developing leaders and multiplying churches.

At Vickery Baptist Church in Dallas, public corporations in the community (hospital, police, schools) sought the church to support its outreaches and to partner together in initiatives to raise the quality of life in the community. For instance, one day I received a call from a man who had just purchased several apartment complexes in the community. Though this man was Jewish with no commitment to Christ, he offered to give our church two free apartments if we would place somebody from our church to serve as an "activities coordinator" for an apartment complex. Urban apartment complexes in cities across our country tend to be among the most underchurched and ripe for starting new churches.

Doing the Unexpected

New churches should be characterized by new ways of doing church. It is inconsistent (and unnecessary) for a new church to do church in any way that doesn't achieve maximum connection with the people it is trying to reach. The use of the arts in reaching out to people in the community is only one example of how important it is to be *creative* in our approach. Too often our approach is so routine and so expected that people don't give it a second thought. In reaching out to the Asian-Indian community the challenge was to find a way to connect with the Hindus who tend to be very suspicious of Christians. An opportunity came through the death of Mother Teresa. Observing how even Hindus had great respect for her, we planned an outreach that would show a video of her life and follow that with a testimony from a man who converted to Christ from Hinduism. An initial indication that this would go well came when one of the top Asian-Indian restaurants offered to cater the event. When the day came, the small room that we had procured in the heart of the Asian-Indian community in Chicago was packed with Hindus, so full that another event had to be planned! Still another creative outreach has been giving out the *Jesus* video as a Christmas gift to all the Asian-Indian shop owners. Videos are very popular among this population.

Our God is creative and He endows His people with creativity as they pray. We must pray with the passion of Daniel and his friends in Daniel 2:17–23 who needed God-given insight or they would be destroyed. When God gave that insight, they praised a God who reveals Himself and makes known what could never be known otherwise. This is so important in an environment where the emotional dynamics are sometimes not very advantageous for churches. Too often urban people know how churches have abandoned the city and the poor. Or they see others that have stayed but excluded people of other racial or ethnic groups. The sheer brokenness in communities where "evil is in your face" (you don't have to go looking for it), the overwhelming need for resources (financial and personnel), and the fact that many in the community would rather not live there but have no choice are factors that virtually compel us to cry out to God for what He alone can give us.

Community Impact Through Diversity

Churches need to lead, not follow the culture in being inclusive of all races and ethnic groups. Though not everyone will relate to the multicultural church, it is a tremendous witness. Urban Christians have a unique opportunity to affect not only their communities but the world through this witness. How churches can intentionally move toward becoming multicultural is shown below.

PRINCIPLES FOR GROWING MULTICULTURAL CHURCHES

Build Conviction About Diversity

    A. Biblically: People must know biblically *why* we should have multicultural churches (see Rev. 7:9–12; Acts 6:1–7; 11:19–26; 13:1–3; Matt. 28:19–20; Eph. 2:14–22; Gal. 3:26–28).

    B. Strategically: The urban reality is multicultural, and the church must not lag behind the world in diversity but instead demonstrate a healthy model of unity in diversity in Christ to the world.

Affirm Diversity as Part of the Church's Identity and Vision

A. From the pulpit: The pastor must speak about it frequently in his sermons.
B. Through planning: Diversity usually does not just happen; there must be intentionality in our plans to grow as a diverse church.
C. Through worship, outreach, and ministries: Worship should be enriched by elements from diverse cultures, and ministries should be developed or refined to be sensitive to concerns of diverse cultures.

Build a Multicultural Leadership Team and Staff

A. Pray for God to direct you to the people of other cultures He has to grow and serve with you.
B. Pursue those people, challenging them with your vision and their role in it.
C. Disciple/train them to grow and serve with you.

Enjoy Progress and Anticipate Problems

A. Celebrate diversity: It's a foretaste of heaven that we can relish right here and now!
B. Evaluate dynamics: Be alert to how people are interacting on deeper levels.
C. Learn to identify warning signals: factions, undercurrents, and "mysterious disappearances." The church may be a foretaste of heaven, but we're not in heaven yet!
D. Facilitate communication: This is an ongoing need to not only solve problems but *maximize what God intends for diversity to be.*

Keep Growing and Plant New Multicultural Churches

A. Recognize how the dynamics of a multicultural church affect the already complex issues of assimilation, mobilization, and change in a local church.
B. Affirm your vision for multicultural churches by enlisting a multicultural team from your church to start another multi-cultural church.

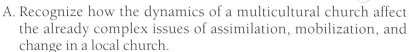

Conclusion:
The Need to Pray and Multiply

The Great Commission demands that we get serious about starting new churches in cities. We're way overdue for Christians to end their retreat from the city and begin to engage cities through prayer. In the urban context, it takes great intentionality and focus to grow a reaching, nurturing, equipping, mobilizing, and sending church that will multiply itself.

We must look at the city with the eyes of God and not the eyes of Jonah. Whereas Jonah only saw the wickedness of Nineveh and so distanced himself from the city and desired its punishment, God anticipated a city that would respond in repentance to the proclamation of His message. Prayerfully seeking wisdom from God, we can go to the city in the spirit of Proverbs 21:22: "A wise man attacks the city of the mighty and pulls down the stronghold in which they trust."

In the movement of history, the twenty-first century may well be the "century of the city." The Lord of the Great Commission is gathering the nations to the cities so that there might be unprecedented kingdom harvest. Will we seize the opportunity? Even now the Harvest Master is commanding His laborers to start new churches in the cities of the earth. Is He calling you? A response to the compassion and the command of Jesus will move us to the greatest era in history of starting churches in the city.

Reflection Questions

1. Why is prayer strategic for birthing and growing churches in the city?

2. Where do we find the leaders to plant churches in the city?

3. How is urban church planting different from starting churches in other contexts?

4. What are some key principles for impacting urban communities?

chapter eleven

THE USE OF ARTS IN URBAN EVANGELISM AND DISCIPLESHIP

AN OVERVIEW OF NEW FLIGHT ARTS MINISTRY

BRIAN BAKKE

Introduction: My Awakening to Art in Ministry

Upon the invitation of the late Rev. Larry Davis (the executive director), I spent one night a week during the summer of 1989 at the Olive Branch Mission in Chicago, drawing portraits of the street guests. I learned some powerful lessons there that still affect me today.

When we started, Larry introduced me to a gentleman whose features resembled those of African royalty. Larry asked Mr. Cecil Partee's permission for me to sit down with him to draw his portrait. Mr. Partee was stunned and then embarrassed at the request, but he ultimately consented. After he agreed, I sat down and began to draw. I had never done portraiture before, and I was really nervous. What made things worse was that a loud and rowdy group of people had gathered around us. Our activity quickly became the focal point of the entire mission that night. His friends in the crowd started making comments like, "Wow is that ugly . . . man that is disgusting . . . it looks just like you!" Then they would all roar with laughter.

Meanwhile, I was trying to maintain composure and be as professional as I could, knowing that my work and my worth as an artist could be judged by this first attempt. Cecil's friends really got him going, and he kept trying to peek over my sketch pad to see how it was going. I politely asked him to sit up straight and look the other way. He immediately complied. I soon realized that I had control over his every movement. He could not look one way or another, smile, or cough without my permission while I did his portrait. By the grace of God, everyone around really liked the drawing. Another man even pushed Cecil out of the chair and jumped in, demanding his likeness be done. I did several other portraits that night.

After a couple of hours the entire mission bid me farewell, thinking they would not see me again, but assuming I would sell the pictures I drew of them. These street people were all too familiar with being ripped off.

When I returned the following week, people happily formed a line at my table as I sat down and pulled out my pencils. While drawing these guests, I would set them in a pose and then begin to give my testimony. In turn, they told me their stories. It quickly became an effective one-on-one evangelism effort. Some of the conversations I had that summer only happened because I came as an invited guest, not as a preacher. I listened to some of the most gut-wrenching personal stories and testimonies I had ever heard. People opened up to me because they saw that I visited with people without any personal agenda.

One very sticky night, I looked up over my sweaty pad of paper and saw bodies being shoved all over the place. Up through the line bulldozed the biggest man I had seen since I left college football. He weighed more than 280 pounds and stood over 6'10" with a mop of unruly hair. His gold front teeth flashed before me as he threatened the person in the chair across from me to get out of his way. As he sat down, he announced, "My name is Sexaphone Rick Best and you're going to do my picture, and if I don't like it, I'm going to kill you!" As I struggled for something to say or do in response, I suddenly noticed for the first time that night that I had forgotten to bring along any erasers. It instantly became a deeply religious experience for me. God gave my hands a sureness and confidence that I myself was lacking at the moment. While I drew, I started asking him questions. He was wearing a tuxedo, and I learned that he had just returned from a "gig" when he heard I was in the mission that night.

He had always wanted his picture done, and, praise God, he liked the drawing! As he got up from the table, he said loud enough for the entire mission to hear, "You alright . . . you come back anytime you like . . . ain't nobody goin' to mess with you." At the end of the summer I gave the mission and the guests the drawings. They appreciated that someone would spend so much time with them, make something beautiful, and then give it to them. I was blessed to learn that I had a gift and that God wanted me to give it away to as many people as possible.

THE COMMUNITY OF UPTOWN

The community of Uptown is a small, densely populated enclave on Chicago's North Side. Imagine it in its finest hour in the "Roaring Twenties," when the neighborhood was the place to vacation. The entertainment district rivaled New York's Broadway theater district. Large, beautiful hotels were built to accommodate the many visitors. Charley Chaplin made the first movies in America at Essanay Studios, and they premiered at the Uptown Theater, the largest movie house in the country. A band was nobody if it did not play the Aragon Ballroom. Vaudeville acts routinely stopped through to play in the neighborhood's many venues. Al Capone got into the act too, starting a jazz club and a speakeasy. He also had his North Side headquarters here.

After World War II, the old palatial hotels were converted into multi-unit housing. The beautiful stone houses were subdivided into small sleeping rooms. Single Room Occupancy Hotels (SROs) began to appear. Waves of displaced Native Americans and rural whites from the South poured into the community. After that time, Uptown led the city in arson fires, armed robbery, assault, and auto theft. Gangs flourished, including the Klan, as people from other cultures and countries filled Uptown, seeking affordable housing.

Through the 1960s and '70s, the community became a human dumping ground of people living in chaos and unmanageability, as the state poured half of its mental patients into the area. Within Uptown's borders are 63,839 people who speak more than sixty languages. Twenty-three percent are African-American, 14.5 percent Asian, 23 percent Latino, and 38 percent Caucasian. Thirty-one percent live at or below the poverty level. It has the highest concentration of senior adults living alone in the Chicago area. Thousands of street people live here now (mentally ill, homeless, addicts), as well as institutionalized adults. There are about twenty street gangs. The drug traffic is so pervasive that the neighborhood has the highest concentration of people living with HIV/AIDS in the Chicago area. It got so bad that, in 1981, the northern part of the neighborhood "seceded" from the south and gave itself a new name, Edgewater, just so it would no longer be identified as Uptown.

According to the 1990 census, 10,440 young people between the ages of twelve and eighteen were living in the neighborhood. The dropout rate at the local high school (where my two brothers went to school) is 24 percent, and it has a graduation rate of 59 percent. In

1997 it led the city's high schools in violent crimes committed by students while on school grounds. More than 90 percent of the students are from low-income households. The school teaches in eleven languages, as more than fifty languages are spoken by the student body.

Throughout the 1980s and '90s, the neighborhood has seen tremendous changes. Real-estate speculation and gentrification is rehabbing buildings and displacing large numbers of the poor. Uptown is marketed as "Lincoln Park North," attaching itself to a very upscale neighborhood south of Uptown. Over time the neighborhood has become a more mixed community economically, and it has grown into a "hot" place to live. The city plans to rehab some of the old entertainment venues in Uptown and create a theater district. Thousands of theater artists live in this part of the city, with new businesses like bookstores and coffee shops drawing more professionals and artists into this community. A massive influx of people from the gay and lesbian community is also moving into the neighborhood, taking advantage of the "condo-ization" of the neighborhood. There are fewer than ten evangelical churches in Uptown.

The Bible and Art

In the beginning I did not know that the Bible had anything to say to me as an artist. When I was studying theater in college, and then later working with professional theater companies in Chicago, I never heard Scripture mentioned. But from time to time I did hear Christians and the church being mocked.

As a theater student, I had the chance to work with some of the world's finest artists in music, dance, and theater. My classmates and I would practically kill ourselves doing anything to help the touring companies and guest artists that came through our school. All students were welcome to attend artistic special events, workshops, and conferences and learn from these artists. Some of us even got paid to help mount or run the shows on our stage. One day it was announced that a Christian theater conference had booked our facility, and paid positions were available for students to work the weekend. Everyone, theater faculty and students alike, avoided this event like the plague. They knew that this event would be really bad art couched in spiritual language. My supervisor cornered me (after he had been cornered), and said he needed a huge favor—would I work the conference? He bribed me, and I hesitatingly accepted. As I ran sound and lights from the booth above the house seats, I watched with horror as brothers and sisters in Christ displayed their talents. They were awful. I was embarrassed in front of my peers to be a Christian.

It really was only after being talked into visiting the Olive Branch Mission and getting "thrown into the deep end," so to speak, that the connection was made for me. My Christian walk was maturing at the same time I was growing and improving as an artist. After joining the staff of Uptown Baptist Church and getting involved in a variety of different art ministries, I began to see God's Word with a sense of how it could apply to the artist.

Reading Exodus 31:1–11, where God gave the gift of art to His people, I saw how I have been gifted by God, and am to use His gifts to glorify Him and not myself. Since I have relationships with many professionals in the arts who are nonbelievers, I am constantly struck by their all-consuming desire to "get their work out," or to become "known." If my friends are known, they will be able to command greater money for the use of their gifts and abilities. This causes many talented people to take that which God has given them and use it to glorify themselves and not the Giver of all good gifts. I am sobered by the fact that, in Exodus 32, the very next chapter after the giving of the artistic gifts is recorded, the people created an idol and worshiped it as a god. This issue of who the artist gives glory to (through the creative process) is as old as the Bible itself.

I have been blessed by the writer of the Psalms, who told us in Psalms 149:1–4 and 150:1, 3–5 to worship the Lord with musical instruments and dance. It was only after Larry Davis donated his own pottery wheel to the church's art program and I tried to throw a pot on the wheel that I fully comprehended the meaning and power of God's words to the prophet in Jeremiah 18:1–6. After I was introduced to Dr. Sam Gore, Chairman Emeritus of the Mississippi College art department, who travels across the hemisphere sharing the gospel through sculpture presentations, I realized that the Bible used sculpture to speak powerful, prophetic words to a pagan king and to the people of God in Daniel 2:31–45.

I read with great interest the parables that Jesus told the people. He was the Master of the long Jewish tradition of storytelling. Many of the great films and plays of today are stories used by gifted people to communicate a conviction. The best ones communicate the truths found in the Bible to a worldwide audience.

PHILOSOPHY OF MINISTRY: LESSONS LEARNED

Asking permission of the people who are already living in, or who are a part of, the mission field to gain entry into their world is the biggest lesson I have learned. Giving my life and art away has been the norm since that wonderful experience at the Olive Branch Mission.

Being willing to learn from, and listen to, the people I am serving is another principle. Being willing to listen to the people I hope to minister to gives the message, "I value you as a person, and I want to get to know you, because you know things that I want to learn." All of the art projects and programs that are happening at Uptown Baptist Church are in effect because people from the community (both outside and inside the church) have asked for them. The ministry happens and God blesses the works of our hands when we make ourselves listen to the desires and needs of the people and respond to them. God calls us to "consider others better than [ourselves]" (Phil. 2:3).

Stepping out in faith, trusting that God will direct my path—even if I cannot see where the path leads—is another thing I have learned. In 1987 I started to attend Uptown Baptist Church. When I experienced the worship there, I felt the love of the church for the Word of God and the church's burden for reaching the neighborhood with the gospel of Jesus Christ. Pastor Jim Queen invited me to join the church staff and gave me his approval and permission to work with the arts along with a mandate to reach out into the community with the gospel. He said, "Make up a job description, choose an advisory board and put me on it, and write a funding proposal . . . and let's get going." I have had to cling desperately to the Lord, as I have never had a clear idea if any one of the projects would be a success. For example, after accepting a commission from a local bank for a huge outdoor mural, I realized it would not be accomplished unless God raised up a gifted team of Christian artists who could all work in perfect harmony with one another and would volunteer to paint for five weeks in the blazing hot sun. God did just that!

Then when I was stumped with how to get from the scale drawing on a sheet of paper to a design fitting the 25' x 90' wall, God had Dr. Sam Gore call from Mississippi at that very moment to ask what I was doing. When I told my dilemma, he revealed that he had painted billboards as a way to put himself through graduate school. "Call a billboard company and ask them to make a pounce pattern for you." A "pounce pattern" is a wall-sized drawing on paper with holes in it to use as a guide to put a design on a wall. During this conversation I remembered that one of my biggest supporters used to own a billboard company. I constantly risk humiliation and defeat, but I am always ready to cry out to God when I start a project.

When word got out about the success of my first mural project, building owners started calling me. I was asked to do mural after mural. Nobody would pay me to paint, but they all offered to buy the supplies. I agreed to this on the condition that I would keep whatever was left of the paper, paint, and brushes. So I started checking art stores to look for the best prices. At one large place a store employee, a bearded man with a baseball cap, asked if he could help me. I told him what I was doing. He asked why I was doing these things, and I told him about how God was opening doors for me to express the love of Jesus through the arts. He removed his cap and revealed a yarmulke, a head covering worn by orthodox Jews. He said that he was a Jew and lived in a commune, but his group did not have the respect for the arts that my church seemed to have. He told me right there on the spot that he would help me find whatever I needed and that he would give me a 60 percent discount! When I first started the art ministry at Uptown Baptist, I had a two-dollar watercolor set in my desk drawer. All of a sudden I was buying the finest supplies I could find at rock-bottom prices and filling a storage locker with top-quality supplies!

Giving my gift away has been a joy ever since my time at the Olive Branch Mission. Whether it has been giving away my personal prints or paintings to others who might need some encouragement or giving time to other ministries and agencies in art projects, the Lord has shown me that it is a far greater thing to give my gifts to Him in the service of others. Another way of giving for me has been in the actual designing of the murals that I work on. Of the more than forty mural projects that I have directed, I have actually designed five. The rest of the designs have been collaborative efforts with others or opportunities to challenge younger Christian artists. It has been a lot of fun to work with younger artists who may not have worked in large scale, to see their struggle through the process and then their joy upon the completion of the project. People who have worked with me are now designing and painting murals in every part of the country.

SPECIFIC PROGRAMS AND ACTIVITIES OF NEW FLIGHT ARTS

Homeless Workshops

The workshops for homeless adults use painting, drawing, and crafts to demonstrate the love of Jesus to street people. In an informal setting, while working on arts and crafts projects, relationships are built and the gospel is presented. It is an opportunity to build people's confidence as they do things that they had not thought possible. A store and a catalog have given us the opportunity to sell items created by these homeless artists. They will promote them in their catalogues and sell them in their stores with 100 percent of the profit returning to the individual artist who created the piece. We are working to develop these items now.

In the past, New Flight also offered a sewing class/Bible study, where the ladies from a shelter learned to alter and mend their clothes, as well as make household items to use in their new apartments when they moved out of the shelter.

Outdoor Concerts

When we first began our summer outdoor concert series in the bank parking lot across the street from the church, we had to borrow a small P.A. system from another church. The sound system could not be heard across the lot, let alone across the street! I asked friends with choir connections to ask their choirs to perform for free as we did not have the funds to give any kind of stipend for their efforts.

Over the eight-year history of the concert series, a variety of different musical styles, including reggae, contemporary, rock, blues, gospel, Latino, Caribbean, rap, and folk music, have been used to bring the gospel through music to the diverse community of Uptown. We now give the musicians a stipend, and we have slowly pieced together an outdoor sound system. The concerts always include a direct presentation of the gospel and an altar call, followed by a time of prayer and fellowship. The average attendance has risen from almost fifty in the beginning to well over three hundred per event. Hundreds more listened from their apartments surrounding the parking lot.

For two years in a row, this program was awarded National Endowment of the Arts funding for these evangelistic events due to the caliber of the musicians playing at these concerts. They knowingly gave us grants to fund evangelism in Uptown!

Just prior to the 1999 season, the bank informed us that we could no longer use its property for concerts. A Concert of Prayer rose up in our congregation for these events. Just two days before our first scheduled concert, one of the local public schools gave us permission to use its grounds. Now even more people come and we watch God work to draw the homeless, disabled, families, and youth to hear the gospel and enjoy fellowship.

Murals

Starting with the spray-paint graffiti mural on my apartment building in 1990, the mural company has produced more than forty murals, most of which are in Uptown. We work with a variety of people groups, including homeless, senior adults, children, and youth. (Some have been done with the cooperation and protection of street gangs.) All murals present the gospel, either by the visual content, and/or through the process of designing and painting. Mentoring occurs while the painting is under way, as older artists (students or professionals working with the project) share their life and calling with the younger artist or nonbeliever working on the mural.

Media have included spray paint, tile mosaic, found objects (e.g., old jewelry, dominoes, mother-of-pearl buttons, broken tile) and tempera, acrylic, and oil paint. The murals have ranged in size from 4' x 8' to 18' x 130'. Projects have taken from two weeks to six months to complete.

In the last couple of years, the company has worked on several large pieces, including an outdoor mural (15' x 50') at the playground of Jesus People USA's shelter for mothers and their children (also in Uptown). It depicts Jesus as a man of color, playing with children from a variety of ethnic backgrounds (representing the neighborhood). Other recently completed murals include the "Uptown Good Samaritan" on the wall of the Salvation Army drop-in center. It shows a black man reaching out to help a white man who has been beaten and left for dead under the El (subway) tracks down the street from the center. This 6' x 10' piece was designed by street people at the drop-in center and a group of artists from Moody Bible Institute working with New Flight. As this book goes to print, we have begun a 15' x 50' Uptown version of the Prodigal Son.

Recently, a local junior high school offered us the opportunity to work with its students to paint murals on the walls of the school. Workshops began in November 1997, and designs for the first two walls (4' x 9') were approved by the school administration in January 1998. The subject matter, chosen by the students, was "The struggle between good and evil." This provided some great opportunities for teaching biblical truths to the kids while they worked on the project. We are currently working with the students on more projects during the school day, in the class. The school wants us to do murals on the entire building.

Art Camps

The first two weeks of August, the annual children's summer art camp targets neighborhood and church children between the ages of eight and fifteen. Each day the "campers" are split up into age-specific small groups and spend an hour in each of four different disciplines: music, theater, dance, and studio arts. High-school-aged arts interns from the neighborhood (including former campers) are assigned to each of the teaching artists. This helps to keep the campers focused and on-task, as well as helping the teenagers learn how to teach others. The camp gives a public performance and an art show at the end of the camp. Campers and teachers meet around art and the gospel, which motivates and directs their work. Children have accepted Christ as their Lord and Savior while participants in the camps. We charge a registration fee for the camp, and we also raise funds so we can offer scholarships. The fee, as well as other fund-raising, helps give a stipend to the artists and purchase the supplies.

For the past seven years, camp participants have produced a number of the large collaborative murals that decorate the church. After the children completed a mural in a room in which the senior adults meet regularly, the "Young at Hearts" made their desire known to join the art ministry. "Why should the children have all the fun? What about us? We want an art camp and a mural of our own!" So, for the past six years we have held a week long camp in June as an all-day multi-disciplinary outreach ministry to the senior adults of Uptown.

The participants learn from professional senior adult Christian artists who have been using their artistic gifts for the Lord all their adult lives. Painting, ceramics, jewelry making, sewing, quilting, and collage are some of the arts and crafts we offer. The participants keep all that they make, as well as work on a collaborative project for the church. We offer free rides and lunch. During lunch the artist teachers give their testimonies. After five years at UBC, the camp now meets in the community in the activity rooms of various residential facilities for senior adults. We raise funds for artist stipends and supplies.

The participants from this art camp have produced a mural made from found objects that is in the Young at Hearts' room, a number of wall hangings for the church, and "stained glass" windows for doors throughout the church building.

Graphic Design

The vision of the graphics ministry was given to me by Greg King, another artist who said that he would be willing to train youth in computer design if I could get a computer. I could not even turn on a computer without fear of damaging something. But with Greg King's encouragement and prayer I approached a supporter who said that he would love to get involved. Other graphic artists jumped in with gifts of software. We recently received a second system as a gift from an artist who wanted his computer to be used in this ministry. The goal of the computer graphics workshop is to train up Christians who will enter art schools and the professional art world and be a strong witness to their peers.

Youth receive hands-on training from experienced professionals who teach on the Power Mac system. Software includes Illustrator, Painter, Photoshop, Quark Express, Pagemaker, Animator, and Director. This Saturday morning class is purposely kept very small, and at times it is made available to students during the after-school hours or on weeknights. The class schedule includes Bible study and teachings on various aspects of graphic design. The members of the class have produced posters, books, CD covers, and yearbook covers for their schools and friends.

We have just finished signing a formal agreement with the Juvenile Justice system to receive youth offenders who will take the class as a part of fulfilling their community service hours.

Sanctuary Banners

The sanctuary of Uptown Baptist Church is an octagon-shaped room with a forty-foot-high domed ceiling. Many of the windows, original to the building, had been broken or were in danger of collapse from neglect. The plaster walls were lined with cracks and holes where plaster had fallen out. It had once been beautiful but was pretty gloomy when our congregation moved into the building in 1987. A church gave us a gift of some banners. They were professionally done but didn't fit the wall space in which they were hung. And they all used the English language. Currently seven different language congregations call UBC home. After several years of looking at these and hoping for a change, I approached the elders with a design for new language banners.

For the past two years New Flight has been creating language and liturgical sanctuary banners. The language banners simply state the names of Jesus in seventeen languages, most of which are spoken by members of UBC. They are uniform in style—black lettering on a white strip of fabric placed on brightly colored backgrounds. The languages and dialects represented are Arabic, Bulgarian, Cambodian, Chinese, Efik, English, French, Hebrew, Hindi, Housa, Korean, Russian, Spanish, Tagolog, Twi, Vietnamese, and Yamba. These banners have been helpful in making guests to our church feel more welcome. They have also served to hide some really ugly walls.

The liturgical "banners" are actually 10' x 12' painted canvases that serve as focal points above the sanctuary altar. They commemorate the liturgical seasons of Advent, Christmas, Epiphany, Lent, Easter, and Pentecost. Those completed so far have been designed and painted by members of the church. As we are, in a sense, creating a new iconography for our congregation, we introduce each new piece during the morning worship service to describe the symbols depicted, as well as their meaning. All of the banner designs have been brought before the elders and pastors for their comment and approval prior to their being constructed.

Ceramics and Pottery

The vision of using ceramics and pottery in ministry was given to me by the Rev. Larry Davis, who did sermons and chapel services while working on the pottery wheel. Larry donated his pottery wheel to the church when he could no longer use it. A couple of years later Dr. Sam Gore came in for the seniors' art camp, and after he saw what we were trying to do with the arts, he shipped a new kiln up from his native Mississippi to the church. Then a couple more wheels were given, along with another smaller kiln. As I am just a student in that craft, I began to pray for experienced Christians who wanted to develop a pottery studio in the church basement. God has answered the prayer and we are reorganizing a storage room to accommodate this new ministry. We will offer a pottery workshop, which includes teaching the wheel, hand building, glazing, and firing. The class targets young adults, with a desire that it will grow into a small group, and even an outreach Bible study, to attract some of the new residents of Uptown who will not otherwise come to a church.

In the past, we have set up the wheels outside the church on the sidewalk. This usually draws a crowd. As people watch the clay being formed, their defenses drop and they become curious about the process. Some want to try it for themselves, and always people ask a lot of questions. We have been used by God to direct the conversation toward the passage in Jeremiah 18 where God tells us that He is working with us as the potter works with the clay. People who otherwise would not read this chapter learn about God's Word through this descriptive example.

TRANSFERABLE PRINCIPLES

Not every church is going to stage outstanding theater, dance, or music or have the people to teach computer design. But God has given gifts in this area to some of His people. Some principles to follow when getting started are listed below.

○ *Give permission to the artists in your midst.* Give creative people a chance to use their gifts! Imagine artists training neighborhood youth not only in their craft, but in the ways of the Lord. Help to provide an atmosphere of permission and then get out of the way. Think of all the creative people in your church or circle of friends who have artistic ability. Can they be challenged to share their skill and their faith with another person who can benefit from their expertise and experience?

○ *Encourage the artists in the body of Christ.* Helping to build bridges (if necessary) between those who respond to the arts and those who react to them can go a long way toward building trust and freeing people to use their gifts. Giving roles to artists in your local congregation will make this happen. We have been using young artists from across the country who are seeking opportunities to get training in art ministry. Because of this, a number of churches in other parts of the country are now starting art camps for children.

     Empower people. A lot of poor people could begin to provide for themselves if they had a little training, or even just the refining of a natural gift. What kinds of gifts need to be improved upon? How can the arts give someone hope so that a person can have a choice between gang membership and art school? Many churches have guest soloists, and others have church members on a rotation of providing special music for worship services. What is stopping the church from rotating banner artists, bulletin covers, public signs for outside the building, or yearly T-shirt designs?

    Decorate your house of worship. Invite a group of creative people to get together and challenge them with the question, "What would you like to see happen here?" Allow people to see how they might use their skill in carving, glasswork, weaving, sewing, painting, calligraphy, stenciling, jewelry, assemblage, sculpture, or woodworking to beautify the church. Some really ugly rooms can be made to sing the praises of the Lord with a lot of creativity and a small amount of money. Our tired old building is now a colorful and vibrant place of worship that is filled with people who have ownership in the church because they have helped to decorate the building.

     Present the gospel to the world. Martin Luther said, "It is better to paint pictures on walls of how God created the world, how Noah built the ark and whatever good stories there may be, than to paint shameless worldly things. Yes, would to God I could persuade the rich and mighty that they would permit the whole Bible to be painted on houses, on the inside and outside, so that all can see it."[1] How might artistic people be turned loose on your neighborhood sidewalks, activity centers, train viaducts and overpasses, schools, libraries, or parks?

Conclusion:
Recommendations for Art Ministry

I have seen how the arts enable God's people to worship Jesus, decorate churches, spread the gospel, give prophetic witness, and make the Scripture come alive to a lost generation that is searching for truth. I have seen God work powerfully to make Himself known to people through the creative process. I have seen people healed, delivered, and saved while participating in the creative arts. I have seen the power of the gospel brought to people of other religions, cultures, and languages, through the universal language of dance, music, and percussion.

My prayer is that more congregations within the body of Christ will encourage artists to use their gifts. My prayer is that pastors will seek out the creative people sitting in their pews and give them opportunity to use their abilities. The specific creative media a given church will employ depends on the people God has given to that specific church. The ceramic and graphic arts, for example, are not my gifts, but the gifts of other artists. By giving place to those people, they have, in turn, attracted still more talented people to Uptown Baptist, both nonbelievers and Christians.

It is my prayer that artists will use their gifts with grace and humility. I pray that artists will not only feel free to use their gifts, but that they will feel free to be held accountable by their churches for what they do as Christian communicators. Based on the many conversations and discussions I have had over the years, healing will not come until artists and pastors admit their fears and respect each other. We need artists who can use their gifts to reach a variety of different people groups.

I cringe when I see art (music, theater, dance, etc.) done in churches with a disregard for the high standards that nonbelievers in the secular world hold for their given craft. I pray for the day when churches will present special creative worship only when it is ready to be offered to God and seen by others, and not because they are beholden to a rigid church calendar. I pray for gifted artists who are Christians accepting the call of being salt and light to the very dark world of the visual and performing arts. What a beautiful church that will be!

Reflection Questions

1. Do you know of someone who has a burden for the professionals working in the graphic and/or fashion design, theater world, dance schools, or movie industry in your area? What would you be willing to do to help that person cultivate a burden into a call of ministry that begins a new outreach to these lost people?

2. Do you know of artists who are personal friends or members of your congregation? Are they using their gifts in the worship and ministry of your church? If they aren't using their gifts, why not?

3. Do you know artists who are not involved in a church? Why do they not attend church?
4. What kind of ministries could your church offer to draw the nonbelieving artist?
5. Have you done a demographic survey of the kinds of events that draw nonchurched people? Do they have to come to your church building, or can other venues be used to attract them?

For further information about art ministry contact:

Camden Printworks, 3706 Westfield Ave., Camden, NJ 08110

Warren W. Caterson, Executive Director, Urban Art Institute, P.O. Box 608, Chattanooga, TN 37401

Christians in the Visual Arts, Box 18117, Minneapolis, MN 55418-0117

Joan and Allen Eubank, c/o Christian Communications Institute, P.O. Box 48, Chiang Mai 5000 Thailand

Mako Fujumoura, Executive Director, International Art Ministry, 69 Murray St., 2nd Floor, New York City, NY 10007

Dr. Ruth Glaze, Chairman, Art Department, Mississippi College, P.O. 4205, Clinton, MS 39058

Jesus People USA Cornerstone Festival and Magazine, 920 W. Wilson Ave., Chicago, IL 60640

Lively Arts, c/o Timothy Botts, 367 Oak St., Glen Ellyn, IL 60137

Mastermedia International, Inc., 330 North Sixth Street, Redlands, CA 92374-3312

Tim Meve or Helen Pickett, Eastbrook Church (gallery and art ministry), 5353 N. Greenbay Ave., Milwaukee, Wisconsin 53209

Rosemarie Oheler, Executive Director, Arts for Relief and Mission, 1800 Ridge Ave., Evanston, IL 60201

Patchwork Central, 100 Washington, Evansville, IN 47714

Byron Spradlin, Executive Director, Artists in Christian Testimony, P.O. Box 395, Franklin, TN 37065-0395

Creola Thomas, c/o Alpha and Omega Ministries, 218 N. Pine Street, Chicago, IL 60644

chapter twelve

RETHINKING THE CHURCH TO REACH THE CITY

THE CITY–SIZE VISION OF NEW LIFE COMMUNITY CHURCH

MARK JOBE

Introduction: What This City Really Needs...

I was twenty-one years old and had just been called to pastor a small struggling church in the heart of a rough Southwest Side neighborhood in Chicago. I was eager to learn from any Chicago pastor who would give me advice. That morning I was especially excited to have breakfast with an experienced pastor who was leading a thriving church in another part of the city. At the restaurant I rattled off question after question, soaking up the practical advice and wisdom he offered. Then suddenly the pastor stopped, looked up from his cup of coffee, slowly leaned toward me, and in a deep voice betraying both sadness and anger said, "Urban churches have been raped!" He said this with such conviction I was taken aback. "The worst thing," he continued slowly, "is that they have been raped by aspiring pastors using inner city churches as stepping-stones for their next ministry." He looked straight into my eyes, took a long pause, and said, "What this city really needs is long-term pastors willing to lay down their lives for the people of Chicago." Implicit in his statement was a personal challenge.

THE THRILL OF URBAN MINISTRY

I have been a pastor in the city of Chicago now for thirteen years, and I can add my voice to echo that challenge. The struggling little church that I began to pastor now has more than 1,100 people at our weekend services and is growing at an average of 25 percent a year. We hold worship services at five different locations and meet in seventy different home groups throughout Chicagoland. In the last four years we have baptized more than four hundred adults. We have seen 65 percent of the church added through conversion growth. Last Sunday, at our monthly baptism, eleven adults took the step of believer's baptism in front of a celebrating church. Three of them were white university students, two were young urban professionals, four were second-generation Hispanics in their twenties and early thirties, and two were baptized at our Spanish-speaking service. Nine out of the eleven baptized had committed their lives to Christ in the previous six months. It is an exciting thing to be a part of a life-giving urban church.

My desire is to see God raise in this generation urban churches that affect entire cities for Christ. Yet I believe the leaders of those future churches are being formed even now as I write these words. Who knows? You might be one of them.

THE CITY AS THE TESTING LAB FOR THE FUTURE

Why is it so urgent that we reach our cities? Urban centers like Chicago represent a microcosm of what the future holds, a glimpse into the future through the keyhole of urban experience. I believe that the testing ground for the churches of the future is the lab of urban culture. If the church cannot survive and thrive in the tempest of urban environment, then it will struggle with surviving in the America of tomorrow. Not too long ago Bob Bufford's organization, Leadership Network, faxed me an article challenging ministers to look to cities to discover the trends of the future.[1] The article pointed out that everything from music to fashion, language, and politics is dominated by urban trends. Ministry approaches needed for the next decade will likely emerge in the hardest edges, the intense urban crucibles, of this generation. If I were an energetic twenty-year-old, passionate about preparing to reach this next generation for Christ, I would head straight for the city. It is in the heat of urban ministry that some of the most creative, energetic, entrepreneurial ministries are pioneering paths for the church of tomorrow.

For the past few years, I have had the opportunity of speaking to the incoming freshmen each year at Moody Bible Institute through the Practical Christian Ministry Department. I tell the students that MBI's location in the heart of Chicago is one of its greatest assets in training them for their future ministry. I encourage them not to view the city as an inconvenience to be endured but as an opportunity to be taken.

The Test of Multiculturalism

To answer how well the church will reach the America of tomorrow we must look at how well we can reach the cities of today. Consider, for example, just the aspect of ethnicity. During the 1990s the African-American segment in the United States grew by 15 percent, the Hispanics by 39 percent, and the Asian community by 40 percent.[2]

In Chicago, multiculturalism is already a reality. A recent article in the *Chicago Tribune* entitled "Chicago's Racial and Ethnic Evolution" underlined the dramatic ethnic changes over the last forty years. In 1940, Chicago was 92 percent white and 8 percent black. In 1999 Chicago is 32 percent white, 37 percent black, 5 percent Asian, and 26 percent Hispanic. At least seven neighborhoods in Chicago are so integrated that they have no dominant racial group.[3] Churches in Chicago today are grappling with issues that most churches in America will grapple with in the near future. As the church struggles to deal with urban issues, it literally is struggling with its own destiny.

The Sad Facts About America

Statistics cannot measure the intangibles like love, faith, and hope, but they can give us a pulse on the number of people we are affecting around us. A quick look at the numbers reveals that America is a mission field in great need. A recent Gallup poll estimated the American unchurched population at more than 195 million.[4] According to Charles Arn, half of the churches in America did not add one new member through conversion growth last year![5] That means that more than 175,000 churches in this country did not baptize or celebrate the conversion of a single new person. No wonder church experts state that the greatest problem the church of today faces is lack of morale.

During the last ten years, the combined communicant membership of all Protestant denominations declined by 9.5 percent (4,498,242) while the national population increased by 11.4 percent.[6] Research expert George Barna tells us that over the past fifty years evangelical churches have failed to gain an additional 2 percent of the American population. In other words, we are not even reaching our children.

In North America we lose about seventy-two churches per week or ten per day, and gain only twenty-four per week or less than three per day.[7] We are closing churches three times as fast as we are planting them. Add to this the fact that 85 percent of churches in America are stagnant or declining. Of the 15 percent that are actually growing, only a small percent are growing through conversion growth; most are simply reshuffling believers into other churches.[8]

I was at a church-planting conference several months ago in which the speaker said that a study of growing churches across America indicated that the only common denominator was that they were almost all in growing communities. He indicated that these were typically emerging suburbs that were attracting many transfer Christians.[9] This seems to imply that the plight of the urban church is even more dismal than the national averages.

The Encouraging Bigger Picture

Thank God it is not all bad news. Incredibly, missiologists tell us that we are living in one of the greatest times of global spiritual harvest this world has ever known. We hear of incredible church growth in China, India, Africa, and Latin America.

I write this chapter more as a practitioner than as a scholar. I have invested the last thirteen years of ministry on the assumptions that the church can reach the city and that there is hope at hand. I am incredibly optimistic about the future of the church, not because the statistics are great, but because I personally know the God behind His church. The church is the divine organism that Jesus said "the gates of Hades will not overpower" (Matt. 16:18 NASB). In my class on Urban Issues and the Church, the first thing I try to ingrain in the students is that the church is God's response to a world in need, despite its shortcomings. I challenge them not to give up on the church, but rather to embrace it and work to restore and revive it.

PREPARING THE CHURCH FOR ITS URBAN FUTURE

As the church crosses the bridge to its future it must be aware of the giants in the land. Let me introduce you to some of the current giants killing urban churches.

Urban Church Killers

I have come to the conclusion that the urban pastor's greatest enemy is discouragement. Years ago, when I told my pastor that I thought God was calling me to minister at a church in the heart of the city, he said to me emphatically, "Churches in Chicago chew up and spit out pastors left and right, so you'd better be sure you're called." It sounded harsh at the time, but he was right. I have helped pick up the pieces of some urban pastors and their families, and it has not been a pretty sight. Although the list could be longer, I have identified six of the most common urban church killers I've seen in Chicago.

The Inability to Adapt to a Changing Neighborhood

Missiologist Peter Wagner calls it the deadly disease of "ethnicitis"[10] —the inability of an old ethnic group to reach the new groups moving into the community. A friend of mine from Europe was helping his son-in-law buy a house in Chicago. He was amazed to discover that a big factor was how the neighborhood is expected to change ethnically in the next five to ten years. In the slow changing, more homogenous Western European market that was not even an issue.

In Chicago, it is common to find church buildings built in the 1940s, when the city was more than 90 percent white, with a congregation suffering from ethnicitis. It's typical to discover between twelve and twenty-five older white people meeting in a deteriorating building in a neighborhood that is now primarily Hispanic, black, or Asian. Many of those attending on Sunday have moved out of the neighborhood, but they commute in to the place where their parents were buried, they were married, and their children were baptized. The worship service in most cases does not appear to have changed in fifty years and has trouble attracting the community around it. A young Hispanic man from the neighborhood walking into the service would probably feel out of place no matter how friendly the group tried to be. These congregations usually close after they can no longer afford to pay the bills, or they opt to sell to an ethnic congregation already in the community.

The Difficulty of Attracting Visionary Leadership

Because of low pay, poor schools, and older congregations, many urban churches find it difficult to attract trained, visionary leadership. Without that kind of leadership, however, in a fast changing, complex society, congregations tend to struggle and die out. I've heard that years ago, when New Life (the church I pastor) was looking for a pastor, some candidates would not even get out of their cars before driving off in fear of the neighborhood. In a neighborhood that is known for drive-by shootings, we called them the drive-by candidates.

The Lack of Creative Financial Resourcing

When I started at New Life, the church was able to pay a total salary package of $8,000 a year, which meant I could not afford medical insurance and could barely pay my rent. Because I was single and debt free, I was able to work full time on that salary, but that is not the case for many urban pastors with families who are forced into bivocational ministry.

The Challenge of Leading Change-Resistant Congregations

The problem is not with age, but rather with resistance to change. Most of us, as we get older, value stability and consistency rather than creativity and change. A reporter once said to a one-hundred-year-old man, "You must have seen a lot of change in your lifetime." The old man quickly replied, "Yep, and I've been against every single one of them." In the fast-changing urban landscape, the church must continually evaluate its methods and its changing community. Someone once said that the only person who likes change is the baby with a dirty diaper. I have a newborn son, and even he doesn't like to be changed that much. Every church in today's society, but especially the urban church, must be flexible enough to reach its surrounding communities.

 ### The Loss of Upwardly Mobile Families

Many upwardly mobile families looking for better schooling and a safer environment in which to raise their children move out of the city and leave their churches. This in turn creates a vacuum of young leadership and economic stability. Unless the urban church convinces these families to stay in the city or restructures to keep them involved, it will have a deadly turnover rate among its leadership.

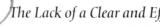 ### The Lack of a Clear and Effective Evangelistic Strategy

In doing research for my master's project related to mentoring and assimilation, I was surprised to find how few churches had actually developed any coherent plan for discipleship and assimilation of new believers. This is not just a problem for the urban church, yet for the city church, as opposed to a church in a growing suburb, it can be lethal since little transfer growth is occurring in most cities.

Now that we have identified the killers, our next challenge is to rethink what the urban church should look like in order to take the land.

Rethinking the Urban Church

George Barna contended that the church does not need a little tinkering, but an all-out revolution. He argued that revolutionary movements are organized around passion and purpose. When there is sufficient dissatisfaction, people are moved to bring about radical change.[11]

In my observation as a pastor and trainer, I have found three key areas that urban pastors need to rethink. I have posed them as several questions.

Is Our Vision Big Enough?

We need a vision as big as the city. It is reported that D. L. Moody, the famous evangelist, told his sons while on his deathbed, "Sons, if God is your partner then make no small plans." Those are fitting words for the former shoe salesman who took Chicago by storm. Someone once asked me, "Does the ministry shape the vision, or does the vision shape the ministry?" I think it is probably a little bit of both. It has been said that "once your mind has been stretched by a great thought it can never go back to its original size." I think vision has that same effect on people. We desperately need urban pastors who are stretched by city-size visions and who cannot return to business as usual.

Over the last few years I have been wrestling with what the church would really look like if it began to make a real impact on Chicago. Three years ago all the pastoral staff and various members of New Life took on the challenge of a forty-day juice fast. We were inspired by Bill Bright's challenge to fast and pray for spiritual awakening in America. It was a tremendous time of prayer, seeking God, and soul-searching, both corporately and individually. Although I lost thirty-five pounds, I did gain a fresh vision for our city. The last day of the fast I rented a hotel room and spent the day alone with God. It was in that hotel room that for the first time I prayed that God would give us 1 percent of the city of Chicago. That did not seem like much at the time until I calculated that Chicago has around three million residents—which means I had just prayed for 30,000 people! Henry Blackaby said, "Vision is not invented by man, but rather discovered in the presence of God."[12] I agree. God's kingdom vision is usually much bigger and broader than ours.

What Do We Do with Vision?

After the initial shock, the pastoral team and I began working through what a church with a city-size vision would look like and feel like. The first thing we tried to do was write it down. We developed a vision statement.

NEW LIFE VISION STATEMENT

It is our aim to cooperate with God in building a church that is great enough to impact Chicagoland and focused enough to make genuine disciples. This picture includes a growing church reaching 1 percent of Chicago (30,000 people). New Life will gather to worship weekly in auditoriums across Chicagoland called satellite churches. These satellites will come together regularly for city-wide celebrations. Black, white, Hispanic, Asian, street people and

CEO's, young professionals and teens, suburban and inner city; each individual will be involved in a small group of about ten people that meets nearby and seeks to keep people connected to each other, God and those in need of God. Prayer and fasting will permeate every aspect of ministry. A twenty-four hour prayer chain will be functioning seven days a week along with a Prayer Center that will help network, train and coordinate people for prayer in Chicago. A Training Center will help equip, educate and empower believers for ministry throughout the year. An equipping track will be in place to form and launch pastors and missionaries into ministry. A Compassion ministry will help the church meet the needs of needy communities. A Networking Center will seek to build bridges, bless, partner and share with other life giving churches and ministries in an effort to reach Chicago and other parts of the world. We will seek to do this; to the glory of God, by the grace of Christ and in the power of the Holy Spirit.

At the bottom of our vision statement we have this phrase "We would rather attempt something great for God and fail then attempt nothing and succeed."

What Does Vision Do to Us?

In the last few years plenty has been written about vision, so I will not elaborate. But I would like to point out how our vision has affected our thinking. When we first began talking about a church with a city-size vision, we had to ask ourselves several questions: Is it biblical? Is it achievable? Is it worth it? Where would we meet? How would we structure? What do we have to become good at? How would we cooperate with other churches? How will we need to change? Are we willing to own this vision? Where do we start? The greatest benefit is that it forced us to think in terms of movement, people, and city rather then buildings, programs, and just our church.

Another by-product of clarifying our vision was the realization that it would take more than a few years to reach it. Each member of the pastoral team has individually expressed his long-term commitment to the team and to making this vision a reality. We understand that it may take longer than we anticipate or even that the next generation may be the ones to see its fulfillment, but we have already made plans through 2010.

Does Our Structure Liberate or Tie Us Down?

Structures do not automatically create growth; but they can remove obstacles, or sometimes they even create them. In 1986, when I began pastoring the congregation of eighteen people, I followed a traditional church structure. For the first few years I was involved in practically every ministry that went on in the church. I thought it was my duty as a good pastor, and at first I didn't have enough people to do it any other way. I preached Sunday morning and evening, led the midweek prayer meeting, headed up the visitation on Tuesdays, led our elders' meeting on Mondays, attended men's fellowship on Fridays, played guitar for music practice on Saturdays, and filled the rest of my time with counseling, discipleship, and administration. I even cleaned out the church's bell tower of twenty-five garbage bags of pigeon droppings shortly after I became pastor. The pace was manageable for the first two years until the congregation was running about two hundred and I was coming apart. About that time my father, a veteran missionary who was visiting from Spain, gave me a little "Jethro" advice and helped me realize I was bottlenecking the ministry. I had three options: I could change, stagnate, or burn out. This forced me, literally, into a new phase of shared ministry and rethinking the church.

Have We Adapted to the Shape of the City?

The church has often been like Cinderella's stepsisters and the glass slipper, trying to force the city into the shape of our prefabricated church. We often hold one worship service intended to reach everyone in the city. We have opted for the "one-size-should-fit-all" mentality. I believe the urban church needs to be more like a movement spawning creative efforts to reach each segment of our city.

At New Life we have come to realize that one style, in one location, and in one language cannot reach all. So we have devised a plan to adapt to the city rather than expecting the city to adapt to us. At the worship level we have become multisite and bilingual. We currently have worship services at five different locations, targeting different people groups in and around the city through what we call satellite churches.

One site targets the primarily Mexican community of Little Village on the Southwest Side of Chicago. That satellite holds its services in Spanish and is located in the heart of that community. The youth, who are mainly second-generation English speaking, attend our youth service with many other young people at a location we call the "Warehouse." The Warehouse has a high-energy "in-your-face" worship band and preaching team.

On the Northwest Side of Chicago, a long drive away, is our second Spanish site targeting more Central and South American Hispanics from that area. Just south of Chicago is New Life South meeting on Saturday evenings at a community center and targeting English-speaking residents of the near south suburbs. New Life Central meets on a university campus off the expressway and attracts primarily white and Hispanic urban dwellers between twenty and forty years old. We plan on having two more satellites up and running by the end of this year. A couple times a year we have joint worship services with the whole church at one location and afterward a meal we call "Taste of New Life."

In addition to the satellites, we have also tried to adapt to the color and shape of Chicago through our home groups. Each home group meets weekly and reflects a geographical area or a certain affinity group. From university campus students and suburban groups, to Spanish-speaking immigrants, we seek to take the church right to people's doorsteps. We have found that for evangelistic purposes, affinity groups work best, whereas for worship celebrations and community we relish the beauty of our diversity.

Although we are organized as one church with one name and one leadership team, we have chosen to decentralize in order to more effectively reach our various communities. Our entire staff comes together weekly at our main offices for training, praise reports, and prayer, and much of the ministry training is carried out in a centralized way. Our goal is to enable a team synergy to flow through the entire ministry.

The Bottlenecked Church

Church experts have been telling us for years that 50 percent of churches in America have fewer then seventy-five people in attendance and that only 4 percent grow beyond three hundred people. One pastor can only handle up to one hundred people in a pastor-centered structure. In an urban culture, problems are even more intense, adding incredible pressure to the solo pastor. In the early days I would walk in the door of my apartment and find ten to fifteen messages on my answering machine, all expressing that someone was in urgent need of my assistance. Adding to the problem was the fact that I also believed they needed *me*. Releasing ministry and empowering others was both difficult and liberating. If this does not occur, the church will bottleneck around the pastor's time and energy limitations.

In my experience this transition involves three major steps that tend to be more difficult for the pastor to accept than for the congregation.

Releasing the Ministry That Others Can Do

Leadership consultant John Maxwell gives a good rule of thumb for releasing ministry. He says that if someone else can do the job 80 percent as well as you can, then release it. With a little time and experience the other person will probably do it better than you. I have found that as pastors we tend to hold on to ministries a lot longer than we should. I now challenge my staff to constantly be working themselves out of a job.

Many urban pastors are buried under the tremendous responsibilities they carry. For a long time I did all the baptizing of new believers. One time I was in the water so long that my teeth were chattering and no one could understand what I was trying to say. I was baptizing people I had never met until they walked into the water. Now, their home group leader and spiritual mentor leads them in baptism. That person knows them well and has been working with them.

Moving from Just Doing Ministry to Training Others for Ministry

I love to mentor new believers in the faith and watch them grow. When my wife, Dee, and I started, we were discipling people during dinner, at Dunkin' Donuts, during people's lunch breaks, and whenever we could fit them in. Eventually we ran out of time slots, and I realized we needed to train others to do what we were doing.

Now I spend a good portion of my time in coaching, training, and empowering my staff and lay leaders to do ministry. I feel as though I have moved from addition to multiplication.

Adopting a Structure That Unleashes Ministry

In 1990, I knew that our structure was pastor-centered and left little room for others to learn to fly in ministry. We had plenty of space for "workers," but I began looking to raise ministers. It was at this crucial juncture that we transitioned to a small-group structure. This might not be the best model for every urban church, but we have discovered it is well suited for evangelism in the midst of diversity.

- Small groups make room for more people to use their spiritual gifts.
- They help take the church out of the building and into homes.
- They help build community and a sense of belonging.
- They create a great platform for discipleship.
- They eliminate many growth barriers.

The home-group model is especially well suited for the intensity of the urban life because it is so flexible and adaptable to any environment. From a group of young singles who meet over latte in a quaint coffee shop to gang-bangers who meet around a park bench on the Southwest Side of Chicago, the model is the same.

Conclusion:
When the Church Meets the City's Needs

A few months ago we had a joint New Life celebration with 1,300 people present. White businessmen worshiped next to Mexican immigrants. Young professionals shared a row with inner city teens. The young and the old, the wealthy and the poor, the black and the white embraced one another. As we worshiped in English and in Spanish, I thought how blessed I am to be a part of a life-giving urban church.

If I could sit down personally with some of you readers, I would look you in the eyes and say slowly, "What we really need are people ready to make a long-term commitment and willing to lay down their lives for the people of this city. Will you?"

Reflection Questions

1. Why is the city the testing lab for the church of the future? What cultural/socioeconomic issues challenge church growth in your city?

2. What urban church killers do you see in your church? How can you help to identify and resolve them?

3. What are the key issues your church needs to rethink in order to prepare itself to reach the city?

4. Does your church have a vision for urban ministry? If not, how can you be a part of shaping its evangelistic strategy in the city?

chapter thirteen

NEW WINESKIN— SAME VINTAGE WINE

FIVE PATHS OF EFFECTIVE URBAN EVANGELISM

Michael N. Allen

Introduction: Urban Evangelism

Abraham was wrong. Sodom did not have ten righteous! That afternoon when he and God parted, Abraham thought judgment was averted because the Almighty promised that if there were ten righteous people in the city, it would not be destroyed. What a surprise the next morning when he saw that the Lord rained down "burning sulfur" on Sodom and Gomorrah! (Gen. 19:24). Mind you, Abraham got his primary wish because Lot and his family were spared, but the city was destroyed nevertheless.

This powerful story is a reminder that a few righteous people in a city will preserve it. The four who were righteous had to leave Sodom before the fire of God came from heaven. We can say with confidence that were it not for the church, our cities would have been under God's judgment long ago. Like a rotting limb that falls from its own weight, so our cities would have already sunk into the moral and spiritual abyss, apart from the people of God. The church has been the salt keeping our urban areas from total decay.

I am convinced that our greatest contribution to the health of our cities is to evangelize, leading men, women, and children to faith in Christ. As we shall see, the challenges are great, but so are the rewards.

Talk to those who live in the inner city, and they will tell you that they are so preoccupied trying to eke out one more day's existence on earth that they have no time to think about heaven. Those in our ghettos are more concerned about dodging bullets than reading Bibles. And yet we know that it is precisely because the problems in our cities are so daunting that the need for evangelism is most pressing.

We have the privilege of living at a time in history when God is doing a new thing. No longer is it necessary to cross an ocean to experience cross-cultural evangelism. He is bringing the peoples of the world, with their various religions and cultures, to the great urban areas of America and the United Kingdom. And happily, in some instances, the church in other countries is also growing, proving once again that God has a worldwide plan for planet Earth. Earl Parvin in his book *Missions in North America* accurately observed that the church

> can see at a distance the needs of the 558,000,000 black Africans and send nearly 8,000 missionaries, investing $255,000,000. This is not to suggest that such outreach is wrong, but rather to point out its success, for today black Africa is nearly 50 percent Christianized, whereas black America may be only 30 percent.[1]

Can we catch the larger vision? More than half the world's six billion people live in the cities. For example, New York City boasts a population of twenty million; Mexico City, twenty million; Sao Paulo, eighteen million; Chicago, eight million; and London, eleven million (all figures are approximate and include suburban areas).[2] Is the church equipped to reach the masses of its cities? According to the U.S. Bureau of the Census, 75 percent of Americans live in urban communities. That translates to approximately 195 million people![3] Without question, the urban cities worldwide have become the "foreign mission field"—across the street, not only across the ocean.

The Bible is not just a rural book, but also a distinctly urban book. The word *city* occurs more than 1,200 times in Scripture, and 119 different cities are mentioned by name in the Bible.[4] When God began the New Testament church, He decided to plant it in the metropolis of Jerusalem, a world-class city of its day. God then created the circumstances that caused the great Diaspora. This fleeing of Christians from Jerusalem to the other great cities of the Roman Empire ensured the greatest possibility for the worldwide propagation of the gospel. Cities are the great reservoirs of human souls from almost every nation, tribe, and tongue.

To speak of urban areas means much more than a reference to masses of people. We even mean more than the social dynamic that binds these people together. That word *urban* includes cultural, political, and economic seats of power. What Washington, D.C., or London is to politics, New York and Paris are to commerce. Different cities play different roles in our global village.

EVANGELISM 101: WHAT COULD IT LOOK LIKE?

Chicago, a sprawling Midwest metropolis along the shores of Lake Michigan, is home for many things. It's home for the Bulls, the Bears, and the Cubs; it's also home for many, many people from almost every country on the planet. Like its world-class counterparts, Chicago not only continues to grow in geographical and numerical size but also in the kind and class of people who enter her borders annually. People who speak strange languages and wear colorful foreign clothing. People who think differently than Americans and have weird customs and religious practices. At the end of the day, they are people created in the image of God who will spend eternity somewhere . . . either heaven or hell.

The question is, Is the church in the city (the urban church) willing and able to minister to the ever-growing and changing metropolis? If so, how? What will it take to reach the unreached people groups in our cities? Will mass evangelism, door-to-door evangelism, or Christian radio/TV do it? These methods may all be a part of the answer to reaching the urban community, but more innovative ways need to be added to this standard list. If the urban church is going to not only survive but thrive, it must learn how its multiethnic, multiclass urban neighbors hear and understand the gospel. If a church does not mirror the people in its community, it will ultimately die.

So what could urban evangelism look like in your city? Each church must study its own urban community and know its own resources in order to effectively minister there. What works in Chicago may or may not work in New York. We know that the gospel works worldwide, but how it is told is somewhat unique to each church. The following are some ways the Moody Church of Chicago communicates the gospel.

Evangelism Could Include:

1. Evangelistic preaching and teaching from the pulpit
2. Evangelistic Bible studies in the home, in the workplace, on the college campus, etc.
3. Evangelism Explosion (training the laity to present the gospel one-on-one or in a small-group setting)
4. Churches within the church (hosting various ethnic groups for worship —we are currently hosting Spanish, Iranian, and Arabic services/ Bible studies)

5. Moody Business Network (monthly business luncheons that provide a forum for personal testimonies of America's most successful Christian businessmen and women)
6. Branch Ministries (we are partnering with eleven independent ministries that are ministering to people with urgent urban problems such as homelessness, drug abuse, gangs, incarceration; tutoring/mentoring children, helping people learn life skills, etc.)
7. Participation in city-wide cultural/political events (art, music or food festivals, a marathon, a fund-raiser walk-a-thon, etc.)— Christian volunteers show kindness and love
8. Prayer-walking the neighborhood
9. Serving on counsels such as the Local School Counsel (LSC), neighborhood crime watch, or community-assisted policing strategy (CAPS)
10. Networking with other churches and religious organizations for ideas on pursuing solutions to particular community-wide problems

Is it possible for the urban church to saturate its city, its local world, as salt and light and at the same time to hold fast to the essential truths of the gospel? In order to accomplish this, the urban church must learn how to view both the city and the gospel with new eyes. We must see every urban dweller as made in the image of God and a potential true worshiper of God. We must understand the gospel more like a process than an event (i.e., examine the life of Jesus' disciples and ask yourself, "When were they saved?").

URBAN PATHS TO FULFILLING THE GREAT COMMISSION

I believe that if the urban church would learn to walk the following five paths of urban evangelism God would be glorified, because the church would be spiritually and numerically strengthened: (1) reproductive leadership; (2) unconditional love; (3) wise compassion; (4) close partnerships; (5) versatile strategies.

Reproductive Leadership (2 Timothy 2:1–2)

The first path to evangelism in any context is reproductive leadership. In Scripture, whenever God wanted to lead His people He always solicited the help of a man or woman to help Him and them. Whether He chose a Moses to lead Israel out of Egypt and into the Promised Land, a Solomon to lead the kingdom, or a Paul to establish and lead the church in Europe, leadership is important to God. God has designed people both to be led and to lead. When one or more people in any group being led are raised up to succeed the current leadership, a certain measure of success is accomplished.

To put it in terms of the New Testament church, reproductive leadership is essential for the church to exist. The terms *leader* and *leadership* refer to any of the following offices: pastor, elder, deacon, deaconess. At the heart of reproductive leadership is discipleship. Bill Hull explained the importance of making disciples, "To be a discipling church, a congregation must maintain its unity, discover its giftedness and respond to its leadership."[5] It is incumbent on the leadership of the church, in part, to intentionally build into the lives of God's people until God raises one or more people out of that group to assist the shepherd in carrying out the work of the ministry. This work of discipleship is included in the job description of the New Testament shepherd.

Reproductive leadership begins with the transformed life of the leader. (This step is preceded only by God's preordained design for his/her life in terms of calling and equipping.) Once the leader understands his God-given purpose and gifts, he is to exercise these gifts in the community he leads in order to direct them toward the God-given vision for that community.

If he is a teacher, let him teach in such a way that others may learn not only the content of his subjects but how to feed themselves and ultimately others also. If he is a worship leader, let him worship privately and publicly with the hope of teaching future worship leaders how to do the same. If he is a preacher, let him preach in such a way as to communicate the truth in love, power, and imagination while asking God to grant him a Timothy or Titus who will help him bear the great and awesome responsibilities of God's church. If he is an evangelist, may he bring along with him those who need and desire to learn how to communicate the faith so that they may teach others also.

Dr. James Kennedy of Evangelism Explosion concurred, saying, "It is better to train a soul winner than merely win souls."[6] This personal evangelism ministry is the only one of its kind that is now operating in every country of the world after some thirty years of training two by two, by two . . . and so on and so on. We clergy have often failed our God-given obligation to equip His people for His work. The sheep of God can only go as far as the shepherds of God lead them.

This wearisome yet rewarding task of discipleship is not a one-way street from discipler to disciple. We must learn to listen to the people to whom we minister. Rich, poor, and middle class can all teach us something of how to better minister to them. They also teach us something of what it is like from God's vantage point in dealing with His appointed leaders.

The discipleship process involves bringing people to Christ, bringing Christ to people, training people, and strategically placing them into the world so that they may get involved in the great harvest. Remember that Jesus made disciples before they became converts. The key to discipleship is a leader committed to God and to the process of discipleship.

Unconditional Love (John 15:12–17)

This present world does not know the unconditional love of God the Father, yet longs for it. Homosexual activists stew in rage against "ultra-right-wing, fundamentalist Christians." Millions of women and men despise those who seek to limit "their choice" to abort the unborn. Even the homeless often bring sharp criticism against the church, which, in many cases, is their primary source of help. On the one hand, the church must consider the source of harsh criticism and vehement opposition. It is Satan who is using the unconverted to accomplish his purposes. Those human beings who fight against the work of God are puppets (albeit self-willed, responsible puppets) in the hands of the devil. On the other hand, the church must see to it that everything it does is done with great care, godly wisdom, and unconditional love. There should be no just cause for anger, hatred, and malice toward the church because of our failure to exercise a balanced response to the prevailing evil and the needs around us.

What if the church became informed on how to love the homosexual? According to Exodus International, when their converts were children, an adult who was a close friend of the family or a close relative within the family sexually abused more than 90 percent of them.[7] If we could only understand their past, riddled with pain, guilt, shame, and anger, we would weep as Christ did for the sinners of Jerusalem.

What if the church made it known that we would adopt any and all unwanted babies heading for abortion and furthermore would assist in all financial responsibilities of the unwed mother so that she could carry the baby to term? Suppose Christians came alongside that mother for the purpose of befriending her and leading her in the paths of righteousness "for His name's sake"?

What if more Christian families moved beyond charity and absorbed a homeless person into their family, taking all necessary precautions and risks to demonstrate the unconditional, sacrificial love of God the Father? Like Jesus we may be called foolish or weak, but at the end of the day they will know us by our love. The world will have to say, "They are indeed the children of God."

Wise Compassion (Matthew 10:16; 1 Timothy 5:3–14)

Unwise compassion, such as giving indiscriminately just because a person says he needs our help, breeds a spirit of unhealthy dependency (i.e., welfare). On more than one occasion, I have heard the bitter remarks of a disappointed and disgruntled homeless client who did not receive from the church what he demanded. Some even quote Scripture to remind me of Jesus' actions toward the poor and needy. They go on to instruct me about the biblical responsibility the church has toward any and every person who calls out in distress. It is at this point that most ministers and laypeople alike cringe inside while feelings of guilt begin to rise.

An impotent and ignorant church is unable to effectively minister to the poor in crisis. In our unwise attempts to be compassionate we become, like the government, a part of the problem instead of part of the solution. We are impotent because we fail to produce fruit that remains. For example, the homeless people we "help" keep coming back with the same needs and sometimes greater ones. The real need is for them to learn how to bear fruit for themselves and for others. The church should therefore realize that supplying the temporary felt need at the moment is really not the person's greatest need. Somehow we must seek to help individuals understand the reason for their poverty. We are constantly trying to relieve the real and urgent symptoms of poverty while ignoring the evil causes of poverty.

The Christian who seeks to exercise wise compassion must first understand how God Himself responds to poverty and what He instructs His people about poverty. Wise compassion is spending time with individuals to first understand their expressed felt need, then moving deeper to the reason those needs exist. After obtaining permission of the needy client, one must gently probe into his life to help him see the real cause of his need. For most of the hundreds of poor families and individuals I have encountered, the cause is personal sin or the sins of others. I agree with Viv Grigg that it often is an unending cycle: Certain personal sins (drunkenness, drug abuse, sexual immorality, etc.) cause poverty, and poverty causes certain personal sins (stealing, lying, gambling, prostitution, murder, etc.).[8]

Perhaps the number one root cause of poverty that I have uncovered is open and willful rebellion against every God-ordained institution of society (family, government, church, and work). What I try to explain to clients is that these institutions are indeed given by God for our personal and societal benefit, and without them there can be no personal or social order, only chaos. I tell them how these institutions

are like a big umbrella of life that serves as a shelter and support during all stages of life if we learn to respectfully use it as designed. But
when misused and abused by rebellion, holes are created in the umbrella, which allow for the storms of life—the lightning, rain, and
thunder—to come upon them with a vengeance.

Breaking this destructive cycle of poverty takes the intervention of
God. In this, the church acts as the body of Christ today—His incarnation. Once the cause of the individual's poverty is established and
clearly seen by both parties, then the minister (lay or professional)
needs to determine if the client wants to remain in the status quo or
make a change. I often ask, "What are your dreams and aspirations?
What do you want to do or be?" I am delightfully surprised to hear the
lofty goals some homeless people have. The problem is they have no
clue as to how to achieve the worthy goals to which they aspire.

I again gain permission to tell the necessary information they need
to begin dealing with the heart of their problem. I then draw what I
call a life map. This shows them a sort of time line marking out where
they are in relation to where they want to be with all the intermediate
steps needed to achieve their goal. By this time I have earned the right
to explain the necessary character traits (self-discipline, humility, gratitude, delayed gratification, hard work, self-sacrifice, respect for all
God-given authority, etc.) it takes to be a productive member of society. Finally I explain how Christ alone can reconcile us back to God
and to all of the God-given institutions, which we have all rebelled
against at some point in our lives. If the individual is still tracking with
me at this point I ask another question: "Are you ready to learn how
the church can help you accomplish your long-term dream as well as
supply your short-term need?" If so, we go on to discuss our next topic, close partnerships.

Close Partnerships (2 Corinthians 8:23)

The fourth urban path to fulfilling the Great Commission in our
cities is close, focused partnerships. To understand the pressing problems facing the urban community is to understand the great need for
the body of Christ to unite and act as if we really are joined together
with spiritual muscles and ligaments. What every church in the city
needs is an honest evaluation of the challenge and a sobering realization of our utter dependence on Christ, other churches, and other
agencies to overcome the challenge for the glory of Christ and the welfare of our cities.

When various individuals from the Moody Church congregation
came independently to the leadership expressing their desire to see the

church more actively engaging the many social problems around the church, we listened intently. The leadership then joined with the laity in thinking, praying, and planning a God-honoring response that would strengthen both our local fellowship and the citywide body of Christ.

God helped us realize we had neither the human nor financial resources to effectively tackle the immense social ills such as homelessness, drug addiction, child abuse, gang warfare, and AIDS with which we became increasingly burdened. So we asked the question, "What is God already doing through other Christian and secular organizations in these identified areas of need?" God heard our question and began to show us the following existing ministries with which we could partner, many of which are highlighted in this book: Alpha and Omega Ministries, Chicago Care Pregnancy Centers, Chicago Christian Industrial League, Good News Jail and Prison Ministry, Inner City Impact, Jesus People USA, Pacific Garden Mission, Prison Fellowship's Angel Tree, Ronald McDonald House, Teen Challenge, and Love and Action Midwest.

We approached these ministries and asked if we could enter into a mutually beneficial partnership that would bring honor to Christ, blessing to His people, and hope to those not yet His people. By partnership we mean two primary things: human and financial resources. We covenanted together to provide people who would come alongside each ministry as a learner, helper, organizer, and/or recruiter, and we covenanted to provide financial resources as needed and as available. Branch Ministries was then formed at the Moody Church. Each branch ministry took on the responsibility of training our volunteers (Branch Ministry Liaisons) to be effective ministers of the gospel in its portion of God's urban vineyard. Together we say with Bill Hull, "The unified, trained body of Christ is the most powerful expression of God on the face of the earth."[9]

The Moody Church family is constantly being challenged by these partnerships to develop new ways of deepening our relationship, and we too challenge Christian ministries to grow deep in God's Word. We have come to realize that no one organization has the theological or ministerial corner on the market, but together we can learn from and strengthen one another for the glory of God.

Versatile Strategies (Matthew 9:17)

One of the great tragedies of the church in recent history are these seven last words, "We've never done it like this before." We fail to recognize the distinction between the message and the method. Although the very essence of the message, namely, who Jesus is and what He did, cannot change, the presentation of the message must.

People differ. Each ethnic group has its own worldview, its own way of seeing, understanding, and interpreting the world around it. Furthermore, mankind is constantly changing, even though the gospel never will. We live in what is now known as postmodern America, where pluralism is the order of the day. People assume that there is no right or wrong when it comes to moral and religious thinking. Tolerance of every worldview is at the heart of postmodern America, but the only thing intolerable is the intolerant view of the Christian faith, which proclaims Christ as the exclusive *Lord* of all.

We understand that man's basic problem is his sinful heart, that "the heart of every problem is the problem of the heart." So why not preach a simple gospel message of sin, repentance, and faith in Jesus Christ? For the same reason that overseas missionaries do not start without first studying the language, culture, and worldview of the people to whom they are being sent.

We also know that it is the Spirit of God who convicts the world of sin and convinces it of righteousness, but for some unknown reason He loves to employ certain people, places, languages, and ways by which to communicate His message. Who are we, therefore, to hinder the work of God by saying, "We have never done it this way before"? Let the Holy Spirit have His way; let Him be creative in us. Let us not only exegete our Bibles, but also our culture made up of the peoples God has sovereignly brought to us. And then let us be innovative when proclaiming the risen Christ in a God-honoring way that is winsome yet doctrinally sound. Joe Aldrich has defined three types of evangelism; I believe all three are to be employed because they are biblical: (1) proclamational (primarily preaching to groups); (2) confrontational (personal/intentional—to strangers); (3) incarnational/ relational (friendship evangelism).[10]

Many in this book have dealt with ministry to the "down-and-outs," but let's look briefly at ministry to another category, the "up-and-outs"—those who earn more than $75,000 a year. Our Lord Jesus said, "It is easier for a camel to go through the eye of a needle than for a rich man to enter the kingdom of God" (Matt. 19:24).

Why is it so difficult to reach the rich? The answer is evident both to them and to those who look on. Their unspoken assumption is often, "I have no need of God; look at all I possess." Little do they know that money and the possessions it affords them are their gods and that the money really possesses them. Money is the first brick, the cornerstone, if you will, in the wall of the up-and-outs. So how does the Christian man or woman lead such individuals to God?

First, you need not be intimidated by the size of his or her bank account or the possessions the person has, knowing that the Christian has infinitely more wealth, lasting wealth, in heaven. Ask God to help you develop a casual relationship with such people. Seek every opportunity to steer whatever conversations you have with them toward their family and hobbies, their goals and dreams, etc. Once a relationship is established, look and listen for "divine appointments." "Divine appointments" are carefully God-orchestrated events in the lives of people (rich, poor, or middle class) that make them more open to spiritual things than at other times.

Such divine opportunities may come just before or after a major family ordeal (wedding, birth of child or grandchild, death of a close family member, etc.), or during national or religious holidays (Christmas, Chanukah, Easter, Yom Kippur, etc.), change of job or housing, a great stock market rise or fall, national or international disasters or wars. All of these things can and should be used to stir up the mind of the unbeliever, undermining his implicit trust in temporary and impotent gods like money. The Bible is clear about the uncertainty of wealth. Proverbs 23:5 says, "Cast but a glance at riches, and they are gone, for they will surely sprout wings and fly off to the sky like an eagle."

What good deeds are you intentionally doing to gain a credible hearing of the gospel by your wealthy colleague in business? God may choose to cause you and your family to experience your own uncomfortable life changes. When He does, ask Him for wisdom on how to respond to the circumstance before your watching colleague, neighbor, or relative. Howard Hendricks wrote, "People are watching us to see if our words are real. Our message and our lives are inseparably related, so the closeness of our walk with God will determine how effectively we communicate His message."[11]

The love of money isn't the only brick that makes up the urban wall of the rich; another is the ego. Sometimes the size of the ego is directly proportionate to the size of the bank account. The most wealthy man who ever lived wrote, "Pride goes before destruction, a haughty spirit before a fall" (Prov. 16:18). If God has blessed you with the ability to create wealth, be careful not to get sucked into the ego trip of your non-Christian counterpart. The sinful ego of the wealthy is built on the shoddy foundation of materialism and accomplishment. It is wrapped up in exquisite restaurants, a certain make and model automobile, and just the right neighborhood or office address. The rich man's ego fosters a false sense of security and self-sufficiency.

So what does he need in order to see Christ? He needs a Christian peer, preferably in his financial bracket, whose hope is not found in this world's delectable goods but in the sacrificial and bountiful Giver of every good and perfect gift. The wealthy must come to the cross of Christ and die to self, to security, to their own culture, and to their wealth. In the Old Testament, wealth and strength were signified by horses and chariots. The psalmist boldly proclaimed what every Christian ought to display, "Some trust in chariots and some in horses, but we trust in the name of the Lord our God" (Ps. 20:7).

Again, you cannot get close enough to the rich unless you have a personal relationship. Out of these established relationships you may invite another person to an evangelistic breakfast or luncheon designed for the high-powered executive or professional. Perhaps your church could be instrumental in starting a chapter of one of several ministries geared to reaching the up-and-outs (Executive Ministries, Christian Business Men's Committee [CBMC], or a similar ministry).

Here is a practical suggestion for innovative ministry. Study the lives of Esther, Ezra, Nehemiah, Jesus, and Paul and discover for yourself the myriad ways by which, in which, and through which God accomplished His purposes in the lives of the urban rich, poor, and middle class. Do not be afraid to try new methods of evangelism. Do not fear failures. Learn to admit them if and when they come. Then be willing to change strategies and try again. Study, pray, and consult with local church leaders, but by all means try new wineskins when delivering this precious vintage wine of the gospel.

Evaluating Progress
(Revelation 5:9–12; 2 Timothy 2:2; 1 Corinthians 4:14–17)

How does the church know that it is progressing in this vital area of urban evangelism? After the work of evangelism, which will never really be finished until we get Home, the next most difficult thing is evaluation. Because evangelism is an ongoing process of discipleship and because no one enjoys looking disappointment in the eye, the church's self-evaluation is difficult, though crucial.

Bill Hull wrote, "The real evidence of success will be the constant production of reproducing disciples and leaders who become multipliers."[12] Perhaps the singular reason Evangelism Explosion (EE) is such an effective personal evangelism program is that D. James Kennedy not only saw the reproducing power of this biblical principle but also committed himself to it. It is this very principle that I stress in the EE ministry at Moody Church. I often remind the trainers and trainees that this ministry should not depend on me or Roy Schwarcz, our co-leader. When I implemented EE at Moody four years ago, I learned that the elders had been praying for ten years for someone to restart this dynamic ministry. Although I was honored to know that I was an answer to specific prayer, I lamented the ten years of drought without spiritual harvest, not to mention the stunted growth of believers who wanted and needed to tell of their faith but had no training, no discipleship in the harvesting of souls. This should never be.

I have already begun praying and looking for a faithful man whom God would use to take over this ministry, if and when God leads me elsewhere. I hope to judge my success based on the strength and vitality of the ministry long after I am gone. The strength and vitality of the ministry closely correlates to the multiplication of godly leaders who will train others also.

It is fascinating to know that the Lord Jesus did not write one word of the Bible, though He is the Word. Rather, He spoke the word and lived the word around twelve men who turned the world upside down with His power. The apostle Paul wrote most of the New Testament, but not to the neglect of making disciples wherever he went who would carry on the important work of making further disciples to carry on the work of the ministry. Bill Hull has some sobering words for the church to ponder: "The church has seriously responded to 'blue water' mission, while neglecting 'in Jerusalem' mission or 'at home' disciplemaking. Both Foreign missions and the American church have suffered for this mistake, because 'at home' disciplemaking is the key to world evangelism."[13]

One telltale sign of a successful urban ministry is the extent to which the local fellowship reflects urban diversity in terms of ethnicity and economic strata. Does the church leadership (staff and laity) also reflect this kind of diversity? Does the worship style accommodate the diverse representation, or does everyone have to conform to a limited scope of worship? Is there a true appreciation of economic and ethnic diversity? How is this expressed? These and other questions help us evaluate our corporate sanctification in the urban community.

Conclusion:
The Transforming Power of the Gospel

The church must be engaged in urban evangelism. This is the purpose of our existence in the city. Fulfilling our calling to the city includes overcoming our fears with God-given boldness. Complacency will give way to God-given passion for souls. We will cultivate and satiate our spiritual appetites with God Himself, not the things He affords us. While becoming the men and women God has called us to be, we will step up to the wealthy and stoop down with the poor for the purpose of telling the life-transforming power of the gospel that can set them free.

If we are going to be salt and light to our dark and decaying cities we will love unconditionally, extend compassion wisely, lead reproductive lives, establish close partnerships, and employ versatile strategies. As we go about our Father's business, He always provides all that we need to obey whatever He commands us to do—for the praise of His glorious name.

Reflection Questions

1. What roadblocks stand in the way of your church doing urban evangelism, and how can you help remove them?

2. Are you making friends with the up-and-outs? The down-and-outs? If not, how can you begin to do so?

3. What are your misplaced affections that hinder your love of God and people?

chapter fourteen

THE CHURCH BEHIND BARS

THE WORK OF GOOD NEWS JAIL AND PRISON MINISTRY

LEN MASELLI

Introduction: An Invisible Church

Most cities in America have a hidden church—the church behind bars. This church reaches a captive audience of 1.7 million potential members all across the nation in jails and prisons. No offering is ever taken, and no elders are appointed. The chaplain is the pastor, the inmates are his congregants, and the jail or prison is his church. Business is booming. The church behind bars is growing.

As a missionary chaplain with Good News Jail & Prison Ministry (Good News JPM), I pastor one of the largest single-site juvenile detention centers in the United States. The Cook County Juvenile Temporary Detention Center in Chicago is "home" to nearly seven hundred youth on any given day and eleven thousand total each year. The young men and women range in age from ten to seventeen and live at the Juvenile Detention Center anywhere from three days to three years, with the average stay being three weeks. Two miles away, three of my fellow Good News JPM chaplains minister at the Cook County Jail with a daily count of more than eleven thousand adult inmates and ninety-six thousand annually. Truly, a huge field of human souls is ripe, ready for reaping. Sadly, these vast, ripe fields go largely unharvested and unnoticed.

CURRENT STATE OF CORRECTIONS
AND CRIME IN THE UNITED STATES

Anyone considering working in the urban setting must consider reaching the incarcerated. We should remember that much of the daily jail and prison population of 1.7 million men, women, and youth will one day be returning to a city near you. From 1990 through midyear 1997, the incarcerated population has grown, on average, 6.5 percent annually. That means the total population has risen more than 577,000 since 1990. In our three largest cities, New York, Los Angeles, and Chicago, a total of 48,679 people were incarcerated each day in 1997.[1] The fuel for this rising jail and prison population is the crime rate.

From 1960–94, the total violent crime rate for the United States increased 345 percent. Murder and non-negligent manslaughter rose 76 percent. Forcible rape went up 309.1 percent, robbery rose 295.3 percent, and aggravated assault skyrocketed 399.9 percent.[2] In one generation our country has degenerated at an alarming pace.

The media have expressed much happiness recently that the crime rate has been going down. In Chicago, the violent crime rate went down, but the rate of thefts rose, bringing the overall crime rate up 0.08 percent from January to March 1998. Percentages do not always convey the true picture of crime. In 1997, Chicago had 65,110 violent crimes, of which 757 were homicides. In the first quarter of 1998, 58,245 serious crimes were reported. This is 480 more than the first quarter of 1997.[3] People are being violated and victimized at an intolerable level. But the picture looks bleaker for the juveniles of our urban areas.

News stories of children killing children have stunned Americans. School shootings have exploded the myth that violent crime only takes place in the inner cities among black youth. Youth between the ages of fourteen and seventeen are the fastest growing group of offenders. For example, the murder and non-negligent manslaughter rate more than doubled from 1976 to 1994. Juveniles committed eight offenses per 100,000 residents in 1976; however, in 1994 that same age group committed nineteen offenses per 100,000 residents.[4] Many criminologists predict that this trend is just starting to rise.

Professor John DiIulio, of Princeton University, wrote in a 1995 *Chicago Tribune* editorial[5] that the nation's approximately 40 million youth under the age of ten is the largest number of juveniles in decades. By 2005, the number of fourteen- to seventeen-year-olds will rise by about 25 percent overall and 50 percent for African-Americans. DiIulio stated, "To some extent, it's just that simple: more boys beget more bad boys."[6] California authorities have predicted that since their state population of eleven- to seventeen-year-olds will grow from 2.9 million in 1993 to 3.9 million in 2004, they expect a 30 percent rise in juvenile arrests.[7]

THE WORLD'S RESPONSES
TO CRIME AND CORRECTIONS

In May 1996, a Gallup poll found that crime and violence were the number one problem facing this nation, according to Americans who were polled.[8] Gangs, guns, crime, and drugs are a great concern to all who live in this country—especially to those who live in the major cities of the United States. Politicians, policymakers, academics, and the average citizen are scrambling for solutions to the national epidemic. The world has responded to crime and corrections in three major ways: making tougher laws, building more prisons, and designing more programs.

Laws: Legislating Our Way Out

A recent flurry of activity in federal and state legislatures has regarded crime and corrections. Generally, laws are being made tougher to deter potential offenders and punish convicted offenders.

In 1994 California passed Proposition 184, which is known commonly as the "Three Strikes You're Out" law. Though it was controversial, it had enough support to pass. Under the law, a person who has been convicted of two violent crimes can be sentenced to life in prison if convicted of a third crime. The effectiveness of this law is hotly debated among politicians and criminologists.

Dan Lungren, who was attorney general of California, hailed this law as the reason that his state has seen a 5.5 percent decrease in violent crime.[9] However, groups such as the Justice Policy Institute note that states without the "three strikes" law have experienced an even bigger drop in violent crime. They conclude in their report, "Ultimately, three strikes legislation and other quick fix panaceas point out the futility of piecemeal approaches to achieving a safer society."[10]

Nationally, the United States Congress and Senate have been considering a number of bills aimed at halting the crime and corrections nightmare. The bills under consideration deal with a range of legal solutions from overhauling the juvenile justice system to tougher sentencing.

Although we all agree that society must have laws and consequences for breaking those laws, we also recognize as Christians that the establishment of law does not stop someone from rebelling against society's agreed-upon laws and codes. In other words, laws do not change people or their behaviors.

Construction: Building Our Way Out

If you are looking for a booming new business to start, try jail and prison construction. Between 1990–95, 213 new prisons were built, with 280,000-bed capacity.[11] This figure does not include county jails, which make up a huge piece of the construction pie.

In Cook County, a new state-of-the-art jail was constructed for $105 million. Since it contains 768 cells, it cost $136,000 per cell. That price would buy a decent house almost anywhere in the United States.

Though jail and prison construction is a good business venture, it is a failed method of deterrence and rehabilitation. Granted, the most violent and antisocial people need to be locked up for punishment and to protect society; however, incarceration does not change behavior.

I read about a man who was convicted in 1991 for robbery and was sentenced to eight years in prison. Eighteen days after his release he went back to the same bank and tried it again, only to be recognized by an employee who had been there during the previous robbery.[12] As Scripture says, "A dog returns to its vomit" (2 Pet. 2:22).

A well-verified statistic notes that eight out of ten inmates will go on to commit new crimes when released, usually within the first year. Unfortunately, the public has a general perception that inmates are being rehabilitated while incarcerated. However, most corrections officials readily admit that they have no other real program or policy other than warehousing prisoners.

Programs: Achieving Our Way Out

Since it has been clearly demonstrated that simply incarcerating people will not change their behavior, many educators, social workers, psychologists, and ministers have placed a great emphasis on developing programs within the facilities. They are knocking on the door of the local jails and prisons with passion and plans to help change the prisoner.

The educator believes education is the key to empowerment; the social worker believes in the need to change the socioeconomic position; the psychologist suggests classical and operant conditioning to alter the deviant behavior; and the minister preaches that religion and church attendance alone will set the lost, demented soul on a new course. All these well-meaning people believe they have the silver bullet that will slay the habitual criminal mentality. Although each of these measures is helpful, none of them stands alone as a panacea.

In my six years working with gang-bangers, drug dealers, murderers, and the like, I have found that programs do not change people.

I met an educated man in the Cook County Jail, where fellow chaplain Steve Thompson presides. For the Tuesday night Bible studies, this guy played the piano like a professional. It turns out he had a master's degree in music. Education does not change people.

Environment does not make criminals. An increasing number of inmates are coming from quiet, middle-class, two-parent homes. Behavior modification programs work well in the short term, but once the visible reward fades, so does the positive behavior. Church attendance and "belief" in God does not stop crimes. George Gallup noted that nine out of ten adults go to church occasionally[13] and 84 percent believe in God.[14] Church attendance and a simple belief in God do not change people.

Please do not think that this chaplain has gone crazy by dismissing church attendance and belief in God as the answer to rehabilitation. I'm saying the answer must go deeper. Jail and prison chaplains have agreed that rehabilitation cannot happen without regeneration. "Therefore, if anyone is in Christ, he is a new creation; the old has gone, the new has come" (2 Cor. 5:17). You cannot change the behavior of a person until you change the person. Change comes from the inside and then progresses to the outside. Any program that does not involve regeneration through a personal relationship with Jesus Christ is likely doomed to dismal failure. We must get to the root of man's problem.

THE CHURCH'S RESPONSE
TO CRIME AND CORRECTIONS

Henry David Thoreau once said, "There are a thousand hacking at the branches of evil to one who is striking at the root." A wicked tree of violence and rebellion has sprung up in our midst. As believers in Jesus Christ, the church has the axe to strike at the root. Laws, education, environment, economics, and prison construction all aim at the branches. These well-meaning and at times valued means only target the symptoms. But my prayer is that believers around the country—maybe you —would work to adopt a Church Behind Bars in their area. If you have a relationship with the living God and possess a heart of compassion for the "least of these" (Matt. 25:40), you have the axe that can strike at the root of this wicked tree.

In fact, the world is starting to agree with the church. The Princeton professor cited earlier in this chapter studied juvenile delinquents personally and evaluated the current research on juvenile delinquency. His conclusion is, "In sum, whatever their material circumstances, kids of whatever race, creed or color are most likely to become criminally depraved when they are morally deprived."[15] Professor DiIulio calls this theory of root causes of crime "moral poverty." In his article he also noted Harvard economist Richard Freeman's startling discovery. In his 1986 study, Freeman found that "among black urban youth, church attendance was a better predictor of who would escape drugs, crime and poverty than any other single variable."[16]

In a June 1998 *Corrections Today* article, Byron Johnson, a professor of criminology at Lamar University, reviewed studies examining the influence of religious variables upon various measures of juvenile delinquency. He found that 85 percent of the studies reported that "higher levels of religious commitment were associated with lower likelihood of juvenile delinquency."[17] May the urban church rise up and empower the Church Behind Bars!

Biblical Basis for Corrections Ministry

I am convinced that sometimes we as Christians are looking for Jesus in all the wrong places. For years I sang the chorus, "Open my eyes Lord, I want to see Jesus," but I ignored the biblical map to locate Him.

One day we will all stand before Jesus the Judge. He will separate us into two groups: the ones who did and the ones who did not. In Matthew 25:31–46 Jesus separated the people as sheep and goats, or righteous and unrighteous.

Both groups will be surprised to learn that Jesus was hungry, thirsty, naked, homeless, sick, and in prison. The righteous and the wicked will both answer, "Jesus, when did we see You hungry, thirsty, naked, homeless, sick or in prison? I mean, Lord, you know that we're on Your side. We've got You covered. So, Lord, we are a little confused because we didn't remember seeing You—Jesus, our Savior, in these conditions" (see Matt. 25:37–39, 44). Jesus then says that if you did (or did not do) anything for the least of these brothers you did (or did not do) it for Him. Are you looking for an encounter with Jesus? Go to jail. Visit a rescue mission. Stop by a nursing home. Connect with a food pantry. You just may run into the living Lord. This is what sheep do. Remembering the least of these does not make you righteous; however, it does express your righteousness in Christ.

If you or your relative were in jail, what would you want for yourself or for that person? Hebrews 13:3 urges us to "remember those in prison as if you were their fellow prisoners." We are exhorted to a ministry of identification with the incarcerated. Paul experienced this first-hand. We often forget that Paul spent a large part of his ministry behind bars. In fact, some of his prison letters are our eternal Word. In 2 Timothy 1:15–16, Paul was deeply discouraged by Phygelus and Hermogenes, who abandoned him in his greatest hour of need. Conversely, Paul praised Onesiphorus for diligently seeking him out and visiting him. God had at least one soul to encourage one of the greatest apostles of Christianity. I often think of whom I will see in heaven. I pray that one of the youths I minister to will become a mighty man of God. My joy will be made full. But as a chaplain I cannot do it alone. Chaplains across America need the church on the outside to minister to the church on the inside.

The Role of the Local Church

Our vision for the Chicago area Good News Jail and Prison Ministry is to "enable the Christian Community to fulfill Christ's mandate in Matthew 25 by providing avenues of action to the incarcerated." We as chaplains view ourselves as gatekeepers, people to hold open the door of the jail and detention center so the church can do its Matthew 25 business. Without the local church involved within the Church Behind Bars, these inmates will probably never know there is another way besides gangs, guns, crime, and drugs. Many youth have told me that the only men they see are the drug dealers and gang chiefs. They feel doomed to the same destiny.

Volunteer in the Church Behind Bars

The compassionate urban church has many opportunities to serve the hidden church. Every institution has different avenues of action. What I propose is only a start. With a sensitive and patient approach, you are bound to find an avenue of service appropriate for your church or group that is concerned about the prisoner.

One of the surprising elements I found when I first started volunteering at the Cook County Juvenile Detention Center was a sincere eagerness from the youth to learn about God. Like most new volunteers, I was very nervous and unsure of what to expect when I encountered the incarcerated. I thought that these gang-banging, gun-toting, drug-dealing youth would be the most resistant and hard-hearted souls I ever met. After all, the "nice kids" in the suburban churches I was part of were not very interested in the things of God, so how much more uninterested would these troubled youth prove to be? I was dead wrong.

All of a sudden John 4:35 came alive to me. The fields are really ripe unto harvest. How many times I looked in my neighborhood, workplace, or family and found fallow ground. I longed to see the fields of human souls as Jesus saw them. I praise God that I have found my field of human souls that are ripe and ready for reaping. From then on, I discovered one day a week was not enough time to meet the requests from the youths for prayer and Bible study.

After volunteering for three years, God chose me to be there five to six days a week as the Good News JPM chaplain. Dear friends, let me tell you six days a week is still not enough time to conduct all the Bible studies, counseling, prayer sessions, and worship services. I often feel that I am in the old apricot orchards of my hometown of Fremont, California. There my brothers and I would eat the ripe apricots until we were nearly sick. The ripe fruit was falling off the tree and rotting on the ground faster than it could be picked. We as chaplains in the criminal justice system need the help of the local church desperately. The fruit is ripe and ready to be picked.

Here is a general list of volunteer opportunities. Remember, every institution is different; therefore, all of these may not be applicable.

Bible Study Teachers/Leader

Many jails and prisons are open to the church community coming in to do Bible studies. I suggest you put an experienced Bible teacher with some less experienced teachers. In times past, the local county jail was seen as the bottom rung of ministry where inexperienced people could make all their mistakes in order to get polished for the "real" ministry beyond the jail doors. There could be no greater disservice to an inmate than to give him or her the totally inexperienced of our congregations. We surely will keep them out of the church when they are released. Nevertheless, prison is a good training ground if there is an experienced leader modeling effective Bible teaching and discipleship. Some ministries, like Good News Jail & Prison Ministry, offer training for volunteers, while others simply facilitate the ministry group.

The most common call I receive from churches is asking about opportunities to teach the Bible in some fashion. At the Cook County Juvenile Detention Center, we match Bible teachers with small groups of residents numbering from one to ten participants. In an adult facility, the opportunities tend to be for a larger group with a more formal setting such as a regular church service. At Cook County Jail, my fellow chaplains generally have a formal service or teaching time and then break down into small groups with volunteers facilitating more informal sessions.

Sunday and Special Services

Most institutions have slots throughout the week for church groups to provide a formal worship service. This is a great way to get started in jail and prison ministry. The church can bring in a team of people to conduct a service, involving musically gifted people in special music and congregational singing. One of the closest glimpses of heaven I have yet experienced was singing "Amazing Grace" with more than one hundred men and tears streaming from our eyes. These inmates know their sin; therefore, they appreciate God's expressed grace.

Have people give their personal testimonies. Often, we feel we must have a "gone to the gutter" testimony in order to minister to those who are incarcerated. I asked some of the residents their opinion of the Sunday services. These kids are brutally honest, which is helpful if you can take it! A couple of them said they were tired of hearing testimonies like "I've been where you are; I sat where you sat." They just wanted to hear some teaching from the Bible from regular people. It is good once in a while to bring in an ex-offender who can relate 100 percent with the life of some of the inmates; however, that testimony is no more effective than the testimony of my wife, who was saved in kindergarten. The issue is not necessarily where you have been but what God has done in your life.

Along with musicians and testimonies, bring someone who can preach the Word of God. This is where you will want to know your audience. Find out the ethnic and age breakdown in the facility. The same message that went well at the nursing home will flop in a juvenile detention center. The preacher should pray to God for His message to be delivered.

Generally, one point with many illustrations works best. I tell my church groups that I am looking for three general areas to be covered: worship, evangelism, and edification. Volunteers must remember that saved and unsaved people will be in their audience. Many times churches preach on John 3:16. However, perhaps another group preached on John 3:16 last week! Most inmates want to move beyond evangelistic messages.

Finally, a church group should bring a few casual participants to open or close with prayer, read a Scripture, or simply observe God at work in the hearts of the incarcerated.

Special Projects

A way to test the waters of jail and prison ministry is to offer to do a special project. The holidays bring natural opportunities. Many churches present Christmas programs. One church brings a small group to sing Christmas carols through the halls of the detention center. It is a joy to see young people smiling innocently when they hear familiar Christmas carols. Another group has a Christmas program in the chapel and gives gifts (cleared by the security staff well in advance) to each resident as he or she exits. My own church once made up bags of cookies, candy, and tracts for distribution to each resident and staff member. Another church brought hardbound study Bibles and placed them on all thirty living units. The ideas are endless. Special projects tell incarcerated people you love them, because you simply took the time to come and give. This provides a great one-day outreach, which introduces your church to jail and prison ministry.

Inmate Families

Another mission field is the family of the inmate. Mothers call me frequently, pleading with me to minister to their son or daughter. Relatives struggle with the fact that their son or daughter or mom or dad is in jail or prison.

Good News chaplain Marcus Baird partnered with his own church to start a "Christmas for the Children" program. Chaplain Baird and his church members carefully screened and interviewed inmates and their families to be a part of this program. Gifts and food were personally delivered to the inmates' families as a way of encouragement. The results were so positive that the church continued with the program the next year. The family does not feel as alone, and many doors are opened to further ministry by this one act.

Our other Good News chaplain, Harry Roundtree, has done a Thanksgiving program for many years. Chaplain Roundtree and his wife, Helen, receive donations of food, money, clothes, and other necessary items from many churches and individuals in order to make Thanksgiving care baskets. Volunteers from local churches make the deliveries. Long-term relationships have been forged with some of these families whose loved ones are incarcerated. Thanksgiving now takes on a new meaning for these families.

When you build up the inmate and his or her family, you greatly increase the possibility for full restoration to take place, which will slow the recidivism rate (the rate at which ex-offenders go on to commit new crimes).

Aftercare

One of the first questions I asked as a new volunteer was, "What happens to these guys once they are released back into the community?" To my initial surprise I found that most of them went back to the same destructive pattern unless a church took an interest in helping them through the transition. I was also surprised that many churches were not interested in helping ex-offenders. The reasons range from fear to honest ignorance. If we are to see the cycle of crime and sin broken in these ex-offenders, the church must risk herself for the "least of these." Admittedly, young Christians just released from jail or prison are often hard to serve. Many of them are struggling with their new freedom, are fighting intense temptations, and are sometimes uncomfortable with church attendance. The key to success in following up on a releasee is relationship. If the church sends a member or family to build relationships with ex-offenders and their families, the chances are greater that the ex-offender will soon be assimilated into the broader church community. You must look at aftercare as an adoption process. The whole church must take ownership in this process, or it will not work.

Some other opportunities might be:

- Pen pals
- Administrative help to the chaplain
- Sports ministry
- VBS programs
- Life skills seminars
- Family counseling
- Victim support groups
- Tutoring

For a more comprehensive list, contact your local institution and ask for specific needs.

Pray for the Church Behind Bars

Chaplains, correctional staff, and volunteers work in a stressful and adversarial environment. Sometimes I have physically felt the oppression that permeates these kinds of facilities.

One day I was taking some youth to a conference room for Bible study; however, a young man in the room was making a phone call. I told him he should move to the hallway, where he should have been in the first place. He did not like my plan. He told me that I had no authority to tell him what to do. I repeated my request that he calmly exit the room and talk to me respectfully. He then said, "You better watch who you're messing with cause I'll hurt you and your family if you don't watch it!" By this time my flesh was rearing its ugly head. I felt like taking this seventeen-year-old boy and throwing him against the wall, but chaplains do not do that! The three youths who were with me were watching my response. Suddenly, the truth of Ephesians 6:12 hit me like a cold shower. God reminded me that my struggle is not against flesh and blood. My enemy is not this rebellious boy but the spiritual forces of wickedness he has yielded to. The battle is spiritual; therefore, spiritual means are necessary for victory. I have a prayer team of approximately fifty-five people who lift me, my family, and the ministry up in prayer daily. Every month I create a monthly calendar with a different request for each day.

Everyone may not be able to personally volunteer at a jail, detention center, or prison, but everyone can regularly pray for the ministry and the chaplain of the facility. Call the chaplain and ask him for issues you and your church could pray for on Sunday with the congregation. Offer to start a prayer team for the Church Behind Bars.

Give to the Church Behind Bars

According to Don Smarto, former vice president of Good News Jail & Prison Ministry, there are more than 450 jail and prison ministries across America. In his former position as the director of the Institute for Prison Ministries at the Billy Graham Center at Wheaton College, Mr. Smarto had the privilege of working with many of these fine ministries.

Most jail and prison ministries receive no government financial assistance. Good News JPM has been offered many times to be placed on a county, state, or federal budget. Though it may at times be tempting, Good News JPM has for more than thirty-five years said "No, thank you!" The leadership simply believes that God's work should be funded by God's people.

Many states are laying off their salaried chaplains. In this era of downsizing, private agencies are being called on to provide services. Good News was asked by the state of Colorado to fill all its state prisons with Good News Chaplains. We have invitations from all over the world, including Costa Rica, Puerto Rico, and Latvia, as well as other areas within Illinois for more chaplains. Without the church on the outside financially supporting the church on the inside, we cannot advance into this ripe field of souls.

If your area has an effective jail and prison ministry, support it. As always, with any mission organization, check it out. Ask for a financial audit to see how the money is spent. Get references from other churches and the institutions that they serve.

Another way to give to the Church Behind Bars is in material gifts.

All jails and prisons could use more Bibles, tracts, and good Christian books. For many years International Prison Ministry has provided Bibles and literature to inmates who request them. However, with the high turnover in jails, there is an ongoing need for the printed Word. Inmates often have lots of time. We should make sure each inmate has a Bible to read. Tracts and Christian books are great ways to introduce inmates to God and keep them encouraged. Videos are another positive way to give to the Church Behind Bars. Often the chaplain has a VCR or projector. I have had great success showing Campus Crusade's *Jesus* movie. Inmates like all the Bible movies, such as the *Ten Commandments* with Charlton Heston. The new series of movies put out by TBS are fairly accurate. In fact, the movie *Joseph,* starring Ben Kingsley, won an Emmy Award. The youth loved the movie, which solidified the story of Joseph in their minds.

Some other ideas for giving to the Church Behind Bars:

- Stationery – Inmates love to write letters. Anything beyond white binder paper is a treat.
- Toiletries – Many inmates do not have family to supply basic needs such as shampoo, deodorant, toothpaste, towels, etc.
- Clothes – Some institutions allow people to give underwear, socks, and shoes to inmates.
- Office supplies – Computer supplies, postage, and general office supplies are usually an ongoing need for any ministry. Many jail and prison ministries are not supplied with basic office supplies.

Check with your local institutions, as each facility has different policies and needs. Remember, the offering plate is never passed at the Church Behind Bars. Support and encourage a church that cannot support itself.

Conclusion: Striking at the Root

Believers in Jesus have the axe that can strike at the root of evil. As urban ministry workers, let us not strike only at the leaves or the branches of the tree.

Unfortunately, the needs of an urban ministry are great. Your attention can be pulled in many directions by numerous good causes. In your efforts to advance the kingdom of God in the cities, please do not forget the least of Jesus' brothers and sisters, especially in the hidden church, the Church Behind Bars.

I believe that Jesus specified the ministry to the hungry, thirsty, naked, foreigner, sick, and prisoner because we as a church tend to forget these fields. When we wake up in the morning, we do not see the tearstained pillows of a repentant prisoner. As we go through the day, we may not think about the old and dying in our hospitals and nursing homes. We may be too accustomed to seeing multiple cultures in our city to identify with the stranger's loneliness. The hungry may not knock on your door. But please do not forget the least of these.

Pray for God's heart, for His compassion. Then search for opportunities. He will lead you into the vast field of human souls—ripe and ready for reaping.

Reflection Questions

1. Be honest. Do you have a heart of compassion for those people Jesus describes in Matthew 25:31–46? Why or why not? How could you develop a heart of compassion for these types of people?

2. Think of all the criminals and prisoners in the Bible. How does understanding these biblical accounts motivate and encourage you for action to the incarcerated?

3. Why do you think seminarians and Bible college graduates have often looked on jail and prison ministry as a third-class ministry or at best a "steppingstone" to a "real" ministry?

part five

ETHNIC COMMUNITIES

chapter fifteen

INCARNATIONAL MINISTRY IN THE LATINO COMMUNITY

IDENTIFYING WITH THOSE IN THE BARRIO

NOEL CASTELLANOS

Introduction: A Special Day

Our family could hardly wait for my daughter Anna's fourth birthday party. My two sons, Noel Luis and Stefan, were looking forward to all the fun that Mom and Dad had planned for their little sister's special day. The best we could come up with was to have a cookout in our big backyard with some kids and families from our church. Living on a corner lot has some advantages: the front and side streets to park on and more space for the kids to play. It also means more work: more lawn to mow, more noise, more cars speeding by, and a garage that is constantly being "tagged" with graffiti, as we live on the border between two rival gangs who are constantly marking out their territory for all to see.

Finally, the big day of the birthday party arrived. Together as a family we got the yard decorated for the big fiesta: streamers, banners, pin the tail on the donkey, and, of course, a piñata. We were ready for all of our friends to arrive. As expected, most of them were right on time—Mexican time, that is. We were all enjoying the fun, fellowship, and the expressions on the faces of our children as they played, ran around, and devoured all the food and candy.

All of a sudden, we heard a familiar but disturbing sound—young men yelling profanities, threats, and gang slogans at each other at the top of their lungs. Along the side of our backyard, a car full of Latin Kings began to confront members of a rival gang, the Two-Sixers, who were all on foot. It was a strange mix of twelve- to fifteen-year-olds, and a man in his early thirties. We quickly rushed everyone inside, picking up the smallest children and carrying them into our home, while yelling at the older kids to rush inside. I grabbed my cell phone and dialed 911, and I ran into the street with my phone as my only weapon. I screamed at the mob, "Get outta here—the police are on their way!" with my cell phone high in the air for all to see. I did that only after observing that there were no guns in the group: only crowbars, bats, and bottles. Almost as quickly as the commotion started, all of the young men scattered, but not before one of them exhorted me to go inside and mind my own business.

After debating what to do next, the party moved outside again, and we finished our celebration and cake, threatened more by light rain than by gang-bangers for the rest of the afternoon. Feeling a need to do something in response to all I had just experienced, I got out some white latex paint and covered some fresh graffiti on our garage door. I wrote in large letters, "Jesus Died for You!" and painted a bust of Christ's head with the crown of thorns, not sure if I wanted to convict them or scare them with my evangelistic artwork.

Throughout this whole episode, I felt much more anger than fear. I felt angry that my family and friends were not safe in our own backyard. Angry that my children's lives were in danger for no good reason. Angry that the police took more than half an hour to respond to my call for help. I also felt sad to think that the gangs have so many of our Latino kids caught in their deadly web and to realize that to these young men, gang life has much more appeal than church life. At Anna's party, we came face-to-face with some of the challenges of living and ministering in the barrio.

DISCOVERING THE SLEEPING GIANT

In 1992, I received a phone call from InterVarsity Press, asking if I would read a draft of a book they wanted to publish, *The Hispanic Challenge* by Dr. Manuel Ortiz. I was excited when the book finally came out, because it fills a void in the church for an informative and inspiring look at the Latino community in the United States. Dr. Ortiz's exhortation in his book is for the church not to ignore the ever growing presence of the Latino population in our country, which he refers to as the "Sleeping Giant."

In *The Hispanic Challenge,* Dr. Ortiz provides a great overview of the growth and demographic trends of Latinos nationwide. A staggering statistic is the 53 percent growth from the 1980 U.S. Census of 14,608,673 to the 1990 count of 22,354,059. In 2010, the Census Bureau projects, there will be 40.4 million African-Americans in the United States and 39.3 million Hispanics. Shortly thereafter, by 2015, Hispanics will outnumber African-Americans (44.0 million to 43.1 million, respectively), making Hispanics the largest minority group in the United States.[1] Recently I saw Latino actor Edward James Olmos being interviewed on television about his newly released book entitled *Americanos* that seeks to celebrate the fact that "Americans" come in all shades and from many different cultures, including those of Latino descent. He stated what many Latino activists and others believe, that there are already more than 40 million Latinos living in our nation today. Whatever the true numbers, it is clear that the sleeping giant has awakened and that our nation is taking notice.

A recent *Chicago Tribune* article about the growth of the Latino population in Chicago stated that in 1997 there were approximately 867,000 Latinos in Cook County alone.[2] Another *Tribune* article quoted the estimate that by the year 2020, 22 percent of the population in the Chicago area, or 2 million people, will be of Latino descent.[3]

WHO ARE THESE LATINOS OR HISPANICS?

Who are these "persons of Spanish-Hispanic origin" that the census claims to have found in the United States?

The short answer is: between 25 and 40 million people who don't know much about each other; who, though bound by the Spanish language, don't all talk alike; who don't all eat the same foods (not all Latinos eat tacos); and who, until coming to the United States, have not seen themselves as "one people."

I can't tell you how many times Anglo or African-American friends or acquaintances have approached me to clarify whether they should refer to "us" as "Latino" or "Hispanic."[4] The reality is that while the terms have come to be used interchangeably to refer to persons of Spanish-speaking descent, we are more accurately called Mexicans, Puerto Ricans, Cubans, Dominicans, Ecuadorians, and so on. We have different customs, different histories, different problems, and different cultural identities.[5]

Listen to the words of Edward James Olmos as he talks about why he would name a book about Latinos in the United States *Americanos*.

> *Why **Americanos**? Why would we give this title to a book on Latinos? There are several reasons. One is that too often society sees us not as Americans but as*

*strangers to this land. We have worked hard to help build this country and we
continue to do so everyday. The face of America should include us. Second, as
Latinos we often think of* **Americanos** *as the others in this country, not us. We,
and especially our children, need to see that we are an integral and equal part of
U.S. society. Third, we wanted a title that would recognize and honor our bilingual heritage and would be easily understood in both English and Spanish. And,
finally, we wanted to illustrate that, much like a quilt woven intricately with
many beautiful fibers, Latinos are a proud and diverse people interwoven with
indigenous, Spanish/European, African, and Asian roots. We are citizens not
only of the United States of America, but also of all the Americas and of the
Latin American countries around the world.[6]*

Earl Shorris explained in his book *Latinos* that, despite the title of
his book, "The theory of it is that there are no Latinos, only diverse
peoples struggling to remain who they are while becoming something
else."[7] *Latinos* and *The Hispanic Challenge* provide important insights
and information about the different peoples and their unique histories
which we, in the U.S.A., lump together into one common category.

THE CHALLENGE OF REACHING THE BARRIO

A continual trend for our community is that a high concentration
of Latinos live in urban centers or "barrios." (A "barrio" is a predomi-
nately Latino community that is usually poor and urban.) In 1980, 50
percent of Latinos lived in large cities, with an additional 37 percent
living in metropolitan areas outside the central cities, making a total of
87 percent urban dwellers. By the 1990 census, this percentage of urban U.S. Latinos had grown to 91.4 percent.[8]

Twenty years ago, the majority of Latinos were concentrated in six
states: California, Arizona, New Mexico, Texas, New York, and Flori-
da. Although these states continue to have the highest percentage of
Latino residents, today an increased number of Latinos live in most of
the major cities of our nation. I was recently in a meeting with the assistant to the mayor of Indianapolis, Indiana, talking about the needs of
the growing Mexican population in that city. He mentioned that over the
past ten years, the Latino population had tripled. He cited the avail-
ability of jobs, affordable housing, and the larger Spanish-speaking
population as factors that were drawing more Latinos to his city. Along
with the growing numbers, his city also was having to address issues
of racial diversity, immigration, and a need for Latino and bilingual
city workers. Cities all across our nation, both large and small, are having similar experiences with the emergence of a new Latino presence
in their communities.

In a very controversial book entitled *Out of the Barrio,* Linda

Chavez takes the position that many Latinos in this country are "pulling themselves up by their bootstraps" and moving out of poverty. She noted that the images of the poor farmworker and welfare mom are not the norm for most Latinos, especially those who have been in this country for more than one generation.[9] Although it is true that many Latino middle-class persons and professionals live throughout our nation, the majority of Latinos still live in adverse poverty and suffer from underemployment. Because many Mexican and Central American workers are here illegally, many are forced into jobs that pay less than minimum wage and have no security or benefits. As you can imagine, this creates a great hardship for families that are struggling to make a living with the constant fear of being deported.

Listen to what Dr. Justo L. González had to say about poverty in the Latino community in his book, *Santa Biblia: The Bible Through Hispanic Eyes:*

> *Poverty, as experienced by vast numbers of Hispanics in our barrios and in our migrant camps, is dehumanization. It dispossesses, not only of money, but also of dignity, of tradition, of identity. At the same time and on the other hand, exile itself is a form of poverty. It does not rob one of money. Perhaps it even improves one's economic condition. But it is also a form of poverty inasmuch as it deprives one of identity, traditions, roots, dignity, family.[10]*

The increased growth, urbanization, and marginalization of Latinos represent an increasing challenge to the evangelical church here in Chicago and in the rest of the U.S.A. The question of if and how we will respond to our Latino "neighbor" is important for all of us, but is of utmost importance for those of us who sense a call to minister in the urban communities of our world.

The Church and the Latino Community

Recently, Dr. Manuel Ortiz wrote an article for *Shout* magazine, a journal for Latino youth workers, in which he categorized four types of church models in relation to youth ministry. I would like to reference these four models to help us think about the church's responsibility to minister in the urban Latino community.[11]

The first model is the "Stay Out Church." In this model, a mostly Anglo congregation finds itself in a community in transition. What for years has been a middle-class, exclusively white community is now turning into a Latino one. (Interestingly, Latinos are often allowed into an Anglo community to keep African-Americans from moving in. As you can imagine, this dynamic can create great tension between these two groups.) What you find in this model is a small group of individuals who refuse to acknowledge the changes that are taking place in the community and who attempt to continue to function as if the demographics of the community were still the same as in the past. Although many of their new neighbors are now Spanish speaking, they have no desire or intention to reach out to them. In fact, they find many ways to communicate that outsiders are not welcome. The result is that they are no longer effective in living out the biblical mandate of loving their neighbor.

The second model is the "Move Out Church." Here you find a congregation in which most of the members eventually move out of the community, either because it has changed ethnically or because of the urban problems that exist. In either case, while the church building is still in the barrio, the people of God no longer are there, except for Sunday mornings. Again, the result is no relationship and no interaction with the people and no true impact for the cause of Christ in the community.

The third model we find is the "Sold Out Church." After possibly years of fading ministry and declining membership, this church finally throws in the towel and decides that it can no longer be effective in that community, so it moves out of the barrio. Often this is the case with older denominations that can consolidate members into other congregations, or with churches that can afford to build or buy a facility in a "nicer part of town." The result here is that Christian witness is diminished and individuals with valuable leadership abilities frequently leave the very communities where they are most needed.

Finally, the "Reach Out Church" is a model that not only keeps its building in the barrio, but also has a commitment to have its members engaged in the life of the barrio, and, in many cases, to have a significant percentage of its committed members living in the community. This is the only church that can bring about the social and spiritual transformation of our barrios. In order to reach out effectively, we must become informed about and involved with the Latino people and community. The more we know and understand the struggles, cultural distinctives, and dynamics of the barrio, the better prepared we will be to be used by God as agents of hope in the Latino community.

Latino Culture and Christianity

Although it is impossible to summarize the experiences of all Latinos in this country in any one story or family history, I would like to tell a bit of my experience as a Mexican-American growing up in California, and how my life was changed by hearing and accepting the call to follow Christ.

Like most Mexican-American families, ours was culturally immersed in the Roman Catholic tradition. Although I never remember "church life" as being particularly important, I knew that I was "Catholic" and that being so was essential to our family identity. Again, Dr. Ortiz did a fine job of documenting the significant issues related to our Roman Catholic roots in *The Hispanic Challenge.*

Given my family's strong cultural and emotional ties to the Catholic church, it was no small thing when, as a junior in high school, I attended a "Christian" camp and returned home declaring that I had given my life to Jesus and had become a Christian. I knew as I was hearing stories about the love of God and the person of Jesus Christ that these words sounded familiar, but I also knew that I was entering strange territory that would challenge my family and cultural loyalties. My Roman Catholic loyalties were the only expression of spirituality and church life that I had ever known.

I am telling this because, for myself and for many Latinos who decide to follow Christ outside of the Roman Catholic church, it represents not only leaving sin behind, but also turning away from an essential part of our cultural identity.

That week of camp in 1976 gave me two pivotal things: a new relationship with God through the forgiveness I found in Christ, and the discovery of a lifelong call to work in the barrio. I will never forget crying under a big tree as I thought about God's incredible love for me. I will also always remember feeling burdened by the fact that only three other Mexican-Americans were present at that camp of two hundred high school kids. Even then, I felt a sense of call to see that other kids "like me" had an opportunity to experience the life-changing encounter I had had with Jesus.

Two years later, upon arriving at a small Christian liberal arts college in the Northwest, I again experienced the culture shock of being in a predominantly Christian setting where few others identified themselves as Hispanic or Latino. In fact, the school had only one other such student. It was a challenge to maintain my call to the Latino community as I was so isolated from the barrio. Despite the challenge, God was faithful in expanding both my worldview and the understanding of myself in relationship to the rest of society, and in keeping the fires burning in my heart for "my people." It didn't hurt that my mother often sent me care packages that included chorizo and homemade flour tortillas.

Julia Alvarez, in her book *How the Garcia Girls Lost Their Accents,* told the story of a family being uprooted from its home in the Dominican Republic. The family moved to New York, where they found a life drastically different from the tropical island they called home. The book chronicles how the four Garcia sisters plunged into the American mainstream, forgetting their Spanish, but remained caught between two worlds.[12]

In the midst of the humor found in this story, I can identify with the pain and confusion of being both Mexican and American. To make things even more interesting, in my case I also had the struggle of finding my place in a new Christian, middle-class, and Anglo culture.

Upon graduating from Whitworth College in Spokane, Washington, I was offered a full-time ministry position with a national youth ministry organization and assigned to live and minister in San Francisco. At the time, I never thought much about whether I was brought on staff for my ministry ability, spiritual maturity, or ethnic background. I suspect all three factors had a bit to do with why they took a chance on a twenty-two-year-old Mexican-American young man from the Sunnyhills barrio in Milpitas, California.

DISCOVERING INCARNATIONAL MINISTRY

From the day I arrived in San Francisco, I never considered living anywhere but in the barrio. Even though I had forgotten much of my Spanish and found myself many times identifying more with my Anglo brothers and sisters than with the poor, uneducated, first-generation Mexicans and Central Americans who were my new neighbors in the Mission District, I always felt it important that I live in the neighborhood.

In those early years of youth ministry I must have heard the term "incarnational ministry" a million times. It was not only a concept for me, but a way of life, as an older adult entered my life and built a relationship with me. In a very real sense, during those years Bob Kellogg incarnated his life into my life, and in so doing became God's instrument to help me find Christ. The idea of entering into the youth culture was easy for me to embrace, but I also knew that entering the neighborhood where kids lived helped to give me credibility with them because I was willing to live where they lived. Somehow, this concept of incarnation was ingrained in my mind and heart.

Though I did not know Dr. John Perkins at the time, his words in *With Justice for All* describe how I felt about living in the community.

> *How then shall we proclaim Good News to the poor? Once again Jesus is our model. "The Word became flesh, and dwelt among us, and we beheld His glory, glory as of the only begotten from the Father, full of grace and truth" (John 1:14). Jesus relocated. He didn't commute to earth one day a week and shoot*

back up to heaven. He left His throne and became one of us so that we might see the life of God revealed in Him.

> *Paul says that we are to have this same attitude Jesus expressed when He humbled Himself: "Have this attitude in yourselves which was also in Christ Jesus, who, although He existed in the form of God, did not regard equality with God a thing to be grasped, but emptied Himself, taking the form of a bond-servant, and being made in the likeness of men. And being found in appearance as man, He humbled Himself by becoming obedient to the point of death, even death on a cross" (Phil. 2:5–8).[13] (quotations use the NASB, 1977 edition)*

After two years of training in the Mission District, I was given the opportunity to return to the San Jose area to establish an urban outreach in the public high schools. Again, I quickly found a home in the heart of the barrio in East San Jose. This time, though, I moved in with my new wife, Marianne, who had just signed up for the adventure of her life. She had been involved in full-time urban ministry for five years when we got married, but all of her experience had been in the African-American community. Now she was moving into a Mexican barrio, having to adjust to a different culture, and moving to the other side of the country—all in her first days of marriage.

The longer we worked with high school kids in the "hood," the more we realized that it was impossible to do effective youth ministry without also working with the parents. Especially in the Latino culture, we found it essential that we include the parents and even siblings whenever possible. I will never forget getting to know a young man from Guatemala named Wilbert. Quickly I became very good friends with him, his brothers, his aunt with whom he lived, and his *abuelita* (grandmother). Very naturally we had great opportunities not only to reach kids for Christ, but also their whole families, as we were invited into their homes and their lives.

We also began to feel that we had to start working with youth at an earlier age, as by the time they were in high school many were already totally involved in gangs and exposed to tremendous difficulties and problems. We were discovering, as well, that almost none of the kids we were reaching out to were finding their way into a local church. Finally, we were discouraged to see that the neighborhood where we lived, and where these kids had to grow up, was in desperate need of transformation, revitalization, and leadership. We knew that focusing only on changing individual kids' lives was not enough to sustain the healthy transformation of our barrio.

After five years of working primarily with youth in East San Jose, we joined an urban ministry in San Jose that was working more wholistically in the community. Among the many exciting new ministry skills we learned during this time was how to evangelize and disciple children and how to develop urban and suburban partnerships. In the third year of our new ministry venture, Dr. John Perkins was invited to address our staff. I was excited to hear him speak passionately about serving the poor and about what he called Christian Community Development. So many of the things he addressed resonated with my longing to see a church in the Latino community that was addressing the spiritual and social needs of the barrio.

Developing a Model of Incarnational Ministry in the Barrio

In October of 1989, I attended the first Christian Community Development Association conference at Lawndale Community Church in Chicago. Listening to Dr. Perkins teach about what he calls the 3 Rs of Relocation, Reconciliation, and Redistribution convinced me that I needed to embrace and apply these biblical principles in the Latino community. Not only did I leave from that conference in Chicago having discovered this CCD philosophy of urban ministry, but I also discovered the Mexican neighborhood of La Villita directly south of the Lawndale community.

Key in the igniting of my passion for La Villita was seeing the wholistic ministry approach of Lawndale Community Church being lived out in its urban African-American neighborhood.[14] I had never seen a health clinic, educational learning center, and full-sized basketball gym side by side with the worship area and pastoral offices of a church. I knew that this form of "incarnational ministry" was exactly what was lacking in the barrio—a church-based ministry, committed to meeting the spiritual and social needs of Latinos, all motivated and empowered by the love of Jesus Christ. I left Chicago with a deep sense that God was calling us to live and minister in La Villita.

A few months after visiting Lawndale and speaking to Pastor Gordon about working in partnership to establish a new ministry in La Villita, my wife, Marianne, and I traveled to Chicago to meet with him on a bitterly cold December weekend. I remember going into our meeting expecting to hear about the excitement of living in the barrio and to get Marianne all fired up about moving to Chicago and starting a church. Instead, Pastor Gordon wisely gave us a clear and realistic picture of the challenges that awaited us if we decided to move to La Villita.

Although the story of how we began the ministry in La Villita can be read in the book *Restoring At-Risk Communities: Doing It Together and Doing It Right* edited by Dr. John Perkins, I would like to highlight a number of key principles that we have learned and have attempted to apply here in Chicago, and that I believe are essential for bringing about the transformation of the barrios of our nation.[15]

A Whole Person Approach to Ministry

After nine years in La Villita, I am more convinced than ever that in order to truly affect the Latino communities of our nation with the gospel, we must be committed to a wholistic (whole person) approach to ministry.

The gospel of Mark has two accounts of Jesus multiplying bread and fishes to feed the multitudes. In chapter 6, where Jesus fed five thousand men, verse 34 tells us that He was moved with compassion, because the people were like sheep without a shepherd.

In response to this need that Jesus saw, Mark tells us that Jesus began to teach them many things. In chapter 8, Mark gives the account of the feeding of the four thousand. On this occasion it says that when Jesus saw that the multitudes had gone so long without food, He was moved to immediately organize the troops to feed them. I love the whole-person concern of Jesus.

In the Latino community, where cultural Catholic roots are so deep, I have found that people are not really looking for a new or different religion. The church has played an important role in the lives of many families as they have celebrated baptisms, weddings, special holidays, and funerals in their local parishes. But, although many Latino families and individuals have great loyalty to the church of their upbringing, a great many are not very involved in the life of the parish. Our experience has been that in order to get beyond the resistance of many Latinos to any religious activity outside of the Roman Catholic experience, we must begin with establishing a genuine relationship, or by meeting a pressing "felt need."

Two years after establishing La Villita Community Church, we began the process of starting a community development organization that would be formally connected to the church, but that would focus on mobilizing the members of our body and the residents of the community in addressing the issues they felt were important in La Villita. We held numerous meetings and had many people fill out a questionnaire that helped us to identify the most significant concerns of our neighbors.

We found that parents were very concerned about the safety of their children. They were worried about their sons and daughters being intimidated by local gangs and being enticed to join, either out of fear or rebellion. We heard concerns about kids doing poorly in school and about the need for recreational and social activities for children and youth. The lack of jobs was mentioned, as well as immigration problems, affordable housing, and substance abuse issues. As we looked at all of the input of the people and assessed our organizational capacity and the passions of the people we had in the ministry at the time, we realized that the most strategic focus we could have was to work with children and youth. We were especially concerned about developing strong leaders who would have a vision for living and investing in La Villita.

At that time, part of our team included a couple from New York who joined us as interns, an urban missionary assigned to our church by International Teams, and Sergio Martinez, a Mexican brother who had been helping with the development of our children's ministry. Together we began an after-school tutoring program to meet the educational needs of kids in elementary school and to build relationships with them and their families. We knew that if we served these children and loved them in the name of Jesus, we would eventually earn the right to present the gospel in a way they would not reject.

In those early days, we had a handful of kids, a few tables and chairs, a couple of old computers, and some Moody Bible Institute volunteers working with us to develop a ministry that would begin to meet the whole-person needs of these kids. We knew they needed to know Jesus, but they also needed to learn how to read and gain the learning skills that would help them excel in school. We were on our way to developing the next generation of leaders for our barrio and our church.

One of the many families we have had in our program the past years is the Bravo family. Jose Luis and his wife began to send their three children to Si, Se Puede (Yes, You Can) after they visited the Lawndale Christian Health Center and the Latino chaplain informed them about the program. Right away it became obvious to them that their children were not only doing better in school, but that they were enjoying learning about the Bible. The more they stayed involved, the more they began to feel comfortable talking with the leaders of the program and interacting with other parents. Eventually, the Bravo family visited a Sunday morning service, and each made a commitment to follow Christ. What began with a clinic visit and an educational program for their kids has become a new way of life in Christ for the entire family.

Just last year Jose Luis and his family moved into a new home that our development corporation built with volunteers from our congregation and from Willow Creek Community Church. Their children are fully involved in the ministry's youth programs, Herminia is a small-group leader in the church, and Jose Luis is an usher at our Sunday morning service. He makes new visitors feel as welcome as he felt just a few years ago. By meeting the practical needs of the Bravo family, and many other families like theirs, the Holy Spirit is giving us a multitude of opportunities to befriend, evangelize, and disciple entire families in the barrio.

In the last nine years, we have attempted many ways to meet the felt needs of our neighbors. We have established a state-of-the-art computer center to prepare our young people for the coming century. We are working with a truancy program at the local high school to help youth stay in school. We are helping dozens of men and women find jobs. We are teaching English to our Spanish-speaking neighbors. And finally, we have even built a new home in the community to help a family become a homeowner. Why have we spent the time and energy to establish all of these ministries and projects? To offer our neighbors a cup of cold water as they thirst for the basic needs of life. And to put us in a great position to minister the Good News of Jesus Christ with extraordinary power and authority. When we meet the practical needs of people in our barrio like Jesus did while He was incarnated in our world, lives are changed for all of eternity.

An Incarnational Approach: Relocating, Remaining, or Returning

Almost every day I drive past a huge, beautiful house one block from our home in La Villita. Nine years ago when we arrived in the city, that house was a disaster. It was overgrown with trees, filthy with garbage inside and out, and had been abandoned for many years. Like many others in the neighborhood, I passed by many times both disgusted with the condition of this place and intrigued with the thought of being able to acquire this giant house to restore. Once, I told my wife these thoughts, only to be reminded that we already had one home in need of major repairs. Another major obstacle to anyone doing anything with this property was that the owners were not open to selling to anyone who was Mexican or African-American. Not many white families were dying to tackle this project—that is, until Mike and Terry Kijowski felt called to join us in the planting of the church in La Villita and called to move into the community themselves. They were able to buy the house, and after a few years of heavy praying and hard work, they finally completed the rehabilitation. Today it is a beautiful brick house, filled with kids and many visitors. Over the years many individuals and especially women in crisis have found refuge and hospitality in this home. These visitors have seen a family very different from their own, a family living out their faith in Christ.

Families like the Kijowskis have been an example of how an Anglo family can move into a mostly Mexican community and win the hearts of their neighbors through their love. Both Mike and Terry work at the Lawndale Christian Health Center, which serves the needs of thousands of needy and uninsured residents from La Villita. Both have learned to speak excellent Spanish, and Mike has been the key leader of our children's ministry for the last few years. Without relocating into the barrio of La Villita, it is doubtful they would be having the same impact in the lives of the Mexican residents who are now their neighbors.

Through the ministry of the Lawndale Christian Health Center, I met a Mexican man who became one of my first friends in La Villita. Although my friend has had a hard time fully surrendering his life to Christ, God has had an incredible impact on the rest of his family. His ex-wife, Juanita, and her son Manuel Jr., and daughter Christina, have become some of our best friends over the years.

A few years ago, Juanita talked to me about her desire to buy a home. She had been taking care of her family as a single mom for a good while and was working a lot of overtime to save money to sustain her family and purchase a home. I will never forget when she told me that she wanted to stay in La Villita to make an impact in her community. I was affected by the decision she made, because so many Mexican families are just waiting to leave the barrio as soon as possible. It is a scary decision to raise a teenage daughter in La Villita without a husband, but Juanita made the choice to stay and work to reach her community for Christ, even though it could have been easy to leave for the suburbs. God has blessed Juanita. Her son, his wife, Reina, and their three beautiful kids live in the neighborhood as well, and they are very involved in the junior-high ministry of our church. Also, Juanita's daughter, Christina, is on fire for serving Christ. She is working to help her high school friends come to know Jesus. The Valdez family are shining lights for the gospel in La Villita. Their commitment to remain in the barrio to be instruments of change and transformation will make all the difference in the world for many of the neighbors and family members they encounter every day.

When I first decided to move to La Villita in 1990, one of my greatest fears was having to speak Spanish in public. Although I was born close to the Mexican border in Texas and grew up speaking only Spanish until I entered kindergarten, I had all but forgotten how to speak the language by the time I got out of college. At home and with my grandparents, Spanish was spoken to me, but I answered in English. Can you imagine the challenge I had coming to a neighborhood where the majority of the Mexican-descent residents spoke primarily Spanish? What scared me the most was the realization that I was not only going to have to speak Spanish, but that I was going to have to preach in Spanish as well.

Many people are surprised that I could not speak the language. The truth is, that is not uncommon for second- and third-generation Latinos. In fact, I believe it is one of the barriers that keep some U.S.-born Latinos from returning to live and minister in the barrio.

Recently, two young women from Santa Ana, California, graduated from Moody Bible Institute in Chicago. Lori was looking for a place to do youth ministry, and she soon found herself interviewing and accepting the role of directing our after-school educational program and summer day camp program. Elsa came back to Chicago wanting to live in the barrio and wanting to use her social-work skills in the Latino community. Lori and Elsa have chosen not only to work and minister in the barrio, but to worship in our congregation and live in La Villita as well. It has not been easy for Lori and Elsa to live in La Villita, as they have had their car windows broken a few times and they are so far from home. But the fact they have been willing to return to the barrio is making a huge difference in their lives and in the lives of others.

When we live in the neighborhood, we demonstrate in a powerful way to our neighbors that we love the barrio. I love to hear my mentor Wayne Gordon talk about how great Chicago is. Unlike many Chicago residents who brag about the championship basketball teams, the beautiful lakefront, and all the wonderful restaurants, Pastor Gordon loves to talk about the neighborhood of North Lawndale where he and his family have lived for more than twenty years. He sees this urban inner city community as a community full of assets and resources. Where sociologists and city planners only see problems to be solved and people to be managed, "Coach" (as Pastor Gordon is called) sees people with great potential living in a neighborhood full of promise. He believes that the neighborhood, through Christ, is a blessed place to live, worship God, and raise a family.

Listen to the words of King David in Psalm 132:13–14 that speak about God's love for the city of Jerusalem: "For the Lord has chosen Jerusalem; he has desired it as his home. 'This is my home where I will live forever,' he said. 'I will live here, for this is the place I desired'" (NLT). Do we love our city like that?

John 3:16 tells us that the motivation for God sending, or incarnating His only Son into a dying world, was His love. If we are going to have a real impact in the barrio, we must love the people and the community we are called to serve in. Effective ministry in the Latino community must begin with pastors and other committed believers who are filled with love and compassion for their barrio and have a desire to make it their home.

Conclusion: Are We Ready?

T oday, the church has new and exciting opportunities to affect the barrios of our nation with the gospel. If we are willing to take the risky step of living in the community and of meeting the whole-person needs of our Latino neighbors, not only will individual lives be turned around, but whole communities will be renewed by the power of Jesus Christ. In fact, not only will cities in our country be affected, but also cities all over Central and South America as well. The question is, Will we rise up and meet this challenge?

Reflection Questions

1. The Latino community in the United States has been called the "Sleeping Giant" because of its amazing growth in demographics. What have you learned reading this chapter about the approach the church must take to reach the Latino community with the gospel?

2. Using the incarnation of Jesus Christ as our model, what implications would being called to minister in the Latino community have for your life and ministry? What would it mean for you to incarnate your life in the barrio?

3. What next steps could you take to gain a better understanding of the Latino culture or cultures in your city? What has been the most significant insight you have gained from reading this chapter?

4. How could your church become involved in ministering to the Latino community in your city or state?

chapter sixteen

REACHING THE CHINESE COMMUNITY

THE CHINESE CHRISTIAN UNION CHURCH/PUI TAK CENTER

DAVID WU AND MICHAEL TSANG

Introduction:
The Chinese-American Population

According to the United States Bureau of the Census, Asian-Americans are the fastest growing ethnic group by percentage growth in the United States. From July 1990 to February 1998, the Asian and Pacific Islander population grew 35 percent to an estimated population of 10.2 million. Chinese people account for nearly 2 million of the Asian and Pacific Islanders in the United States.[1]

Asian-Americans and Chinese-Americans are as diverse as the many regions and cultures from which they come. Some came as students and are now highly educated professionals. Some came from war-torn countries as refugees. Others were sponsored by relatives and came as immigrants with limited education and resources. Still others are second-, third-, fourth-, and, sometimes, fifth-generation individuals who often identify more with American culture than with their Asian heritage.

This chapter focuses on the Chinese Christian Union Church (CCUC) and the Pui Tak Center in Chicago's Chinatown and their role in reaching Chinese living in Chinatown and the nearby Bridgeport community. Many principles in this chapter are relevant to Christian ministries seeking to reach other Asian and immigrant communities in Chicago and beyond.

CHINESE IN CHICAGO

Chinese people began moving to Chicago in the late 1800s. The earliest Chinese immigrants in Chicago arrived after the completion of the transcontinental railroad. Before that time, most Chinese immigrants had settled on the West Coast. The first Chinatown in Chicago was located downtown near Clark and Van Buren. Due to rising housing costs in that area in the early 1900s, most of the Chinese population moved to the neighborhood near Cermak Road and Wentworth Avenue, the location of today's Chinatown.[2]

By the early 1970s, Chinatown's housing was filled to capacity. Families began moving to the nearby Bridgeport community, which is southwest of Chinatown. By 1990, the Chinese population in Bridgeport had grown to exceed the Chinese population in Chinatown.[3] At the start of the 1990s, 10,379 Chinese lived in the Chinatown and Bridgeport communities.[4] Most community leaders estimate there are now more than 20,000 Chinese living in this area. Population growth is attributed to the facts that immigration continues to bring more Chinese to Chicago and that more families are staying within the community as new and better housing is made available near Chinatown.

A typical new immigrant family comes to the United States legally under immigration provisions that allow for family reunification. Most new immigrants share an apartment with relatives in the Chinatown or Bridgeport community. Quite often, all working-age adults will quickly find work in a Chinese restaurant or another Chinese-owned business that does not require English proficiency or technical vocational skills. Usually by the end of the first year, the new immigrant family has saved enough money to move into its own apartment and will begin saving money for a car and other material goods. After a number of years, many immigrant families try to purchase a two-flat apartment building. They will typically live in one apartment unit and rent out the other unit to help pay for household expenses.

Traditionally, Chinese families are extended and intact. It is still common to find three generations living together in Chinatown. Since in many families both parents work, grandparents are often responsible for child care. This arrangement works well while the children are young but often is tension filled when the children reach junior high and high school age. Children learn English quickly and begin adopting American values. The grandparents struggle to learn English and have a difficult time accepting new values.

Recently, marital problems are on the rise. The stress of immigration to an unfamiliar culture, long working hours, and a newfound social freedom for women has given rise to a growing number of marriages experiencing separation and divorce. CCUC's nursery school program rarely had children from broken homes fifteen years ago. Now it is not uncommon to have at least one child each year from a broken home. Although this suggests that the divorce rate is still much lower than among other Americans, it is a break from traditional Chinese culture.

To the casual observer, Chinese living in Chinatown are not formally religious. Most do not regularly attend religious services, whether Protestant, Catholic, or Buddhist. Besides the Chinese Christian Union Church and its sister church in Bridgeport, religious institutions include a Catholic church in Chinatown and a Buddhist temple and a Lutheran church in Bridgeport. But the power of the supernatural does play an important role in the minds of many new immigrants. Many Chinese believe in spirits and practice forms of ancestor worship.

> *In China, ancestor worship is an act of veneration, honor and obligation. People venerate their deceased relatives because they have an obligation to care for their souls who now live in a shadowy afterworld. . . . Neglect of paying proper respect will displease an ancestor, who will then punish his descendants like naughty children . . . even those modern urban Chinese who have abandoned the belief that ancestors actually need the livings' offerings continue the practice, for to abandon these commemorative rites makes most families feel uncomfortable.[5]*

CHINESE CHRISTIANS IN CHICAGO

In most places in the world, the percentage of the Chinese population that is Christian ranges from none to 10 percent.[6] This low percentage also holds true in Chicago, where there are twenty-nine Chinese churches with a membership of about three thousand.[7] Even with a growing number of Chinese Christians attending non-Chinese churches, probably fewer than 10 percent of the 43,016 Chinese living in the Chicago metropolitan area are Christians, although those numbers are fluid.[8]

Most of the Chinese churches are located in the suburbs and have between fifty and two hundred regular attenders. Typically, these churches conduct their programs using a Chinese dialect (Mandarin, Cantonese, or Taiwanese). The larger churches may have a smaller ministry serving English-speaking Chinese. The churches work together through the United Chinese Churches of Chicago. This network organizes monthly prayer meetings for the pastors, pastoral retreats, joint Easter sunrise services, and annual revival meetings.

Chinese Christian Union Church and Pui Tak Center

In the early 1900s, five Protestant denominations (Baptist, Congregational, Presbyterian, Methodist, and the Disciples of Christ) sent home missionaries to conduct Sunday school classes to reach Chinese families living in Chinatown. This effort led to the formation of the Chinese Evangelical Church in 1915. By the mid-1940s, the church had become financially independent and had a growing core of Chinese Christian leaders. It was renamed the Chinese Christian Union Church (CCUC) to reflect the important role that the five denominations made in helping to establish the church.[9]

During the early years, most of the church's programs were conducted in Cantonese, which was the Chinese dialect spoken by most of Chinatown's residents. These residents were originally from the Guangdong province in southern China. Due to the growing number of American-born Chinese (ABCs), the church began conducting Cantonese-English bilingual services in the 1950s and eventually established an English service in the early 1960s. Also in the 1960s, the church added an educational wing and gymnasium. The gym has played a strategic role in reaching children and youth in the community since there are no other gyms in the community open to the public.

As a result of normalized relations with the People's Republic of China a new wave of Chinese immigrants came to Chinatown in the early 1980s. Although many continued to come from the southern parts of China, others came from other regions of China and primarily spoke Mandarin, the official language of China. In the early 1980s, CCUC established a Mandarin-speaking ministry to serve this growing group. A large part of this congregation's ministry has been to serve Chinese international students who are pursuing undergraduate or graduate degrees at local colleges or universities.

In colleges and universities in the United States during the 1997–98 school year, there were 42,503 students from China, 30,487 students from Taiwan, and 10,942 students from Hong Kong.[10] Outreach to these students is strategic for world evangelism since many of these students will return to their home countries after they finish their studies. Once home, many of them will become leaders in business, government, and higher education and will have access to people and situations that are unavailable to traditional missionaries.

Today, nearly eight hundred adults and four hundred children participate in CCUC's programs each week. Ranked by size, the largest congregation of the church is the Cantonese congregation (average attendance of 350), then the English congregation (average of 275), and finally the Mandarin congregation (average 125). The church also has a small Monday morning service. This service was started in 1970 to serve restaurant workers. Restaurant workers typically work ten to twelve hours per day, six days per week. Often, restaurant workers have Mondays off when many small family-owned Chinese restaurants are closed. Since they work on Sundays and evenings, they are unable to attend regular church activities.

Recently, the church has emphasized small groups. Each language congregation is subdivided into fellowship groups based on age and/or marital status. Since many visitors attend the church, the small groups and fellowship groups play a critical role in integrating visitors into the life of the body.

In the 1980s, CCUC planted two sister churches. These sister churches were started in response to demographic shifts in the Chinese population. In 1984, CCUC established a Gospel Center in Bridgeport to target new immigrant families. A church was eventually established that has ministries in both Cantonese and Mandarin.

Another growing segment in the Chinese population of the Chicago area is that in the far north suburbs. These tend to be professionals who are either American-born Chinese or overseas-born Chinese who came to the United States to attend college or graduate school. Foreign students are allowed to stay in the United States after they receive their degrees if an employer petitions the INS for permission for them to stay based upon their unique training and qualifications. CCUC-North was established in the north suburb of Highland Park in 1986 and seeks to reach Chinese individuals and families who live in that area.

In 1993, CCUC was looking for space to expand its programs in Chinatown. At that time, the federal government was selling the former On Leong Association's building, which had been seized in the late 1980s due to illegal gambling activities. Due to the impressive architecture and role of the On Leong Association, this building was once considered Chinatown's "City Hall." In the past, the On Leong Association had operated an apartment building for new arrivals from China, Chinese cultural programs for children such as Chinese lion dancing, a community court that helped resolve civil disputes between community members, and a small business development program. Many organizations were interested in bidding for the building, including various business groups and a Buddhist temple that was trying to increase its presence in Chinatown.

Through many miracles, the church's bid was accepted and funds were raised to purchase and renovate the building. In the fall of 1995, the church dedicated the building and renamed it as the Pui Tak Center. In Chinese, "Pui Tak" means "building moral character and virtue." This was the name of the church's Chinese school and nursery school, which were established in the early 1950s and already well recognized in the community for the church's efforts in meeting the community's physical and social needs. Through its educational, family, and community services, the Pui Tak Center seeks to be a witness to God's love in both words and action.

Meeting Community Needs

Throughout its history, CCUC has sought to be a witness to the Chinatown community through acts of compassion and service. It was not uncommon in the early years for church members to spend time after church tutoring new immigrants in English. The church developed a Chinese language school because many parents in the community wanted their children to improve their Chinese language abilities. The nursery school was started to meet the needs of preschoolers. Since many young children are cared for by grandparents, they often speak Chinese at home and begin school with a limited grasp of English. The nursery nchool helps to bridge that gap by teaching the children English and exposing them to a formal learning environment. Other efforts include English as a Second Language classes, hosting a volunteer medical clinic staffed by Chinese Christian doctors, and opening up the church's gym to community children and youth.

This concern for the social needs of the community, combined with a desire to reach the community with the gospel, led to establishing the Pui Tak Center. The Pui Tak Center now serves more than one thousand individuals each year through its adult English classes and tutoring services, children and youth programs, activities for senior citizens, and new immigrant services. One of the Pui Tak Center's visions is to be a lighthouse for new immigrants. The center hopes that everyone in the community, nonbelievers as well as believers, will point new immigrants to come to the center because there they will be helped by caring Christians.

Language-Based Ministries

Most ethnic churches begin with their ministries conducted in the native language. Worship services, fellowship groups, and Sunday school programs are conducted to meet the needs of the new immigrants. But over time, more and more of the children in the church and in the community speak English better than the native language and their values are shaped more by American culture than by the native culture. This problem of meeting the needs of the second generation is not obvious until the children become older. Younger children are brought to church by their parents and do not have the ability to say that they will not go to church. But as teenagers, they often can choose for themselves whether to go to church. If the ethnic church is seen as irrelevant because all the programs are conducted in the native language and the gospel is presented only in a manner relevant to the new immigrants, the youth may decide that the church has nothing to offer.

From an outside perspective, it seems obvious that ethnic churches should develop some ministries to serve the spiritual needs of the younger generation. But cultural and financial issues affect this decision. Some in the older generation want the children to learn and respect the native culture. They hope that the church can play a role in teaching the native language and preserving the cultural heritage, and thus they resist incorporating English into the life of the church. In addition, more staff may be needed to start an English-language ministry since the current staff may not speak English well and may not understand the American culture enough to be effective at reaching American-born Chinese youth. Many small ethnic churches may not be able to afford even a part-time youth worker and will have to depend on recruiting lay volunteers.

Multiple-language ministries vary to a great extent. Usually, the first English-language ministries in an ethnic church are Sunday school classes or fellowship groups for children and youth. The next step is to have side-by-side translation of the sermon from the native language into English. A final step is to develop separate language ministries so that there are both English and Chinese services.

The handling of this language and cultural issue is one of the most critical decisions that ethnic churches face. Some avoid addressing this issue and lose their second-generation youth and young adults. Sometimes, the push for separate-language ministries divides the church because the pace of change is too fast or too slow. Recently, there has been a growth of Asian-American churches that seek to reach American-born Chinese, Japanese, and Koreans. These churches feel that many second- and third-generation Asian-Americans are dropping out of the ethnic churches and that there must be a new kind of church to win them back.

Some of the important factors that churches consider when establishing separate-language ministries include:

* How do we maintain unity while allowing each language group to develop programs that effectively evangelize and disciple its peers?

* How do the language ministries honor and value one another in spite of the ministries' differences in style, size, and the age of their leadership?
* Is the resistance to change or the desire for change driven by cultural values (American or Chinese) rather than by Scripture and God's leading?

As a large church with a long history of separate-language ministries, the Chinese Christian Union Church deals with different issues than a small church that is only beginning to feel the cultural tensions between the generations. One constant issue facing the CCUC is "What is church unity?" Over the years, all three congregations have tried to worship together a few times per year. The logistical difficulties of space and the need to interpret twice discourages combined worship services. Unity has been aided by a joint process to develop one mission statement and set of goals for the entire church. The various committees and boards (Christian education, youth board, foreign missions department, deacon and trustee boards) draw representatives from each of the congregations. The use of English at these meetings occasionally precludes some from feeling that they are a part. At the level of individual members, it remains a challenge to get every member to be concerned with issues affecting other language ministries in addition to their own.

 ## Metropolitan Church

Traditionally, most churches draw from a relatively close geographic area. But many Christians are willing to travel long distances to participate in an ethnic congregation. Chinese Christian Union Church is no exception. Some CCUC members commute up to an hour from the far north and western suburbs or Northwest Indiana to get to church. Some of these long commuters grew up in Chinatown and still have relatives living there. Along with CCUC being their home church, coming to Chinatown on Sundays allows them to see parents and grandparents and shop for the week's groceries. Others who don't have these kinds of ties to CCUC still may be willing to drive because they want to be in a larger Chinese church that has programs meeting the needs of each of their family members. Others are attracted by the desire to serve in one of the many church ministries.

There are numerous challenges to being a metropolitan church. First, some church members may be hesitant to invite friends because of the long commute. This commute is often compounded by the fact that their neighbors, friends, and co-workers may not be Chinese or may not feel comfortable in a Chinese church. Second, there have been times in which the church was viewed as not caring for the community. Some neighbors perceived church members as people who take their parking spaces but do not give back to the community. CCUC and Pui Tak Center have tried to foster positive feelings between them and the community by getting involved in community issues as well as through community service efforts. Third, since many leaders of the church do not live in Chinatown, Sunday afternoons are often used for committee and board meetings. This may result in leaders feeling that Sundays are long days of ministry and meetings rather than days of worship and rest.

Children and Youth Ministries

Ministry to children and youth has always been a strong emphasis of CCUC. Although parents may be personally resistant to the gospel, they readily send their children to church because they feel that Christians are good people and will teach their children how to be moral. Throughout its history, CCUC has been blessed with people committed to reaching the children and youth in the community. In their lives, the children find role models. Although most young people admire the sacrifices that their parents have made to immigrate to the United States and provide a new life for them, relationships with parents can be strained because of the demands of their parents' work and the growing cultural tensions.

In terms of evangelizing adults, CCUC has found parents of preschoolers the most receptive in learning about Christianity. Although non-Christian parents with older children just drop off their children for church, parents with younger children enjoy talking with other parents and watching their children interact with others. This has given Sunday school teachers opportunities to get to know the parents and discuss the gospel with them.

Building Connections Through Small Groups

In today's highly stressful society, people have a need for relationships. Many churches have rediscovered what the early Christians found: Small groups are essential to the growth of Christians. CCUC has had a long history of dividing the congregation into fellowship groups according to language and age characteristics. Although this was effective when the church was smaller, many of these fellowship groups have themselves grown so large that the needs of some individuals could not be effectively met. In recent years, CCUC has found that small groups are the best vehicle for discipling. These small groups care for the needs of group members as well as outreach to newcomers.

Role of Non–Chinese in Ministry to Chinese

During many times in the church's history, the church would have greatly struggled if not for the help of non-Chinese Christians who served as youth workers and Sunday school teachers. The earliest work among Chinese in Chicago was carried out by home missionaries from the various denominations that helped establish the church. Even after the church became more established, a group of non-Chinese Christians served as Sunday school teachers. They made it a point to pick up their students from their homes and gain the confidence of the parents. One of these individuals developed a vision for serving pre-school children. She became the founder of the church's nursery school and directed this ministry for more than thirty years.

More recently, CCUC and the Pui Tak Center have benefited from students who were studying at Wheaton College or Moody Bible Institute. Many of these college students wanted to learn more about the Chinese culture because they were interested in becoming missionaries in Asia. At CCUC, they have served primarily as Sunday school teachers. At the Pui Tak Center, they have served as English tutors to new immigrant children and adults.

Tutoring has been a good experience for both the college students and the new immigrants being tutored. For many new immigrants, this relationship with a tutor is the first time that they have ever talked in length with a person who was not Chinese. Even if they have been studying English for a few years, they may not use English every day since they can get the things they need in Chinatown where the store clerks speak Cantonese and Mandarin. Through tutoring, new immigrant students have a chance to practice English, gain confidence that they can communicate, and develop a friendship with someone who can help them understand the culture. A number of college students who have been English tutors at the Pui Tak Center have gone on to pursue training in teaching English as a Second Language (ESL) or have gone overseas to teach English. They have found that their experience at the Pui Tak Center gave them an invaluable introduction to using ESL ministry in sharing the gospel.

BARRIERS TO THE GOSPEL IN CHINATOWN

Lack of Awareness of the Gospel/Relationship with Christians

The most important barrier facing many living in Chinatown is a lack of awareness of the gospel. In China, they never had the opportunity to hear the gospel. Now that they are in the United States, Christianity continues to be irrelevant to the lives of many.

One of the crucial aspects to the Pui Tak Center's ministry is its pre-evangelistic work. Through the community service work, new immigrants have an opportunity to meet Christians and to experience God's love through their concern and compassion. Whether or not they become Christians, their experience of how Christians were willing to help them in their time of need will leave a lasting impression. They may allow their children to be more involved in the church ministries and they may turn to the church during times of personal and family crisis.

The Pursuit of a Prosperous Life

Many new immigrants come to the United States with a dream of providing a better life for their children and grandchildren. The initial years in the United States are often a struggle trying to provide for the financial needs of the family. All of the adults and sometimes the teenagers will work long hours in restaurants or factories. After the initial struggle, these families want to move out of the apartment that they have been sharing with relatives to their own apartment, as well as buy their own car. An even bigger apartment, a television, or a nicer car seems to be within their grasp if they continue to work hard and save. Once these goals are met, they might consider buying a home of their own rather than renting. This constant pursuit for more material possessions leads many to continue working long hours and put aside any interest in spiritual matters.

Syncretism

Religion is viewed differently by Chinese than by Westerners. For traditional Chinese, "there is no feeling that one 'truth,' or doctrine, is superior to others. Chinese follow not only 'the three great truths' (Confucianism, Taoism, and Buddhism) but also pay homage to numerous minor gods who bring good luck or ward off illness."[11]

Most parents think that going to church is good for their children because it provides moral teaching. They get more concerned later in life when the children spend more time at church, and they may begin to see the church as a threat to their own family time. Another threat comes when youth want to be baptized and they tell their parents that Christianity calls for exclusive allegiance. Parents begin to realize that some of their beliefs are being challenged.

For example, Christians from families that practice ancestor worship are often torn between family obligation and their Christian faith.

Parents teach their children to respect their ancestors by bringing food and offerings to their gravesites. The parents want their children to develop this habit so that when they pass away, their children will continue this practice. But this conflicts with Christian teachings and becomes a dilemma for young Christians concerning whom they will obey: their parents or Christ.

Gambling

One of the growing concerns in the community is the rise of gambling. Illinois and Indiana legalized gambling in 1991 in order to increase state revenues.[12] Soon after the riverboat casinos opened, casino operators began contracting with private bus companies to transport Chinatown residents to their casinos. Within months, long lines of Chinatown residents began waiting for the buses on different street corners. Various estimates range from three hundred to one thousand persons going to the casinos each day from Chinatown. Some go because of the free meals and other enticements given to the gamblers. Others go because there are limited recreational and social outlets in Chinatown. But a growing number go to the casinos because they have become addicted to the chance of getting rich quick. This has led to a rise in personal bankruptcy, divorce, and substance abuse.

Conclusion:
Meeting Needs

In the miracle of the feeding of the five thousand, Jesus said to His disciples, "You give them something to eat" (Matt. 14:16). Jesus' command was that we need to be involved in meeting the physical needs of people in order to meet their spiritual needs, but He was also challenging them to realize only He could really meet their needs. He gave us the best model by coming not to be served, but to serve, and giving His life as a ransom for many (Mark 10:45). As followers of Jesus, the Chinese Christian Union Church is trying to obey Jesus' call to demonstrate His love by meeting people's needs and presenting the gospel.

Reflection Questions

1. How might evangelistic strategies be different for trying to reach Chinese in Hong Kong versus ministering to them in Chicago or any other American city?

2. What strategies used in Chinatown might be used to reach other new immigrants coming to Chicago or your city, such as Central Americans or Bosnians? What ministry challenges might there be if these immigrant or refugee groups did not live as closely together as the Chinese do in Chinatown?

3. If you were going to live in Chinatown as a summer short-term missionary, what are some things that you could do to prepare yourself?

For Further Reading

A Winning Combination: ABC/OBC (Understanding the Cultural Tension in Chinese Churches). Petaluma, Calif.: Chinese Christian Mission, 1986.

Cao, Lan, and Himilee Novas. *Everything You Need to Know About Asian American History*. New York: Penguin, 1996.

Yep, Jeanette, editor. *Following Jesus Without Dishonoring Your Parents*. Downers Grove, Ill.: InterVarsity, 1998.

chapter seventeen

OUTREACH TO THE JEWISH COMMUNITY

THE PRINCIPLES AND POSSIBILITIES

MICHAEL RYDELNIK

Introduction: The Question of Evangelizing Jewish People

In my observation, Gentile Christians who want to witness to lost people are generally somewhat reluctant when it comes to Jewish people. When believers hear a Jewish person say, "Oh, I'm Jewish!" all too often they back off, as if Jewish people have a spiritual inoculation against ever hearing about Jesus or as if being Jewish meant they didn't need Jesus. Those believers who actually do forge ahead and explain their faith are often frustrated by their own ineffectiveness at communicating the gospel with Jewish people. As a result, there is a tendency to relegate Jewish evangelism to Jewish believers in Jesus or to professional Jewish outreach agencies. Nothing could be further from God's heart for the Jewish people. This chapter is designed to help believers overcome their hesitance and provide some insights into more effective outreach to God's chosen people. It will examine Jewish people as an American ethnic group, consider a biblical basis for Jewish evangelism, present the most common barriers, offer some basic principles of witnessing to Jewish people, and finally observe some of the approaches taken to reach Jewish people in Chicago, a major Jewish population center.

JEWISH PEOPLE IN AMERICA

In 1654, twenty-three Portuguese Jews, fleeing the Inquisition, arrived in New Amsterdam (later named New York), becoming the first Jewish people in the New World. Today, close to six million Jewish people live in the United States. Throughout the colonial period, Jewish people came to America sporadically, as entrepreneurs, merchants, and traders. But the first significant migration took place between 1840 and 1860 when about 250,000 arrived. Coming predominantly from Germany, these middle-class immigrants settled throughout the Midwest and worked as shopkeepers and artisans. They came seeking greater freedom and found it.

The greatest influx of Jewish people into the United States took place between 1880 and 1920, when a tidal wave of Jewish immigrants arrived from Eastern Europe, primarily Russia. Fleeing anti-Semitic restrictions, pogroms (organized violent attacks on Jewish communities condoned by the government), and intense poverty, two-and-a-half million Jewish people made their way to the *goldeneh medina* (golden land, the term Eastern European Jews used for the United States) to find freedom, opportunity, and safety. Most settled in major urban centers, with more than half going to New York City, where they worked as street peddlers, tailors, and shopkeepers. The children of these immigrants took advantage of American opportunity and within a generation became teachers, lawyers, doctors, and business owners. Today, about one in twenty United States citizens is Jewish. Most Jewish people have congregated in major urban centers, with the New York metropolitan area having the largest population of 1,900,000 Jewish people.

FIGURE 1. ESTIMATED TOP FIVE JEWISH
POPULATION CENTERS IN THE UNITED STATES

New York, NY	1,900,000
Los Angeles, CA	585,000
Miami, FL	535,000
Philadelphia, PA	315,000
Chicago, IL	250,000

Jewish people remain a distinct ethnic minority within the United States. However, despite Jewish people continuing to identify as Jews, religious devotion to and affiliation with Judaism is decreasing. According to the Council of Jewish Federations (CJF) 1990 survey of the Jewish community, only 7 percent of the Jewish population identifies with Orthodox Judaism, the most observant and traditional branch. Another 38 percent prefers the less rigorous Conservative branch of Judaism, while 42 percent favors the liberal Reform branch of Judaism. Even these figures are misleading, since they only register the *preferences* of the surveyed community. Although almost 90 percent of the Jewish community expressed a preference of which branch they identify with the most, only 41 percent of Jewish households officially affiliate with a synagogue or temple. And this statistic only reflects households in which both parents are Jewish. If households in which one parent is Jewish were included, it would reduce the affiliated percentage even more drastically. Additionally, of those households that do affiliate with a synagogue or temple, the vast majority of members only attend services for major Jewish holy days (Rosh Hashanah and Yom Kippur) or significant life cycle events (Bar or Bas Mitzvah). American Jewry seems to be increasingly identifying as an ethnic/cultural group and decreasingly as a religious group.

American Jews hold to such varying degrees of religious observance and maintain such a wide variety of religious beliefs that it is hard to classify their theological position. Michael Medved, a media critic and an Orthodox Jew, aptly summarized the faith of the American Jewish community:

> The chief distinguishing characteristic of most American Jews is not what they do believe, but what they do not believe. They do not believe in Jesus as the messiah. Period. End of sentence, end of story. Tragically, for all too many members of today's Jewish community, this rejection marks the sum total of their theological commitment, the beginning and end of their ideological identity as adherents to what is still misleadingly described as "the Jewish faith." . . . Acceptance of Jesus is the one theological permutation that Jews of all persuasions find unacceptable, the only issue on which Jewish Americans from the militantly secular to the militantly Hasidic are ready to draw a common line.[1]

While, by and large, resistant to faith in Jesus, the Jewish community is becoming more secularized and assimilated than ever before. However, the American Jewish community continues to exhibit some distinctive tendencies. For example, it continues to be highly educated. According to the CJF study, "The American Jewish population has a remarkably high level of educational achievement. . . . The Core Jewish Population shows very high proportions of college graduates and a declining gender gap in education." Additionally, American Jews are represented as professionals, entrepreneurs, corporate managers, and academics at a proportionally higher percentage than their population would anticipate.[2]

Despite the changing nature of the Jewish community, Medved maintains that "the deep seated and nearly universal Jewish resistance to claims of the divinity of Jesus will ensure that even the most engaged and energized sort of Christian evangelism will yield few outright converts."[3] Is he correct, or is there an opportunity for Christians to reach their Jewish friends with the good news that Jesus is the Jewish Messiah? Most believers still approach Jewish people as if they were part of a closed, highly religious, tightly organized community. By understanding the shift to secularization and communicating with that in mind, believers could very well see a greater responsiveness to the gospel on the part of the increasingly secularized and intermarried Jewish community. But is Jewish evangelism still part of the church's mandate? It is to this question that we turn by examining a biblical basis for Jewish evangelism.

A BIBLICAL BASIS FOR JEWISH EVANGELISM

The Great Commission (Matt. 28:16–20) extends to all people groups in the world. This should be sufficient reason for believers to reach Jewish people with the gospel. However, the Scriptures indicate that God has a special mandate for Jewish evangelism, beyond the Great Commission. Two key verses in the book of Romans demonstrate God's continuing concern for a particularized outreach to the Jewish people.

The frist verse, Romans 1:16, is a significant verse both for interpreting Romans and for establishing a biblical basis for Jewish evangelism. Unfortunately, believers too often misquote it by cutting off the final clause, which relates to Jewish evangelism. Paul wrote, "I am not ashamed of the gospel, for it is the power of God for salvation to everyone who believes, *to the Jew first and also to the Greek*" (NASB, italics added).

Interpreters have taken the final phrase of this verse in a variety of ways. Some have held to a historical view, arguing that the gospel was formerly offered to the Jews but it is presently being offered to the Gentiles. There are several problems with this interpretation. To begin with, although the gospel was given to the Jewish people first, it nevertheless continued to be offered to Jewish people after it was given to the Gentiles. Second, if Paul had meant the historical view he would not have used the Greek word *proton* (first). Instead he would have chosen the Greek word *proteron,* which means "formerly."[4] Third, this view implies that the word *first* is to be taken in a chronological sense. However, Romans 2:9–10 uses *proton* with a non-chronological meaning: "There will be trouble and distress for every human being who does evil: *first* for the Jew, then for the Gentile; but glory, honor and peace for everyone who does good: *first* for the Jew, then for the Gentile" (italics added). Clearly Paul does not mean that "trouble and distress" and "glory, honor, and peace" will come to the Jews *before* the Gentiles. Since Paul is not using the word *first* in a chronological sense in Romans 2:9–10, it is unlikely that he required a chronological sense in Romans 1:16.

Other interpreters have taken the phrase "to the Jew first" in a *methodological* sense. This view mistakenly takes the verse as an evangelistic strategy and method for world evangelization. According to this position, wherever the gospel is preached around the world, it must first be presented to the Jewish people. This interpretation is weak for several reasons. To start with, it relies on taking the word *first* in a chronological sense, just as the historical view does. Moreover, Romans 1:16 describes the nature of the gospel, not a mode of proclamation. In other words, it tells what the gospel is, not how to present it. Finally, it seems impractical and illogical to evangelize Jewish people fully in every given community before proceeding with Gentile evangelism.

It is best to take "to the Jew first" in an *elective* sense, meaning that the Jewish people are the elect or chosen people of God and therefore the gospel is preeminently a Jewish message. This view is strong for the following reasons: First, according to the standard Greek lexicon, the word *proton* should be translated "above all" or "especially" in this context.[5] Second, this translation would fit with Romans 2:9, in which Paul stated that condemnation will come to all nonbelievers, Gentile or Jewish, but "especially" to the Jewish people because of their privileged status as chosen people. Third, it conforms to the overall argument of Romans, which recognizes the equality of Jews and Gentiles but also the elective priority of the Jewish people (see Rom. 9–11, particularly 11:29).

Noted commentator John Murray explained Romans 1:16 this way:

> *The power of God unto salvation through faith has primary relevance to the Jew, and the analogy of Scripture would indicate that this peculiar relevance to the Jew arises from the fact that the Jew had been chosen by God to be the recipient of the promise of the gospel and that to him were committed the oracles of God. Salvation was of the Jews (John 4:22, cf. Acts 2:39; Romans 3:1–2; 9:4–5). The lines of preparation for the full revelation of the gospel were laid in Israel and for that reason the gospel is preeminently the gospel for the Jew. How totally contrary to the current attitude of Jewry that Christianity is for the Gentile but not for the Jew.[6]*

Simply stated, the gospel was, is, and always will be a preeminently Jewish message. The gospel was promised to the Jewish people by Jewish prophets; it was established by a Jewish Messiah; it was proclaimed by Jewish apostles. Even though the gospel was designed for all people, it was particularly prepared for the Jewish people, whether or not they accept it.

The second verse, Romans 11:11, gives both present and future hope to Jewish people. In this verse Paul began by asking rhetorically if the Jewish people had "stumbled so as to fall." The answer he gave was a resounding, "No!" His point was that Jewish people, despite their rejection of Jesus, had not fallen headlong so they could not get up again. Their stumbling was not beyond recovery. Paul's argument was that Jewish people are still savable.

This hope for Jewish people is evident in two ways in Romans 11. First, Paul argued that Jewish rejection of Jesus is not final. At the end of Romans 11, Paul maintained that when the fullness of the Gentiles has come, Israel's partial hardening will cease. All the Jewish people alive at that time will turn to Jesus as their Messiah. This national acceptance of Jesus precedes the second coming of the Messiah, at which time "all Israel will be saved" (Rom. 11:26).

Second, Paul argued that Jewish rejection is not total. At the beginning of Romans 11, Paul affirmed that there will always be a remnant in the present day. As proof that God had not rejected Israel (despite their national rejection of Jesus), Paul maintained that God has always worked through a remnant. Just as a remnant of seven thousand Israelites did not bow to Baal in the days of Elijah (Rom. 11:1–4), so there was "at the present time a remnant according to God's gracious choice" (v. 5 NASB). God's faithfulness to the Jewish people is evident in that in every generation of the church age, there has always been a segment of the Jewish people who have trusted in Jesus as their Messiah and Savior. Paul was an illustration of this in his day (v. 1), just as Messianic Jews are examples of this truth at the present time.

Having established that Jewish people are savable, Paul explained how God will go about reaching Jewish people. He argued that their transgression (the national rejection of Jesus) had brought salvation to the Gentiles. God's purpose in doing this was to make Jewish people jealous.[7]

The phrase "to make them jealous" means *to make people desire what rightfully belongs to them by giving it to someone else.* An example of this is in 1 Corinthians 10:22 where the same word is used of God. That verse speaks of Christians worshiping in pagan temples, thus provoking God to jealousy. Believers, who rightfully belong to God, were making Him jealous, because they were worshiping someone else. With this meaning of the phrase in mind, it is easy to understand the point of Romans 11:11. God gave the gospel to the Gentiles with the express purpose of making Jewish people jealous, so that they would want it back for themselves.

Paul was saying that Jewish people are still savable and God wants to use Gentile Christians to reach them. Max Reich, formerly professor of Jewish Studies at the Moody Bible Institute, has paraphrased Romans 11:11 as follows: "To make the Jewish people's mouths water for the salvation which Gentiles have found in the Jewish Messiah!"

Should Gentile believers present the gospel to the Jewish people? As long as the Great Commission stands, the answer must be yes. Nevertheless, that is not the only reason to witness to our Jewish friends. It is plain from Romans 1:16 that the gospel is a message especially and preeminently designed for Jewish people. Moreover, from Romans 11:11, it is evident that one of God's foremost purposes in bringing Gentiles to salvation is to make Jewish people want what the Gentiles have received.

Since this is God's purpose and plan, why is so little being done to reach Jewish people? The next section will address the reasons Gentiles are so reluctant to fulfill their special mandate for Jewish evangelism.

THE BARRIERS TO JEWISH EVANGELISM

Gentile believers have not taken up their special mandate for Jewish evangelism for countless reasons. Unfortunately, these include anti-Jewish attitudes and theological dispositions. However, those are not the basic reasons believers do not witness to Jewish people. I have found that Gentiles are reluctant to discuss their faith with Jewish people because they are fearful. These fears form the essential barriers that must be overcome in order to reach Jewish people with the good news of Messiah Jesus.

The first barrier to Jewish evangelism is *a fear of wasting time and effort*. Many have the perception that Jewish people are blind to the gospel and therefore unreachable. Many churches and individual believers think that any efforts to reach Jewish people will prove fruitless. They ask, "Why waste our precious time and our limited resources for an effort that will have little or no payback?" They are guided by the principle that outreach efforts should be restricted to more responsive people.

This is an unfortunate and invalid fear for several reasons. First of all, God has called us to the work of evangelizing the world regardless of response. We are not just to obey when we are guaranteed a willing hearer. Even Jesus, in His earthly ministry, came to His own and His own did not receive Him. Yett every believer would agree that the Lord

Jesus was correct in going to the lost sheep of the house of Israel. Second, the whole idea of a unique judicial blindness for Israel is questionable. Romans 11 does indeed say that Israel was hardened. But the Scriptures also say that every lost person has a blindness to the gospel (1 Cor. 2:14). Nowhere do the Scriptures say that Israel's blindness is greater than any other nonbelieving person. Moreover, the church must also accept some responsibility for helping cause Israel's unbelieving blindness because of the church's tragic history of Christian anti-Semitism. Finally, the Scriptures do assure a measure of success in Jewish evangelism. Paul plainly said that there will always be a remnant of Jewish people who will respond to the gospel with faith (Rom. 11:4). Believers should be faithful to God's mandate for Jewish evangelism regardless of their fear of being unsuccessful.

Gentile Christians are also reluctant to witness to their Jewish friends because of their *fear of an unpleasant situation*. Most Gentile believers are aware that Jewish people generally do not believe in Jesus. Having read the Gospels and Acts, these believers conclude that just as Jesus, Peter, and Paul faced unpleasant opposition to their messages, so will they. They do not want to offend their Jewish friends or deal with an explosive reaction from them. But is this valid?

Generally Jewish people do not react in an unpleasant or explosive way when their Gentile friends discuss Jesus with them. Jewish people expect their Gentile friends to believe in Jesus. If approached in a loving way, Jewish people will usually give consideration to the words of their friends, even if it is about Jesus. Even those Jewish people who are disinterested will politely decline to discuss it. Surprisingly, many Jewish people are much more interested than their friends anticipate. Most people, including the Jewish people, are naturally curious and want to learn about other faiths. Some Jewish people are even searching spiritually and will be quite open to consider spiritual truth if people are bold enough to present it.

Years after the Russian Revolution, Leon Trotsky, who was both Jewish and second in command to Lenin during the revolution, fell into disfavor with Lenin and was banished from Russia. While in exile in New York City, he lived for a while with a family of believers. After leaving their home, Trotsky was asked what they were like. He is said to have replied, "Those Christians were hypocrites! They went to church every Sunday morning, every Sunday night, and every Wednesday night. And they didn't invite me to join them once!" Here was a Jewish man open to hearing about Jesus. However, those who had the opportunity to tell him failed to speak up because they were afraid of an unpleasant situation.

Gentile Christians often have a third reluctance in witnessing to Jewish people: *a fear of Jewish knowledge of the Bible.* Too often believers have the mistaken notion that Jewish people know the Scriptures inside out and can quote it in Hebrew. These Christians fear that if they present the gospel to their Jewish friends that the Jewish people will raise objections that cannot be answered. So they conclude it is best not even to engage their Jewish friends in a discussion of the Bible.

This perception about Jewish knowledge of the Scriptures is quite inaccurate. Most American Jews, as already noted, are quite secularized. Most Jewish people are not able to translate biblical Hebrew. Even those who have a Jewish education often do not know the Hebrew Bible very well. Generally Jewish people are amazed at the knowledge that Gentile Christians have of the TaNaK,[8] which is a Jewish book (Rom. 3:2). Believers should not fear Jewish knowledge of the Scriptures. Moreover, Jewish people will frequently be moved to jealousy when they encounter Gentiles who know the Jewish book better than they do.

THE PRINCIPLES OF JEWISH EVANGELISM

Once believers decide that they have a biblical mandate for Jewish evangelism, they are often stymied by their own perceived lack of ability. "I wouldn't even know what to do!" they exclaim. Here are some basic principles that every person can follow that will make for an effective witness to Jewish people.

To begin with, believers must have *a genuine love for Jewish people.* Jewish people have been repulsed from the message of the Messiah Jesus because of the hateful anti-Semitism that has existed in the church. Many Christians object that real believers could not be anti-Jewish. Sadly, that is simply not true.[9] In the Eastern tradition, for example, the most significant Church Father, John Chrysostom (ca. 347–407), who was also known as the golden mouthed preacher, wrote eight homilies against the Jews that are without peer in the whole realm of anti-Jewish literature. A brief sample of his poison tongue follows:

> *The Jews are the most worthless of all men. They are lecherous, greedy, rapacious. They are perfidious murderers of Christ. They worship the devil, their religion is a sickness. The Jews are the odious assassins of Christ[10] and for killing God there is no expiation possible, no indulgence or pardon. Christians may never cease vengeance, and the Jew must live in servitude forever. God always hated the Jews. It is incumbent upon all Christians to hate the Jews.[11]*

Christian anti-Semitism was also evident in the Western Church, in the writings of Augustine. Considered by many to be the greatest theologian of the ancient church and perhaps of all time, both Roman Catholic and Protestant traditions look to him as their theological patron. He developed the theory of the Jews as a "witness people" to explain their continued existence. Allegorizing the story of Cain and Abel, with Cain representing the Jews, according to this theory the Jewish people were marked by God when they murdered Christ. Hence they cannot be destroyed, but their dispersion and misery serve as testimony of their evil and of Christian truth.[12]

Martin Luther (1483–1546), the father of the Protestant Reformation, vehemently attacked the Jewish people in his writing when he stated:

> What then shall we Christians do with this damned rejected race of Jews, since they live among us and we know about their lying and blaspheming curses. We cannot tolerate them if we do not wish to share in their lies, curses and blasphemy. . . . [We must] set their synagogues on fire, and whatever does not burn up should be covered or spread over with dirt so that no one may ever be able to see a cinder of stone of it . . . in order that God may see that we are Christians. . . . Their homes should likewise be broken down and destroyed. . . . They should be deprived of their prayer books and Talmuds . . . in which idolatry, lies, cursings and blasphemy are taught . . . their rabbis must be forbidden to teach under the threat of death. Let us drive them out of the country for all time, for as has been said, "God's rage is so great against them that they only become worse and worse through mild mercy and not much better with severe mercy." Therefore, away with them.[13]

These are just three examples of two thousand years of hatred. It has been so severe that Jewish people fully expect contemporary Christians to harbor a vile prejudice against them. What an amazing surprise to Jewish people when Gentile believers openly express concern and compassion for them. The believer's model of love is Paul, the apostle to the Gentiles. He loved his own people so much that, had it been possible, he would have gone to hell, if that would have enabled the Jewish people to experience God's love in Messiah (Rom. 9:1–3).

Jewish people will greet simple acts of kindness, such as sending a Passover or a Rosh Hashanah card, with surprise and appreciation. When Christians express solidarity with the Jewish community in standing against anti-Jewish attitudes and actions, Jewish people will be amazed and grateful. Once, former New York City mayor Ed Koch was asked why Jewish voters so appreciated Republican Al D'Amato. His reply was, "If there is one thing Jews appreciate more than a Jew who loves the Jewish people, it is a Gentile who loves the Jewish people!" Reversing the Christian tradition of hatred with love will build a platform from which Christians may speak to Jewish people about Jesus the Messiah.

A second principle of Jewish evangelism is that Christians must *live a distinctive lifestyle before the Jewish people.* Too often, Jewish people observe Christians and wonder what is different about their faith. By demonstrating a transformed life, believers can attract Jewish people to the message of the Messiah. I have a friend in Israel who is as blonde, blue-eyed, and Gentile as they come. Not only has she gained a hearing by her genuine love for Jewish people, but she has provoked sufficient jealousy merely by openly living for the Lord in a genuine way. For example, on a kibbutz one day, she was asked, "What's different about you? Your faith seems so real and makes such a difference in your life." We can have the same question asked of us, by allowing people to see our changed lives so they can glorify our Father in heaven.

A third important principle is for believers to have a *sincere respect for the Jewishness of the gospel.* Too often, both Christians and Jews forget that faith in Jesus as the Messiah is rooted in promises given to the Jewish people. Jesus said, "Salvation is from the Jews" (John 4:22). Paul agreed when he said that the gospel is pre-eminently to the Jewish people (Rom. 1:16). His respect for the Jewish roots of Christianity is seen in this description of the Jewish people in Romans 9:4–5, "Theirs is the adoption as sons; theirs the divine glory, the covenants, the receiving of the law, the temple worship and the promises. Theirs are the patriarchs, and from them is traced the human ancestry of Christ, who is God over all, forever praised! Amen."

When Jewish people object to hearing about Jesus because they are Jewish, our most natural response should be, "That's great! I worship and love the greatest Jew who ever lived. He's the One I wanted to talk about with you."

Once, when I was visiting in a retirement village, a Jewish woman objected to my faith in Jesus. She said it was for Gentiles, not Jews. I read her the first verse of my (Yiddish) New Testament, which describes Yeshua, the son of David and the son of Abraham. She looked at me in shock and said, "You mean He's really Jewish!" That Jesus is the greatest Jew who ever was is one great truth that we must communicate over and over to Jewish people.

A fourth principle of Jewish evangelism is that believers must *develop sensitivity to Jewish concerns.* This should be particularly evident in the symbols and speech that we use when communicating. For example, Crusaders brutally murdered Jewish people throughout Europe under the sign of the cross during the Crusades. Christians today should be especially careful to avoid using this symbol, which has come to represent hatred to Jewish people, rather than love. Of course, that is not to say that we ought to avoid the message of the Atonement. Rather, avoid using the symbol and substitute the word "tree" for the "cross," as in "Messiah died on the tree."

Sensitivity involves using terms that are understandable to Jewish people. For example, most Jewish people are not aware that the word *Christ* is the Greek form for the Hebrew word *Messiah*. Most Jewish people think that "Christ" is a last name (Joseph Christ, Mary Christ, Jesus Christ). Since Jewish people generally do understand the Jewish concept of the Messiah, using the word Messiah instead of Christ communicates far better. The following chart lists some words that communicate more understandably and are less offensive to Jewish people.

Don't Say	*Do Say*
Christ	Messiah
Jesus	Yeshua
Cross	Tree
Church	Congregation
Saved	Forgiven, Redeemed
Old Testament	Scriptures, Tenach
Convert, Conversion	Become a follower of Yeshua
Christian (noun)	Follower of Yeshua
Christian (adjective)	Biblical, Scriptural
Jews	Jewish people
Converted Jew	Messianic Jew; Jewish follower of Yeshua
Died for sins	Atoned for sins
Baptism	Immersion
New Testament	New Covenant

For many Jewish people the name of Jesus has become a great offense. Therefore, using His Hebrew name can sometimes minimize the offense. The one word of caution is to make sure the Jewish person knows who you are speaking of when you say Yeshua. A believer might say, "When we speak of Jesus, I would like to use His Hebrew name Yeshua. This is the name He was always called by His family and friends."

Believers should not only be sensitive with speech, but with our attitudes as well. Too often Gentile Christians betray stereotypical but untrue attitudes about Jewish people. False perceptions of Jewish wealth, appearance, personality style, or any other stereotype should be rejected completely, not just avoided in conversation.

Followers of Jesus should also become sensitive to Jewish history.

The Jewish experience in history has shaped Jewish perspectives about life. We must be aware of the deicide charge,[14] the Crusades, the Inquisition, expulsions from European countries, forced conversions to Christianity, pogroms, and assorted other anti-Jewish acts and libels, particularly those propagated by the church. When we talk to Jewish people about Jesus, although we must never compromise or be fearful, we must be sensitive to the way Jewish people feel.

Another principle of Jewish evangelism is that believers must *be informed about Jewish barriers to belief.* One stumbling block to faith is that Jewish people often believe that once they believe in Jesus, they will no longer be Jewish. Nothing could be further from the truth. In the New Testament, Jewish people always remained Jewish when they believed. Even today, when Jewish people become atheists or agnostics or even practice Zen, they remain Jewish. If Jesus really fulfilled the messianic prophecies of the Scriptures, then He is the Jewish Messiah. Belief in Him is thus the most Jewish faith a person can have.

Another barrier to belief is that Jewish people often question the reason anyone might believe in Jesus altogether. The simplest approach is to explain that the Messiah was foretold in the Scriptures and then show how Jesus of Nazareth fulfilled those prophecies. We must ground our faith in the Old Testament if Jewish people are going to believe in Jesus.

The Bible contains many prophecies and fulfillments. The chart on page 288 includes some basic ones of which believers should be aware.

A third block to Jewish faith in Jesus is that many Jewish people find it hard to understand the idea of Jesus dying for their sins. Therefore, it is important to explain the sacrificial system of the Hebrew Bible. Those sacrifices foreshadowed the exchange of life that God would provide through the death and resurrection of Jesus. It is vital to show that substitutionary atonement is not a new concept of the New Testament but one that was anticipated in the Hebrew Scriptures.

Every person is different and may come up with different barriers to belief. Regardless, believers must be ready to help Jewish people hurdle these walls so they can make a reasonable spiritual decision.

Finally, believers must *develop holy boldness in raising the issue of Jesus with Jewish people.* Do not allow fear and intimidation to take over. The best way to overcome intimidation is by using your own sense of humor and the other person's curiosity. For example, a Gentile friend of mine named Gus would frequently tell a Jewish person that the folks in his congregation believed Genesis 12:3. Very often the Jewish person would ask what that verse said. Then Gus would respond, with true surprise, that he was amazed that a Jewish person did not know what was in the Torah. When his Jewish friend insisted on being told what was in this passage, Gus then, and only then, explained the Abrahamic covenant. Before too long, they would be discussing how that covenant found its ultimate fulfillment in the coming of the Messiah.

A SURVEY OF MESSIANIC PROPHECY[15]

Messiah's Birth	Prophecy	Fulfillment
Messiah would be born in Bethlehem.	Micah 5:2	Matthew 2:1
Messiah would be the last in the kingly line.	Genesis 49:10	Galatians 4:4
Messiah would be born of a virgin as a sign.	Isaiah 7:14	Matthew 1:23
Messiah would be born with a divine nature.	Isaiah 9:6	John 1:1–2
Messiah's Life		
Messiah would perform miracles.	Isaiah 35:5	Matthew 11:3–6
Messiah would proclaim good news.	Isaiah 61:1–2	Luke 4:16–21
Messiah would be rejected by His own people.	Isaiah 53:3	John 1:11; 7:5
Messiah's Death		
Messiah would die before the Roman destruction of Jerusalem and the temple.	Daniel 9:26–27	Luke 19:43–45
Messiah would die as an atonement for sin.	Isaiah 53:5–6, 11–12	2 Corinthians 5:21
Messiah would die by crucifixion.	Psalm 22:16	Matthew 27:35; John 19:18, 31–37
Messiah's Resurrection		
Messiah would see life after death.	Isaiah 53:10	Matthew 28:1–10
Messiah would not decay in the grave.	Psalm 16:10	Acts 2:24–32
Messiah's Return		
Messiah will be recognized by Israel as the Pierced One at His return.	Zechariah 12:10	Matthew 23:39
Messiah will establish a righteous reign from the throne of David in Jerusalem.	Isaiah 9:7; Amos 9:11–15	Revelation 19:11–16; 20:4

Gus often pulled out a pamphlet and told a Jewish friend that the booklet told the story of a rabbi who believed in Jesus. Immediately, the Jewish friend would dispute the validity of the tract. Before too long, the Jewish person would insist on reading the pamphlet. Gus would agree, on the condition that they could discuss it together once the person had completed reading it. Gus was a master at provoking curiosity with a smile and a laugh at the same time. Believers would become more effective in all kinds of evangelism, not just Jewish evangelism, by learning to raise their spiritual flag in a friendly and funny way.

It is still not enough to know how to talk about Christ with a Jewish person or even to speak up when the opportunity presents itself. Believers who want to reach Jewish people must be intentional in their strategies. Various ministries have been laboring at reaching Jewish people in the Chicago area for many years. What follows are some of the strategies that these ministries have effectively used to reach Jewish people.

JEWISH EVANGELISM IN CHICAGO

The long history of strategic Jewish evangelism in Chicago includes D. L. Moody bringing Joseph Rabinovich from Kishinev, Russia, to preach to Jewish people at the Chicago World's Fair (1893). By that time, Christian Zionist William Blackstone, in addition to his efforts to see a Jewish state founded, had already established the Chicago Hebrew Mission (1890) with the goal of reaching Jewish people with the gospel. His mission later became known as the American Messianic Fellowship and is now known as AMF International. In 1923, the Moody Bible Institute started a Jewish Studies major in order to train effective workers in the field of Jewish evangelism. Today, a variety of ministries are actively engaged in various forms of Jewish outreach.

Proclamation Evangelism

This form of evangelism is also known as confrontation evangelism. The group most frequently associated with this technique is Jews for Jesus, whose mission statement is "We exist to make the Messiahship of Jesus an unavoidable issue to our Jewish people worldwide." Jews for Jesus staff and volunteers can be seen all around Chicago in their high-profile T-shirts and jackets. They distribute witty and provocative gospel pamphlets (called broadsides) and stop passersby with creative gospel street dramas, both laced with high doses of Jewish humor. Jews for Jesus staffers especially focus their efforts at major events such as the annual "Taste of Chicago" food festival in July or high-traffic opportunities like Christmas shopping. Their goal is to make Jewish people consider that Jesus is the Messiah and make personal, face-to-face contact with those Jewish people who are searching for truth. Jewish seekers often attend a Jews for Jesus Bible study or invite Jews for Jesus evangelists to meet with them personally, to help them examine the claims of Jesus.

Other ministries also engage in this kind of outreach, although without the high profile of Jews for Jesus. For example, Chosen People Ministries (formerly known as the American Board of Missions to the Jews) regularly sends teams to Devon Avenue in West Rogers Park, an old and very Orthodox neighborhood. There they boldly distribute literature and engage the Orthodox Jewish people in conversation about the messiahship of Jesus. AMF (American Messianic Fellowship) International evangelists regularly visit Jewish people door-to-door in Skokie, Illinois, a suburban village with a distinctive citylike feel and an established Jewish community. The results of proclamation evangelism can be mixed, depending on the creativity of the evangelists and the openness of the audience. However, it does give Jewish people an opportunity to investigate the gospel and to identify to whom they can go for further help.

Ministry Centers

The ministry center has been a long-time technique for Jewish evangelism in Chicago. In this approach, an outreach center is established in a Jewish community, in order to hold Bible studies and other special activities. In past generations, this was the preferred approach, but in recent years it has not been used as much. However, a recent joint-ministry effort has established the Russian Messianic Cultural Center in West Rogers Park. Designed to reach recent Jewish immigrants from the former Soviet Union, the center holds Bible studies, services, and special events in Russian. It produces Russian language outreach literature and uses the center for discipleship meetings. In addition to this center, both Chosen People Ministries and Jews for Jesus maintain ministry centers for Bible studies and personal work.

Friendship Evangelism

All groups working in Chicago believe in friendship evangelism. However, AMF International has established this approach as its primary outreach strategy. In this approach, staff workers live in Jewish neighborhoods, attend Hebrew classes, or shop in Jewish-owned businesses, with the intention of making authentic friendships with Jewish people. These friendships, in turn, lead to evangelistic opportunities.

There are two cautions with this approach. First, friendships must be sincere, not mere stratagems to engage Jewish people. Otherwise, Jewish people will mistrust any person seeking to witness to them. Second, it is hard to reach many Jewish people this way, since a person can only have so many friends. It is far more effective to mobilize a congregation to practice this method. Many people can reach a few Jewish friends far better than a few people trying to become friends with every Jewish person they meet.

Church–Based Jewish Outreach

Several predominantly Gentile churches have expressed concern for reaching Jewish people and have been quite effective in doing so. For example, the historic Moody Church has developed a bi-monthly Friday night Jewish outreach, called the Light of Israel Fellowship, which has the goal of reaching the many young Jewish professionals in the Lincoln Park area. Another Chicago area church has hosted Messianic Passover Seders and held special concerts at the church for the entire congregation to invite their Jewish friends. Furthermore, a large church in Chicago has established seeker small groups for Jewish people to investigate the Messiah.

Messianic Congregations

Another method for reaching Jewish people is through the messianic congregation. These are ethnically Jewish congregations that seek to exalt the Messiah Jesus in a Jewish cultural context. These congregations are not exclusive: The membership in most of them are 40 to 50 percent Gentile. The cultural expression is Jewish, not the entire membership.

These congregations exist for the purposes of worship, instruction, fellowship, and accountability, all in a Jewish cultural context. Moreover, Jewish expressions and practices are not only for the purpose of evangelism but for expression of communal faith in a Jewish way. Although they do not exist solely for the purpose of Jewish evangelism, the Jewish people are the ministry focus for outreach. Chicago has a number of messianic congregations, each with a different philosophy of ministry. Adat Hatikvah (Congregation of the Hope) in Evanston, B'nai Maccabim (Sons of the Maccabees), and Congregation Etz Chaim (Tree of Life) have a more liturgical and traditional expression. Olive Tree Congregation in Des Plaines is less liturgical but equally Jewish. Temple Shalom Yisrael (Schaumburg) has its roots in the Assemblies of God denomination and is more expressive in its worship style.

All of these congregations have weekly services in which Jewish people feel comfortable. Additionally, they have special outreach events at Jewish holiday seasons, as well as concerts, seminars, and special seeker services. Although these congregations do not have the sole purpose of evangelistic outreach, they have been effective in seeing Jewish people come to faith in Jesus.

Academic Outreach

The Moody Bible Institute of Chicago has had a Jewish Studies program since 1923. Besides classroom training, it has required each student to engage in practical ministry on a weekly basis. As a result, Jewish Studies students spread across Chicago every week, serving in various Jewish ministries and congregations. Some visit nursing homes, others proclaim the Good News on the streets, and still others follow up on Jewish inquirers.

Each summer both Jews for Jesus and Chosen People Ministries offer two-week training programs at Moody. Besides the intensive classroom training, trainees also engage in street evangelism designed to reach Jewish people throughout Chicago. After these high-activity weeks, the trainees in both programs take their knowledge and experience to New York City for several more weeks of demanding Jewish outreach.

Chicago has the fifth largest Jewish population in the United States. As a result, it provides excellent models for the various intentional strategies that can be used to reach Jewish people. Whether through proclamation, ministry centers, church outreach, friendship evangelism, messianic congregations, or even educational institutions, the gospel is at work with Jewish people in the city of Chicago.

Conclusion:
What Needs to Be Done

Although much is happening in Jewish ministry, much more remains to be done. Someone once wrote, "For 1800 years, certainly for most of that time, Jews have not been given an opportunity to know what Christianity is, or to know what the Christ means. The ignorance of the Jew concerning Christianity condemns not the Jew, but Christendom." What makes this statement all the more potent is that it was not spoken by a Jewish evangelist but by Rabbi Stephen S. Wise, who certainly did not believe in Jesus. Regardless, his words are true—if believers would accept their mandate to reach Jewish people with the

Good News, many more Jewish people would come to know Jesus, their promised Messiah.

Reflection Questions

1. Do you have a love for the Jewish community? If not, are you willing for God to burden your heart for them? In what ways can you develop an awareness and affection for Jewish people?

2. Do you see evidence of anti-Semitism in your community? If so, how can you and/or your church help to counteract it?

3. Do you feel reluctant to discuss the gospel with those you meet who are Jewish? If so, how can you overcome your fears?

4. In what ways could you and/or your church support ministries to Jewish people?

For Further Reading

Einstein, Stephen J., and Lydia Kukoff. *Every Person's Guide to Judaism.* New York: UAHC Press, 1989.

Flannery, Edward H. *The Anguish of the Jews.* Revised. Mahwah, N.J.: Paulist Press, 1985.

Fruchtenbaum, Arnold. *Jesus Was a Jew.* Tustin, Calif.: Ariel Press, 1995.

Goldberg, Louis. *Our Jewish Friends.* Revised. Neptune, N.J.: Loizeaux Brothers, 1983.

Johnson, Paul. *A History of the Jews.* New York: Harper & Row, 1987.

Kaiser, Walter. *Messiah in the Old Testament.* Grand Rapids: Zondervan, 1995.

Rubin, Barry. *You Bring the Bagels, I'll Bring the Gospel.* Revised. Baltimore, MD.: Messianic Jewish Publishers, 1997.

Telchin, Stan. *Betrayed.* Grand Rapids: Chosen Books, 1981.

Wylen, Stephen. *Settings of Silver: An Introduction to Judaism.* Mahwah, N.J.: Paulist Press, 1989.

chapter eighteen

BRIDGING THE GAP TO ISLAM

UNDERSTANDING AND MINISTERING TO MIDDLE EASTERN MUSLIMS

RAOUF BOULOS

Introduction: A Fresh Look at Islam

People have a tendency to label people and groups and to put a title on different countries and nations. For instance, the term "third world" is normally used to refer to an undeveloped nation.

Most people also have certain thoughts and ideas they associate with Islam and Muslim people. Most people in the West think of Muslim people as militant, terrorists, and invaders. It could be difficult to think of Muslims in a different way. You may never have a chance to meet a Muslim person or a real Muslim family. The most common source of our information is the media, which have a great effect in shaping our minds and influencing our thinking, either positively or negatively. To help understand the role of the media in stereotyping people, let me take the opportunity to tell my personal experience and how my views were adjusted after I met "the real people."

Being born and raised in Egypt, the only window available to the Western world and American people was the television and cinema industry. Needless to say, the predominant factors of the widespread American movies and television series are directed toward sexual immorality, violence, gangs, and the like. It was easy to believe that this was the pattern of life in the Western world and the United States. Another dimension should be added here: We Middle Eastern people associate the Western world with Christianity. Believe it or not, many people in the Islamic nations reject Christ and deny Christianity because of the stereotype of the West.

The turning point in my life happened when I came to Chicago in 1987 to study at Moody Bible Institute. During that time, I met many American people, Christian and non-Christian, in different places—at work, at home, and in social interaction. I still remember my first invitation for supper. I had to be intentional about arriving on time. The wife had just finished preparing a delicious meal for us. The husband and wife sat at each end of the table. Their three teenage children, two girls and one boy, joined the parents, each one in a designated seat. I observed their manner of eating and talking. To be honest, I was shocked! The family was united, and the children were not loose somewhere outside the home. They were really behaving themselves. That was my first exposure to a real American home.

It took me a substantial amount of time after that to change the traditional picture I brought with me from Egypt. Going through the process was not easy but was worth doing. The bottom line is that we Christians need to allow ourselves to be exposed to real Muslim friends, both families and individuals. Let us meet them with an open mind to change our traditional views and open our hearts to love them as people created after God's own image.

MUSLIM STATISTICS

Islam is growing more quickly than Christianity. The world's second largest religion expanded from 15.3 percent of the 1970 total world's population of 3.7 billion to 19.6 percent of the 1997 total world population of 5.89 billion.[1]

An exact figure of the Muslim population in the United States is not easy to obtain. The table on the next page represents a breakdown by states of the largest Muslim communities in the United States. There are an estimated 3.3 million Muslims in these states. That figure represents 62 percent of the estimated 5 million Muslims living in the United States.[2]

The United States has three main categories of Muslims:
   1. Immigrants
   2. American converts to Islam
   3. Those born to the first two groups as Muslims

TABLE 4

State	Muslim Population	Percentage Total Muslim Population in United States	Percent of Total State Population
California	1,000,000	20.0	3.4
New York	800,000	16.0	4.7
Illinois	420,000	8.4	3.6
New Jersey	200,000	4.0	2.5
Indiana	180,000	3.6	3.2
Michigan	170,000	3.4	1.8
Virginia	150,000	3.0	2.4
Texas	140,000	2.8	0.7
Ohio	130,000	2.6	1.2
Maryland	70,000	1.4	1.4

The following table shows a breakdown by ethnic grouping and its related percentage of the Muslim population in the United States in 1990.[3]

TABLE 5

Ethnic Grouping	Population in 1990	Percent of Total Muslim Populations	Definition of Terms
African-American	2,100,000	42.0	African-Americans: Persons of African descent in America.
South Asians	1,220,000	24.4	South Asians: Those of Indian/Pakistani, Bangladesh, Sri Lankan, or Afghan descent.
Arabs	620,000	12.4	Arabs: People from Arabic-speaking countries of the Middle East and North Africa.
Africans	260,000	5.2	Africans: People from the African continent who are not American citizens.
Iranians	180,000	3.6	Iranians: People of Persian descent, usually from Iran.

Ethnic Grouping	Population in 1990	Percent of Total Muslim Populations	Definition of Terms
Turks	120,000	2.4	Turks: People of Turkish descent.
South-East Asians	100,000	2.0	South-East Asians: People of Thailand, Malaysia, Indonesia, Indochina, or the Philippines.
American Whites	80,000	1.6	American Whites: Those of West European descent.
East Europeans	40,000	0.8	East Europeans: People from various regions of Eastern Europe.
Other	280,000	5.6	Other: All other groups.

UNDERSTANDING ISLAM

Life of Muhammad

Islam is an Eastern religion that began in A.D. 622 at Yathrib, the Medina, a city in what is now Saudi Arabia. Muhammad, the founder and prophet of Islam, was born in A.D. 570 in Mecca, Saudi Arabia, and died in A.D. 632.[4]

Muhammad means "the prized one" in the Arabic language. His father, Abdallah, which means "slave of God," died shortly before the birth of his only son, Muhammad. Muhammad's mother, Amina, which means "faithful one," died during Muhammad's early childhood, leaving him in the care of his grandfather Abd Al-Muttalib. Two years later his grandfather also died, putting Muhammad in the care of his uncle Abu-Talib.[5]

At the age of twelve, Muhammad joined his uncle on trading trips from Mecca to Damascus. During those trips he was exposed to both Judaism and Christianity.[6] When Muhammad turned twenty-five, he married his first wife, Khadija, a wealthy widow from Mecca, who was forty years old.[7]

Muhammad began to meditate at a cave called Hira, where he was visited by a spirit. Muhammad was shaking and shivering and in doubt about the nature and source of that spirit. Khadija, his wife, and later on her cousin, Waraqah ibn Nawfal, assured him that the spirit was the angel Gabriel who spoke to Moses.[8] The Quran (also spelled Koran) was revealed to Muhammad in the Arabic language (Quran 43:3). Muhammad was first rejected by his own tribe, Quraish, forcing him to flee to Yathrib in A.D. 622. Muslims claim that event as the beginning of the Islamic era.

Holy Books and Beliefs of Islam

The Quran

The Quran, the holy book of Islam, contains 114 Suras or chapters. A sincere Muslim has to memorize the Quran in its entirety in the Arabic language. Muslims regard only the Arabic Quran as a miracle from Allah sent down from heaven and the Arabic language as the language of heaven.[9]

Islam is an Arabic word that means "submission," and a Muslim is a person who submits himself to Allah. Allah is the name of God mentioned in the Arabic Quran and the Arabic Bible.[10] It is therefore used by Arabic-speaking people, both Muslims and Christians alike, in various Middle Eastern countries.

Muslims believe the Quran was revealed to Muhammad during the month of Ramadan. For that reason, sincere Muslims fast the whole month of Ramadan from dawn until dusk. The Quran regards the Torah or Old Testament of Moses and the Gospel or New Testament of Jesus as the Holy Scriptures, but Muslims believe that both Jews and Christians corrupted their Holy Scriptures. Therefore, Allah had to reveal the Quran as his final word to correct and replace them.[11]

The Quran regards many prophets including Adam, Abraham, Moses, David, Jesus, and Muhammad. According to the Quran, Jesus foretold the coming of Muhammad (Quran 61:6). Isa is the Quranic name of Jesus, but Yasu' is His name in the Arabic Bible. The Quran, in various texts, refers to Jesus as Isa, Messiah, Son of Miriam. Miriam is the Arabic name of Mary in both the Quran and Arabic Bible. The Quran regards Isa as a special prophet close to Allah (Quran 3:45).

Hadith

Hadith is the sayings and deeds of Muhammad. Some Muslims believe that the Hadith has the same authority as the Quran, but the majority of Muslims give the Quran higher value. Muslims may quote the sayings of Muhammad as authoritative words to support their viewpoints. There are many collections of the Hadith. Sahih Al Bukhari and Sahih Muslims are normally given high credit.[12]

2. The Pillars of Islam

Sincere Muslims have at least five or six basic principles to follow.[13]

1. Shahada: Confession of Faith

    "There is no god but Allah. Muhammad is the messenger of Allah." Muslim people rehearse the Shahada in various occasions during the day.

2. Salat: Prayer

    Sincere Muslims pray five times a day. First at dawn, second at noon, third between noon and sunset, fourth at sunset, and fifth at nighttime.

3. Sawm: Fasting

    The majority of Muslims around the world fast the whole month of Ramadan from dawn till dusk. Islamic fasting includes abstaining from food, water, smoking, and sexual relations between spouses during the daytime.

4. Zakat: Almsgiving

    A Muslim must give at least 2.5 percent of his income to help poor people, build or renovate a mosque, and spread the cause of Islam.

5. Hajj: Pilgrimage

    A Muslim should visit Mecca at least once in his or her lifetime if it is affordable both physically and financially. Muslims believe that during the Hajj all their sins will be forgiven. It is important to notice that non-Muslims are prohibited from entering Mecca at any time.

6. Jihad: Holy War

    Abu Said al Khudri said, "I heard the Apostle of Allah, peace be upon him, say, 'If any one of you sees something displeasing him, let him change it with his hand, or with his tongue, or with his heart, and that is the least of faith'" (Hadith Sharif, an honorable saying).[14] Muhammad instructed his followers to fight against non-Muslims (Quran 9:29). Some Muslims may use the pen to fight; others may use the sword.

7. Day of Judgment

    Every person has two recording angels, one on each side, to count the good and bad deeds (Quran 50:17–18). In the final day of judgment Allah will determine the destination of each soul based on that report (Quran 50:21–25). Only those who die during either Hajj or Jihad may go straight to paradise.

C. Common Ground Between the Bible and the Quran

It is interesting to note that the similarities between the Bible and the Quran are much more than outright contradictions. Here are just a few examples:

The Quran agrees with the Torah, or Old Testament, in the following verses:

1. God is One and no one is like Him.   Quran 112:1–2 & Deut. 6:4
2. God created the heavens and   Quran 2:29 & Gen. 1:1
   the earth.
3. God created Adam and Eve,   Quran 2:35 & Gen. 2:16, 17
   instructing them to dwell in the
   garden and eat freely its fruits,
   except from one tree.
4. Satan deceived Adam and Eve   Quran 2:36 & Gen. 3:6
   and caused them to disobey God.
   As a result, God kicked them out
   of the garden.
5. God favored the children of   Quran 2:122 & Isa. 14:1
   Israel and preferred them over
   all mankind.
6. The Quran regards Abraham,   Quran 2:136 & Heb. 11:9
   Isaac, and Jacob as the forefathers
   of the nations.

The Quran regards many prophets, including Moses, who received the Torah, and David, who wrote the Zabour or Psalms, and Jesus, who they believe received the Gospel or New Testament (Quran 3:2). The Quran also agrees with the Gospel, or New Testament, in the following verses:

1. Jesus was born of the virgin Mary.   Quran 19:16–20
      & Luke 1:26–33
2. Jesus is a good prophet.   Quran 19:30 & Luke 7:16
3. Jesus is supported by   Quran 2:253 & John 1:32–34
   the Holy Spirit.
4. Jesus is the Word of God.   Quran 3:45, 4:171 & John 1:1
5. Jesus performed many miracles,   Quran 3:49 & 5:110
   such as:
   a. He opened the eyes of the blind   John 9:5–7
   b. He fed the multitudes   John 6:11–14
   c. He healed a leper   Matt. 8:2–3
   d. He raised the dead   John 11:43, 44
6. Jesus is a sinless prophet.   Quran 19:19 & John 8:46
7. Jesus ascended to heaven.   Quran 19:32 & Acts 1:9

8. Jesus will come back again   Quran 19:33 & Rev. 22:7
   in the end times.

 ## Major Differences Between the Bible and the Quran

1. Trinity of God

The Trinity is considered the stumbling block in an Islamic view. Allah is only one God and not three. "They are surely blasphemers who say: Lo, Allah is the third of three; when there is no God save the one God" (Quran 5:73).

Christ's baptism in Matthew 3:13–17 and His transfiguration in Matthew 17:1–5 are good pictures of the Trinity. They may help a Muslim to see the difference between the physical trinity—God, Mary, and their son, Jesus—rejected by the Quran and the spiritual Trinity embraced by the Bible.

2. Jesus Is God

The Quran denies that Jesus is God or the Son of God. "They are surely blasphemers who say: Lo, Allah is the Messiah, son of Mary. The Messiah (himself) said: O children of Israel, worship Allah, my Lord and your Lord" (Quran 5:72).

3. Death and Crucifixion of Christ

The Quran denies both the death and crucifixion of Jesus Christ. "And concerning their saying: "We slew the Messiah Jesus, Son of Mary, Allah's messenger. They slew him not, nor crucified him, but it appeared so unto them, and Lo! But Allah took him up unto Himself. Allah was ever Mighty, Wise" (Quran 5:157–158).

4. Concept of Sin

The Quran regards various categories of sin and different actions of sin. For instance, sexual immorality is the highest level, stealing is a medium sin, and lying falls into a lower category. In addition, there is no recognition of a sin nature or the original sin inherited from Adam. Because of this, a Muslim believes that he or she does not need atonement or ransom for sin. Consequently, Jesus did not have to die on the cross for the sin of mankind. Furthermore, a Muslim has no need of a new nature. "God is good and He created me good." It is true a Muslim may commit sin, but good deeds will make up for bad deeds. In the Day of Judgment, Allah will weigh the bad deeds against the good deeds and then decide where a Muslim may go: either Paradise or Hell.

Muslim Evangelism as a Way of Life

There are about 400,000 Muslims and almost 75 mosques, Islamic centers, and institutions in the greater Chicago area, about 40 to 45 percent of those being black Muslim groups.

Muslims, as many other religious groups, consider the United States a land of opportunities. So they come to the United States to look for new jobs, nice houses, big cars, profitable businesses, higher education, new careers—"the American dream."

Muslims occupy a variety of positions in public places, such as physicians, teachers, and students. They are also owners and customers of various Middle Eastern grocery stores and waiters in many ethnic restaurants. Barber and coffee shops are often good sites to meet and talk to Muslim men.

Reaching Muslims is not as complicated as it may seem. They are very religious and have a sincere heart to worship Allah and follow Muhammad. In addition, Muslims do not turn you off when you ask about their language, culture, or native country. In fact, they love to talk about their customs, traditions, and religious background.

Basic ways to reach Muslims may include teaching English as a Second Language, exchanging recipes, and general orientation of new immigrants. There are two different categories of relationship in which to communicate the Good News:

- First: Long-term relationships, such as co-workers, neighbors, classmates, roommates, and so on. In this case you have sufficient time to develop a solid relationship based upon love, care, and trust.
- Second: Short-term relationships, including short bus or train rides or a ride with a taxi driver. In this case you have only one chance and a short period of time. Telling your personal testimony and what Jesus has done in your life, after laying the necessary foundation, is one of the most effective tools for evangelism. The man born blind and healed by Jesus, when challenged by his townsfolk, replied, "Whether he is a sinner or not, I don't know. One thing I do know. I was blind but now I see!" (John 9:25).

General Rules in Presenting Christ to Muslims

The Personal Life of the Christian

1. Constant Prayer
   It is the power of the Holy Spirit that changes the heart of individuals. Pray for your friend by name.

2. Fasting
Fasting is highly recommended to gain Muslim souls.

3. Study the Scriptures
Focus on the gospel of Jesus Christ according to Luke, which includes much common ground with the recollection of Jesus' birth in the Quran.

4. Sincere Motive
Make sure that the sole motive of your ministry is love. Ministry motivated by hate shall surely fail, but genuine love will prevail. Love God and love your neighbor (Luke 10:27).

5. Genuine Goal
You may win an argument against your Muslim friend, but lose his/her soul. Keep your eye on the goal, not on "winning" an argument and proving your point.

6. Be Humble
It cost Christ to humble Himself and to be made in the likeness of men so that we may have everlasting life (Phil. 2:7–8).

Methodology and Culture

1. Be Available
Muslims are event-oriented, not time-oriented people.

2. Take Your Time
Most Muslims are laid-back and not used to a fast-paced life.

3. Family vs. Individual
Muslims in general are family-oriented, not individual-oriented people.

4. People vs. Material
Most Muslims are more concerned about a person than his/her material possessions.

5. Elders vs. Youth
Muslims respect older men and women and listen to them.

6. Same Gender
Man to man and woman to woman is a vital and effective method in order to avoid misunderstanding and to correct the distorted picture of immoral Christians.

7. One on One
Presenting the gospel to a Muslim has to be a personal conversation. There is a deep intimidation and peer pressure between Muslims.

Communication

1. Be Considerate
Speak slowly and clearly. Most Middle Eastern Muslims speak English as a second language.

2. Be Clear

Your Muslim friend is intelligent; do not beat around the bush.

3. Do Not Use Slang

Say "children," not "kids." Say "men," not "guys."

4. Do Not Use Abbreviations

Nothing is more confusing to your Muslim friend than abbreviations.

5. Use Common Biblical Principles

Muslims accept and regard the Bible as long as it agrees with the Quran. So we should carefully study both the Bible and the Quran to understand where Muslims already are in their spiritual journey as we reach out to them.

The following are useful examples of biblical principles:
- "Do to others what you would have them do to you" (Matt. 7:12).
- "What good will it be for a man if he gains the whole world, yet forfeits his soul?" (Matt. 16:26).
- "A man reaps what he sows" (Gal. 6:7).

Hospitality

1. No Alcoholic Beverages

According to the Quran, Muslims should not consume alcohol. Offering an alcoholic drink may offend your Muslim friend and confirm his traditional view that Christians are immoral people.

2. No Pork

Most Muslims are sincere about their religious traditions. Offering pork may badly affect your relationship with your Muslim friend.

3. Proper Seating

Keep your feet on the floor. Do not let your Muslim friend see the sole of your shoes, and do not place your Bible on the floor.

4. Be a Servant

As a host, you should serve your Muslim guest. Do not set out the food and say, "Help yourself."

5. Be Flexible

You may sit on the floor if there are not enough chairs to accommodate each guest. You may use your hand to eat when appropriate.

6. Be Conservative/Serious

Muslims enjoy serious conversations. A lot of joking and laughing may risk the relationship.

The Story of Zechariah

Zechariah is a good Muslim fellow from the Middle East. He came to the United States with a business visa to start a new Middle Eastern restaurant in the Greater Chicago area. Zechariah started to work as a waiter in a Middle Eastern restaurant, where I met him. It took me about six months to develop a solid, friendly relationship. During that time I often dined with my wife and children and other friends in this restaurant.

As usual, every time we eat there, we hold hands and pray before the meal. Zechariah noticed our behavior but did not make any comments. We talked with him about his land, family, food, customs, and traditions. One time I was there by myself and the whole place was almost empty. We started a religious discussion about the Bible, Quran, Jesus (Isa in the Quran), and Muhammad. Zechariah is an open-minded person with a great zeal to learn, listen, and ask questions. After a good talk, I offered him an Arabic Bible, which he received with clear gratitude. I noticed Zechariah hid the Bible right away. He did not want any curious person to know what he just received.

A few weeks later, I stopped by the restaurant for a cup of tea and to ask Zechariah about what he had been reading in the Bible. I had a deep joy as I listened to him. He told me he had not been sure where to start. As he opened the Bible, Zechariah was surprised to find his own name in the Old Testament. He went directly to the book of Zechariah and read it. Then he moved to the beginning of the Bible, the book of Genesis. I had the privilege to walk through the Bible with him and answer some of his related questions.

1. General Observation

   Seeking and reading the Bible, Zechariah had to confront serious barriers. First of all, Muslims believe that the Bible has been changed, tampered with, and corrupted. Second, the Quran, the final word of Allah, exists to correct and replace the Bible.

2. Recommendation

   Most Muslims respect sincere Christians who pray and read the Bible. Do not shy away from praying in the presence of your Muslim friend.

3. Walk Through the Bible with a Muslim Friend[15]

   This walk may take fifteen or twenty minutes. Start from Genesis chapter 1, the creation of heaven and earth. Then go to the story of how Adam and Eve disobeyed God in the Garden of Eden, and how they discovered their nakedness and were kicked out of the garden (Gen. 3). A similar story is told in Quran 7:19–22.

   The first murder occurred when Cain killed Abel (Gen. 4:8–9). Sin increased so that God had to destroy all of mankind by a flood (story of Noah—Gen. 6:5–8). Abraham obeyed God's calling

(Gen. 12:1–3). Also look at Joseph's dreams and how his brothers sold him into slavery (Gen. 37:5–8, 18, 28).

God sent Moses to deliver the children of Israel from Egypt (Exod. 3:10). God instructed Moses to offer the sacrifice of the Passover (Exod. 12:5–7). Moses received the Law of God (Exod. 20:1–3, 13–16). David wrote the Psalms, which are called the Zabour in the Quran. You might read Psalm 23.

The birth of Jesus Christ is given in Luke 1–2, the spread of the church in Acts 2:8–12. Many nations are mentioned there, including Arabs, Egyptians, Libyans, and other Middle Eastern countries.

Finally, look at the promise of the second coming of Jesus the Christ (Acts 1:11) and the final judgment of the whole world in the book of Revelation. It is a very effective way to show your Muslim friend the unity of the Scriptures.

Conclusion: Our Work—and God's

First and foremost, Muslims are people. They have their own needs, concerns, and problems. They are sincere to worship Allah and follow Muhammad. They deserve our genuine love, care, and respect. Above all, they need to see Christ in our lives and touch Him through our deeds and listen to Him in our words. You may be the only available gospel for your Muslim friend to read.

Finally, remember that Jesus called us to plant seeds. It is the work of the Holy Spirit to save a lost soul.

Reflection Questions

1. What is my motive for reaching Muslims?

2. Where are the Muslims in my area? How large is their community?

3. How can I help them? What can I do to be better prepared?

4. What more do I need to know about the Bible and Quran in order to be effective?

All Quranic references are from Pickthall, Marmaduke M. *The Meaning of the Glorious Quran* (New York: The Muslim World League, U.M. Office, 1997).

chapter nineteen

MISSIONS IN REVERSE

EVANGELIZING AFRICAN IMMIGRANTS TO AMERICA

SUNDAY BWANHOT

Introduction: Meeting Africans in America

In August of 1995, the second day after moving into our house in Chicago to begin ministry to African immigrants, my wife was taken to a grocery store where she met an East African man. In the course of their conversation she told him that we had just moved in as missionaries from Nigeria. Surprised, the man told her his story. He came into this country as a Christian, but he had since abandoned his faith. He claimed, "It is impossible to survive in this land and remain a Christian. The time is just not there to practice your Christianity." He then "prophesied" that my wife would soon forget about Christianity. Since then, we have met many others with similar tragic testimonies.

A few weeks later, we received a call from a Nigerian lady raising three little children in a suburb of Chicago. She was lonely and she wanted to find out if she could visit us, just to have someone to talk with. She even offered to pay us if we would accept her visit. This is an unheard-of situation in the African culture where people live communally. Her plight is the plight of many other immigrants in this society who are not used to living independently.

Recently, we met an African-American named Emmanuel who practices Islam. We were baffled that a Muslim would be named Emmanuel. He told us that when he chose Islam, he did not see the need of changing his name. He told us he chose Islam because it is a way of life and is also the original religion of Africans, as opposed to Christianity, the "white man's religion." Both points he made are a fabrication of the truth.

How can situations like these and others be best addressed? SIM (Society for International Ministries) is on the cutting edge of meeting these challenges. Our story is a unique one and a suggested pattern for missions as we enter the new millennium.

THE SIM STORY

SIM is a mission agency with headquarters in Charlotte, North Carolina. More than two thousand SIM missionaries are ministering in all the continents of the world today. SIM pioneer missionaries arrived in Nigeria, West Africa, in 1893. The fruit of one hundred years of ministry is the planting of a national church—Evangelical Church of West Africa (ECWA) with four million worshipers today. ECWA also has a missions department with 1,250 missionaries serving mainly in seven West African countries, the United Kingdom, and America.

A few years ago, SIM leadership observed the growing communities of immigrants in American cities and saw that many of these immigrants were coming from the traditional countries served by SIM missionaries. They also discovered that these immigrants were not the target of most traditional American churches. Therefore, SIM established a local ministry—Ethnic Focus Ministry (EFM) to address this need. A team of veteran missionaries who have served in different parts of the world with different gifts and abilities were brought together to begin this ministry. SIM also requested its daughter church—ECWA in Nigeria—to send a missionary to be part of the team and help in reaching out to African immigrants in Chicago and other cities.

God's call to meet this need came to my family, and we accepted the challenge to step out as the first ECWA missionaries to partner with SIM to reach immigrants in American cities.

Coming from the Muslim-dominated northern part of Nigeria, Thomas Archibald, the first SIM missionary to come to my town (Kagoro), arrived May 7, 1927, while my great-grandfather was the chief of the town. After he had labored for a few years, several people responded to the gospel. This golden heritage resulted in my salvation before I became a teenager. Ever since I have desired nothing more than to be where God wants me to be and to do what God wants me to do.

God has a way of repeating history without anyone interfering. I left my hometown May 7, 1995, for America as a missionary—sixty-eight years to the day after the first missionary entered my town. What could be more exciting than to see and be a part of how God is changing the face of missions in our time? It is indeed "missions in reverse."

Missions in Reverse

Parents want to see their children take after them and even surpass them in every area of achievement. When this happens, parents are proud and feel that they have successfully fulfilled their responsibilities. I desire to leave such a legacy for my children. This is what "missions in reverse" is all about. In his editorial comment in *Missions Frontiers*, Ralph Winter noted this evolving process. Reflecting on an interview with Jim Plueddemann, the general director of SIM, he said:

> *Once mission efforts on the part of the national churches (often called "Third World Missions") have finally burst into view (often without the initiative of the expatriate missionaries) truly amazing and wonderful mission structures have often emerged. Certainly that is true for SIM, which Plueddemann rightly points out.*
>
> *Note that the final appearance of these new missions completes a potent "reproductive cycle." 1) Expatriate mission agencies plant churches and 2) those churches sprout their own mission agencies, and 3) those new field mission structures then become a new generation of "Standard Missions."[1]*

A confirmation of this process is the statement by the Evangelical Missionary Society (EMS)—the indigenous mission agency of ECWA in Nigeria—that "As the year 2000 approaches, the EMS prayerfully wants to mobilize more missionaries and supporters to refocus and particularly have our eyes focused on reaching the people of African descent scattered around the world, more especially in Latin America and North America."[2]

It was with great excitement that SIM received us (ECWA missionaries) to partner together in reaching out to internationals in the cities. An article on our family in *SIM Now* stated:

> *The arrival of Sunday Bwanhot and family in Chicago in 1995 completed a cycle that began more than half a century before with SIM missionary outreach in Nigeria. The coming of this young African as a missionary to the West represents the ultimate harvest of any missionary effort—those who have heard the message going forth as missionaries themselves.[3]*

Ralph Winter continued in his editorial comment:

> *In the 1920's people spoke of "the great new fact of our time" as the marvel of national **churches** planted within hundreds of different languages and cultures*

*all over the world. Today "the great new fact of our time" is the marvel of nation-al **mission** structures as those same overseas church movements add their own missionaries to an ever-increasing world total. Thus, the **mission fields** of the world are becoming **mission bases**.*[4] *(bold type in original)*

This is not a new phenomenon; the history of the Christian church has seen other epochs of missions in reverse. Western missionaries serving currently in several locations in the Middle East are actually a case of missions in reverse. The pioneer missionaries from North America in the second decade of the nineteenth century headed east.[5] The church in the Middle East is virtually extinguished, and the need to reach out is important and urgent. The church in North America is still alive, but it has real issues that beg for missionaries from developing countries. As we begin a new century and a new millennium, this trend of missions in reverse will become more and more crucial.

North America has been described as the third-largest mission field. The Navigators, in their Spring 1998 ministry report, *One to One*, titled the issue "America: A New Mission Field." They cited researchers and analysts who described North America as the world's third-largest mission field behind Western Europe and Japan.[6] No nation in this world is so spiritually sound that it does not need help from outside its borders.

The Mandate

The mandate Jesus Christ gave the disciples just before His Ascension to heaven was to "go" and "make disciples" of "all nations" (Matt. 28:18–19). Earlier, Jesus recruited these disciples with the firm purpose to "come, follow me . . . and I will make you fishers of men" (Matt. 4:19). Three and a half years later, the focus and mission remained unchanged, and it has not changed since. The disciples came to Jesus, followed Him, learned from Him, then went as He commanded and started evangelizing nations. Their first shot at the job was in the metropolitan city of Jerusalem where they had to minister to more than fifteen nationalities in one day (Acts 2:5–12).

Today, God is actively bringing different nationalities to our cities, giving the organized church and every individual Christian the opportunity of reaching the nations right at our doorstep. For most of us believers today, the "go" is only a street away. Some others, though, will still have to cross the mountains, the seas, and the deserts to "the uttermost parts" of the world. It is important to start thinking straight here that the nations we are to reach as the Bible commands are people groups and not necessarily geographical destination points. A lot of these nations are now conveniently located in the neighborhoods of our cities.

Our home on the North Side of Chicago is less than a block from Devon Street. Driving for ten minutes on this street, one will pass through Jewish, Russian, Indian, and Pakistani communities.

Further east and a little south are Chinese, Vietnamese, Cambodians, Thai, and other Asian communities as well as Africans. West and a little south are the Polish and Hispanic communities.

THE GROWING MISSION FIELD OF NORTH AMERICA

Two decades ago no one would have thought that America would become a large mission field in such a short time. A brochure prepared by the EMS summarized this phenomenon, stating that America is home to millions of immigrants who are spiritually starving. Islam and other world religions are gaining much ground.[7] Islam is considered to be the fastest growing religion in America today.

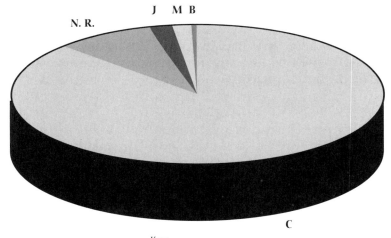

WORLD RELIGIONS IN AMERICA

Key:

C–	Christian	86.5%
N.R.–	Non-Religious	8.7%
J–	Jews	2.4%
M–	Muslim	1.8%
B–	Buddhist (0.4%), Hindu (0.2%) = 0.6%

GROUPS LISTED AS CHRISTIAN

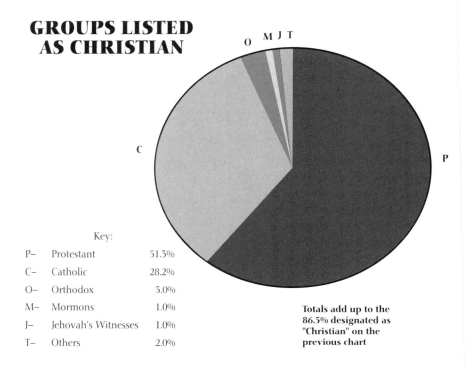

Key:

P–	Protestant	51.3%
C–	Catholic	28.2%
O–	Orthodox	3.0%
M–	Mormons	1.0%
J–	Jehovah's Witnesses	1.0%
T–	Others	2.0%

Totals add up to the 86.5% designated as "Christian" on the previous chart

The above charts reflect statistics of "professing" Christians and not necessarily those who really are saved and living the Christian life. A realistic estimate of the actual number of true believers in America would be difficult to project.

The Stew Pot

The diversity of cultures in North America has become the symbol of what America really is. Population growth in America today is more of a factor of immigration, as well as a high birthrate among immigrants already living in America. For instance, the annual growth rate in 1990 was 0.82 percent and immigration accounted for 0.54 percent.[8] A greater percentage of the new population is non-Christian. The implication is that America is becoming more and more "unchristian" every year given the estimated one million legal and illegal immigrants[9] coming into the country.

Large communities of different nationalities that have migrated into the U.S.A. live in the cities. Terry Muck observed, "Immigrant communities find it easier to settle and establish new roots in the cities."[10] Kenneth B. Mulholland rightly substituted the old vision of "America the Melting Pot" for "America the Stew Pot."

Just as softened, but largely unassimilated and quite discernable chunks of meat, potatoes, carrots, celery, and onions swim in the gravy of the stew, so ethnic minorities—Mexicans, Liberians, Poles, Vietnamese, Iraqis, Samoans—seek to find their place in American society without surrendering their cultural heritage.[11]

In an address by Dr. Daniel Sanchez, he confirmed:

There are more Jewish people here than in the nation of Israel; more Blacks than in any country of the world except for Nigeria; more Samoans than in Samoa, and more Hispanics than in any nation except for Spain and Mexico. Miami is the second largest Cuban city in the world. Only Warsaw has more Polish people than Chicago. The majority group in Atlanta, Augusta and Oakland is African American. Los Angeles is the second largest Mexican, Armenian, Filipino, Korean and Salvadorian city in the world.[12]

Patrick Johnstone, editor of *Operation World,* gave statistics for the racial makeup of the United States, which I've translated into the following graph.[13]

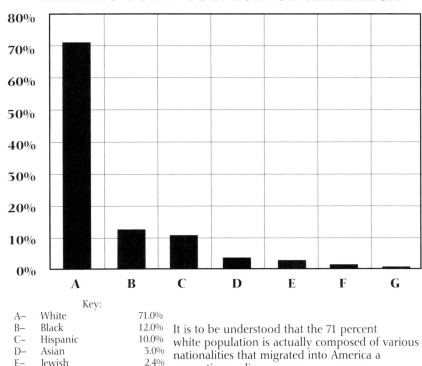

ETHNIC COMPOSITION OF AMERICA

Key:

A–	White	71.0%
B–	Black	12.0%
C–	Hispanic	10.0%
D–	Asian	3.0%
E–	Jewish	2.4%
F–	Arabic	1.2%
G–	Armenian	0.4%

It is to be understood that the 71 percent white population is actually composed of various nationalities that migrated into America a generation earlier or more.

Respecting Cultural Differences

From my experience so far in working with immigrants, a church for every culturally different group should be the first step. Integration will take place in a natural process as the two cultures become more and more compatible or as the individuals feel adjusted to the host culture. The beginning place is not integration, but a church that relevantly meets the needs of the immigrant. For example, at a Thanksgiving dinner organized in Wheaton, Illinois, by my colleagues in the Ethnic Focus Ministry in 1997, different nationalities were invited. When the Somalis were asked if seating them at tables with different people so they could interact with new friends from different backgrounds was OK, they resented the idea. In their words: "We either stay together, [i.e., at one table] or we will not come." This experience brought to mind a similar situation I encountered in Nigeria a few years ago.

Before coming to Chicago as a missionary, I served the Lord in the Prayer and Church Renewal Ministry at the ECWA Headquarters in Jos, Nigeria. Apart from praying for the church for revival, we also conducted prayer seminars in churches and groups. I was invited to teach on prayer at an adult Sunday school class in a church in Jos in 1992. To my surprise there was only one Nigerian in a class of about thirty people, mainly Westerners. I thought it was wrong for the Westerners (most of them missionaries) to be apart by themselves instead of integrating with the national churches, but certainly I did not know the struggles they were going through. Now that I am an immigrant myself, I understand better. The Westerners went to this particular church to get their spiritual needs met in a cultural way that appealed to them before returning to do cross-cultural ministry during the week. It is a real need everywhere one goes.

Most of the people groups in America are unreached, as they do not have sufficient gospel witness to evangelize their own people. As long as the shift in the demographics is in favor of urbanization, the problem of pockets of unreached communities will plague us. We must learn to address this need.

THE NEED FOR MISSIONARIES
FROM DEVELOPING COUNTRIES

A Christian Nation?

The general view held by Africans and many other people is that America is a Christian country. Christians from around the world want to come to America, believing that this will afford them the opportunity to see true Christianity practiced and to grow in the Lord. Muslims are concerned that if their young people are allowed to go to America, they will all be converted to Christianity, so they encourage them to go to the Middle East or elsewhere. Unfortunately, the true situation is captured in an SIM Ethnic Focus Ministry brochure: "Most internationals come here believing this to be a 'Christian' country . . . yet fewer than 10% will be invited into an American, let alone a Christian, home."[14] To confirm this, one Kenyan, in response to an interview, said that many Kenyans do not go to church but prefer to listen to Christian radio because of the absence of comfortable fellowship in the churches.[15]

Some years ago, Christian leaders in Nigeria raised concerns over the lifestyles of young people returning from America. The zeal and enthusiasm they used to exhibit as Christians before going to America was observably absent upon their return. The question raised was: What is happening to our young people in America? Philip Barker, who did research on the "African in Chicagoland," answered the question through an interview with Leslie Pelt, who is a Chicagoan currently serving as a missionary in Nigeria with SIM:

> Africans are also "devoured by U.S." because they innocently accept the secular values of America and it "blows out their spiritual light." They are "surprised by the materialism and entertainment and then gradually get sucked into" the unbiblical practices of the post-Christian era. Evidence comes of this when their obligations and loyalty to community fades and they actually take up materialism. Over time they innocently watch television and accept the messages of it as indicative of morality in what they perceive as a Christian country.[16]

Unfortunately, the American church is not quite equipped and braced to face these problems. This is why the Ethnic Focus Ministry is trying to mobilize and train churches to do that. But with the millions of immigrants scattered in different parts of America, it could take years to make a significant impact. This is where missionaries from the originating countries of the immigrants could assist the church here in reaching out.

The Plight of Hidden Minorities

Immigrants go through a lot of adjustment, fear, uncertainty, language barriers, loneliness, spiritual starvation, excessive working hours, etc. The three examples given at the opening of this chapter describe just a bit of the plight of immigrants into this country. A Nigerian friend of mine moved from Wheaton, Illinois, to Mississippi with his family a few years ago and was quite delighted to discover that their house was very close to a church. The first time they visited they discovered they were the only people of color. Nobody talked with them. They returned the following Sunday and the pastor met them after the service. He told them that if they wanted to keep coming to the church, a motion and vote had to be taken by the church before they could be accepted. To summarize it, they were not welcomed.

In my four years of ministry among African immigrants in the Chicago area, I have seen spiritual rottenness and family breakups infiltrate many immigrant families. Most of the problems stem from culture clash and a breakdown in communication. Couples spend little or no time together as each spouse is working two jobs or a full-time job along with full-time schooling.

The Response So Far

Commendable work has been done on campuses by various student-led organizations and ministries like Campus Crusade for Christ, International Students Inc., InterVarsity Christian Fellowship, Navigators, and so forth in getting internationals situated and integrated into the mainstream of the society. However, the majority of immigrants into America today do not live on campuses but in the neighborhoods of the major cities. It is this large percentage of immigrants that we are concerned about today.

Chicago, for example, has an estimated fifty thousand African immigrants. Fifteen thousand of these are Nigerians, while Ghanaians, Liberians, Somalis, and Ethiopians have significant numbers also. World Relief, which targets refugees and is profiled in another chapter in this anthology, SIM Ethnic Focus Ministry, and just a handful of churches are known to have some ongoing work with immigrants in Chicago. This field is still largely unreached.

Kenneth Mulholland's response is:

> I am not advocating that (IFMA) missions abandon mission work in their traditional fields in order to plant churches in North America. Rather, I suggest that in partnership with existing ethnic churches or with churches which would like to launch new work among lesser evangelized people groups distinct from themselves, they seek to leverage their experience and expertise among the ethnic enclaves in North America.[17]

Michael Pocock, of Dallas Theological Seminary, was quoted by Mulholland, and Pocock pointed out that the "school systems already train teachers for the multi-cultural situation facing them, but the evangelical church has been slower to take steps to increase awareness of their congregation and their appreciation for the opportunity the Lord is giving them."[18]

Churches could be equipped through training programs by the Ethnic Focus Ministry of SIM to reach their ethnic neighbors by teaching English as a Second Language, church planting, discipleship, and friendship ministry. The church, on the other hand, could come alongside its ethnic neighbors and help them bring in trained workers from their countries of origin to effectively minister to them as a short-term measure and help train others who will remain in America to carry on with the work on a long-term basis.

It is worth emphasizing here that trained workers from these immigrants' countries of origin will more likely impact their community than someone who is not from that culture.

The Struggles African Immigrants Face

Culture shock generally summarizes all the difficulties an immigrant into a different culture experiences. When we moved into Chicago a little more than four years ago, we had our share of culture shock, which every member of our community here in America has experienced.

1. Weather: For most Africans, snow, temperatures below freezing, sunset at 5:00 P.M., sunrise at 5:00 A.M., rain every month of the year, trees without foliage for months, hurricanes, tornadoes, etc. are new experiences and not easy ones to adjust to.
2. Clothing: Different types of clothing are used during the different seasons, and sometimes one may not easily distinguish a male from a female from the person's apparel. Africans wear the same clothes year-round, and men dress as men while women dress as women.
3. Relationships: Communal life is visibly absent, especially among Americans living in the cities. Everybody lives by and for himself. Africans, even in our large cities, still maintain some level of communal life. This is one of the most devastating experiences for Africans in America.
4. Family: Most American families have only one or two children, and some couples are not interested in raising children at all. This is shocking to most Africans, who rear large families and easily become polygamous if the wife is not able to bear children or does not bear a male child.
5. Discipline: Many in America consider spanking children to be child abuse. Africans, on the other hand, consider a parent to be spoiling a child if that child is not spanked when the occasion warrants it.
6. Communication: Americans generally speak straight to the point and sometimes the message seems more important than the person

spoken to. Africans talk in circles using parables, riddles, and popular quotations to make a point. What an American can communicate in five minutes may take an African nearly an hour.

7. Language: Although many Americans are surprised that some Africans speak English well, they turn around and embarrass us with remarks that we have an "accent." It is an unkind remark to Africans who speak several other languages when most Americans know only English.

8. Eye Contact: People who cannot look at others eye to eye while conversing are considered insincere in this culture. To the African, it is disrespectful to look at the other person directly in the face. Only enemies who are about to fight challenge each other eyeball-to-eyeball.

9. Hugging: Hugging is a common practice in this society, even between sexes. Hugging the opposite sex is a taboo in Africa.

10. Holding Hands: Same-sex friends who hold hands while walking are considered homosexuals in this culture. In Africa, it is a sign of good friendship and has no other meaning.

11. First Names: In American culture, children sometimes call their parents and other adults by their first names. This is a shock to Africans. Children dare not call adults by their first names in Africa. Adults, out of respect, use pet names to call each other. I was a teenager before I knew my mother's actual first name. Children have fought many times because another child dared to mention their father's name.

12. Left Hand: It is common practice in this culture to give and receive things with your left hand. It is a serious offense to do so in Africa. The left hand is considered culturally dirty and connotes evil.

13. Time Orientation: Americans are ruled by the clock, whereas Africans are ruled by events. African time simply means no time restriction.

14. Hospitality: Visitors to most American homes call ahead, and when the door is opened they come into the house and wait to be seated. The visitor is asked if he or she would like a drink, and choices are offered. Food is rarely part of the entertainment unless prior arrangement was made. Africans, on the other hand, walk into homes unannounced. When the door is opened, the visitor comes in and makes himself or herself comfortable, taking whatever seat desired. A drink is served instantly by the host without seeking the consent of the visitor. Even if the family has just finished eating dinner, the hostess has to prepare a meal for the visitor. Seeking the visitor's consent before serving a drink or food is interpreted to mean that the host is miserly, inhospitable, or lazy.

In four years we have made some adjustments like the rest of Africans, and we now live in a culture that is neither purely African, nor completely Western. One has to be in this new culture to be able to understand the immigrants more fully.

Advantages of Having an Indigenous Missionary

1. Acceptability: A missionary coming from the same ethnic community he is reaching out to does not need any credentials or years of faithful service before he can be accepted. Africans, for example, suspect "visitors" who are not from their community. It takes a long time before an "outsider" is accepted and trusted. Since our coming to Chicago, almost every African we have met has welcomed us and taken time to talk with us as if we had lived next door back in Africa. Someone from another culture will not be accepted as quickly.

2. Understanding: Experiencing culture shock, making adjustments, living in another culture, and going through all that an immigrant goes through equips the indigenous missionary to better minister to his people than anyone else can. He can relate to their problems and help them walk through them.

3. Boldness: An indigenous missionary will be naturally bold and confident in witnessing among his community. He has no fear of wrong communication or wrong approach. Someone from another culture will first have to learn how to effectively communicate with this community, and errors of approach that could adversely slow down his effectiveness cannot be ruled out. For example, as I communicate the gospel with Africans, I will also directly challenge them to quit drinking, smoking, and attending parties and begin to go to church—a type of "John the Baptist message." This is what works for an African—direct confrontation. Most Western ministers are not comfortable in using this approach.

4. Suspicion: Africans do not accept people who are not from their community at face value or instantly believe what they say. It takes a long time of relationship building with such "strangers" before an African can open up and speak from the heart. This hurdle can be bypassed by having a fellow African minister to them.

5. Accessibility: Africans do not care much about "private" time and will more gladly have someone visit than be alone. In addition, unannounced visits are very much appreciated because that reveals how much one cares. Africans are able to do that, but someone else from another culture may find it hard to do so.

6. Freedom: What amuses a Westerner does not necessarily amuse an

African. Most Americans will start off conversations with weather, ball games, and the like. These are all events. Africans want to talk about people because their lives are entwined around people. But as noted earlier, an African will hardly be free to have a heart-to-heart talk with someone he has no relationship with. This is why Africans do not go to professional counselors. That business is nonexistent in Africa.

Our Ministry

Although our target group for ministry is West African English-speaking immigrants, we find ourselves ministering to almost every nationality along the way while pressing on toward our target. We minister mainly in the following ways:

1. Prayer: We invest a lot of time in prayer for our people. We believe we will do a better job talking more to God about them than just talking to them about God.
2. Visitations: We build relationships through visiting our people in their homes, the hospital, etc.
3. Bible Studies: We hold Bible studies in small groups and on a one-to-one basis.
4. Counseling: A very important and demanding task. About a quarter of our ministry time goes into this. We do direct, telephone, and correspondence counseling.
5. Church Planting: We started Goodnews Evangelical Church—a multinational church with an African bias to meet the spiritual needs of our people and also to provide an alternative to the syncretistic African churches in Chicago that our people attend.
6. Preaching and Teaching: We have opportunities to preach or teach in churches, conferences, schools, etc. and to challenge Christians to reach out to immigrants around them.

The Challenge

It is an established fact that nationals can best reach their own people irrespective of where they are located. An African can best reach Africans in American cities. A Hispanic can best reach the Hispanic community, a Korean or Chinese can best reach the Korean or Chinese communities. Steve Hawthorne has put it well:

People groups are God's idea. . . . There are many different ways that people band together in people groups. Common language is obvious; and of course common ethnic background glues people together. But cultural, social, economic, geographic, religious, and political factors all combine to give different groups a distinct corporate identity. From the view point of evangelization, a "people group" is the largest possible group within which the Gospel can spread as a church planting movement without encountering barriers of understanding or acceptance.[19]

We cannot consider North America as a whole as a people group. It is composed of different people groups that are culturally diverse. We have seen that the larger society is either indifferent or does not know how to handle these new neighbors whose ways are quite different. The definitions that apply to countries overseas are valid here as well. I believe Steve Hawthorne's remark is applicable to America:

Other people groups are without a strong church-based witness to their culture. They are beyond the reach of normal neighbor-to-neighbor evangelism. These are the Hidden Peoples or Unreached Peoples. Only cross-cultural church planting efforts will be able to make the Gospel compellingly clear and invitingly accessible. The national churches could possibly penetrate their culturally distant neighbors, but in most cases do not.[20]

This is where the change is beginning to take place. Ethnic missionaries (like our family) are crossing land and sea to get to their culturally related people in other countries who are spiritually unreached. Missions in reverse is taking place. How can the existing church at large assist?

Ministry in the cities is very costly and requires full-time devotion. The ethnic communities being reached are not organized or financially able to support a full-time worker. The church in America can help. Individuals, churches, independent mission agencies, and other organizations can come alongside and assist in some of the following ways:

1. Prayer: Pray for the spiritual and emotional stability of the immigrants.
2. Friendship: Determine and step out to befriend an international. Be a true friend. Do not try to Americanize him or her. Love the people just as they are.
3. Churches could adopt an immigrant community, start a Bible study in their facilities, and supply whatever a good host could provide. Give the immigrants the freedom to grow independently. Do not incorporate them into your congregation or denomination unless they so choose.
4. Help support an indigenous missionary to work among these immigrants.

5. Consider a partnership with a home church of the immigrants and team up with them to reach out to their community. It has been noted in two issues of *Mission Frontiers* that Africa is a sleeping giant that must be awakened to take its parts in sending missionaries to the 10/40 window and beyond.[21] Countries like Nigeria and Indonesia have started but will need encouragement and help to get such programs going.[22]

Conclusion:
The Future of Missions

Although the number of missionaries from the West is slowly declining, there is an upsurge of missionaries from developing countries whose presence in the West has been hampered by lack of finances. The first and second decades of the twenty-first century will witness even more missionaries coming from the developing countries to Europe and North America after making a mark in the Middle East, Asia, and North Africa. Missions in reverse is here. May God help us all to do our part.

Reflection Questions

1. Immigrants are coming to America by the thousands every month. Do you see this as a problem or as an opportunity?

2. Imagine you were an immigrant in another country. How would you like the Christian community to respond to you?

3. With the large ethnic communities coming into America, would you say that the church is equipped to minister to them effectively? How could they best be ministered to?

4. Is the idea of "missions in reverse" the need of the hour to be pursued with all vigor, or is it something to be allowed to take its natural course? What role could you play?

part six

DISENFRANCHISED
SUBCULTURES

chapter twenty

RESTORING DIGNITY TO THE HOMELESS

THE HISTORY AND WORK OF BREAKTHROUGH URBAN MINISTRIES

ARLOA SUTTER

Introduction: Experiencing Homelessness for Myself

In the spring of 1997, in my sixth year of providing services to homeless people in Chicago with Breakthrough Urban Ministries, I decided I wanted to experience what it was like to be on the receiving end of the services that Breakthrough offers. For four days I left my home and family, my shower and coffeepot, and ventured out to the South Side of Chicago for a plunge into homelessness. I wore red sweatpants with a hole in the knee over long underwear, a T-shirt, a blue sweatshirt, a white sweat hood, a blue steelworkers union jacket, a Nike hat backward, and sunglasses. I had taken off all of my jewelry, including my watch, and had left my contacts at home.

I carried a double grocery bag with a book, lotion, a little journal, three pens, a highlighter pen, a spoon, a Styrofoam cup, a hairbrush, and a little jug of water. I stuck my Chicago library card in my book so I could be identified in case something happened to me.

My experience was life changing.

It was frightening not to know where I was going to sleep or how I would survive without money or my refrigerator. It was raining, so I ventured into a Catholic church in Pilsen, a Mexican neighborhood in Chicago. The church was holding services in Spanish. At the end of the service I asked the priest if he knew of a place in the neighborhood where I could stay for the night. Following his directions, I walked for four hours and over five miles to find there was no shelter at the address he gave me or any other spot on the route there. Finally a policeman directed me to a women's shelter. The shelter was in a little storefront church. It had no toilet paper, soap, or towels in the bathroom. For breakfast we ate a little spoonful of oatmeal without milk or sugar. There was nothing but water to drink. We slept on blue mats provided by the city's Department of Human Services.

During the day I followed the women as they moved from place to place to find food and shelter from the cold and rain. When the days were sunny I sat in the park. When it was cold or rainy I found a library to sit in. I used bathrooms in public parks. We ate at different ministry centers during the day. By following the trail I was able to eat five meals each day, but few were substantial. Our whole day was organized around the location of the next meal and staying warm and dry.

It was disturbing for me to realize that although ministries provided food and shelter, none of them seemed to care to know me personally. I had developed a story about why I was out on the street, but I never had to use it. Only one of the volunteers ever asked my name.

CONSULTING EXPERTS ON HOMELESSNESS

To understand what it is like to be homeless, I decided to turn to experts, the homeless people themselves. I interviewed them to learn about their experiences on the street and how they got there. I tried to investigate their thoughts and feelings regarding their experiences of homelessness and the services and relationships provided to them by the staff of shelters and service centers that they had turned to for help. I wanted to learn how the experience of being without housing had affected their self-esteem and about the effective and ineffective ways they were serviced by the staff who operate the places they went to receive help.

If the troubling circumstances of their lives have not already stripped homeless people of their sense of dignity, it is quite likely that their experiences on the street and in shelters will.

Standing in food lines and waiting outside shelter doors while onlookers seem unaware of their existence or even bothered by their presence is depressing and humiliating. Homeless people often feel a loss of identity and hope. Their sense of self-worth becomes crumpled as again and again they face rejection in their search for an income and struggle to survive. Heavily preoccupied with bureaucracy, numbers, and statistics, the poverty industry, American society, and even the church have tended to contribute to the depersonalization of homeless people.

The social, political, psychological, and spiritual factors that produce homelessness are compounded by the experience of homelessness itself. Individuals without homes face the daily pressures of survival on the street. Without strong support, it is difficult for the homeless to overcome feelings of fear and hopelessness. Paul told me that he was so devastated when he learned that he had AIDS that all he could think about was drinking to numb the pain. "I didn't think my family cared. I didn't think that there was a God that could help ease the pain of my world crashing down around me. I was blinded with self-pity, resentment, and anger."

Stephen didn't think he would ever have a home. "I never thought I was capable enough to handle life on my own. I was afraid because I thought I was inferior, a mess-up. I ran around with a mask on like I didn't like anybody. For the first time in my life I can just be me. I can say I'm afraid. I am forming a strong support system."

Of the thirty-two homeless men and women I interviewed, 45 percent had feared not knowing where they were going to sleep at night, 35 percent feared getting sick, and 32 percent worried about not having anything to eat.

The attitudes of government workers and shelter staff can be demeaning. Some shelters are run by homeless people who have been deputized as staff, but are not really ready for the responsibility. JoAnne explained her frustration: "They hire people to run the shelter that was homeless before and they kind of sort of forget where they came from. That bugs me. They put themselves above everyone else."

The manner in which staff members communicate with homeless guests makes a big difference to Sam. "You got some guys that just don't know how to talk to people with a positive attitude. They're like the world owes them something; they don't work like that. They might of had a bad day. Some of them get a little loud and 'Well, you ain't got to be here' or 'Oh, you're barred out. Don't come in. See me tomorrow.'" He told me,

> Some of the guys talk to you in the food lines like you ain't nothing, you ain't no-body. Staff, like at one center, I'll never go back up there again. They be cussin'. "Take your _____ hat off! Sit down and shut up" and all that, you know? I'm a grown man just like you're a grown man. Just say, "Mr. M, have a seat, please put off your hat." You all sit around with you'all's hats like this, cocked to the side and all that. That's not showin' no example. Some of them guys need to change their attitude. I'm already mixed up a little myself. I'd either be dead or locked up goin' through someone else's trials or tribulations. Some of these guys do need to change their ways about talkin' with people.

Relational tension and violence on the street and in shelters is a big concern of the people with whom I talked. More than 30 percent of the homeless people I interviewed indicated that they had been shot or stabbed. About a third said they had come to a shelter to find safety.

Angie expressed her feelings about being homeless. "It's a very ugly feeling. It's scary not knowing where your next meal's coming from, what you're going to do for the day. That's scary. People are very nasty to you when you're homeless. I was raped a couple of times. It was very terrible. Very."

Sam's way of handling the negativity he found on the street was to isolate himself. "I'm more of a loner. I keep to myself. You stay out of trouble that way. A lot of these guys run in a pack. I don't like that because it seem like they lookin' for trouble and trouble is easy to find. So that's why I stay to myself."

Twenty-nine percent of the homeless people I interviewed said they had been harassed by the police. "When you get stopped by the police, you know . . . they treat you terrible," reported Angie. "Cold, you know. Like you're just another person. Terrible. They automatically assume 'cuz you're out there homeless you're either whorin' or, excuse my language, or into drugs and all that. That's not the case with me."

During my homeless excursion, a Chicago policeman called me over to his squad car and asked me with a snicker to go out with his partner for a date. When I said no, he followed me in his car and mocked me over his loudspeaker. It was my most frightening experience on the street. I felt powerless. If the police were going to harass me, then where could I turn for help?

Addictions to drugs and alcohol are common among the homeless. In my home I sometimes go to my freezer for a bowl of ice cream when I need a little lift. Many of those who live on the street have a difficult time refusing the flow of addictive substances. While homeless, I was offered crack on several occasions. A guy asked me if I would go in with him to buy a bottle of wine. Anyone who thinks that using drugs and drinking is a continual party probably has not known the tragic desperation of an addict who can't stop using. Mike, one of the men I interviewed, had fallen on his head twice, requiring stitches, during his two-month binge. He had slept on park benches, under a loading dock, at a bus stop, and under a back porch. He begged for bus tokens in front of churches so that he could sell them for vodka. He had not showered for weeks, and the smell of his urine-soaked clothing followed him wherever he went.

Mike told me his experience as an addict. "I panhandled, stole, and conned people to come up with $75 to $100 a day so I could stay high. I slept anywhere I could, underneath porches, by garbage cans, on old mattresses, in abandoned buildings, in cars that I broke into just to sleep in, anywhere. My life centered around where my next bag was gonna come from. That was all."

One of the men I interviewed complained about people who get government checks and stay in the shelter so that they can spend their money on drugs. "That ain't right," he said. "They should be put out if they get checks."

Sam expressed feeling bored. "All we do is walk around all day. I have nothing to do during the day other than get in trouble out on the street. It's very cold and windy outside and I have no place to go. My relatives won't see me or give me money. I have the choice of walking the streets all day from 7:30 in the morning until 8:30 at night, pan-handling money and drinking, or going to AA meetings and filling my day with things that are good for me."

THE DEMOGRAPHICS OF HOMELESSNESS

An estimated two to three million homeless people live in the United States. Most of them live on the streets of America's largest cities.[1] In Chicago nearly sixty thousand people will go homeless throughout the course of one year, twelve to fifteen thousand on any given night.[2] They are the poorest of the poor, the destitute, the un-wanted. They can be seen picking through dumpsters, begging outside supermarkets, huddled in doorways and on park benches at night, and sleeping over steam vents on the sidewalk.[3] They are the most vis-ible modern example of what Jesus called "the least of these brothers of mine" (Matt. 25:40).

Stereotypes regarding people without homes are often unfounded. A common stereotypical profile of a homeless person is the image of a middle-aged alcoholic man. In actuality, 38 percent of the homeless population are families with children. Twenty-seven percent of the homeless are under the age of eighteen. The number of homeless fami-lies with children has increased significantly over the past decade. Families with children are currently the fastest growing group within the homeless population.[4]

Single homeless adults are more likely to be male than female. The 1996 survey of the U.S. Conference of Mayors found that single men comprised 45 percent of the homeless population and single women 14 percent. The median age of the thirty-one homeless adults that I surveyed in Uptown Chicago was thirty-six. My survey was conducted in shelters for adults.

One of the most obvious causes of homelessness is the simple fact that not enough affordable housing units are available to the poor. Between 1973 and 1993, 2.2 million low-rent units disappeared from the market in the United States. These units were condemned, burned and abandoned, or converted into condominiums or expensive apartments, or they became unaffordable because of cost increases. During the same period the number of low-income renters increased by 4.7 million.[5] In 1993 11.2 million low-income renters needed the only 6.5 million low-rent housing units. In the state of Illinois, for every 100 low-rent units available there are 250 people who need low-income housing. This crisis has led to overcrowding and substandard housing and has driven many of those at risk out of their homes and onto the streets.

As housing costs have continued to rise, work and income opportunities for people with low or moderate skill levels have stagnated. Well-paying entry-level jobs in manufacturing have been replaced by less secure and poorly paid jobs in the service sector or by no jobs at all. In Illinois, there are four people needing every available entry-level job. The number of applicants is even higher when one considers living-wage jobs.[6] Unemployment statistics do not include those who have given up and are not seeking jobs. The homeless people with whom Breakthrough ministers are often in that category.

THE STRATEGY OF
BREAKTHROUGH URBAN MINISTRIES

Breakthrough is a faith-based church partnership ministry whose mission is "to foster healthy community and empower individuals with the love of Christ."

Breakthrough's Neighborhood

In the 1960s Uptown was known for its burned-out buildings and abandoned cars. In the late sixties and early seventies, the state of Illinois, in an attempt to save money, instituted a policy of deinstitutionalizing mental health patients. Uptown, with its vacant apartment hotels and rooming houses, became a prime neighborhood for placement of these former wards of the state. According to a spokesman for the Chicago Region of the Illinois Department of Mental Health, some seven thousand "deinstitutionalized" patients were shipped to Uptown in one year alone.

In recent years Edgewater and Uptown have begun to experience a turnaround. A Woodstock Institute report released in 1995 found that between 1979 and 1989, the North Uptown and South Edgewater area experienced one of the biggest economic revivals in Chicago. Factories that once provided entry-level jobs are being turned into expensive loft apartments for the well-to-do. Low-rent units are disappearing from the market. The rising cost of housing has jeopardized the stability of those on reduced or fixed incomes, forcing some of them out of their homes and onto the street.

Breakthrough's History and Mission

Breakthrough was founded in 1992 by members of the First Evangelical Free Church in Chicago in order to more responsibly help the street people who were coming to the church requesting assistance. In January 1992, Breakthrough began serving a daily lunch in a small storefront room. Breakthrough Urban Ministries was incorporated in February of 1992 and received not-for-profit status in December of 1992. The vision of Breakthrough's Homeless Service Center is

> *that everyone who comes through the doors will receive assistance in assessing their own real needs and will be empowered with appropriate tools to help them help themselves to satisfy those needs whether they be finding employment, locating decent and affordable housing, achieving freedom from addictions, or obtaining counseling regarding issues associated with mental health and spiritual and emotional growth.*

The foremost goal of Breakthrough's Homeless Service Center is to bring homeless people to faith in Christ and to assist them to grow in the Christian faith. Breakthrough seeks to equip believers with the basic knowledge of Scripture and to encourage their participation in a local church.

Personal Relationships

Breakthrough's staff view the ministry as a vehicle to help homeless people return to society. Guests who want to be served lunch are required to sign in before 10:00 A.M. so that staff have an opportunity to provide more than just a hot meal. Each guest is required to state a goal for the day. Staff sit down with each person and help him or her to determine a plan of action for his or her life. Staff members help them to set achievable goals and continue to check in with them daily to see how they are progressing.

As guests sign in for the day they are also given the opportunity to have a "one-on-one" talk with a staff person. Those looking for housing or needing government benefits might sign up to meet with Breakthrough's case manager. Individuals needing employment sign up to meet with Breakthrough's job trainer. Those struggling with addictions might sign up to meet with one of Breakthrough's addictions counselors, attend Christ-centered twelve-step recovery groups, or enroll in

Breakthrough's intensive outpatient treatment program. Those who need referrals to mental health centers are given appropriate guidance. Those desiring to grow in their Christian faith sign up to meet with staff for discipleship training. Others may need time to take care of some of their most basic needs such as food, shelter, clothing, use of a phone and an address, personal storage space, laundry, or a shower before they are ready to begin to think about more long-range goals for their lives. Treating people as unique individuals and giving them personal attention is always key.

Cooperation and Participation

A spirit of cooperation is encouraged at Breakthrough. Guests are encouraged to share helpful information with one another and to work together. Every day the guests are asked to sign up to do a chore to assist in the operation of the center. Chores include such activities as setting up tables for lunch, helping with the dishes, and mopping floors. About fifteen of the guests punch a time clock and go to work at Breakthrough. They will receive a paycheck for their work.

Employment

Breakthrough's job trainer conducts job readiness training at Breakthrough. Some of the trainees receive salaries while they experience on-the-job training. Some of the workers' salaries are reimbursed to Breakthrough through the Public Aid Earnfare program. Some will work as paid janitors. Breakthrough's partnering church, First Evangelical Free Church, has contracted with Breakthrough for janitorial service. This arrangement provides Breakthrough's job trainer with an on-the-job training site to prepare Breakthrough guests to be employed as custodians.

Other workers will go out into the community to sweep trash from the streets. Breakthrough has contracts with seven community organizations throughout the city that pay Breakthrough to hire homeless people to clean their streets. This "Cleanstreet Program" provides entry-level jobs for about ten of Breakthrough's guests. For those who have no work history or who may be in the early stages of recovery from addictions, the street-cleaning jobs provide an opportunity for them to move into the workforce. It is a stepping-stone employment opportunity that provides just enough income for them to get a room and move off the street. Breakthrough has learned that it is much more dignifying to give a paycheck instead of a handout to a person in need.

Housing

Breakthrough is able to provide supportive housing for ten men and women. Their rents are subsidized by the Chicago Low Income Housing Trust Fund. Breakthrough provides individual counseling, case management, recovery and support groups, life-skill training, and budgeting guidance for the residents. The goal is to help them to be able to eventually manage on their own. Breakthrough also operates an overnight shelter called "the Dwelling Place" for thirty men in the church's gymnasium in the winter months. Breakthrough's case manager maintains a list of low-income housing in the neighborhood and assists homeless guests in locating housing suitable for them.

Spiritual Growth

Discipleship is integrated throughout all of the activities of Breakthrough. Staff members model intimacy with Jesus throughout the day. Recovery groups emphasize dependency on God for the power to overcome addiction and use the basic scriptural principles of confession, forgiveness, restitution, redemption, and healing. Job training emphasizes a biblical work ethic and principles of personal responsibility taught in Scripture. Prayer and Bible study take place in group settings and in one-on-one times with the guests.

Every morning at the center and every evening at the Dwelling Place, Breakthrough's night shelter, staff lead the guests in an interactive devotional time. Scripture is used as the basis for discussions regarding issues relevant to the lives of the guests. Guests are encouraged to give their opinions, and they often have deep insights that are helpful to the group. Staff guide the group toward life recovery through the teaching of biblical principles.

Atmosphere and Safety

A positive atmosphere is maintained at Breakthrough. If the atmosphere is threatened by the behavior of an individual, that person is firmly but lovingly shown to the door. Anyone using drugs or alcohol who is not willing to sit down with an addictions counselor and follow through with a recovery plan is required to leave until he can come back sober. Staff carefully guard the physical and emotional safety of the guests.

Breakthrough is committed to people for the long haul. Part of the recovery process for some involves numerous relapses and discouraging setbacks. Breakthrough is committed to "hang in" with people through these disappointments.

Personal Responsibility

We do not restore dignity to the homeless by providing handouts that keep them from taking responsibility for themselves. Marvin Olasky talks about what a tragedy it would have been if the prodigal, when he was in the far country, had run into a really great social service program that would have fed him, clothed him, and given him food. He never would have gone home.[7] We try not to enable people to stay in bondage to drugs and alcohol. We want them to feel the consequences of that bondage, but we want them to know that when they're ready to come home, we have our arms open. We will celebrate their return with a great meal and with help. We are there for them.

Breakthrough's strategy is to provide a variety of services to meet the wide variety of needs the homeless have brought through our doors. Our goal is to give in such a way that the recipients will no longer need our gifts—to provide a hand up instead of a handout. In 1997 Breakthrough served 16,299 hot meals. We distributed 5,132 bags of groceries to low-income families in the community. We helped 169 people into living-wage jobs, assisted 84 people into treatment for their drug addiction and alcoholism, and found permanent housing for 134 people.

Input and Feedback

Breakthrough provides opportunities for people to give their input and feedback. During my homeless plunge I ate dinner every day in a cramped basement room of a church where a nun provided dinner four evenings a week for about sixty homeless men and women. One evening all of us nearly gagged as we made our way down the stairs to eat, because a mop bucket at the foot of the stairs was full of putrid water that smelled like vomit. We all filed past that bucket on our way to eat, but nobody told the sister in charge about the bucket. We had no opportunity to give feedback. I wanted to say, "Sister, thanks for the great meal, but really, could you please get rid of the mop bucket?"

As I was leading the devotional discussion one morning at Breakthrough, I overheard someone talk about the cold water in the shower. I asked what he meant and discovered that for a full week the men and women at Breakthrough had taken their showers without hot water. I investigated and discovered that the temperature control on the hot-water heater had inadvertently been turned down, a simple problem that was remedied by a twist of the dial. It was stunning to me that for a full week no one had informed the staff about the problem. Evidently they were so accustomed to poor service that none of them felt they had the option of bringing such a major inconvenience to the attention of the staff. Since then, we have regularly solicited feedback from our guests.

Church Partnership

Breakthrough is church-based. Breakthrough is a separate 501c3 corporation from the church, but considers itself a community outreach arm of First Evangelical Free Church. The partnership between the church and Breakthrough is written into the bylaws of each entity. Breakthrough's bylaws state that Breakthrough is an "outreach ministry under the spiritual guidance of First Free." More than half of Breakthrough's board members must also be members of an Evangelical Free church. A member of First Free's governing board sits on the Breakthrough board. In its bylaws the First Evangelical Free Church recognizes Breakthrough as a partnership ministry of the church and pledges its support to the mission of Breakthrough.

The staff of Breakthrough recognizes the importance and value of drawing homeless people into the wider community of faith. Fifteen guests of Breakthrough joined First Free at a recent church retreat. Several of the men and women of Breakthrough have been active participants in First Free. Others have become involved in other churches in the community. Laypeople are encouraged to welcome Breakthrough guests into the church community and to build relationships with them. By volunteering at Breakthrough, church members get to know the homeless and are able to welcome them to the church.

Breakthrough benefits immensely by being able to share facilities with First Free. The church initially allowed Breakthrough to use the little storefront room for its day center for one dollar per year. As the ministry grew and began to use more of the church facility, the ministry began to pay a more substantial fee for rent. Breakthrough has been able to draw in some funds for rehab work on the church building. An unused space that had become an eyesore off the church's fellowship hall was made into a nice food pantry room, and the church kitchen was renovated with funds raised by Breakthrough from a local foundation.

The church has benefited by gaining a reputation in the local community and in the evangelical community of being a church that cares and is active in responding to the needs of the poor. Several new members of the church have stated that one of the things that drew them to attend First Free was its ministry to the community through Breakthrough.

Faith–Based

Breakthrough is faith-based. Fifty percent of its funds come from the donations of individuals whom God has led to support the mission of Breakthrough. Through the years Breakthrough staff have seen direct evidence of God's passionate love for the poor through the gifts of His people. As David wrote in Psalm 34:18, we have come to see how "the Lord is close to the brokenhearted" as we have watched His tender care for them.

In 1992 a very large man came into the center. It was freezing outside and he had only a light sweat hood to wear. He asked if we had a warmer coat for him. I went to check the back room where we had some coats, but could not find one that would fit him. I had just begun to tell him that we could not help him when the front door of the center opened and a man entered with a beautiful large down jacket that fit the needy man perfectly. "The Lord led me to donate this coat," the man said. "Can you use it?" With my mouth open in disbelief, I was able to take the coat from the donor and give it to the man in need and say to him, "Jesus loves you, Buddy! Jesus really loves you!"

In the summer of 1994, Breakthrough's food pantry and bank account were empty. Our director of homeless services told me at a Friday staff meeting that we would not be able to provide meals the following week. Together as a staff we lifted our need to God in prayer and decided to take it one day at a time and see what God would do. That Sunday I was greeted at the door of the church by an excited usher who told me to go look in the food pantry. To my astonishment it was filled to capacity with groceries. The postal workers of a suburban community had organized a food drive. They did not know about our need, and we did not know about their collection. A man from our church who worked there had loaded up two van loads of groceries and had stocked our food pantry from floor to ceiling with postal service boxes filled with groceries. We were able to provide lunches all week and have our usual food pantry distribution on Saturday.

It has been a great privilege for me to see God at work through Breakthrough. We serve a God who loves people, especially the broken, poor, and needy. To know God is to defend their cause. As we get near the broken we are drawn near to God.

BIBLICAL PERSPECTIVE ON
COMPASSIONATE CARE OF THE POOR

Dignifying care of the poor is a consistent theme throughout Scripture. It is a vital part of every fiber of God's plan. Through the Old Testament Law God established the tithe to care for "the Levite, the alien, the fatherless and the widow, so that they may eat in your towns and be satisfied" (Deut. 26:12). One tenth of all the produce of the land was designated to care for the priests and their assistants and the poor.

"There should be no poor among you," declared the Lord in Deuteronomy 15:4, "for in the land the Lord your God is giving you to possess as your inheritance, he will richly bless you." Ten percent would be enough to care for the less fortunate. He went on to explain the process: "If there is a poor man among your brothers . . . do not be hardhearted or tightfisted toward your poor brother. Rather be openhanded and freely lend him whatever he needs" (vv. 7–8).

Harvesters were instructed not to reap to the very edges of their fields. They were to leave gleanings of the harvest for the poor. This beautiful system of welfare provided an opportunity for the poor to work and to harvest their own food with dignity (Lev. 23:22).

Throughout the book of Deuteronomy the Lord gave instructions regarding how the Israelites were to care for the poor, challenging them to "remember that you were slaves" (Deut. 16:11–12; 15:15; 24:18, 22).

They were to remember what it was like when their spirits were broken and their hearts discouraged as a result of their painful forced labor. They were to identify with the poor through their own experience of oppression.

Deuteronomy 10:18–19 describes God's special care for the poor and the aliens. "He defends the cause of the fatherless and the widow, and loves the alien, giving him food and clothing. And you are to love those who are aliens, for you yourselves were aliens in Egypt."

Ezekiel 16:49 describes the sin of Sodom, "Now this was the sin of your sister Sodom: She and her daughters were arrogant, overfed and unconcerned; they did not help the poor and needy." The people of Sodom were judged by how they treated the poor. Our God is a God who sees the afflictions of the oppressed. He hears the cries of the poor and acts on their behalf (Ps. 10:14). He is near the broken and saves those who are crushed in spirit (Ps. 34:18). To really know God is to defend "the cause of the poor and needy" (Jer. 22:16). God does not stand by and do nothing in the face of human need.

By far the most powerful representation of God's love and commitment to the poor is the incarnation of Jesus Christ. Jesus "being in very nature God, did not consider equality with God something to be grasped, but made himself nothing, taking the very nature of a servant, being made in human likeness. And being found in appearance as a man, he humbled himself and became obedient to death—even death on a cross!" (Phil. 2:6–8).

Jesus endured the excruciatingly painful death of the cross. On the cross He triumphed over the Enemy and made a public spectacle of him in order to bring justice and redemption to this dark unfair world (Col. 2:15).

Jesus came to us. He identified with us. He felt our pain. He ate our food. He left the riches of glory and came to live among us. He hung out with drunkards and swindlers and prostitutes.

He let people touch Him. He even let a prostitute wash His feet with her hair! He bent down and touched the lepers. By the example of the way He lived we learn about God's heart for the poor and broken.

Matthew 25:32–46 clearly teaches that the nations will be judged by how they respond to "the least of these," the down-and-out, the poor and disenfranchised, as they represent Jesus Himself.

As Jesus began His ministry on earth, He declared His mission statement. He asked for the scroll of Isaiah and read, "The Spirit of the Lord is on me, because he has anointed me to preach good news to the poor. He has sent me to proclaim freedom for the prisoners and recovery of sight for the blind, to release the oppressed, to proclaim the year of the Lord's favor" (Luke 4:18).

Jesus' mission on earth was a mission to the poor, those in bondage, the blind, and the oppressed. His Spirit is still carrying out that mission today through His body, the church.

Jesus described neighborly love in His story of the Good Samaritan in Luke 10:30–37. The merchant was the victim of violence. He was beaten up and left to die. The religious leaders and outstanding citizens of the society passed him by. When the Samaritan noticed him lying along the road, he was moved by compassion and immediately got involved. Though the broken man was from a different culture, the Samaritan reached down and touched him and bound up his wounds. He lifted the man up on his own donkey, personally transported him to the nearest treatment center, and paid for his entire rehabilitation.

James 2:14–17 says, "What good is it, my brothers, if a man claims to have faith but has no deeds? Can such faith save him? Suppose a brother or sister is without clothes and daily food. If one of you says to him, 'Go, I wish you well; keep warm and well fed,' but does nothing about his physical needs, what good is it? In the same way, faith by itself, if it is not accompanied by action, is dead."

Faith that does nothing in the face of human need is not true Christian faith.

WHO IS SERVED BY RESCUE MISSIONS?

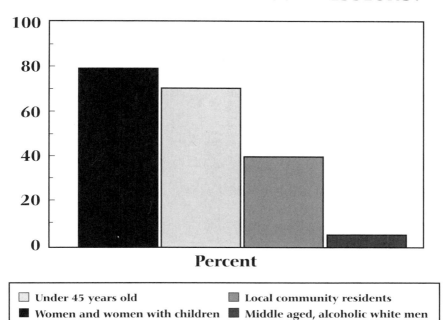

Legend:
- ☐ Under 45 years old
- ■ Women and women with children
- ▨ Local community residents
- ▨ Middle aged, alcoholic white men

HOMELESS IN THE USA

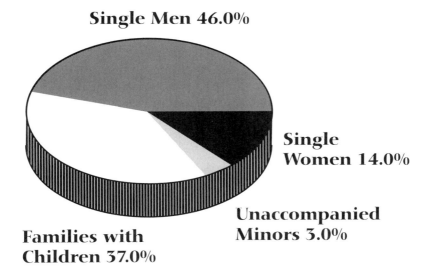

Single Men 46.0%

Single Women 14.0%

Unaccompanied Minors 3.0%

Families with Children 37.0%

From the 1995 U.S. Conference of Mayors Report

AFFORDABLE HOUSING 1970 – 1990

Millions

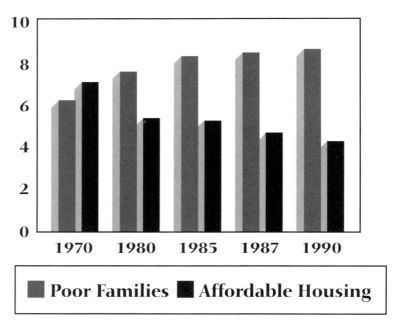

Housing that costs 1/3 or less of total income is considered affordable. The families in this graph are the poorest 1/4 of all American families.

TYPES OF FACTORS AFFECTING PERSONS WITHOUT HOMES

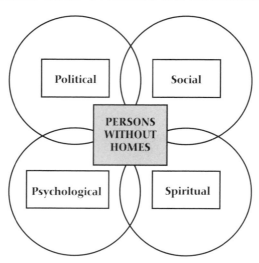

THE SHELTER
INTERVENTION PROCESS

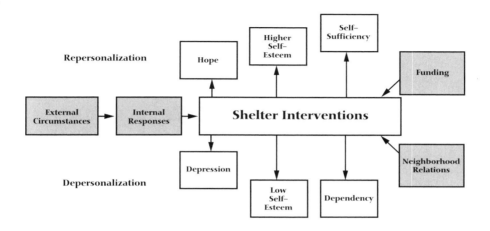

Conclusion:
Our Calling

My heart has been gripped by the stories of the homeless persons I have met. The scenes of suffering many of them have experienced are heartbreaking. Most are gentle people who have been ravaged by the sins of others and have been left to flounder in confusion and hopelessness. We are called to love all people with the same love that Jesus showed us when He restored our dignity through the redemption of the Cross.

Though we cannot possibly befriend everyone, we are compelled to reach out with the compassion of Christ and affirm the dignity of every person created in the image of God. I believe God brings specific people across our path who are ours to touch with His special love. As we listen to the Spirit's leading, He directs us to have lunch with someone asking for help, to volunteer at a city mission or homeless shelter, to befriend that difficult person at church who is often avoided, or to make financial contributions to works among the poor.

Jesus confronted the church at Laodicea for their self-sufficiency. "You say, 'I am rich; I have acquired wealth and do not need a thing.' But you do not realize that you are wretched, pitiful, poor, blind and naked" (Rev. 3:17). It is when we recognize our own neediness and identify with the poor that we find the "gold refined in the fire" (v. 18). When we associate with the broken, we draw near to God and experience the blessings of Isaiah 58.

> *Is not this the kind of fasting I have chosen: to loose the chains of injustice. . . . Is it not to share your food with the hungry and to provide the poor wanderer with shelter—when you see the naked, to clothe him . . . ? Then your light will break forth like the dawn, and your healing will quickly appear. . . . If you spend yourselves in behalf of the hungry and satisfy the needs of the oppressed, then your light will rise in the darkness and your night will become like the noonday. The Lord will guide you always; he will satisfy your needs in a sun-scorched land and will strengthen your frame. You will be like a well-watered garden, like a spring whose waters never fail. (Isa. 58:6–8, 10–11)*

Reflection Questions

1. Who has God placed in your pathway that is in need of special compassion? How can you be God's hands and arms to that person?

2. What broken places in your life have made you more sensitive to the needs of others?

3. What are some contemporary systems of injustice? What can you do to oppose them?

4. How have you experienced the blessings of Isaiah 58 as you have shown the compassion of Christ to the less fortunate?

chapter twenty-one

AN OLD LIGHTHOUSE FOR A NEW WORLD

THE PACIFIC GARDEN MISSION IN TODAY'S WORLD

PHIL KWIATKOWSKI

Introduction: The Plight of the Homeless

It is night. It is cold. You are on the streets with nowhere to go. You have a substance abuse problem. You dropped out of school years ago and have burned all of your bridges with your family. Now you cannot find work. You have lived in shelters, been in rehab centers, and at times earned a little money through temporary jobs. But now you are alone, uncertain; in short, you are homeless.

The plight of our nation's homeless is increasingly apparent. At any time, numerous individuals and families can be seen roaming our cities' streets, sleeping outside, or begging for food. In fact, statistics suggest the number of homeless individuals has increased over the last decade, with no end in sight.

Local and national efforts to address the needs of homeless people have focused on temporary shelter, food, clothing, emergency health care, and public aid. Though these address momentary needs, they are woefully inadequate in finding any long-term solution.

Historically the church has sought to address the problem through the traditional rescue-mission approach. But has this method been as effective as it could be, or does more need to be done? What, if any, is the church's role and responsibility to meet the needs of this vast population of people?

FACTORS IN HOMELESSNESS

Many factors contribute to a person being homeless. In the 1980s, mental health programs were cut back almost a third. The Center for Mental Health Services revealed that thirty states have acknowledged they can serve only 40 percent of their severely mentally ill residents in community mental health centers. This leaves a large population of people with nowhere to turn. According to U.S. government estimates, 200,000 homeless people are mentally ill, or a third of the homeless population.[1]

> Over the course of the 1970s, public policy favored the deinstitutionalization of the mentally ill. The result of this direction was a dramatic decrease in the census of public mental hospitals. Between 1955 and 1974, the resident census of public mental hospitals declined from 559,000 to less than 130,000. In 1955, 73 percent of all patient care episodes occurred in hospitals; by 1980, that figure was reduced to 27 percent.[2]

Another determinant is drugs. The stereotypical image of a homeless individual is that of a drunk. In fact, until the mid-1980s a large percentage of the homeless population fit that description. The reasons were simple: Alcohol was legal, accessible, and cheap. The arrival of crack cocaine changed this picture dramatically.

At first, cocaine was seen as a rich man's drug, but crack made the pleasures of cocaine readily available to people who had little cash and would readily spend it for the first high they could get. A "rock" of cocaine typically goes for ten dollars.

A third component is the decline in low cost housing. Many single-room occupancy hotels were torn down in the 1960s and early 1970s and replaced with office buildings, stores, and high-rent apartments, only to send the residents to the streets. In 1958, eight times as many Chicago residents lived in cage hotels as in shelters. (A cage hotel is a cheap space surrounded by chicken wire where the homeless can flop for the night.) By 1986, about three times as many people took refuge in Chicago's missions and shelters as in its two remaining cage hotels. Low-rent apartment units are also harder and harder to find.

Unemployment is another ingredient. During a ten-year period, 1985–94, a quarter of a million companies downsized in the United States. A half million business failures and 80,000 firm mergers all resulted in lost jobs. Chicago has lost more than 115,000 blue-collar jobs over the past ten years. Between 1971 and 1991, Chicago lost

334,000 manufacturing jobs. During the same period, service jobs increased by 68,926. Most service jobs pay minimum wage, provide no benefits, and offer little hope for promotion.[3] These are just a few of the many issues that lead to a person being homeless.

"THE OLD LIGHTHOUSE"—
THE PACIFIC GARDEN MISSION

In early February 1996, when Chicago temperatures went sixty-seven hours well below zero and at times the wind-chill factor approached -50 degrees, thousands of homeless people found refuge in missions and city shelters. Every night Pacific Garden Mission (PGM) crowded more than five hundred people into its two main facilities, providing warm, comfortable quarters. However, the numbers accommodated during this period were not unusual, for almost every night throughout 1995, PGM provided shelter for an average of 480 homeless men, women, and children. A total of 206,759 people were helped in all divisions of Pacific Garden Mission in 1995; to these people, the mission provided 2,455,859 meals and distributed countless items of clothing.[4]

Pacific Garden Mission ("The Old Lighthouse") is known for its ministry to homeless men. The mission provides food, clothing, sleeping quarters, medical help, and a hearing of the gospel. For men who come to Christ, we have designed a one-year program where they receive counseling, Bible teaching, and life-skill training. We have partnerships with various employers so that upon completion of our one-year program a graduate can be guaranteed meaningful employment. We also have a facility for women and children, called the Gospel League Home, located two miles west of our State Street facility in downtown Chicago. Women with children are among the fastest growing segments in the homeless community.[5] In addition to food, shelter, clothing, and the Word of God, homeless women receive counseling and an opportunity to join our women's program. Once in the program, the women are assigned chores and must attend Bible and life-skill classes. Women and their children are not separated and can go through our program as a family. After completing one year, the women are assisted in looking for meaningful employment.

God's Heart for the Poor

Scripture informs us that the poor and homeless have always been close to the heart of God. In Luke 4:18 Jesus read a prophecy that He fulfilled, "The Spirit of the Lord is on me, because he has anointed me to preach good news to the poor. He has sent me to proclaim freedom

for the prisoners and recovery of sight for the blind, to release the oppressed." Jesus also stated in Matthew 25:35–36, "For I was hungry
and you gave me something to eat, I was thirsty and you gave me
something to drink, I was a stranger and you invited me in, I needed
clothes and you clothed me, I was sick and you looked after me, I was
in prison and you came to visit me." Psalm 41:1 says, "Blessed is he
that considereth the poor" (KJV). The Lord also stated in Mark 16:15,
"Go ye into all the world, and preach the gospel to every creature"
(KJV). Our heavenly Father is concerned not only for the poor, but for
every member of society, and He also wants His followers to be concerned. But Scripture reflects specific provision for the marginalized in
society, "When you are harvesting in your field and you overlook a
sheaf, do not go back to get it. Leave it for the alien, the fatherless and
the widow, so that the Lord your God may bless you in all the work of
your hands" (Deut. 24:19). Continuing this theme is Zechariah
7:9–10, "Dispense true justice, and practice kindness and compassion
each to his brother; and do not oppress the widow or the orphan, the
stranger or the poor" (NASB).

The History of Pacific Garden Mission

It was in this spirit that Sarah and George Clarke opened the nation's second rescue mission on September 15, 1877. In an area of
Chicago notorious for its vice and corruption, the Clarkes opened a
mission seating about forty people but offering no overnight accom-
modations, and not even soup! The gospel was preached as the audience crowded together on backless, wooden benches, in a simple
auditorium, with Scripture verses gracing the walls. "Saloons on either
side, with their banjos and accompanying instruments, were a great
combination," Sarah Clarke wrote in describing the opening of the
mission. "However, we held the fort—Mr. Clarke preached, and I tried
to keep crooked men straight."[6]

The time came when more space was needed, so in 1880 George
Clarke was led to a building recently vacated by the notorious Pacific
Beer Garden, "a place where the vilest and toughest were accustomed
to coming for beer . . . the most murderous joint west of New York
City," according to an early description.[7] It was at the suggestion of
Dwight L. Moody that the word *Beer* was stricken from the name and
the word *Mission* was added. Thus, the Clarkes' mission became the
Pacific Garden Mission.

The list of famous converts soon began, culminating with the conversion of a rough and tough baseball player named Billy Sunday. Billy,
a baseball player for the Chicago White Stockings, and some friends

were out drinking when they stumbled across the corner of State and VanBuren. On this corner a group of men and women from the Pacific Garden Mission were singing hymns that were familiar to Billy. That evening he accepted an invitation to visit the Pacific Garden Mission and he liked what he heard. After repeated visits to the mission, Billy decided to come forward and publicly accept Christ.

After becoming a Christian, Billy continued playing professional baseball and became an eager student of the Bible. As his faith grew, he began to speak whenever he got the opportunity, and crowds came because he was a baseball player. In 1891, Billy quit baseball and began ministering at the YMCA. Then he became an advance agent and promotion man for evangelist J. Wilbur Chapman. In 1896, Chapman took a pastorate in Philadelphia, and that left Billy to preach. Huge crowds came to hear the gospel from this animated former baseball player. It was estimated that at the time of his death in 1935, Billy Sunday had preached to 100 million people.

The story of Billy Sunday has stood as a model of success for Pacific Garden Mission. But is this story representative of the current homeless profile on the streets of our cities going into the twenty-first century?

Needed: A More Wholistic Approach

Most evangelical missions have historically majored on the "spiritual," while minoring on the social or physical aspect of ministry. As a reaction to liberalism or the social gospel at the turn of the twentieth century, many evangelical missions offered only this "soup, soap and salvation"[8] approach to homeless ministry. In the tradition of Billy Sunday, the emphasis was on "preaching to 'em" and "getting 'em down the aisle." Success equaled "how many got saved tonight." But the problem in using Billy Sunday as a model of a rescue-mission convert lies in the fact that Billy was not homeless, had no addiction, and had a career before and after he came to Christ. I came to Pacific Garden Mission in 1988, as a student from the Moody Bible Institute. My first position was as a counselor. I witnessed to the homeless and gave out clothing tickets. It was a real eye-opener to see men with such great needs who were so open to the gospel. As I prayed with some men to receive Christ, my excitement grew, and I asked to be transferred to the men's division full-time.

I was given the position of transient supervisor, where I was able to witness, preach, and meet the physical needs of all the homeless men. I saw lives transformed and I made friends, and God gave me a burden for the homeless. I had a great desire to see them discipled, so I was given the responsibility of the men's program and soon after became director of the men's division. I would meet with the men, take them out ministering in the subways and on the streets, and try to place them in jobs upon completion of our program. In 1997, I became vice president of ministries. Now I have the responsibilities of all the ministries, both to men and women.

Success Stories?

When I first came to the mission, I was excited by the large number of men who received Christ. Soon I also noticed the large percentage of men who failed once they left the mission. This trend disturbed me. As I became familiar with the program I saw that the focus was on numbers of salvation decisions, not long-term results.

I met Dennis soon after he came to the mission. His problem was a drug habit that he could not kick. He made a profession of salvation and then joined our program. I soon began to disciple him, taking him with me to churches to give his testimony and even to the subways of Chicago to preach and pass out gospel tracts. He was seen by many as a "model" rescue-mission convert who said all the right words. But soon after he graduated from our program I noticed a change. The prospect of leaving the "comfort zone" of the mission and facing the real world was having an effect on him. He began to disappear from his work station and eventually stole a large sum of money from a staff pastor to purchase cocaine. At a later date we tried to restore him, but he broke into a staff member's room looking for more money to buy drugs, so we had to let him go. Today he wanders the streets of Chicago no better off than when he arrived.

Then there was Carlton. He came to us with an addiction to crack cocaine. Upon arrival he made a profession of faith and began to grow. He loved to witness and could be frequently found preaching on street corners. He was a leader to many men in the program and gave a stirring testimony. Today he is still homeless, in and out of jail, and back on crack. What happened to these men and many more like them? We know the Lord does not fail, but have we done all that we could for them?

I was at a meeting many years ago where we discussed computer training for our men and women. The objections were simple: We are a Christian ministry, not "secular" in our approach. On the basis that "our goal is to train preachers," we decided not to involve ourselves with any such enterprise. So the trend continued. Our percentage of people who were successful after they left was so low we had to keep promoting the same old testimonies from years gone by.

The problem seemed to be that we were using models of success from the 1940s and 1950s and transferring those principles to the 1990s. Most homeless men who come to us now have little or no education. Most who come have no marketable skill that will pay any livable wage. Most who come have had a serious drug addiction, usually crack cocaine. So do we address the problems in a tangible way and do what is best for the homeless, or do we just continue to pile up statistics that impress our donors and testify how we have never changed since we opened in 1877?

John came to us from the South with an addiction to crack cocaine. After coming he prayed to receive Christ and joined our program. He was in our Bible classes; he was passing out tracts in the city and testifying to others how he had changed. Upon seeing John's life change, his cousin, who also had a problem with crack cocaine, came to the mission and professed Christ. Soon after, John's wife and children came, and they too accepted Christ. Things were going well for John and he was indeed a model of what the mission wanted to portray. When it came time for him to leave the mission, he went to Motorola looking for work, and the company required him to take a simple test. I will never forget when he called me after taking the test. He said, "Pastor, you guys taught me how to find John 3:16 in my Bible, but you did not teach me how to pass this test." In short, John failed the test, was not hired, and was soon back on crack. To this day he is still not reunited with his wife. Did we fail John as well?

His story really made me consider the methods we were using in ministry. The pattern was the same: A homeless person comes to the mission, receives Christ, joins the program, and does very well while he is here. But the real test came when they left the mission. Most departed with no improvement in basic life skills and would go back to where they were comfortable and accepted—the streets.

What Was Missing?

It was with this background that I attempted to address the problem of our failure rate. How could we give homeless men and women a strong spiritual foundation and also equip them with the proper skills to "make it" in the world? We settled on a one-year program. For the first sixty days after a person professes faith in Christ he receives nothing but Bible training. Since many are dealing with an addiction they need to focus on victorious living and the basics in the Christian life. After sixty days they take a GED-equivalent math and English test and are placed in an appropriate class. They have to pass both the math and English tests in order to move to our next phase, which is career development. This phase consists of computer training, job-interviewing skills, résumé writing, and various other life skills. We have partnerships with several companies that will hire individuals upon our recommendation and the completion of our program.

People often wonder what we do about drug rehabilitation. We detox the men right here. Located in what has now become an upscale neighborhood, men who are easily tempted have difficulty finding drugs in the area. We have a full-time doctor and nurse on our staff who can assist with any medical complications. In a short time we have seen encouraging results.

Steve came to us as a forty-five-year-old who was homeless and strung out on drugs. After professing faith in Christ, he joined our Bible program. After one year of Bible and vocational training he was ready to graduate. We had partnered with a church in Minnesota that would find employment for some of our men and would keep them accountable. We decided to send Steve to Minnesota. Upon arrival he was employed by Quality Pork Processors and assimilated into the church. Steve has become an usher in the church, bought a car, has a savings account, and recently received his first credit card. When his pastor visited the mission not long ago, he testified how successful Steve was and said he wanted others like him.

Gordon came to the mission as a heroin addict and soon accepted Christ as his Savior. He joined our program and excelled at his Bible classes while working as a tour guide for the mission. He successfully completed a computer training class with Chicago Bridge and Iron along with his other vocational training classes. After graduation he enrolled as a full-time student at Pillsbury Baptist College to major in Bible/pastoral studies. Gordon is also leading a "soul-winning" team of college students in the local community. He has been a blessing to the school and looks forward to graduation.

Consider this testimony from one of our women:

> The Lord brought me to PGM's Gospel League Home a little more than two years ago when I was homeless. I needed direction, encouragement, and hope. I joined the Bible program and received direction and guidance and also discipline according to God's Word. After a year I graduated with my class, the largest class to complete the Bible program. This qualified me to attend GED and computer classes in connection with the new career development program begun by PGM. These classes help to encourage graduates to seek employment. Many speakers came to speak to us and help prepare us to get employment. Finally, I did start working for a health care organization after attending a job fair. When I came here, I did not have any goals in my life. I really did not know what to do. Now my life is being used by God to serve others.

Or excerpts of a letter from Toner Express, which recently employed one of our graduates here in Chicago:

> *I want to thank you for the services of Don. It has always been an honor to serve PGM with my business services. But now it is even a greater partnership to provide a safe work home to one of your graduates. It is clear Don has had important training from you and others at PGM. It is so important Don received résumé, budgeting, and other necessary real-world training to go along with his spiritual discipleship. Again, thanks. Hopefully our business will grow, and we will need more PGM graduates!*

Finally, a letter from McCormick Place in Chicago:

> *I would like to thank you and the rest of the team at Pacific Garden Mission. The partnership that has been formed not only with the Levy Restaurants but more specifically here at McCormick Place has been spectacular. One example of a partnership success story would be that of Tony. Tony began working with us a few months ago and has quickly become a vital contributing member of our team. Our entire management team looks forward to a long, prosperous, and positive relationship with the Pacific Garden Mission.*

Where would these men and others like them be if not for the wholistic approach of assimilating them back into society? Ministering effectively to the homeless takes more than a "quick fix" approach. Luke 2:52 states, "And Jesus grew in wisdom and stature, and in favor with God and men." This verse describes a proper balance in the development of a human being. "Wisdom" is intellectual development. "Stature" is physical development. "In favor with God" is spiritual development. "In favor with man" is social development. In any program that deals with ministering to the homeless these four elements need to be equally united in order to see lasting results.

Conclusion:
The Opportunity and the Need

The church has a tremendous opportunity to minister to the needs of the homeless community. A mission field is roaming our city streets. What can be done to help? In a recent article on city rescue missions Roger Greenway stated,

> *First, they [missions] need financial support, for these are not inexpensive operations. Every church, including upper middle class suburban churches, should*

take two or three offerings each year for city rescue ministries. Second, city res-
cue missions need help from churches in the process of enfolding converts from
the street into the mainstream of life and Christian fellowship. . . . A third way in
which churches should support city rescue missions involves the mission workers
as individuals and fellow Christians. These workers are all related to local con-
gregations where some of them are treated as "second class" missionaries and do
not sense much support or understanding.[9]

Many missions, shelters, and inner city ministries are looking for volunteers. Contact them and see what opportunities are available. Organize work groups in your church to go to a shelter or mission and lend a hand in any work that needs to be done.

I have seen great success with individuals who have chosen to work with one man or woman. Begin by coming to a shelter and taking one person under your wing; just be a friend. Then take the person to church or help him or her find employment. Involve the person in the life of your family. Robert came to us as an angry drunk with no direction in life. He joined our program and began to excel. He conquered the bottle but had a difficult time with his temper. When it came time for him to graduate, we were worried how he would fare away from the security of the mission. He began to go to Cicero Bible Church on Chicago's West Side, and the church took an interest in him. He began to meet with the pastor and got involved with the people. The church offered him a custodial position with room and board. He accepted, moved out, and went to work with them. It has now been a couple of years and he is still there, still meeting with the pastor, and well adjusted and happy.

Ministry to the homeless is difficult yet rewarding. It has been my experience that the only way we can be effective in seeing permanent change is through a wholistic approach. A spiritual foundation is primary, but it must be followed by intellectual, physical, and social aspects, or long-term impact will be minimal. More than 120 years old, the Pacific Garden Mission has a rich history of seeing lives that have been changed by the power of the gospel. We have sought and continually seek to be to this generation as "men of Issachar, who understood the times and knew what Israel should do" (1 Chron. 12:32). So whether society's problems are alcohol, poverty, drugs, mental illness, joblessness, or the lack of affordable housing, a wholistic gospel message is still the answer. May God help us to keep shining brightly as an old lighthouse for a new world.

Reflection Questions

1. What stereotypes does society portray of those that are homeless? Why do you think these persist? What is needed to help dispel them?

2. Is anything keeping you from ministry with the homeless? Are you willing to explore some form of personal involvement? If so, what practical steps can you take?

3. Brainstorm ways your church could become involved more wholistically in ministry at your local rescue mission. This could include helping feed, tutor, donate clothing, or participate in a service. In what ways could you intentionally involve them in your fellowship?

4. Are you aware of businesses in your community that could possibly employ a homeless person? Could you connect these with the leadership of your local mission?

chapter twenty-two

WHO IS MY NEIGHBOR?

MINISTERING TO THE WORLD'S REFUGEES

CHAD ERLENBORN

Introduction:
Through the Eyes of a Refugee

The dinner was warmly steaming on the table as we bowed in thanksgiving. Since we were eager to eat the delicious food, the prayer was over quickly. Soon family and friends were laughing and sharing, unaware of a rumbling sound in the distance.

Suddenly, into the house bursts a small contingent of solders, spraying bullets at the ceiling and screaming racial attacks. Panic-filled adults tried to shield young children while others fled toward the back door. Some of us were unable to escape, and the soldiers grabbed us and threw us up against the dining room wall. Our hands were in the air, and the soldiers began to mock us and spit on us. "You stupid Christians! You believe in this stupid Jesus! Don't you know it's just a fable!" they shouted. Another soldier grabbed my father by the hair and knelt him down before the rest of the group. Yelling for our attention, he waved his revolver in the air, saying, "If any of you move or show any sign of emotion, I will kill you too." BANG, BANG, BANG! My sister screamed and collapsed at the sight of our dying father. Another round of bullets was fired at the ceiling, as a soldier yelled, "Get out of here, you stupid Christians!"

Leaving everything, we ran out the front door. More soldiers then forced us into an already filled school bus. People were crying, bleeding, and terrorized by what they had just experienced. As the bus began to move, I looked back to see our house looted and in flames. Fear and rage ripped through me as we moved to an unknown destination. I lost my father, my home, and my possessions. I am a refugee.

This is not a Hollywood movie script, but reflects actual refugee experiences. Nearly fourteen million people in the world today have a similar story.[1] That is twice the number of people in greater Chicago. Somalians, Iraqis, Bosnians, and many others have become our new neighbors. They are fleeing war, persecution, and oppression in their homelands, seeking a safe place to rebuild their broken lives. They are coming from countries that have been neutral, highly resistant, or even closed to the gospel. Their powerful stories tell of an unthinkable journey of tragedy, heroism, and hope.

A REFUGEE'S JOURNEY

The journey begins in a refugee's homeland. It has been said that the mother of all refugees is war. War breaks out in the homeland, requiring refugees to make the involuntary decision of abandoning their families, homes, and community. Persecuted because of religious beliefs, ethnic background, or political association, refugees are forced out of their homes. Seeking shelter, some refugees travel great distances through difficult terrain with little food or water. Some are captured, some die, but a few escape to a neighboring country.[2]

The journey slows here for most refugees with a lengthy wait (the average is five years) in a refugee camp.[3] Usually closely guarded by armed soldiers, the camps are holding centers where refugees are warehoused until the fighting stops in their country or a new country accepts them. Camps consist of close quarters in tents or campers with shared facilities. Limited food and clothing are handed out on a regular basis. One refugee youth from Liberia complained that the camp was "boring [because] there is nothing to do but eat and sleep." Because refugees in camps have little access to work or school, inactivity creates a greater awareness of all that they lost, and depression is inevitable.

Occasionally, a change in power in a refugee's homeland will allow for a safe return. Most refugees apply to the United Nations High Commissioner for Refugees (UNHCR) to resettle in a host country with a similar language and customs.[4] Only those who can prove they are escaping persecution are eligible to find freedom in a new country. Some refugees interview with the Immigration and Naturalization Service (INS) to live in the United States. Because of the large number of refugees seeking to come here, most interviewing refugees need to have family members in the United States to welcome them. Family members "sponsor" refugees by providing necessary assistance for the first three months.

After thorough interviews with UNHCR and INS, some refugees receive the long-awaited news that the United States has accepted them. Then the Intergovernmental Committee for Migration (ICM) arranges travel plans. Refugees pay travel expenses with money borrowed from a revolving loan fund. The United States Government allows about eighty thousand refugees into its borders each year.[5] More than four thousand refugees come to Chicago annually from war-torn countries like Ethiopia, Somalia, Iraq, the former Soviet Union, and Bosnia.[6] Most of the current refugees arriving in Chicago are from Bosnia (three thousand over the last five years) including Namka, a fifty-year-old woman.

I met Namka and her family in a small apartment on Chicago's North Side. Some youth from a local church had gathered household essentials to welcome the refugee family. After giving the items, we sat down to exchange names and drink some juice together. The interaction started off festive and free as we saw pictures of Bosnia and other family members. Our conversation quickly became heavy when a picture of her husband appeared, and Namka told her story.

Namka had lived in a rural town of about fifty thousand people. While her husband worked road construction, Namka cared for their two children and maintained a home with a large garden. The family was stable and self-sufficient. Then, without much warning, the Serbian army entered Namka's town. A group of soldiers invaded Namka's house looking for her husband. Her husband, hearing that the Serbian soldiers had killed the adult males in other towns, hid inside the house. In an attempt to get information about the father's location, the soldiers took Namka's fourteen-year-old son and beat him with the back end of a machine gun. (Scars still remain above the boy's eyes.) To free his son, the father surrendered himself to the soldiers. The soldiers beat the father, tied him up, took him into the woods, and killed him.

Listening to Namka tell her story caused my heart to weep. Looking into the tear-stained eyes of her children, I could see their pain and humiliation. As I was listening, I looked down at my hands. I realized that I held in my hands one of the only pictures of her dead husband, and my heart broke. I thought to myself, *These are the people that God is bringing to our city, wives without their husbands, children without their fathers, and people without a home. How is God calling us to respond?*

BIBLICAL RESPONSE

God has a deep concern for the fatherless, widows, and refugees. Although you will not find the word *refugee* in the Bible, you will find God actively involved in caring for refugees.[7] The Bible refers to refugees as "aliens," "strangers," and "sojourners." Throughout the Scriptures we find God loving and providing for refugees, as Deuteronomy declares: "He [the Lord] defends the cause of the fatherless and the widow, and loves the alien, giving him food and clothing" (Deut. 10:18; see also Pss. 9:9; 146:9). Jesus described His own ministry with the words from Isaiah: "The Spirit of the Lord is on me, because he has anointed me to preach good news to the poor. He has sent me to proclaim freedom for the prisoners and recovery of sight for the blind, to release the oppressed, to proclaim the year of the Lord's favor" (Luke 4:18–19).

God also instructs believers to love, defend, and provide for refugees. "When an alien lives with you in your land, do not mistreat him. The alien living with you must be treated as one of your native-born. Love him as yourself, for you were aliens in Egypt" (Lev. 19:33–34). We are to "defend the cause of the weak and fatherless; maintain the rights of the poor and oppressed" (Ps. 82:3). Moreover, a beautiful picture of "true fasting" is portrayed through the prophet Isaiah:

> Is not this the kind of fasting I have chosen: to loose the chains of injustice and untie the cords of the yoke, to set the oppressed free and break every yoke? **Is it not to share your food with the hungry and to provide the poor wanderer with shelter**—when you see the naked, to clothe him, and not to turn away from your own flesh and blood? (Isa. 58:6–7, emphasis added)

Jesus, a refugee Himself, said, "For I was hungry and you gave me something to eat, I was thirsty and you gave me something to drink, I was a stranger and you invited me in. . . . I tell you the truth, whatever you did for one of the least of these brothers of mine, you did for me" (Matt. 25:35, 40). The Lord not only cares for refugees but identifies Himself so closely with their suffering that to minister to refugees is to minister to Him. To love those He loves is to love Him.

In short, our God is a God of compassion, and He expects us to be like Him (Luke 6:36). The work of compassion is to the kingdom of God what water is to the kingdom of nature. As water is present almost everywhere, as it is an essential element for life, so compassion is present almost everywhere in the Bible as an essential element in every Christian life. In Matthew 9, Jesus instructed the Pharisees to "go and learn what this means: I desire mercy, not sacrifice" (v. 13). The emphasis is on learning, but mercy is not something that you can learn by reading a book or taking a class. Mercy is learned as you go to those who are hurting. Later in the same chapter Jesus demonstrated how to learn compassion. "Jesus went through all the towns and villages, teaching in their synagogues, preaching the good news of the kingdom and healing every disease and sickness. When he saw the crowds, he had compassion on them, because they were harassed and helpless, like sheep without a shepherd" (Matt. 9:35–36). Compassion can only be learned when we see with our eyes, hear with our ears, and respond with our hearts.

OUR RESPONSE

For more than fifty years, World Relief has worked with local churches to bring help to hungry and hurting people.[8] As the relief and development arm of the National Association of Evangelicals (NAE), World Relief's mission is "to work with the church in alleviating human suffering worldwide in the name of Christ." Internationally, World Relief works with churches in developing countries by teaching basic health care, training in agriculture, responding to disasters, and providing small business loans. Here in the United States, World Relief has twenty-five offices working with churches to assist refugees, immigrants, and the homeless.

World Relief Chicago fulfills the mission by seeking to meet the wholistic needs of refugees. The Chicago office provides refugees with a host of services, including providing household furnishings, adjustment counseling, English classes, job training and placement, and mental health counseling. Of the eight refugee resettlement agencies in Chicago, World Relief is the only evangelical church-based agency. World Relief is committed to connecting arriving refugee families with caring Christian volunteers. World Relief trains and prepares Christian volunteers to help refugees rebuild their broken lives. Volunteers, along with World Relief, stand together to meet the wholistic needs of refugees.

Refugee Needs

Refugees arrive with little more than the clothes on their backs and bags of emotional pain. Although their needs can feel overwhelming, their needs can be synthesized into two terms, survival needs and friendship needs. Survival needs are the pressing physical needs that require immediate attention. They include housing, food, beds, and clothes. Unmet, these survival needs constantly ring in a refugee's mind. "How am I going to feed my family?" "Where are we going to live?" "What are we going to do?" Despite the intensity, survival needs are generally satisfied in a short period of time. With the help of World Relief, volunteers can welcome a family at the airport with a "Good Neighbor Kit" of essential household items for the bedroom, bathroom, and kitchen.

Once these survival needs are met, the deeper need for friendship rises to the surface. Many arriving refugees feel a bewildering sense of rejection, isolation, and loss. They need friends to accept and encourage them to rebuild their broken lives. They need people to say, "We heard of your suffering. We are glad that you are here. Welcome to America!" Within the context of friendship, volunteers can assist refugees by teaching English, donating or delivering furniture, helping in the job search, or hosting a family. They also have opportunities to pray and give financially to refugee families. Because friendships make a foreign place feel like home, volunteers are strategically placed as a refugee family's first friend in their new home. As Christian volunteers provide for a refugee's survival needs and initiate friendship, a refugee experiences God's love.

Carol is one volunteer who expressed God's love to refugees in Chicago. I met Carol through a mutual friend at her church. Like many prospective volunteers, Carol was eager to help yet limited in time and resources. As a mother of two kids and a leader in her church and community, Carol was particularly busy. Eventually, her schedule opened up and Carol invited me to speak at her adult Sunday school class. With the help of a Bosnian refugee friend, I explained refugee ministry and God's deep concern for those who suffer. Days later, Carol and a few friends from church agreed to welcome a refugee family with a "Good Neighbor Kit."

A week before the family's arrival, we received news that the one family was actually two related families. Both families needed a church to help them. Although initial interest among the congregation was lacking, Carol agreed to help the second family with a kit. Then God opened the floodgates of heaven. When Carol reported back to the church the urgent needs, God moved people to give. Kitchen items, towels, money, and furniture came pouring into the church. As the donations increased, so did the excitement level. By God's grace, the church was ready to welcome both families.

On the day the families arrived, Carol, a few other volunteers, a Bosnian relative, and I went to the airport to welcome them. The excitement level continued to grow as we waited at the international terminal. The group eagerly watched the entrance ramp, clutching balloons, flowers, gifts, and a banner saying, "Welcome to America." Then our long-awaited guests arrived.

Weary from the flight, the two families of four slowly walked into sight with only a few bags. The Bosnian relative raced to greet her beloved family while we watched in humble amazement. With tears of joy and sorrow they greeted each other. They celebrated their safe arrival and reunion, yet grieved all they lost along the way. We quietly introduced ourselves, and after a few photos, we were off to their new Chicago apartment.

After carrying the "Good Neighbor Kits" into the apartment, we sat around the room and reintroduced ourselves. We welcomed the families to America by saying, "Dobro Doshli u Ameriku (Welcome to America). We are glad that you are here." Although our Bosnian language skills were limited, our love and concern could be clearly understood.

The involvement of Carol and her church did not stop with meeting survival needs. Giving the household essentials was a doorway to a new relationship, one that included her whole church and family. Members from the church continued to visit the families. As one of the families was expecting a child, the church held a baby shower. The Bosnian children also attended the church's day camp, where they had fun at the beach and learned about Jesus. Carol's husband, Ray, hired one refugee, Aladin, as a construction worker. Ray was quickly impressed with Aladin's work ethic and skill.[9]

Before Carol met a refugee from Bosnia, refugee ministry was a vague concept, and Muslims were scary people. Now, she has a Bosnian Muslim friend named Alija who teaches her about baking Bosnian bread while Carol teaches her about the Bread of Life. In her own words, Alija says, "Carol is my friend, and I love her very much." "It's mutual," Carol replied.[10]

Compassion or Conversion

In partnership with World Relief, Carol and her church demonstrated God's love by welcoming two Bosnian families. Although neither Aladin nor Alija has trusted Christ as personal Lord and Savior, the work of compassion is done in the name of Christ. Compassion is a free gift with no strings attached. We cannot assist Bosnian Muslims or other refugees with the unspoken expectation that they must in turn become believers. We can, however, play an active role in God's redemptive purposes by living out the gospel through presence and proclamation.

We live out the presence of the gospel by meeting needs, building relationships, and confessing Christ. Our work follows the principle, "People don't care how much you know until they know how much you care." Being a good neighbor is one way to shine a spotlight on the presence of the gospel. The word *neighbor* comes from a root that means to be near, or close by.[11] To be a good neighbor is to be where people are and love them as God does, unconditionally. A good neighbor crosses cultural lines and enters into another person's world. As we are good neighbors, refugees have a chance to see the hope that is within us and ask questions (1 Pet. 3:15–16). One of the best questions that refugees ask is "Why are you helping me?" At that moment, the door is open to confess Christ as Lord. We can answer, "Because of God's love for you and me, I want to help." Sometimes we can continue with our personal experience of God's love and forgiveness. Our conversion story is a very appropriate and nonthreatening way to share the gospel.

We can also proclaim the gospel. Proclamation is the verbalization or explanation of the Good News.[12] In the midst of meeting urgent needs, we must remember that a refugee's deepest need is for forgiveness and reconciliation with God (Rom. 5:8). People need the Lord (Rom. 6:23). We can explain the Good News at any time because the gospel is powerful (Rom. 1:16). The gospel message does not need to be seen perfectly before it is heard, for the Holy Spirit and the Word of God produce the power and conviction necessary for conversion. "For our gospel did not come to you in word only, but also in power and in the Holy Spirit and with full conviction" (1 Thess. 1:5 NASB).

The balance between presence and proclamation can be difficult. Although both are necessary, refugee ministry is primarily a work of presence or pre-evangelism. We are cultivating the soil. We plant seeds, another person waters, but God causes the growth (1 Cor. 3:6–9). God is the Evangelist. He brings individuals to Himself in His time. We must remember that conversion is a process that requires a long-term perspective.

We also must recognize the barriers that prevent refugees from responding to the gospel. "Christians" tortured, murdered, and destroyed many of the Bosnians' homes and families. Bosnian refugees feel a tremendous amount of hatred and betrayal toward Serbian Christians. Bosnians and Iraqis are Muslim, and their religious traditions and customs unify them as a people. To leave the "faith" is to leave one's family. In converting to Christ, former Muslim refugees are often disowned by family members. Further, Christianity is viewed as cultural rather than relational. People are "born" into a religion rather than choosing to follow Christ.

The Story of Edin

Let me tell you about my dear friend Edin. I met Edin, another Bosnian refugee, a number of years ago when I was volunteering at World Relief Chicago. I delivered furniture and household items to a family. After the furniture was inside the apartment, we sat down for coffee and juice. I remember seeing a group of younger boys laughing on the other side of the room. Unexpectedly, one of the boys, Edin, walked through the crowded apartment and handed me a bracelet with the name "Jennifer" on it. "This is for you," he said shyly. Although my name is Chad, not Jennifer, I was deeply touched by this young boy's tender heart. Edin came to the United States with next to nothing, and he gave me a gift.

That day was the beginning of our friendship. Since then Edin and I have enjoyed playing board games, attending a Chicago White Sox baseball game, swimming at the beach, reading books, and hanging out. As our friendship has grown, so has the trust level. Edin once introduced me to his newly arrived cousin as his "best friend." Edin also opened up and told me about the pain of war. With tears in his eyes, he described how his father was murdered and how he wanted to kill a hundred Serbs to avenge his death. He recounted his terrifying experience in a concentration camp where people were tortured, food was scarce, and his mother signed over their property to escape death.

Because of the time that we spent together, not only did Edin trust me, but his mother, Alma, trusted me too. You can imagine the protective stance that this single mother took toward her twelve-year-old son. Because Alma worked as a housekeeper in the evenings, she made Edin stay home alone after school. Whenever Edin told his mother that he would be with me, he was free to go. This sacred trust blessed and scared me. I wanted to be up front and clear with Alma where I was taking her son. So when it came time to go to the "Say Yes, Chicago" evangelistic campaign with Luis Palau, I explained to Alma that we were going to the park to learn about God, play baseball, and listen to music. Like most Bosnians, she was open with her faith and agreed to let Edin come with me. Little did I know the eternal significance of that single day.

We arrived at Chicago's downtown Grant Park in the middle of the afternoon. After playing baseball in the field, we sat near the band shell to eat and hear Luis Palau. The gospel presentation was clear, short, and to the point. To my amazement, Edin said, "I want to go forward and be a Christian."

I said, "Are you sure that you understand?"

He said, "Yes. Will you go with me?"

"Of course," I responded. Then we walked up front and Edin prayed to receive Christ as his personal Lord and Savior.

Needless to say, I was thrilled to be a part of God's work in Edin. On the car ride home, I reviewed the gospel with Edin and he repeated his faith in Christ. Then he asked me, "Now do I go to church or to the mosque?"

I asked, "What do you think?"

"Both," he answered, "I want to be with my family too." I agreed and said that he could worship Jesus at church and still attend the mosque with his family.

Minutes later, we returned to Edin's apartment. I wondered what I was going to say to his mother. Clearly, she trusted me with her son, and now he was rejecting her faith. Unsure of what to say, I let Edin explain to his mother his new belief in Christ. In Bosnian, he explained all that happened at the park. Again to my amazement, Alma responded positively. Then I asked if I could teach Edin more about Jesus by reading the Bible with him. She replied, "Yes, but what about Muhammad?"

After a quick prayer, I answered, "I'll teach him everything I know about Muhammad." Alma agreed. Then for the next several weeks, we studied the Bible along with the evangelistic campaign's follow-up material.

I wish that I could complete this story by telling you that Edin is growing strong in his relationship with Christ; however, it is a real struggle. I can tell you that he is moving in the right direction. He continues to struggle with what it means to be "born" Muslim and a "born again" Christian. He is also learning how to respond to his friends' ridicule. Edin, like all of us, is in the process of knowing Christ. By God's grace, Edin will grow into the man that God intended him to be. Until then, I must maintain a long-term perspective, cultivate our friendship, and pray.

TOP TEN RECOMMENDATIONS

The following list is my top ten suggestions for helping refugees.

1. Be open to God. God may be leading you to go and learn what it means that He "desires mercy not sacrifice."

2. Take the position of a learner. We can learn a great deal from refugees if we are open. Watch, listen, and observe a new way of living.

3. Listen, listen, listen. The most important thing that you can do is listen to a refugee tell his or her story. Storytelling is one of the best ways to bridge a cultural gap and build a relationship. After listening, tell your own story.

4. Respond to the survival needs of refugees first. Freely provide the obvious needs of furniture, household items, job leads, and train-

ing. One caution: Do not come as one with all the answers. Come with questions. By asking refugees if they need assistance, we move toward interdependence.

5. Strive for interdependence. Never do something for a person if that person is capable of doing it. We must not create dependent relationships. For example, when you help, teach a person how to fill out a job application or school forms, rather than doing it for him. It may take a little longer, but it is worth it in the long run.

6. Be patient. Communicating across cultures is challenging. You will have misunderstandings and conflict. Be patient with yourself and your new friend.

7. Find common activities. We are more alike than we are different. Find common activities and do them together. Many women have enjoyed hours of fun by cooking together. Many boys and girls enjoy sports, and men like a good game of chess.

8. Learn as much as you can about their country. Knowing general information about a country provides topics of conversation and displays interest. Read newspapers and maps. Try to speak a few words in their language. I cannot tell you how much a greeting in their language means to most refugees.

9. Be prepared to explain the gospel. You never know when an opportunity to present the gospel will arrive. Familiarize yourself with Bible verses, the Bridge illustration, or a gospel tract.

10. Stay close to the Vine! Refugee ministry can feel like navigating through a jungle, so stay close to Jesus (John 15:5). He is with you, and this is His work. Ask Him to work in you and through you for His glory and your joy.

Conclusion: What Refugees Need

The world's refugees are escaping persecution and coming to the United States as our new neighbors. They need help to rebuild their broken lives. God has a deep concern for the fatherless, widows, and refugees. Because of His love, we can love refugees by meeting their needs and initiating friendship. The work of compassion is done in Christ's name whether or not a person responds to the gospel. We play an active role in God's redemptive purposes by living out the gospel through presence and proclamation. In doing so, we learn compassion. Compassion can only be learned as we go to those who are hurting and hungry. After helping a refugee family, one volunteer summed it up best when she said, "This is what being a Christian is all about."

Reflection Questions

1. Imagine that you are going on a trip to a foreign country. List all the items that you might need for your journey.

2. Look up the biblical passages on refugees listed in this chapter. Meditate on God's concern for them. Ask God to give you the same concern that He has for refugees.

3. We never forget the friends who help us in times of need. Describe a difficult time in your life. Who were the people there to help you? How did they help?

chapter twenty-three

REACHING THE HOMOSEXUAL COMMUNITY

FACE-TO-FACE MINISTRIES IN THE EYE OF THE STORM

BRAD GRAMMER

Introduction: Diversity on Parade

On the fourth Sunday of June, an annual event takes place in Wrigleyville, a Northside Chicago neighborhood famous for baseball and chewing gum. Some people come to gawk. Others come to jeer and ridicule. Many come to celebrate a particular community—the gays of Chicago.

The Gay Pride Parade draws thousands of participants and spectators every year. People line the streets to get a glimpse of the imaginative floats and flamboyant personalities. Throughout the parade, banners are carried proudly by special-interest groups such as "Gay Teachers" or "Dykes on Bikes" or "American Baptists for Gays." The warm temperatures assist in various displays of nudity. Some individuals wear little more than their underwear. The parade is entertaining for many—an ostentatious display of sexuality and liberality. For the Christian community, however, this event can be a picture of Old Testament carnality and sexual degradation—Sodom and Gomorrah in full swing. Unfortunately, it is often this snapshot of the gay community that is revisited in the discussion of homosexual issues.

Many Christians avoid homosexuals because of those who take angry, militant stances or who flaunt promiscuous lifestyles. Many Christians fear that befriending a homosexual might result in a temptation to sin or to relax a strong moral stand. They are afraid associating with homosexuals seems to mean advocating the lifestyle. And many people assume homosexuals are inclined toward child molestation. Can they be trusted?

FACE-TO-FACE: A LIGHT IN DARKENED CORNERS

Face-to-Face Ministries has sought to reach out to a community of people that has been shunned by the church for many reasons and many years. The ministry is based upon the hope that regardless of the presence of homosexual desires in an individual's life, a growing relationship with the Lord Jesus Christ and meaningful relationships in the body of Christ can provide an avenue for a transformation of these desires.

We know from Scripture that this is not a new issue. Former homosexuals were in the New Testament church. Paul reflected on this situation in 1 Corinthians 6:9–11: "Or do you not know that the unrighteous will not inherit the kingdom of God? Do not be deceived; neither fornicators, nor idolaters, nor adulterers, nor effeminate, nor homosexuals, nor thieves, nor the covetous, nor drunkards, nor revilers, nor swindlers, will inherit the kingdom of God. *Such were some of you;* but you were washed, but you were sanctified, but you were justified in the name of the Lord Jesus Christ, and in the Spirit of our God" (NASB, italics added). Paul knew of these individuals. They had experienced a transformation because of the work of the Lord Jesus Christ in their lives. This is the hope we carry in Face-to-Face Ministries.

The ministry of Face-to-Face has three purposes: (1) to help Christian men who struggle with homosexuality find freedom in their identity in Christ; (2) to educate the body of Christ about the issue of homosexuality; and (3) to reach out to nonbelieving homosexuals. One-on-one discipleship has been a major aspect of the ministry from the beginning. During this time, the ministry has had the opportunity to investigate the particulars of each man's struggle and to use the Bible and a Christian perspective to transform the ingrained thinking and behavior that perpetuates the homosexual struggle.

God has opened many doors to educate the body of Christ. Speaking engagements have included television and radio spots, as well as conferences and workshops. We have also had opportunities to get a foot in the door in predominantly non-Christian environments, such as a public high school and university. I never cease to be amazed at how God gives life to the simple words that a person uses to pierce another person's heart. Through the telling of my own story, as well as the stories of those served by the ministry, I've seen Christians grow in their compassion for the homosexual community.

The evangelistic branch of Face-to-Face involves frequenting the streets where part of the homosexual community socializes. Pairs of volunteers go into the gay bars on the North Side of Chicago wearing pins bearing a first name and the name of the ministry. We go to tell the gospel. To lay to rest any negative images of Bible-pounding preachers, we take an approach similar to Jesus talking to the woman at the well. We enter the bar and order a Coke. While we sit, we pray and wait for God to work. Invariably, individuals come up to us, and often the pins are a way to begin a conversation. A phrase we use, when asked why we are in the bar, is "We're here to talk about Jesus Christ with anyone who wants to talk." This usually comes up in the first part of the conversation; then the person can decide whether he or she wants to continue or end the dialogue. Much to my surprise, gay bars have often turned out to be places where people seek help, emotionally and spiritually.

TRUTH—AND SOME FICTION

The 10 Percent Myth

To introduce you a little further to the gay community, allow me to take a few moments and dispel some errant thinking. Much of the media has been faithful at communicating incorrect facts about the homosexual issue. Often, media reports will say the homosexual community is 10 percent of the population. This figure is taken from Alfred Kinsey's research study, *Sexual Behavior in the Human Male,* published in 1948. Another research study published by him and his associates in 1953 was called *Sexual Behavior in the Human Female.* Kinsey had a male sample of just over five thousand and a female sample of almost six thousand.

In recent years, Kinsey's studies have come under criticism from some reliable professionals. In their controversial book, *Kinsey, Sex and Fraud,* Dr. Judith Reisman and Edward Eichel discredit Kinsey's research by examining poor methods of sampling (focusing on prisoners, including many pedophiles), inaccurate conclusions, and unethical practices.[1] Many other studies have come out with very different figures than Kinsey's 10 percent.

In their book *Answers to the Gay Deception,* Marlin Maddoux and Christopher Corbett quoted several studies. These studies include the Guttmacher Institute study of 1993 and the University of Chicago study of 1990. The *New York Times* quoted the latter study, which found

that "about 2 percent of the men surveyed had engaged in homosexual
sex and that 1 percent considered themselves to be exclusively homosexual." The National Opinion Research Center at the University of
Chicago is a reputable survey team. Its researchers sampled 1,587
adults over eighteen years old nationwide. The conclusion: At most,
1.5 percent of the sample were male and female homosexuals.[2] These
are only two of the reputable sources quoted in this book. A few other
well-known studies are quoted in this book, as well as other sources. A
survey in France found that 4 percent of men and 3 percent of women
had ever engaged in homosexual activity.[3] Other studies reflect similar
results.[4]

For twenty years Ron and Joanne Higley have been directors of a
ministry located in New York City called L.I.F.E., Inc. They report that
approximately three hundred thousand homosexuals live in New York
City, which is approximately 3 percent of the population—the largest
gay community in the world.[5] In Chicago, estimates in local media
have reported that the homosexual population numbers from five
hundred thousand to six hundred thousand. I believe these figures are
based upon Kinseys' 10-percent figure. Getting official statistics on
this population group is difficult. Most of our information comes from
the research results already cited.

It has been said that the 10-percent figure was merely used by militant gay activists to help the straight world get a visual picture of one
in ten people in this nation being homosexual. Consider the following
statement: "The thing about the 'one in ten'—I think people probably
always did know that it was inflated. But it was a nice number that you
could point to, that you could say 'one in ten,' and it's a really good
way to get people to visualize that we're here."[6]

By using an unreliable figure, gay activists were hoping to solicit
more support from the population by helping to normalize homosexual behavior. If there is a large percentage of homosexuals, the belief is
that this is a common, and, therefore, acceptable phenomena.

The Possibility of Change

One other misconception I'd like to address is the question of
whether an individual can change in his or her sexual desires. Since
we have already looked at 1 Corinthians 6, we have seen that the Bible
does support this position. Psychological research shows the same
support. A true examination of research would show that the psychological community supports change. This is not the perspective most
often reported in the media. Masters and Johnson reported, in the
book *Homosexuality in Perspective*, on a success rate of 71.6 percent

among eighty-one homosexuals desiring reorientation. Their conclusion: "No longer should the qualified psychotherapist avoid the responsibility of either accepting the homosexual client in treatment or referring him or her to an acceptable treatment source."[7]

Dr. Irving Bieber, former president of the New York Medical College, directed a research team in a nine-year study of male homosexuality. He and his colleagues concluded that "a heterosexual shift is a possibility for all homosexuals who are strongly motivated to change."[8] Dr. Lawrence J. Hatterer wrote a book entitled *Changing Homosexuality in the Male*. He wrote, "I've heard of hundreds of other men who went from a homosexual to a heterosexual adjustment on their own."[9] Dr. Charles Socarides is the attending psychiatrist and professor at the Albert Einstein College of Medicine in New York City. He is quoted in the *American Handbook of Psychiatry* as saying, "The major challenge in treating homosexuality from the point of view of the patient's resistance has, of course, been the misconception that the disorder is innate or inborn."[10]

Many other professionals could be quoted from the past fifty years. There is substantial evidence from the psychological community that homosexuality is a reversible condition. Part of the psychiatric community may disregard such studies to remain faithful to their position. Regardless of psychological research results, the fact that the Bible is supportive of change should be enough for a believer to stand upon and find hope. I know, because I have been in the position of experiencing this kind of change.

My Own Story

Twenty years ago, I faced the fear that maybe I was a homosexual. Having sexual desires for males was a common experience for me. I was fearful of being identified as a homosexual because I had grown up being rejected by peers for being "different." Athletics were not my strength or interest. This simple difference was enough to be the ridicule of most of my male peers. I quickly learned that boys were supposed to be good in sports and to enjoy them. To venture outside of this mold invited a label of "sissy" or "faggot." *Faggot* was not a familiar term in my isolated world. Once I discovered what the word meant, I became anxious that maybe this was my true identity. To face another reason to be rejected was too much for my adolescent mind. But trying to deny that I was a homosexual never took away the homosexual desires.

I had grown up in the church, so I knew that homosexuality was wrong. The practices of prayer and reading the Word were my only formulas for overcoming these desires. After a few years, my formulas proved to be a failure in overcoming these feelings. I wasn't sexually attracted to women, so I didn't believe marriage could be an option. Neither was faking heterosexuality. However, my commitment to my faith prevented me from venturing into the homosexual lifestyle. I did not even know this lifestyle because I had no relationship with others who had the same desires. I made the decision to lead a celibate life. Following Christ, regardless of the cost, was my only recourse. I sorrowfully resigned myself to this decision.

How the process of change took place in my life would probably take an entire chapter in itself. What I can communicate is that an authentic, growing relationship with God and with men who modeled a godly love in friendship were the two pillars of healing in my story. No ministries from which to seek help existed at the time in my area. Few books were published, and they weren't widely distributed. All I learned came from relationships with men who were willing to go beyond the surface and reveal their own lives. My willingness to be transparent and completely honest was the other important ingredient. Through these relationships, I came to identify myself truly as a male. As this understanding connected more in my heart and mind, I began to experience a transformation in my desires, without necessarily knowing why. By the time my desires had completely changed to heterosexuality, I wondered what had happened. Only in hindsight can I identify essential ingredients to experiencing change.

THE NEGLIGENCE OF THE CHURCH

After hearing, briefly, the process of change in my own life, perhaps you can understand why so few have been able to experience this freedom. The church's past responses to homosexuals don't include a record of which to be proud. Countless times, I have heard saddening stories from men who were rejected by the church once they were willing to be open and seek help. The typical response from pastors and other Christians has traditionally come in three forms: (1) ignoring the problem of homosexual desires, hoping they'll go away; (2) rejecting the person, often asking him or her to leave the church; and (3) suppressing the problem, resulting in stronger desires and deeper frustrations. All three responses fail to address the heart of the problem of homosexuality, therefore hindering any process of healing and change.

All of the men I have spoken with are familiar with trite formulas spouted by thoughtful but uninformed Christians. These men know that reading the Bible and praying fervently produces little change in sexual desires. Many have gotten married, hoping that this will solve the problem. Much to their chagrin, no change took place. Sometimes going to a counselor or support group has resulted in little change. Feeling despondent over their situation, many have given up, concluding that their experience must be a result of an innate condition. We often met stray Christians in bar settings. Finding no other place in which they felt comfortable, they sought out the night scene and familiar faces in the bar atmosphere.

Many faces can be found on the streets at night. One might assume that everyone has a similar background or fits a common description. At least, that's what I assumed. Through this ministry, God has broken down barriers of ignorance and prejudice in my own mind. Some assumptions included the following thoughts: (1) that homosexuals aren't interested in the gospel; (2) that I had nothing in common with a male prostitute; (3) that homosexuals were always confident and sure of their sexual identity; and (4) that homosexuals didn't have emotional pains. To counter all of these assumptions, God showed me that homosexuals are interested in God, many are doubting their own sexuality, and many carry pains that no one will walk them through. In addition, God showed me that a middle-class, suburban boy could have something in common with a male who prostituted.

Is It a Waste of Time?

Tom has been living on the streets. His only source of income, when I first met him, was the money he made from men who were willing to pay to have sex with him. How could I forget the moment we first met?

While spending an evening in a gay bar, I was anxious to give one of my best prepared evangelistic sermons to some lost soul. Tom was quick to remind me that I was wasting my time. He had heard about us through the bartender, and he yelled out his greeting across the bar, "Hey, are you some Jesus freaks come to save us?" How does one respond to such an introduction? Should I smile and wave to let everyone know to whom he was referring? My response involved looking him in the eye and smiling. In the bar scene, this is a statement that I'm interested in you. I wanted to let him know that I wasn't intimidated by his mocking remarks.

After a few minutes of laughter and ridicule, Tom calmed down. While everyone was busy in conversation, Tom came over to my partner and me and informed us that we weren't going to change anyone. I assured him that this was not our desire. Our intention was merely to talk about Jesus Christ to anyone who was interested. He quickly retorted, "You're wasting your time."

Was I wasting my time? Was I ridiculous to think that there might actually be someone in a gay bar open to hearing the gospel? How could I convince them that the gospel was good news? The way some Christians have treated homosexuals doesn't seem to reflect much "good news." Most of the men I met already knew that homosexuality was a sin. Many of them had been rudely reminded of that by Christians who had asked them to leave the church at the revelation of their struggle. They knew that God was a mighty judge, with a capital "J." Try to convince someone rejected by the church that God loves him or her. I realized that in one minute, or one hour, I would not be able to convince anyone God is loving.

One aspect of our outreach is that we do not approach people in the bars. We develop a presence and let people approach us. In this way, we earn the respect to speak with someone, rather than earning the reputation of being Bible-pounding legalists. Over the next few weeks, Tom approached me to engage in conversations about life and what I believed. I listened, intrigued at how a man in love with philosophy and poetry crumbled into a worn-out soul whose only pleasure involved sex with men who never really cared for him. My heart ached for his soul.

One night, I walked with a partner into the bar Tom frequented. My partner connected with a familiar face, and I saw Tom sitting alone at the bar. I went over and sat beside him. His head was down, and he was quiet. This was unusual for the boisterous, energetic Tom I knew. He was slightly drunk and completely broken. He still bore a black eye from an encounter he didn't wish to discuss. At first, he made attempts to be funny and get a laugh from the crowd. No one was responding. I sat silently, hoping to offer some comfort. Then suddenly and quietly, he said, "I don't know why you care about [trash] like me."

You see, Tom and I had developed a friendship during the few hours we talked each week. He knew that I *really* cared about him. I wasn't interested in using him. Usually, others were merely interested in him for what he could do for them. Up until this point, I hadn't fully presented the gospel. In that moment, the door opened, and I began to describe the incredible love of God. I told him how I had felt like "trash" at one point in my life, and that God died for "trash" like us because of His incredible love.

If you love someone long enough, he will want to know what true love is all about. Tom wanted to know because he was confused about how a seemingly "clean-cut, put-together" Christian could care about someone who lived such a different lifestyle—an "evil" life.

What great wisdom do I have to tell about how to reach out to a male prostitute? Not much. There are no formulas. There are no special words. I grew up in a middle-class neighborhood. There appeared to be nothing that could connect me with Tom. Except two things: We both know what it's like to feel like trash, and we both want someone to love us anyway. What "training" do you need to be interested in someone's life? How "gifted" do you need to be to sit with someone and let him or her know you care?

A Diverse Community

Tom is just one face in the crowd. Many come from very different backgrounds and experiences. Some are very promiscuous, involved in one-night stands on at least a weekly basis. Some may indeed lust after young children. Some homosexuals are militant activists whose own pain is the driving force behind all the bitterness and anger in their political goals. But many homosexuals are working toward the same goals as you. They are going to school, working honest jobs, and seeking to buy a home and make a few friends. Radical demonstrations or legislation is not a priority on their lists. In fact, many couldn't care less about the radicals' position, even though they may not verbally refute such tactics.

Another group that needs to be mentioned is within the church. These are the individuals who remain silent and struggle alone. They are committed Christians who believe that homosexuality is not in God's plan for mankind, but they wrestle with the fact that these desires are present within their own bodies. My life story fits this category.

Sometimes, as Christians, we lose the focus of our main purpose. Often, we hold up our hands to nonbelievers, keeping them at arms' length, while tossing little tracts that preach the message of truth. We're more concerned about nonbelievers repenting than we are about loving our neighbor (Lev. 19:18; Matt. 22:39), speaking the truth with gentleness and respect (1 Pet. 3:15), and allowing the Holy Spirit to convict the heart (John 16:8). Richard Lovelace reminds us of what is really true: "Most of the repenting that needs to be done on this issue of homosexuality needs to be done by straight people, including straight Christians. By far the greater sin in our church is the sin of neglect, fear, hatred, just wanting to brush these people under the rug."[11]

REACHING OUT BEYOND THE CHURCH

Obviously, the different groups of individuals mentioned warrant different responses. How is one to minister to the unbelieving homosexual? In his book *Desires in Conflict*, Joe Dallas answers such a question:

Remember, the goal of the church is not to make "straights out of gays." It is to preach the gospel. . . . So our first priority, as with anyone else, is to share Christ and treat our fellow humans with courtesy and honor. Often people ask, "How do you witness to a gay?" The question itself shows a certain misunderstanding. Why should witnessing to gays be any different than witnessing to someone else? Their homosexuality is not our main concern. The state of their souls is.[12]

Outreach to the gay community may take different forms. Face-to-Face chose to pursue the avenue of night ministry on the street and in the bars. This approach is low-key and perhaps more risky, depending on the bar where you choose to do outreach. We have gone into different kinds of bars. Some are neighborhood bars where patrons are familiar and frequent. The pace is slower, and the conversations tend to be longer. Other bars are what are called "pretty boy" bars, and they are frequented by young, attractive urban patrons. Dancing, loud music, and a party atmosphere put a damper on conversations at times. In other bars, where men prostitute, there was a more dangerous environment with drug dealing and striptease acts. However, in these settings, more men tended to be broken and open to the gospel. An advantage of bar outreach is being on their turf, which is less intimidating for them. Another advantage is that we don't have to sit and wait at the doors of the church before we have any contact with the gay community. Most homosexuals won't darken the doors of churches that don't accept the lifestyle.

There are many other methods of outreach. Ministries that reach out to those with AIDS often make contact with homosexuals. Love & Action Midwest, Inc., is located in the suburbs of Chicago. Sven and Nancy Cederburg are the directors of this ministry. Through the loss of their own son to AIDS, they are able to offer love and compassion without judgment. They have earned the respect of area hospitals and nursing homes. Through their love and kindness, they are able to visit individuals with AIDS and develop relationships. Many people with AIDS live lonely lives with no one coming to visit or lend a helping hand. Through these relationships, the volunteers with this ministry earn the right to informally present the gospel.

Another way to minister to the homosexual community is through involvement in community organizations. Face-to-Face reaches out in the Lakeview, Uptown, Edgewater, and Rogers Park neighborhoods on the North Side of Chicago. These neighborhoods house the largest population of the gay community in the city of Chicago. Community organizations working to improve these neighborhoods often have homosexual staff or volunteers. Working alongside these individuals for a common good can provide natural opportunities to give the gospel.

A more low-key but more powerful way to reach out to the gay community is to develop a prayer ministry (Matt. 5:43–48; Luke 18:1; Eph. 6:18; Col. 4:2–4; 1 Thess. 5:17; 2 Thess. 3:1; James 5:13–16). As people go to the sections of cities and towns where homosexuals live, work, and socialize, they set out to pray on a weekly basis for the salvation of people in that community. Emmaus Ministries is a ministry in Chicago that reaches out to men involved in prostitution. John Green, the director, has formed prayer teams that walk the streets at night and pray for these men and the gay community.

Ask God to bring people across your path, and pray against the work of the Enemy in these individuals' lives. Allow God to speak to you about how you can reach out to those who need to hear the gospel. Some of the people you're praying for may even come from within the walls of your own church body. Many other creative ways could be used to reach the homosexual community. Beginning a prayer ministry is a great way to open your heart for God to speak about your unique situation.

REACHING THOSE WITHIN THE CHURCH

What about the believing struggler who desires to live a righteous life before God? Starting a support group for those struggling with homosexual desires could be a possible response, although to avoid possible dangers it needs to be carefully structured and headed by someone who does not struggle with homosexuality. Ideally, friendships are the avenue for healing. Through relationships, we experience the greatest pain and the greatest healing. Bob Davies and Anita Worthen coauthored a book *Someone I Love Is Gay*. One chapter addresses how to help a Christian friend. These are the recommendations they give:

1. *Work on deepening your friendship.* Become a "safe" person with whom that man or woman can be honest. Make an effort to be a reliable, consistent friend.
2. *Pray for your friendship.*
3. *Be open about your own struggles.* Be willing to risk your reputation. If you are hoping that your friend will open up at a deep level, you can reach that level of communication by opening up first.
4. *Mention homosexuality in a neutral context.*[13]

Little did I, or my friends, expect that this would be the path God would choose to bring my own transformation and healing—through relationship. If the church trained all believers to take one person and disciple that individual, there would be a remarkable change in the lives of the body of Christ, both for those who struggle with homosexuality and those who don't. Through my relationships with a few straight men, I experienced my own healing. God used me in their lives as well. God is not just interested in bringing healing to those who struggle sexually. Those who don't struggle sexually need Him as much as those who do.

A PROPER PERSPECTIVE

I believe that homosexuality has been labeled a "big" sin because of many Christians who are unwilling to face the depths and darkness of their own hearts. Do we really believe what the Bible says? In Jeremiah 17:9, God says, "The heart is deceitful above all things and beyond cure. Who can understand it?" Do we naively assume that this refers to us only in our unredemptive state? As I examine this passage, I don't see the Lord designating that His words are only referring to the unsaved individual. Would you claim that you became perfect at the point of conversion? Proverbs 20:9 says, "Who can say, 'I have cleansed my heart, I am pure from my sin'?" (NASB). Even more strongly, 1 John 1:8 says, "If we claim to be without sin, we deceive ourselves and the truth is not in us."

During a typical night of outreach, I entered a bar where we had developed a good relationship with the owner. Drug dealing, strip dancing, and male prostitution were regular activities in this bar. As I watched a couple of men playing pool, an older, well-groomed gentleman came up to me and asked about the pin I was wearing. After telling him that I was there to talk about Jesus Christ with anyone who wanted to, he said "Oh" and moved away. I turned to continue watching the pool game, somewhat disappointed that this gentleman wasn't open to talking. About five minutes later, he came back to me and said that he was intrigued by what I said.

This began a conversation in which I gave my testimony and the basic message of the gospel. After we spoke for about an hour, he stated, "I don't know if you're one of these, but I've met a few born-again Christians in my time. They weren't pleasant experiences, but since I've met you, I think I'll be more patient with the next one." Having one pleasant conversation with a Christian can be enough to cause someone to be more open to the next opportunity to hear the gospel.

Conclusion:
Facing Our Own Hindrances to Ministry

Is there a reason this kind of interaction could not happen more often? Perhaps if we don't view ourselves as God does, as miserable wretches in need of His glorious forgiveness and sustaining grace, then we do not really need Him *that* badly. The sin of Adam and Eve was to be independent from God (Gen. 3:22). We have this sinful nature built into each one of us. Realizing our need for salvation, and asking Christ into our lives, does not automatically remove from our hearts all desires for independence. This process spans our lifetime (Rom. 12:1–2). Ignoring the depths of sin in our own hearts is one way for us to keep some independence from our Lord. Our pride also has an opportunity to grow so we can feel good about ourselves and confirm that we do not need God as badly as others do.

We need to address this form of pride. To some degree, we all possess this weakness in our lives. Keeping a view of the depths of our sin is a necessary element in working in ministry—not to discourage us, but to keep a proper perspective and prevent any pride from developing. We *all* need the Lord Jesus Christ *daily*. If you are able to keep this perspective, you provide the avenue to be most effective in ministering to the homosexual.

Reflection Questions

1. How has your perspective on homosexuality influenced your relationships with those who struggle with this issue?

2. In what ways has your church sought to address this issue from a Christian perspective? Are methods used merely political in nature, or do they involve relationship?

3. What have you learned from your own sexual experiences/struggles that could be of help to someone struggling with homosexuality?

4. What scriptural passages would you use to represent your position on homosexuality? Are these passages consistent with your church's position?

5. What, in your eyes, are the greatest needs of the homosexual in your community? How can you be a part of ministering to that need, or needs?

For Further Reading

Ankerberg, John, and John Weldon. *The Myth of Safe Sex*. Chicago: Moody, 1993.

Dallas, Joe. *Desires in Conflict*. Eugene, Ore.: Harvest House, 1991.

————. "Responding to Pro-Gay Theology," *The Journal of Human Sexuality*. Carollton, Tex.: Lewis and Stanley, 1996.

Davies, Bob, and Lori Rentzel. *Coming Out of Homosexuality*. Downers Grove, Ill.: InterVarsity, 1993.

Maddoux, Marlin, and Christopher Corbett. *Answers to the Gay Deception*. Dallas: International Christian Media, 1994.

Reisman, Dr. Judith A., and Dr. John H. Court. *Kinsey, Sex and Fraud: The Indoctrination of a People*. Lafayette, La.: Huntington House, 1990.

Worthen, Anita, and Bob Davies. *Someone I Love Is Gay*. Downers Grove, Ill.: InterVarsity, 1996.

chapter twenty-four

MINISTERING IN THE PROJECTS

THE HISTORY AND CHALLENGES OF PUBLIC HOUSING

DAVID C. BROWN AND DANA THOMAS

Introduction: Taking the Light into Dark Places

The public housing projects of Chicago and other urban centers of the United States are monuments to poverty. Building high-rise apartment buildings to house only people living in poverty has concentrated and intensified problems in numerous areas of the inner city. In addition to a concentration of poverty, high-rise public housing has produced overcrowding, high rates of unemployment and underemployment, greater educational needs in local schools, drug and alcohol abuse, higher crime rates, and the breakdown of the family unit.

As a society, we have created a dark picture for the residents of public housing projects. But we know that Jesus Christ is the Light (John 1:4–9; 8:12), even in these dark places. From a human point of view, the situation is hopeless. From God's point of view, however, there is hope in Christ (Titus 2:13).

As Christians, we should be committed to helping families and individuals get adequate housing here on earth. We should also be committed to making sure that everyone has the opportunity to get the best housing available—an eternal home in heaven through their personal faith in our Lord Jesus Christ.

INTRODUCING GOSPEL OUTREACH, INC.

Gospel Outreach, Inc. is an Illinois not-for-profit organization incorporated in 1987. Its purpose is to present Jesus Christ to the people of the Robert Taylor Homes and elsewhere who live where poverty and other factors make a credible Christian witness difficult to develop and maintain. We also want to promote, encourage, and foster programs designed to help meet the spiritual, physical, mental, social, and emotional needs of such individuals and families. We want to help people —especially young people in the inner city—come to know, love, and follow Jesus.

Gospel Outreach was started after the Lord laid a burden on our hearts to reach out to the people (especially boys and girls) of the Robert Taylor Homes with the gospel. We had been involved with a friend who was a probation officer in Cook County's juvenile court. We worked with several young men from the Robert Taylor Homes. Responding to this exposure, our previous experience in the Cabrini-Green Housing Project, the counsel of godly friends, the partnership with a church in the Robert Taylor neighborhood, and much prayer, Gospel Outreach was launched. During our first ten years, we have seen 335 young people and adults come to put their personal faith in our Lord Jesus Christ. Praise God for this!

At Gospel Outreach, we are concerned about ministering to the whole person. That is why, in addition to our Adventure Bible Clubs, Adventure Day Camps, resident camping programs, evangelistic visitation, and discipleship, we also emphasize advocacy programs, including tutoring, clothing distribution, food distribution, holiday gift boxes, and much more. God has truly blessed these efforts to meet the practical and spiritual needs of people living in the inner city.

Gospel Outreach is a parachurch organization. We endeavor to work in cooperation rather than in conflict with local churches. Gospel Outreach is governed by an independent board of directors (primarily African-American) from a variety of evangelical churches. We benefit from a large number of volunteers who minister with us. Gospel Outreach receives no government funds. We rely entirely on the Lord and His people for the ongoing need of the ministry.

Gospel Outreach's main area of ministry is the Robert Taylor Homes on Chicago's South Side. Robert Taylor Homes' name has become synonymous with stereotypes of the high-rise public housing. It is not only the largest public housing project in Chicago; it is the largest in the world. At its peak, twenty-eight sixteen-story buildings with more than four thousand apartments contained a total population of 18,670 people.[1] An anonymous resident summed up life in Robert Taylor: "We live stacked on top of one another with no elbow room. Danger is all around. There's little privacy or peace and no quiet. And the world looks on all of us as project rats, living on a reservation like untouchables."[2]

Built during the 1950s and the 1960s, the Robert Taylor Homes stretch more than fifteen blocks down State Street, paralleling the Dan Ryan expressway. Although the Chicago White Sox play ball in Comiskey Park, which is literally just down the street, it may as well be in another world. Single mothers head more than 90 percent of the homes in Robert Taylor. The high school dropout rate is 73 percent. More than half of the girls become pregnant as teenagers. More than two-thirds of the children are born to unwed mothers.[3]

Ten-year-old Michael is an example of the young people living in the Robert Taylor Homes. He asked me how white people got rich if they did not sell drugs. In his world, the only rich people were drug dealers. The people he knew who did not sell drugs were all poor. Of course, he did not realize that white people also sell drugs—just not in his neighborhood.

INTRODUCING SUNSHINE GOSPEL MINISTRIES (SGM)

Sunshine Gospel Ministries (SGM) is a parachurch outreach to people living in and around the Chicago housing complex known as Cabrini-Green. Founded in 1905 by Moody Church, SGM was established as an outreach to present Jesus Christ to single mothers and their children on the Near North Side of Chicago. As the immigrant population increased in this area, the number of homeless people expanded as well. SGM broadened its outreach to include compassionate ministry to this segment of the community, providing food, clothes, shelter, and the gospel to these men and women, while continuing to provide programs for youth.

Today, intentional efforts to minister to the parents and guardians of youth are fostered through establishment of relationships centered on the child. A variety of programs and settings are used to minister to the residents of this community. Club programs, small discipleship groups, mentoring relationships, adult Bible studies, camping, and a host of field trips strengthen relationships with youth and their families. Help with everything from homework and tutoring to job training and referrals are offered to meet some of the practical needs of families.

HISTORY OF PUBLIC HOUSING IN CHICAGO[4]

The community recognized as Cabrini today was previously known as "Little Hell."[5] Originally settled by German immigrants in the mid-1800s, it was a truck-farming community that gradually grew up into an urban neighborhood. When the original German settlers achieved the means to move on to more affluent areas of the city, Irish immigrants succeeded them. The Irish were replaced by Swedish immigrants, and the Swedes were replaced by Sicilians. The neighborhood the Sicilians inherited was already run-down and had become a dangerous place for outsiders to enter. Riddled with gangs, it echoed with gunfire so frequently that a place near what is now Oak Street and Cleveland Avenue became known as "Death Corner" because of the numerous gang murders that were committed there. "Little Hell" was already a vermin-infested area with garbage-strewn alleys, gangways, and dangerous streets in which residents endured a rate of violent crime twelve times that of nonslum neighborhoods.

As the Sicilians settled into "Little Hell," another immigrant group began arriving in Chicago in large numbers. These were a different kind of immigrant to the city, however. They did not come from overseas, but were homegrown Americans. They were poor blacks fleeing the Jim Crowism and hardscrabble, sharecropping existence of America's Southern states.

The city, in its effort to address this problem, broke ground three days before the Japanese attack on Pearl Harbor in December of 1941 in the middle of "Little Hell." The city was to build 586 two- and three-story townhouse units. The initial occupancy was 75 percent white families and 25 percent black. During the years of the war, black occupancy increased to 80 percent. Upon the arrival of blacks, the number of families in the neighborhood jumped from 1,800 to 3,600, horribly overtaxing the areas' substandard housing.

A 1951 survey done by the Chicago Housing Authority (CHA) of "Little Hell" revealed a shocking profile of the community. Infant mortality was 2 1/2 times greater than in nonslum neighborhoods, and some diseases, such as tuberculosis and pneumonia, ran rampant. Thirty-five percent of the neighborhood's heads of families were unemployed. Twenty percent of families were single-women households, and the neighborhood truancy and juvenile delinquency rates were the highest in the city.

The city resolved that building additional housing to address the problems of the "Little Hell" district was the answer. Only this time, it had to address a new challenge. CHA found it difficult to acquire land to move blacks into other parts of the city. At the same time, it was determined that apartment units could be constructed less expensively than townhouses. So the planners decided to exclusively build high-rises. It was done in two stages. The "Cabrini Extension" was started in 1955 and completed in 1958, providing 1,896 modern, subsidized apartments in a complex of fifteen buildings rising seven, ten, and nineteen stories. The second stage, called the William Green Homes, was started in 1959 and completed in 1962, adding another 1,096 apartments in eight buildings of fifteen and sixteen stories.

Today more than 95 percent of the inhabitants of Cabrini-Green are African-American, and 76 percent of the homes are headed by single women. By 1985 the unemployment rate had grown from 35 percent in 1950 to 80 percent of the families existing on some form of government assistance for income.[6]

Chicago's economy, like the nation, was experiencing the most severe economic depression of its history by the end of the 1920s. The housing supply was hit hard. The Housing Act of 1937 laid the foundation for low-income persons, slum clearance, and urban renewal. It allowed for the transfer of responsibility for public housing from federal government to localities. This paved the way for the states to create local housing authorities like the Chicago Housing Authority.

The Chicago Housing Authority was incorporated in 1937 under the housing laws of the state of Illinois. Its dual purpose was to provide decent, safe, and sanitary housing to poor families and individuals who could not otherwise afford adequate housing in the private market and to remove slums and blighted areas. The federal government, under various housing agencies, would supply funds and overall direction. For example, the CHA was to keep enough rental income for administrative and operation expenses, but pay a specified amount to the United States Housing Authority as a reserve for repairs and replacement.

The CHA's first undertaking was managing three public housing projects built by Public Works Administration. They were the Jane Adams Homes, Julia C. Lathrop Homes, and the Trumbull Park Homes. These projects were on Chicago's West, North, and Far South Sides of the city, respectively. Because racial segregation in housing was a federal policy, all of these projects were rented to exclusively white tenants.

A 1938 CHA study found that about two-thirds of the units occupied by African-Americans in Chicago lacked complete facilities of central heating, gas, electricity, unshared kitchens, and private baths. Therefore, the African-American community suffered from the worst housing conditions, but it had virtually no public housing. The Wells Project was the first housing project built to help alleviate the substandard housing conditions of Chicago's growing African-American population.

The decade following World War II brought the CHA full swing into urban renewal activities. The CHA's first undertaking in clearing slums for private development was in 1946, when Michael Reese Hospital needed land for expansion. The cleared land also provided sites for private housing developments and other facilities. However, it displaced thousands of families, most of who were poor and African-American. The Chicago city council feared that new housing projects would bring African-Americans into white wards. Therefore, it persuaded the Illinois General Assembly to pass a statute that every public housing site proposed by local housing authorities in cities of 500,000 or more residents be approved by the particular city council. As a result, many of Chicago's housing projects designed for African-Americans ended up next to railroads, factories, and expressways.

In 1949, Congress passed a significant piece of legislation affecting public housing in the post–World War II area. Declaring that every American family should have a decent home and a suitable living environment, the act did two basic things. First, it authorized local public authorities to acquire slum land using the power of eminent domain and to sell it to private developers. Second, the act authorized loans and subsidies for a national program of low-rent housing to be constructed by local housing authorities.

The 1960s were characterized by two trends. First, there was an emphasis on providing decent housing for the elderly. During this period, a total of nine projects were completed. Second, family housing was also completed, including the final component of the 3,578 Cabrini-Green units and the 4,312 units at Robert Taylor Homes.

In 1976, the Chicago Dwelling Association, which provided housing for middle-income individuals—those with income too high to be eligible for public housing but too low to obtain adequate housing in the private market—dissolved into the CHA. By this time, the Chicago Housing Authority, as we know it, was beginning to take shape. Eighty-five percent of CHA units were occupied by African-Americans. With twenty-seven projects and 14,205 units in operation, the CHA was quickly becoming one of the largest landlords in the country.

Congress had passed a law in 1968 that no new family public housing located above the third floor would be approved. This, however, was closing the barn door after the horse had escaped. The CHA population was already almost 150,000 people, 97,000 of whom were minors. A full 50 percent of the families had five or more children, and more than 2,500 families had nine or more members. The proportion of CHA families with both parents present was only 38 percent. Sixty percent of families received public aid, social security, or unemployment compensation. In short, public housing in Chicago had become the permanent residence for a whole underclass of mostly large, poor African-American families.

But what is public housing like today?

General Chicago Housing Authority Information[7]

What Is Public Housing?

Public housing is low-rent housing for low-income people. The Chicago Housing Authority provides public housing in Chicago. Today the CHA operates approximately 40,000 homes and apartments.

What Kind of Housing Does CHA Provide?

The CHA provides a Family Housing Program. This includes 30,212 apartments with 118,000 people, including 43,000 under the age of twenty. The CHA also provides an Elderly Housing Program. This includes 9,822 apartments housing 10,200 persons. The CHA also provides the Section 8 Housing Assistant Program. The CHA's Section 8 program provides rent subsidies to low- and moderate-income families and senior citizens living in 15,696 apartments housing 43,532 people.

Who Pays for Public Housing?

The Chicago Housing Authority operates with money from rents and federal subsidies. The CHA has no taxing powers and therefore receives no real estate tax funds.

What Is the Rent?

The rent is set at 30 percent of a family's adjusted gross income or at a calculated rent ceiling, whichever is lower. The average rent in CHA-owned programs is $114. The average for families is $104 per month. The average for the elderly is $135 per month. The average for Section 8 is $135 per month.

Chicago Housing Authority Statistical Profile[8]

Family Composition: father, mother, and children—3%; one-parent family—74%; adult households without children—22%

Current Population in Public Housing

CHA OCCUPANCY[9]

Developments where demolition and modernization is planned:

	Units	*Occupied*	*Occupancy rate*
Abbott	1,258	770	61%
Adams	991	427	43%
Brooks Extension	465	271	58%
Cabrini-Green	2,625	1,410	54%
Dearborn Homes	800	677	85%
Horner	1,190	486	41%
Taylor	7,725	4,663	60%
Rockwell	1,135	465	41%
Stateway	1,644	998	61%
Wells	3,287	1,900	58%
Washington Park	932	425	46%

Overview of Problems in Public Housing

Many problems are caused or magnified by life in public housing projects. These problems surface to lesser and greater degrees in particular individuals. All of these problems can be seen in almost every building of a CHA complex. In some cases, all of these problems can be seen in individual families.

The high-rise projects generate some obvious difficulties. Poverty is widespread. People cannot legally live in a CHA project unless their income is below the nation's poverty level. Because so many people are jammed into high-rise buildings, overcrowding and the pressures of many people in a small area are an ongoing problem. Most of the residents of the projects are also unemployed. Of those who are employed, most are underemployed. That is, they are in jobs with little or no hope of advancement and at very low wages.

Education is inadequate. Schools are comprised entirely of students from poverty-level families. Parents often have limited education themselves and are unable to be of strong assistance to their children. Dropout rates are extremely high. For example, the dropout rate at DuSable High School across the street from the Robert Taylor Homes is almost 75 percent. Drugs are a way of life. The crime rates keep soaring to new heights. Homicide is the leading cause of death of male residents. Although a higher rate of criminals live in the housing, a higher rate of victims live there as well. Unwed pregnancies continue at high levels.

Everyday living becomes a difficult adventure. A mother comes home with some groceries but must walk to the fifteenth floor because neither elevator is working. A child dies from an appendix attack because the Emergency Medical Service is scared to enter the building. Mothers keep children home from school because of shootings in the neighborhood. Boys in the first grade are recruited by gangs. Preteens are involved in homicides. In short, the housing projects house samples of all of society's problems. In the projects, these problems are not only more widespread, but they also happen earlier in life and with far more intensity.

Roberta and Brad Hanson are Gospel Outreach missionaries, faithfully serving in Chicago's inner city. This article is a portion of a letter written by Roberta:

> Our morning started at 8 A.M. by picking up some volunteers from Moody Church to help with the packing of the Thanksgiving food boxes at Campus Crusade's Agape Center (in the Roseland Community on the South Side of Chicago). Together we joined hundreds of people from ministries all over the city of Chicago in praying, working up a sweat, packing, and praising God in songs of worship. That afternoon, Brad and I, along with some friends and fellow church members, had the privilege of sharing the "boxes and love" with 22 Gospel Outreach families.
>
> At one stop we were greeted by children, at least six of them ages two to ten, all running around the warm apartment in just their underwear. Their smiles and bare feet welcomed us into the dark living room. Someone was working on the electrical circuits, and the mother apologized for the darkness. Dressed in her housecoat, she looked a bit shocked to see us. We offered her the box and began to share why we had come when three women visitors arrived, interrupting our conversation. The next thing we knew Michelle, the mother, was sobbing on her bed. One of the women visitors explained that Michelle's twenty-eight-year-old son had just been murdered. We were able to pray with Michelle and offer our help for the coming days. We also encouraged her to call upon our loving God who knows the pain of seeing His only Son die at the hands of angry men.
>
> At one of the last homes, a mother asked us to come in and sit down. When Brad asked how her daughter was doing, she described the nightmare her family had been through the past month. A young man had plotted and attempted to murder her teenage daughter. He waited for a time the mother and brothers were away, came in and slit the young woman's throat, and stabbed her in the back. She held her breath and played dead even after he left. The offender came back and emptied her purse and pockets of money. He later bragged to others that he would have continued to stab the teen, but the knife lodged in her ribs and he couldn't get it out to continue, so he quit.

Later, the victim was able to get to the front door to let her aunt in. Miraculously the knife dislodged easily.

Her life was spared, but the man continued to stalk her. For the next two weeks the family remained on the move, and she was not able to go to school or anywhere else without his harassment. Finally, because of caller ID, the police were able to trace him and apprehend him. She and her family are back at home and she plans to return to school soon, but noises in other apartments make her jump. She is withdrawn because of the scar on her neck and sleep is still difficult. We prayed for her healing inside and out. We prayed for the perpetrator, that God would show His miraculous power and save his soul. We prayed that one day they would be able, with God's strength, to forgive the man and not let bitterness further damage their lives.

SECULAR RESPONSE TO PROBLEMS IN PUBLIC HOUSING

Relocate the Residents

The most prevalent action taken has been to *relocate residents* from buildings, and in many instances from the community altogether. This appears driven by economic community development rather than concern for the quality of life for residents. Arnold R. Hirsch chronicled the plan behind the rehabilitation of inner city Chicago. He wrote:

> *Although humanistic concern for the quality of life in such areas was often expressed, simple economics governed the Loop's devotion to its hinterland. Chicago's business elite clearly envisaged a postwar building boom on the city's periphery, the flight of the middle class, and the insulation of State Street from its "normal market." They subsequently tried to counter the forces promoting decentralization through the complete rehabilitation of the center of the city. "The real purpose of redevelopment," one knowledgeable observer later noted, was "to re-attract solvent population and investment to the dying areas of the city."[10]*

Others approach the issue of relocation with the belief that the residents' conditions will improve in a new surrounding. Considerable discussion occurs as to how the community will look with new residents, usually more affluent and capable of owning homes that many working two-parent families could not afford. The trend has been to cater to attracting new residents without offering most long-time residents the privilege to remain in their community. Hirsch recorded this as he rehearsed the inception of the redevelopment process in Chicago. He noted, "The objection that rentals in new construction would be uncontrolled was irrelevant to the programs' intent. The promoters wanted to reattract 'solvent' population to the central city, not to provide new housing for those who could not afford it."[11]

This process of relocating residents into different buildings and, in some cases, different communities has left families without critical support systems that help them function in society. At the same time, it has put the youth of these families at risk, moving them into similar poor communities with different gangs controlling them. Many observers are left questioning if history is repeating itself as the wealth of developers and the empty promises of politicians prevail in changing the demographics of the economically poor but land-rich areas housing people living in CHA housing. It has been done before. Hirsch noted the driving force for two of the pioneers leading this movement when the Redevelopment and Relocation Acts were passed in June of 1947 in Illinois. He said:

> *The profit motive would govern redevelopment, and the process itself would remain in private hands. Augmented government powers and support were necessary to aid the private sector, to enable to accomplish that which it could not do by itself. But the priorities, goals, and implementation of the program were left to the traditional forces of privatism.*[12]

Renovate and Replace Structures

Many residents are instructed to move so that their unit can undergo *renovation;* others are told their building is scheduled to be *razed.* Such was the case for the residents living in the 500 through 502 West Oak building in Chicago's Cabrini-Green. This fifteen-story building, a longtime stronghold of the street gang the Vice-Lords, was identified as one that would be razed. With little notice and limited options, the residents were told to move. Although assistance was offered for relocating within or outside the community, this decision was difficult. For families with boys thirteen or older, a move into another building would mean moving into a domain controlled by a rival gang. To move out of the community would not only mean possible exposure to rival gangs, but the loss of support structures that these families rely on.

Many depend on extended family or longtime friends for child care, transportation, or even use of the telephone. On the South Side of Chicago, in what many tenants and observers consider to be deception, six hundred families living in four sixteen-story buildings along the lakefront were moved out in 1985 under the pretense that they were to be renovated. Within two years, CHA officials decided to demolish them instead, pledging to find permanent replacement housing for the displaced residents.

c) Recommend More Programs

The most common suggestion has been to *recommend more programs* as the cure-all for everything from gang violence to teen pregnancy, school dropout to unemployment. Program after program has been introduced in the public housing complexes throughout Chicago. The sad commentary on them has been little to no change in the life of the community or the individuals they were designed to help. Well-meaning people placed emphasis on addressing the fruit of broken lives without considering the root cause of their brokenness. Often, they have been void of that which changes character (the person and work of Jesus Christ); therefore the cause of these conditions go unaddressed.

Many children have been helped scholastically to gain needed skills such as reading, writing, and math. Other programs have assisted youth in gaining entrance into college. However, since they have not dealt with the character or sin issue, many of these youth still follow the detrimental patterns of their families and friends. In other words, they become educated drug dealers, drug users, alcoholics, and gang members. Many will perpetuate the single-parent home situation by having one or more children outside of marriage. Others lose hope as they enter adolescence, embracing the socially accepted lifestyles of the community. The solution to the moral, ethical, and educational problem does not lie in a program, but in the principles taught in Scripture, fleshed out through Christ-centered program design.

CHURCH RESPONSES
TO PROBLEMS IN PUBLIC HOUSING

a) The Biblical Mandate for Ministering to the Poor

The Bible clearly teaches us that we need to be concerned about the poor and oppressed. God exhorts us to care for the poor. "Blessed is he who considers the poor" (Ps. 41:1 NKJV) is one of many examples. God is also concerned for justice for those who are poor and powerless. "Defend the rights of the poor and needy" (Prov. 31:9). The life of Jesus serves as a pattern of social interaction in Christian ministry. Christ saw social action as a natural outworking of His mission (Luke 4:18). Christ demonstrated social concern on behalf of the people whose paths crossed His (Mark 6:5–6; Luke 7:1–10; John 6:1–16). Jesus taught that His disciples were to bring God's standard to the earth (Matt. 5:12–16).

The church today has a responsibility to help those in need. Just like one's first responsibility is to his own family, our first obligation is to fellow believers (Gal. 6:10). Although our primary responsibility to the broader society is to evangelism (Acts 1:8), social concern is often a good pre-evangelism tool (John 4:5–9). The social action of the church is to spill over to the world at large where possible as a means of attracting people to Christ.

Equip and Enable Through Evangelism

The need to do more than evangelism for the residents of this self-contained concrete community screams at those who come to serve in these areas. Detrimental lifestyles perpetuated by hopeless and purposeless living entrap generations. The poverty that pervades is more than simply economical; it is spiritual as well. Yet one cannot be addressed to the exclusion of the other. As Chuck Colson stated:

> *A faith . . . which stops with the belief that being "saved" is the whole Christian experience, is dead and denies Christ's concerns for all mankind. It is like a baby dying in infancy; the child may be born healthy, but his life will have little or no impact on others. Grasping this concept was a turning point for me, as it is, I suspect, for many Christians. God, I now understood, was working a powerful transformation in my thought habits and forcing me to think about what it really means to live as a disciple of Christ.[13]*

Chuck Colson realized that what a person really believes affects how he lives. Therefore, the message of "Good News" should be presented to people in a way that affirms the dignity of each individual. We go beyond merely talking about our faith when we demonstrate it by caring for the practical needs of people as we tell them about the love of God. As we enter the world of public housing with all its needs, dangers, and poverty, we respect the individual worth of those that live there. They are made in God's image; loving them is loving Jesus, and thus we will neither demean nor ignore them.

"Therefore go and make disciples of all nations" (Matt. 28:19) presents simple and clear direction. How one does this in a public housing community seems to be the point of confusion for some. To see lives transformed here, as in any community, the gospel must be the foundation and the reason for all that is done to address needs. So when an after-school program is started to evangelize unchurched youth, it also provides structured, supervised activities for children mainly from single-parent homes. It provides positive male role models to boys who often have no father figure in the home. It provides help with homework and it values education, which often is not valued in the community. These are some of the small, often unnoticed benefits that need to be designed into programs when one is looking to do more than simply tell somebody the gospel.

In our community, reading scores are, on average, years behind student grade level. Knowing that reading is critical to learning and that success at learning is important to remaining in school, we developed a literacy program to address this need. Helping youth learn to read opens enormous doors to tell the children and their parents the reason that we are doing what we do. But it is driven by meeting basic needs.

This has been demonstrated by one of our staff members, Chris, who for the last three years has worked with four youths from the same family. His involvement, attention, and help assisted these children in making great strides in school, although it was his relationship with them that proved most meaningful. Tragically, their mother died suddenly at a young age, leaving these children behind. Chris's relationship with the family has brought stability for the children. His faith, which he has been demonstrating in his interaction with the kids, has become a source of hope when they needed it most. Their progress academically has been a great encouragement, but there is still work to be done. Yet seeing them grow spiritually in the face of difficulty has been the most rewarding experience.

New Life Celebration Church of God in nearby Dolton, Illinois, has partnered with our outreach in a variety of ways for several years. The church has been providing transportation to bring youth to church and preparing lunches for them after the service. It has worked with us to help families in financial crisis, as well as helping young men walk away from gangs.

One such young man named William found himself in trouble with the law. Through contact with Sunshine Gospel Ministries he committed his life to the Lord. However, William needed to be discipled and connected to the church. The men of New Life Celebration embraced this young man, taking him with them to several Promise Keepers events, including Stand in the Gap in Washington, D.C. He was welcomed into the life of the church as if he had no criminal history. In fact, many of the men have totally forgotten that this young man just a few years ago was on the road to prison. Today he is in a leadership development program, serves as an usher, and helps with the juniors in his church.

THE ROLE OF INDIVIDUAL CHRISTIANS

Pray for Outreach in Public Housing

"Ask the Lord of the harvest, therefore, to send out workers into his harvest field" (Matt. 9:38). The actions and words of Jesus speak as clearly today as they did in the first century. Where there are massive people populations, vast numbers of people need to know the Lord. The first instruction to His disciples while He was making them aware of the enormous opportunity was to pray. Prayer is still the primary action for you and me. The tragic stories that pervade the media about these communities should remind believers to intercede for the people living there. We should pray for those involved in the situations reported and for those affected by the conditions, mindful that God takes what is humanly impossible to demonstrate the depths of His redemptive love for people. Prayer becomes a viable means of involvement in what God is doing in these complexes.

Many individual believers from a variety of settings join with us in praying for the power of the gospel to transform the families being ministered to in the city. They receive requests through various outlets such as newsletters, prayer letters, update letters, e-mail, and sometimes even by telephone. The fruit this bears is immeasurable. On numerous occasions we have seen God answer specific requests that were asked of Him by our friends and staff.

One request that we asked people to join us in was petitioning God for the parents and guardians of the children we work with. We wanted God to give us the opportunity to minister to them. Whether giving the plan of salvation or aiding them to mature in the faith, we simply wanted God to open the door with them. These doors have swung wide open. Not only did we see a change in how families received our staff members when they visited homes, but parents have come to the center asking us for "programs" for them. One mother, who for six months would not even respond to me [Dana] when I greeted her on the street, came into the center and asked me why we did not offer any programs like computer training or Bible study for adults. Stunned but elated, I asked her to help us serve the adults of the community, and she has been volunteering ever since. She not only gave her life to the Lord; she joined a local church, started tithing, went back to school, and now is a regular participant in our women's Bible study.

Some people in such a situation might have concluded that they were just so likeable that the unchurched parents randomly came into their center and asked for the very thing that people had been praying about. I am convinced that God placed a burden on the heart of many people, then responded to their request by doing the very thing He wanted all along—to bring these parents into a personal relationship with His Son. Through prayer we have seen single mothers not only put live-in boyfriends out, but terminate the relationship altogether.

Some have joined churches and started living out their faith before their children.

David in Psalm 65:2 exclaimed, "O you who hear prayer, to you all men will come." Donald S. Whitney reminded us, "This is perhaps the most taken for granted principle of prayer—that prayer is answered."[14] We have seen God provide for the ministry, whether one of our missionary staff had a personal need or the mission in general needed space, transportation, or funds. Prayer has been the most powerful way individuals and churches have helped us reach the city.

Volunteer in Public Housing Outreach

Another method of involvement with our missions is seen in the people who volunteer their time. Directly or indirectly their assistance ministers to the families in these housing complexes. Volunteers help with everything from our programs to fund-raisers, from office support to computer repair. Many come once a week, providing consistent help in a specific area of the outreach. Some get involved with a youth one-on-one, providing a godly adult role model. Others help occasionally with special projects. We have had people perform all types of services that our budgets would not be able to afford, from installing phone systems to painting, cleaning, performing neighborhood surveys, replacing doors, repairing vehicles, and sorting through donated clothes.

The need for volunteers remains one of the greatest needs for missions like ours. This has been perhaps one of the most tangible ways people could join efforts with us to reach the city. Each person who aids in some way is part of the team that our Lord uses to draw these dear people into a relationship with Himself.

Support Public Housing Outreach

The final and most obvious method to help reach the families of these communities is through financial support. The resources to make ministry possible come almost exclusively from outside neighborhoods. The Lord uses His church, whether through individuals or a local fellowship, to provide the resources to send missionaries into these concrete mission fields. Often people ask why missionaries remain in this country, especially in a world-class city like Chicago. People who ask that only need to make one visit to a neighborhood such as Cabrini-Green or Robert Taylor to see the vast mission field here at home.

To reach the thousands of hopeless people living in these areas requires resources. It takes a little more than walking up and down the streets telling people God loves them and has a plan for their life, though this is the primary issue they need to realize. Frequently it takes providing groceries or a meal to a family who cannot hear you because they are distracted by hunger pains. It requires meeting some simple practical need like making calls to probation officers or offering a ride to the public aid or Social Security office, substance abuse program, or court or prison. Any act of kindness speaks more of the compassionate love of God than mere words.

For missions like ours, this is possible through the financial gifts people give to make sure the gospel is taken to these people. Like the local church, most missions have no source of income other than the freewill offerings of godly people. The amounts and frequency of these gifts vary, but each plays a vital role of enabling the mission to be the hands and feet of Jesus to people who need to know Him. Compassionate acts bring to life the love of God when the families living in these housing complexes realize that people they have never met care enough about them to show it in a tangible way.

Conclusion: An Uncertain Future

Will the walls ever come tumbling down? Since the late 1960s, we have listened to plans to demolish the housing projects and provide "scattered site" housing to the residents who will be displaced. In the Robert Taylor Homes (and other selected housing projects), some individual buildings have been demolished. Will others follow? Perhaps surprisingly, many have protested the demolition of Chicago Housing Authority buildings. Some politicians see their votes being redistributed. Some community organizers see the destruction of an entire community and even compare demolition to "ethnic cleansing" as in Bosnia. What will happen in the near future? We really do not know yet.

As Christians, we should be committed to helping individuals get adequate housing, wherever that may be. Although some people in million-dollar mansions have rejected God's offer of eternal life, others living in the worst of public housing have received the greatest of all housing plans—an eternal home in heaven. Let's help more learn of that heavenly housing plan!

Reflection Questions

1. Do you think a Christian should interface with the government in regard to public housing? If so, how? If not, why not?

2. What personal involvement do you think that you should institute regarding the people who live in public housing in or around your community?

3. In what ways could your local church minister to those in public housing?

4. What household amenities might you or your church members eliminate, and use those funds to directly help people in lesser housing situations?

part seven

CHILDREN
AND YOUTH

chapter twenty-five

REACHING THE NEXT GENERATION FOR CHRIST

INNER CITY IMPACT AND TODAY'S CHILDREN

WILLIAM PAUL DILLON

Introduction: The Need

In our country is a group of people who are hurting more than ever before. They are scared, they are lonely, they are confused, and many of them are being abused. We have a special name for this group of people—they are called children.

> Every day in the USA
> 1,106 teens have abortions.
> 27 children die from poverty.
> 10 children are killed by guns.
> 6 teenagers commit suicide.
> 135,000 children bring a gun to school.
> 7,742 teenagers become sexually active.
> 211 children are arrested for drug abuse.
> 3,288 children run away from home.[1]

OUR OPPORTUNITY

It does not take long to acquaint yourself with the struggles of today's young person growing up in the inner city. All you have to do is pick up a newspaper, turn on a radio, or park yourself in front of a TV.

The plight and struggle of the urban young person is discussed, reported, and analyzed on a daily basis. Street gangs in particular get high-profile exposure.

But dream with me a little bit. Instead of a life of sin, rebellion, hatred, and violence, is it not possible for us to see young people saved, discipled, and not only a valued part of the body of Christ but also a productive part of society? Why must they be just more high school dropouts? Why must they live a life of drugs and sex? I have been told that as many as 90 percent of salvation decisions occur before age eighteen.[2] If that is the case, a lot of harvesting is possible in this mission field called the inner city.

OUR OPTIONS—
WHERE IN THE WORLD DO WE BEGIN?

Many refer to the city as the "concrete jungle." The need is great and the options numerous. A number of approaches can be taken to the many problems in the inner city.

One is the rehabilitative approach. Here someone comes alongside and intervenes as an advocate for a person who has already encountered a problem. It could be gang intervention; maybe it is drug rehab. Or it could be help for the single teen who faces an unwanted pregnancy.

Others have taken a look at the problems facing today's inner city youth and have decided that enough is enough. Let us beat the system and approach the issue from a preventive, proactive posture. With this scenario, young children are targeted for ministry at very early ages. In the inner city this is critical in one's strategy. The street gangs start their leadership development program with children as young as eight.

Young Freddie grew up in a difficult home setting. One brother died at birth, the street gangs killed a second brother, and a third was locked up and charged with murder. We were competing with the street gangs for Freddie, and the question is always, Who will overcome? But God had His hand on Freddie. At age ten he heard the gospel, responded by faith, and became part of God's extended family. We got him first—before the gangs could impose their stranglehold on his young life. God has kept him to this day from their entanglement.

Another set of decisions involves how to package one's program. Should it be formal? Should it be informal? Should it be both? When I say formal, I mean an organized program, which meets at a set time, usually weekly and usually in a building.

The formal approach has great value, but could the informal approach make a significant impact? The informal approach combines the learner (the inner city child) with a Christian role model. In the life and ministry of Inner City Impact (ICI), missionaries serve full-time as role models. Such a missionary lives within the inner city setting and has many times in a given week when he or she is relating to inner city young people. The relating could be a visit to that child's apartment, it could be a spur-of-the-moment basketball game, it might be eating pizza while watching the latest sporting event, or it may be a shopping trip downtown or a trip to the zoo.

During the course of this relationship building, the young inner city child begins to feel accepted and loved. He begins to mention such things as "My teacher said there is really nothing that bad about marijuana. What do you think?" or "My mom says it is OK to have sex before marriage. What do you think?" We now have the awesome privilege and responsibility to drive the child or teen back to God's Word and provide an answer.

For a hurting inner city kid who desperately lacks love and respect, informal relationship building is fantastic. I will never forget a young teenager by the name of Tito. As we talked one day, I told him how sad I was that so many kids were simply not making it. I said, "Tito, why are *you* making it?"

He said, "Bill, you have to realize, I never knew love before until I met Paul" (an Inner City Impact volunteer). He went on to tell me that Paul had believed in him and had indicated to him that indeed he was very special and that God was going to use him in a mighty way.

Listening to Tito, I began to realize that he was marching to the beat of a different drummer. Here was a kid who had grown up hearing he was dumb and never going to amount to anything, now saying with all the confidence in the world that in God's sight he was special and was going to impact his world for Christ.

In that brief encounter in my office I was reminded of all that Paul had done with Tito and that our approach of informal ministry was having a profound effect on the city and on the kids of the city.

As I think of the informal approach and the "teachable moment," I am reminded of Deuteronomy 6:5–9:

> *Love the Lord your God with all your heart and with all your soul and with all your strength. These commandments that I give you today are to be upon your hearts. Impress them on your children. Talk about them when you sit at home and when you walk along the road, when you lie down and when you get up. Tie them as symbols on your hands and bind them on your foreheads. Write them on the doorframes of your houses and on your gates.*

Maybe the modern translation of this Scripture in today's urban culture might read like this: "These commandments that I give you today are to be upon your hearts. Impress them on your children. Talk about them when you sit in that inner city apartment and when you walk through the alleys, when you are playing hoops with them, when you lie down in the city parks and when you get up. Tie them as symbols on your hands and bind them on your foreheads. Write them on the doorframes of your houses and on your locked gates."

The city contains many needs, many lives that need to be touched by a Savior who died for them and who wept over the city.

A Model

Inner City Impact
Parachurch Youth Ministry
Founded: 1972
Mission Statement: To present the living Christ primarily to inner city children and youth, discipling and integrating them into the local church
The Target Audience: Ages 5–18
2d- and 3d-Generation Hispanics (Puerto Rican, Mexican, etc.), African-Americans, whites

The Communities

Chicago's Humboldt Park and Logan Square

Education

Local high school ACT scores average about 14.2. The city average is about 17. The national average is 20.8.[3]
Facts about Roberto Clemente High School:
• 76.2% of students are "low income."
• 2,408 students are enrolled:
  • 85.3% Hispanic
  • 10.9% African-American
  •   2.2% Asian
  •   1.5% Caucasian
• 52.4% of freshman graduate.
• 71% of students score in the bottom quarter of Illinois high schoolers in reading.[4]

Gangs

• Gangs start recruiting kids as young as eight years old.
• 80% of kids in the Chicago court system have some gang affiliation.
• 60% are on trial as a result of their street activity.

- 125 gangs claim territory in Chicago, with a membership well over 100,000.[5]
- 30 gangs are located in the Humboldt Park area.
- The biggest influence in Humboldt Park is the "Maniac Latin Disciples" and the "Spanish Cobras."

Demographics

- 91% of the neighborhood population are 65 or younger; 46% of the population are 21 or younger.
- 15,000 kids live in the vicinity of the Humboldt Park and Logan Square Inner City Impact centers.
- 65% are of Latino origin (primarily Puerto Rican and Mexican), 19% are African-American, and 16% are white.
- 24,331 people in the community live below the poverty level. That is 37% of the community. (This was based on the 1994 poverty level for a family of 4 = $15,390.)
- The median family income is $18,753, which is 36% of the median income for Chicago, $53,100.
- The unemployment rate is 16%, which is 10% above the city's average. In certain parts of the community it is as high as 30%.
- More than 44% of the people who rent in Humboldt Park are paying more than 35% of their incomes. Some families are paying 50% to 70%. This neighborhood has been called a housing poverty area, which means that a majority of the properties are in poor physical condition.[6]

Illegitimacy

- 80% of kids live in single parent homes.
- 70% divorce rate prevails.[7]

PRINCIPLES OF URBAN YOUTH MINISTRY

Be Visible and Accessible

Our missionary staff lives within a five-block radius of our buildings. We are in the schools, the homes, the churches, and we have contact with community agencies. The staff shop in the community and bank in the community. I think of Ralph, one of our former staff members, who would make contact with young people and families while just walking between his inner city home and ICI. He was definitely a part of the fabric of the community. His house was like Grand Central Station with young people in and out.

We must put a high premium on remaining visible. Young people need to get to us. We must be willing to get to them. Ours is a twenty-four-hour ministry. Are we willing to let them make intrusions into our schedule? I am not advocating ministry at the cost of one's marriage or family. At specified times we are not available except in an emergency. But our actions in caring for people will speak far louder than any of our Bible studies.

b) Go to Them and Meet Them on Their Level

It is more important for us to go to them than to expect them to come to us. ICI has had a strong presence in the local public schools. We know the principals, the teachers, and the aides. In some cases we assist in tutoring. I will never forget the comment of one of the principals. He said, "I know the kids you are working with, and we send them to professional counselors that demand high fees—but you are doing a far more effective job than they are."

We make more than two thousand visits to homes a year. Home visits are important for several reasons:

- We need to build good relationships with parents.
- We can be an advocate for the child in his or her home.
- Parents often introduce us to other families.
- Interacting with children and their parents gives us greater insight.

You cannot simply race around the city, drop off a Bible at each home, and expect to see phenomenal results. We are talking about real people who have real needs. Whether through helping families that have been burned out, finding apartments, or helping pay utility bills, the city contains many opportunities to demonstrate God's love.

c) Spend Concentrated Personal Time with Them

When we talk about developing relationships, it's important to remember that time spent together develops trust and openness. I put it this way: People are primary; programs are secondary.

As a student at a Christian college and a secular university, I was trained to think programs. Any need to be met had to be addressed by a program. I believe in programs, but programs in and by themselves cannot fully meet the needs of hurting inner city young people. People love hurting people. It is the people connection that makes the difference. Remember Paul's words from 1 Thessalonians 2:8, "We loved you so much that we were delighted to share with you not only the gospel of God but our lives as well, because you had become so dear to us."

In some cases we have been imposing programs upon our cities: door-to-door visitation, mass rallies, and so on. God can use many different means to get out the gospel. But if you really want to get the attention of hurting inner city young people and go through the process of loving them to Christ, you must recognize that *relationships* are primary and programs secondary.

The role of our missionary staff calls for investing time with young people. By spending time, missionaries earn the trust needed to present the gospel. Then they have the awesome responsibility to nurture the newborn Christian. For those young people really desiring to grow, the focus becomes discipleship.

Another tool that is a favorite of our inner city kids is our year-round camping program. In the early days of our ministry, we operated only a one-week summer camping program. Then I met Dr. Ted Ward, who currently teaches at Trinity Seminary but in those days was at Michigan State. As we talked, I asked, "What do you recommend in terms of effective programs to impact city kids?"

He quickly replied, "Get them out of their normal environment for an extended period of time. As we reflect on our childhood, it is events like a family vacation, visiting grandparents, or a trip to camp that stand out—times when we were removed from our normal environment."

I quickly came to the conclusion that ICI needed to expand our successful summer camping program to a year-round program. And that we have done. Today we make available more than twenty-five camping trips and camping programs. From Chicago's inner city we go to such places as Colorado, Pennsylvania, Missouri, the Boundary Waters of Minnesota, Michigan, Wisconsin, Indiana, and more.

Love Them

Whether a person is a member of an unreached tribe in South America, a wealthy businessman in downtown Chicago, or a child in the inner city, everyone has a built-in need for love.

A number of years ago I participated in a panel of missions executives at a conference on the West Coast. I was the only "home missions" representative on the panel. After hearing about penetrating the jungles of South America and other remote spots on the earth, I began to tell our strategy for inner city ministry. What I was hearing each of us emphasize was the importance of the love factor. It is one of the universal truths in mission, no matter where a person serves.

Shortly after one of our teens headed to Bible school, I had occasion to visit her on campus. I decided to grab my tape recorder and ask several questions. I began by asking her impressions of Inner City

Impact. Her eyes quickly lit up, her hands began to go into motion, and she said, "There is so much love at Inner City Impact." The love factor had made a significant difference.

Keep in mind that love does not emanate from a program but from people. A strategy built around relationships will not end merely in salvation but in a vision for the convert's entire future. Because of that bond of love, inner city young people begin to imitate the person who influenced them for Christ.

Be a Learner

Most urban youth workers grew up in rural America or suburbia. For them, entry into the inner city is indeed a challenge. If one is to be effective, one must enter as a learner. Ministry in the inner city is a cross-cultural experience.

Be a student of the culture, the people, and their ways. Allow them to teach you, and yet be yourself. Laugh at your mistakes and recognize that sincere concern and compassion on your part will cover a multitude of sins. Remember that the inner city is no place to impress people with your theological jargon. For some, even the introduction of familiar Bible characters is a brand-new insight.

Be a Networker

Network in Terms of Evangelism

I remember the day that Cindy appeared at the offices of Inner City Impact. She had come to know the Lord through a Bible study on Chicago's North Side. With her newfound faith and the heart of an evangelist, she began inviting a small group of her friends for a simple one-hour Bible study. Later the one-hour Bible study was expanded as simple refreshments and game opportunities were made available. Soon it grew to include a potluck supper that preceded the Bible study, followed by a time of fellowship that on many occasions went beyond midnight.

Young adults were being saved and growing in the faith, and new members were enlisted. Eventually God formed a church, and today that church has a vibrant witness, all as a result of networking. In the process, each of Cindy's many friends was exposed to the gospel.

Network in Terms of Community Resources

Many would be amazed if they were to set out to discover what other churches and agencies are doing within their community. It is easy for evangelicals to think we can do it alone. We initially think that we have all the answers. Soon we realize that many people have gone before us, many people who have a vast amount of experience and re-sources that can be tapped.

As we studied our community, it became abundantly clear that we could meet many of the needs our young people and families had by networking with other community agencies. Instead of developing our own medical clinic, food pantry, job placement services, and clothes distribution program, we decided to tap into the many resources al-ready in place. We have developed the position of a full-time child ad-vocate, who had served as a social worker by training and profession in a respected agency in our community. As our missionary staff iden-tify needs of our children, youth, and families, the child advocate is brought onto the scene. She then links the families to valuable existing community agencies that can meet those needs.

Network in Terms of Suburban Resources

On the outskirts of our major cities are suburban churches and suburban Christians. God has prospered many of them, and yet most drive through the metropolitan area and rarely take the time to see firsthand this mission field on their doorstep. For some, it might be a lack of concern. Others simply need a way to connect.

I believe we need to create a new framework for "connecting." In the past, city ministries have met with the missions committees of sub-urban churches and asked for their financial support. In many cases that has worked, but usually the process has been very time consum-ing and produces little.

I believe that suburban Christians can better be challenged on the basis of sharing their expertise. The suburban printer can assist in printing, and the photographer can lend his photography skills to record what God is doing in the lives of some special inner city kids. The possibilities for bringing resources to God's work in the city are endless. We need to open our imaginations and give people a vision to share what they already have.

Be a Long–Termer

The average youth pastor stays a year and a half in one location. Unfortunately that is not going to be successful for urban youth min-istry. Most kids in the city have watched people come into their lives and go out just as quickly. A mere eighteen months of ministry with an urban young person will just be another example of the revolving door, another vivid reminder that no one really cares. No one is willing to provide consistency and stability.

Your staying power can make a significant difference. To be effective, you need to put down roots. Many of our success stories involve young people who at one point responded positively to the gospel and then turned away, only to return later and find us still there. In some cases, years passed before they returned. It was interesting to hear their response. One young man said, "The love was still there."

Scores have rebounded after trying to live their lives without the Lord. The key is that we never gave up on them and were there to invite them back with open arms. Living out the endurance factor is hard, painful, and difficult but so rewarding.

Imelda was one of the first children I met when I began the ministry of Inner City Impact in 1972. She came to one of our clubs and was saved, but like many of our kids she walked away from the Lord. I saw her on the streets from time to time and told her that we missed her, we loved her, and the Lord loved her as well. I sought every opportunity I could to draw her back our direction. Eventually she did return and began to grow spiritually. We steered her to a Christian college, and her faith deepened. While at Bible school she met and married a wonderful Christian young man who is now a pastor.

I am so grateful that we put our roots down and were there when Imelda decided to return to the Lord.

THE PROCESS OF URBAN YOUTH MINISTRY

To get a young person from Point A (unsaved) to Point B (a maturing, growing, committed Christian leader) is quite a challenge in the inner city. The process we use is as follows and has been adapted from Sonlife Ministries.[8]

Pre-Evangelism—A Contacting Ministry

It is important to go to where children and young people are and design programs that will get their attention. The contact could be a visit to a home or to a local school. It could be sitting in a high school lunchroom or serving as a tutor in a local grade school. Other feeders into our programs are block clubs and block parties.

Other possibilities are a Thanksgiving dinner, an Easter dinner, or a Christmas dessert. Young people in the inner city are attracted to sports, and sports leagues have been formed to get their attention. Field trips also have proven to be a good drawing card: a trip to Great America, a baseball game, a trip to the zoo or the beach.

Outreach/Evangelism

We look primarily to vehicles that gather young people and are highly dependent upon a lifestyle evangelism strategy. Year-round camping is used as a tool to attract young people and then to confront them with the claims of Christ. Small-group evangelistic Bible studies and an open gym with a drop-in center are additional opportunities.

Spiritual Growth/Discipleship

First Peter 2:2 reminds us of the need to feed newborn Christians. "Like newborn babies, crave pure spiritual milk, so that by it you may grow up in your salvation."

This process begins with small-group Bible studies. The focus here is on those who want to grow. These are not attracted by creative events or fancy programs. They voluntarily make the trek to our facilities to attend a Bible study. Many of our camping ministries are also designed for the believer to mature in the faith.

A key component is the one-on-one discipleship that takes place. As the young believer begins to grow, he finds himself relating to one of our missionaries. As they interact with each other, trust is built, and a relationship begins to deepen.

The writer of Hebrews scolded the believers because they really had not grown up spiritually.

> We have much to say about this, but it is hard to explain because you are slow to learn. In fact, though by this time you ought to be teachers, you need someone to teach you the elementary truths of God's word all over again. You need milk, not solid food! Anyone who lives on milk, being still an infant, is not acquainted with the teaching about righteousness. But solid food is for the mature, who by constant use have trained themselves to distinguish good from evil. (Heb. 5:11–14)

Might we take on the challenge of "rightly dividing the word of truth" (2 Tim. 2:15 KJV) and raising up a generation of growing biblical leaders in the inner city?

Leadership Development

When they proceed into the seventh, eighth, and ninth grades, key young people become a part of our LIT (Leaders In Training) program. Here they assist some of the younger age groups under the leadership of our full-time staff.

High school brings further responsibility and opportunities for growth. Key young people are carefully selected to serve as interns. These are part-time paid positions. For most, this is their first time to spread their wings and demonstrate some leadership skills.

The next significant step is a college scholarship program funded through ICI. Key young people are invited to apply for these monies, and a committee reviews each request against set policies on distribution of scholarships.

The investment is significant but worthwhile when one sees solid Christian young people graduate from qualified Christian schools. The high school dropout rate in our community is 75 percent, yet we are seeing many complete college.

Some of these same college students are put to work as summer interns, yet another opportunity for them to show and sharpen their leadership skills.

The final step in the leadership process is to invite them to join the full-time staff of Inner City Impact.

Few find their way back on staff full-time, yet we see many young people like Tito, who has returned with his family to the inner city and is now a schoolteacher at the same public grade school he attended as a child. His active participation in a local church within the community is a shining example of God's work of grace.

Others will be strong advocates for our Lord in far-flung places beyond the inner city, but we can have the satisfaction of knowing that ICI introduced them to the Lord, discipled them, and developed them as significant leaders for the kingdom.

Conclusion:
Final Advice

Stay focused. Focus on relationships. Hurting kids need love and will respond to love.

Put your roots down. The city will never be won unless people stick and stay and think long range.

Put in place a plan to avoid burnout. Take ample time off, vacations, and trips out of the city. ICI includes a missionary furlough as part of the plan.

Network. The Lord never intended for you to go it alone. In fact, it is simply impossible to do so in the inner city. Inner city young people have many needs, from inadequate education or dysfunctional homes to the need for employment. Through networking, we can become facilitators and caring advocates.

God is active and alive in the city. We just need to mobilize more of

His resources to have an even greater impact for His kingdom and His glory!

Reflection Questions

1. Visit the youth ministry of one or several local churches or parachurch ministries in the inner city. Could you help connect your church with them to help meet some of their needs?

2. Seek to build a relationship with a young person from an inner city community. How could you help others to do the same?

3. If you are a college student, consider a summer experience or short-term assignment working with young people in the inner city. Do you agree that urban youth are a mission field in our own backyard?

4. Inner city ministry hinges on forming and keeping long-term relationships. What is it that God may want you to learn about the urban youth culture to enable you to be more effective in doing so?

For Further Reading

Dieleman, Dale, ed. *The Bridgebook: Youth Group Ideas for Cross-Cultural Contacts.* Grand Rapids: Baker, 1985.

Feldmeyer, Dean. *Beating Burnout in Youth Ministry.* Loveland, Colo.: Group, 1989.

Harringer, James M. (compiler). *Discipline and the Urban/Disadvantaged Youth.* International Union of Gospel Missions, Box 10780, Kansas City, MO 64118.

Matias, Tito, and Randy Peterson. *Child of the City.* Wheaton, Ill.: Tyndale, 1989.

Roehlkepartain, Eugene C. *Youth Ministry in City Churches.* Loveland, Colo.: Group, 1989.

Van Houten, Mark E. *God's Inner City Address: Crossing the Boundaries.* Grand Rapids: Zondervan, 1988.

Urban Ministry Organizations

Coalition for Urban Youth Leadership, Box 12231, Portland, OR 97212

Open Door Ministries, Box 4248, Seminole, FL 34642

CURE (Chicago Urban Reconciliation Enterprise), P.O. Box 804113, Chicago, IL 60680-4103

Urban Ministries, Inc., 1439 W. 103rd St., Chicago, IL 60643

Kingdomworks, P.O. Box 12589, Philadelphia, PA 19151

chapter twenty-six

CHILDREN OF PROMISE

EDUCATING INNER CITY CHILDREN AT CIRCLE-ROCK PREPARATORY SCHOOL

Lonni Kehrein

Introduction: Children and Violence

The fear of the Lord is the beginning of wisdom, and knowledge of the Holy One is understanding. (Proverbs 9:10)

"Mom, I don't think I'm going to live to be twenty-one." A tall fifteen-year-old with striking physique stood in front of me—my son. "Mom, three of my acquaintances are dead this summer." Words for a response escaped me. Three years later his words struck home again as twice during the summer following Nathan's graduation from high school, my husband and I walked through the doors of a local funeral home to bury his football teammates. They had fallen as victims of gang-related violence, though neither one was a gang member.

For two years a young student at Circle-Rock Preparatory School repeated to his teacher, Dr. Carmen Marcy, "I don't know how I'm going to be able to stay out of the gangs, because they're all around my house." That is an all-too-true statement for many of today's inner city school age children, whose focus during school hours is as much on getting to and from school safely as it is on learning itself. Fortunately, for this young student there is hope; the promise of his life is being fulfilled a day at a time at Circle-Rock Preparatory School on Chicago's

West Side. Near the end of his first-grade year, during a quiet moment in the classroom, he announced, "Dr. Marcy, I'm gonna live for Jesus for my whole life—no matter what!"

In Deuteronomy 30:6 Moses expressed the covenant of the Lord with the Israelites in Moab this way: "The Lord your God will circumcise your hearts and the hearts of your descendants, so that you may love him with all your heart and with all your soul, and *live*" (italics added). For children from the inner cities of America, a major question is whether or not they will live to adulthood. Satan has a plan for our children. His plan is to confuse and to destroy them, as he did with our son's football teammates. His plan is to confuse and destroy this young student at Circle-Rock before he can become the blessing that God intends him to be. But Christ came to "seek and to save what was lost" (Luke 19:10). Jesus said, "The thief comes only to steal and kill and destroy; I have come that they may have life, and have it to the full" (John 10:10).

CIRCLE-ROCK PREPARATORY SCHOOL

Circle-Rock Preparatory School is the response of Circle Urban Ministries and Rock of Our Salvation Evangelical Free Church to put flesh on these words of Jesus. These partner ministries are located on the Far West Side of Chicago in a neighborhood sociologists call a "throw-away community." Together, they have labored for fifteen years to bring the gospel message and much-needed physical help of all kinds to a community that most people go out of their way to avoid. Circle and Rock have consistently made God's love visible with acts of mercy and empowerment. Through Circle, entire families have the opportunity to regain health and self-esteem, to reestablish stability of home and work, and to find a safe place to learn and grow. At Rock Church they find a place of comfort and acceptance and enter a climate in which they can recognize and address their spiritual and emotional needs. Because Jesus came to offer people life "to the full," and because we are His hands and feet in Chicago's Austin neighborhood, we know that "His divine power has given us everything we need for life and godliness through our knowledge of him" (2 Pet. 1:3). Although Satan's plan has thwarted many young lives, instilling the knowledge of God's ways into their hearts—as Moses called it, "circumcising" their hearts—is a major impetus for why we started Circle-Rock Preparatory School.

Thirty-seven kindergarten students stood before an audience of family and friends last June during graduation ceremonies. Their aspirations brought tears of hope and joy to my eyes.

"My name is Irving Taylor, and I will give honor to God by
   becoming an electrical engineer."
"My name is Anthony Ponder, and I will give honor to God
   by becoming a doctor of theology."
"My name is Kristina Cotton, and I will study to become a
   school principal."

WHAT IS THE PROBLEM?

In a recent report by the Chicago Board of Education, the Chicago
Public Schools advised its citizens that only one of the forty-nine general high schools in the city has half of its student body performing at
national norms. In thirty of the general high schools, fewer than 10
percent of the students perform at national norms.[1]

Austin is one of seventy-six communities defined by the city of
Chicago. Austin is the largest of those communities, nine square miles,
and the most heavily populated. In the late 1960s, fueled by the riots
that followed Dr. Martin Luther King's death, racial panic spread
across Austin. Whites left at a rate of 20,000 to 25,000 a year, until
most of the original 138,000 white residents were gone. Businesses,
institutions, and churches soon followed. Into this changing community poured new residents who had not had the benefits of home ownership, excellent schooling, and economic security. Schools built for
smaller-sized families now experienced overcrowding, leading to
burned-out faculty and principals. Now the schools became "throw-
away" institutions with staff who assumed that the parents would just
accept whatever their children got in their new classrooms. Staff expectations for students were low. When children's futures are devalued
or completely ignored, they disengage from the learning process and
meet the expectation of failure at an astounding rate.

Miseducation and undereducation of any child equals lost potential.

> *Poor people, for the most part . . . receive inferior education. We can no longer
> allow the enormous potentials of children to remain dormant. . . . We cannot
> measure, with any degree of accuracy, the human cost to society when talents
> and potentials remain undeveloped. No amount of rhetoric can justify the hope-
> less expression on a child's face when he believes that he has no future and is
> afraid to dream. No amount of effort should be spared in convincing that child
> that he has a right to dream.[2]*

Education of inner city children is beneficial for them, but also for
society as a whole.

Quite apart from issues of social justice, educated people live healthier lives, they earn more, stay married longer, pay more taxes, and give more leadership to their communities than uneducated [or undereducated] ones. Separate from the issue of social justice, education is . . . equally valuable to others and is perhaps indispensable to an orderly, equitable, and achieving American society.[3]

THE PLIGHT OF THE SYSTEM

There is absolutely no doubt that America's inner cities have a horrendous educational track record. Annual school report cards spell this out with mournful regularity, and parents who have an option often do not choose their local public school. Many move to a suburban neighborhood where the school's academic record is somewhat or much better than its urban counterpart. The criticism, of course, is that people with choice who leave the urban schools just add to the problems by silencing their own voice of higher expectation. Truthfully, parents mostly just get tired of the battle and give in to what is an easier route—private urban schools or moving to the suburbs—leaving mostly ethnic minorities and lower-income families to fend for themselves in the inner city public schools. The people who most need the best education available are, for many reasons, the least likely to receive it— sometimes simply because they do not know how to access it, often because they can't afford it. This cycle creates another generation caught in the grip of poverty, miseducation, joblessness, and underachievement, thereby always depriving the world of the contributions these students would have made.

What do inner city parents want for their children's education? Equity of opportunity with strong academic results; high expectations resulting in personal achievement by their child; a structured and disciplined environment with strong behavioral results; moral training; a sense of accomplishment; safety. . . . The list includes pretty much the same things (at least the same results) most American parents want for their school-age children.

Why do many inner city parents select private Christian schools for their children? Are they primarily motivated by purported academic superiority? Is the anticipated safety in private school settings the thing that appeals to parents? Do they want, first and foremost, to protect their children from the influences they know or assume their children will be subjected to in the public schools?

At Circle-Rock Preparatory School, even non-Christian parents are very articulate about their choice. Right up front, parents say they want their children to be in a structured atmosphere where they will have the best chance to really learn and where that learning will include positive Christian morals and values. At the outset, many of our parents do not realize that at Circle-Rock this means their children will be immersed in Bible learning, not only during Bible class time, but throughout the entire day—on bathroom breaks and during lunch period, gym, drama and music classes, and all the way through the after-school program. At the beginning of open registration last year a woman called the school and told the clerk, "I baby-sat for one of your students last week and I can't believe how much Scripture she knew and how well she can read in kindergarten. I *have* to get my son into your school!" Another parent whose third-grade daughter has attended since kindergarten says, "I wouldn't take my daughter anywhere else; she's learning so much about being a young woman of God here."

Too often, in my thirty years in the inner city, I have anguished over stories like this one from a friend of mine: "They told me I was an honor student in my high school, but when I got to college, I could barely make it," she said. "I cried all four years and tried to drop out every chance I got, but my family kept cheering me on and so I stayed and graduated. The people at my high school lied to me—they didn't teach me with the same expectations of my college classmates' schools. I wasn't an honor student at all. *But I could have been!*"

A sophomore from our neighborhood told me, "I thought I was learning in my old school, but now that I'm going to a good high school *where they expect you to learn,* I really can't believe how much I'm learning! I like it!" Self-worth is built when students are challenged with real learning expectations.

As principal of Circle-Rock Preparatory School, Dr. Marcy envisions a school that seeks a rigorous classical and Christian education, with a return to an education grounded in the culture of Western civilization. Latin instruction begins in third grade, and Greek will be introduced in the high school. There will be instruction in formal logic and rhetoric as well as the biblical concepts of (a) knowledge, (b) understanding, and (c) wisdom. The school will educate the student so that he conforms to, and masters, the curriculum. Our goal is to produce students who possess excellent study skills, extensive knowledge of the history and literature of Western culture, and all that it takes to be competitive and successful in the college of their choice. We expect our graduates to be thinkers and leaders.

HOW DO WE SAVE THE CHILDREN?

I once read a fable of a small village located at the edge of a river. The people of the village were kind and generous. One day a villager saw a baby floating down the river, and he rescued the baby from drowning. In the days that followed, other babies began appearing in the swift current of the river, only to be rescued by various villagers. As this phenomenon increased, the village became very organized in its rescue operation, setting up stations for resuscitation, feeding, clothing, and parenting the babies. The village was doing quite well in its attempts to save drowning babies, and the villagers became used to their life as rescuers. One day, though, a villager suddenly asked his fellow rescuer, "Where could these babies be coming from? How are they getting into the river? Shouldn't we get some people together and see what's going on upstream?" Heated discussion followed as to who would take care of the intensive rescue operation if people left their posts to go upstream. But the querying villager continued to raise his voice with the idea that locating the source of the drowning babies might prevent the problem altogether.[4]

How can Christians break the cycle of educational poverty and its grip on a community? For twenty years Circle Urban Ministries has conducted ancillary education programs for children and adults. Resources of staff time, curriculum supplies, countless volunteer hours, money, and love have gone toward assisting the local public schools and bringing students up to grade level in reading and math. Yet we anguished over why we found ourselves attending too many teen funerals rather than high school graduations. In books and over the radio airwaves, child-rearing experts and ministers tell us that if children are loved they will have something to live for and if we demonstrate God's love they will want to honor and serve God too. Are love and ancillary outreach programs not enough?

Circle Urban Ministries and its partner, Rock Church, have consistently served the physical and spiritual needs of the poverty-stricken West Side of Chicago. Health care, housing development, youth programs, legal aid, and many more programs address critical human needs. As significant as these ministries are, often it feels like the village of kindhearted and generous people who keep rescuing the babies from drowning in the river. Few of these prescriptive efforts create long-term improvements and a brighter future. Few leaders emerge from prescriptive efforts. Without leadership, destructive cycles continue.

These twenty years of sincere but time-limited influence through tutoring, after-school, and youth programs have not adequately prepared the next generation for leadership in their community and in the church. After much prayer, a long-term view of Christian leadership development emerged. Given the realities of the education and social needs of our families, it seemed apparent that only a Christian day school could meet the challenge. We felt the Lord prodding us to extend our time, influence, effort, and resources to educate Austin's children in a distinctively Christian, highly academic day school. A school provides the intensive and long-range investment and begins early enough to build solid character and the skills necessary for academic success, leading to improved lifelong conditions. Student families include families with two working parents as well as some of the poorest families who would have no educational choice except that scholarships and work-exchange options are offered in this Christian school located in their neighborhood.

LEARNING FROM THE EDUCATORS

I like the pragmatic emphasis of urban educator Marva Collins. She consistently articulates the belief that we make choices, which then determine outcomes in our life. She believes that it is ignorant and unrealistic to wait for life's opportunities to come your way. Upon this premise she builds a learning base and instills self-esteem in her students. Many of us in urban ministries today believe that all children —yes, minority children—are capable of extremely high learning and achieving. Therefore we press forward to provide tools, keys, and opportunities of learning and achieving. Furthermore, we believe in instilling "old values and morals" so that our students will not grow up to experience mediocrity and failure. Our efforts to teach students to read, write, and think critically and analytically must be coupled with teaching of biblical morality so that their leadership will be based on strong character rather than on self-indulgence: character that is based on the choice to do what is right, even when it costs them something or when no one will know.[5]

Circle-Rock Preparatory School began with a pilot program of nineteen students in a half-day kindergarten during the 1995–96 school year. We reasoned that if God blessed our efforts and confirmed this calling in our hearts during that trial year, we would add a grade each year that followed. The confirmation was overwhelming. The progress of the students was stunning. The dream of a school from kindergarten through high school blossomed. Imagine, as we have, what would happen in the lives of young people after investing more than sixteen thousand hours of instruction, inspiration, and challenge in each one! Very quickly CRPS is gaining a reputation of tremendous student performance by providing high quality education in a well-disciplined environment, with a faculty who believe that every student can and should perform at or far above their grade level. Should God continue to bless, we will continue to expand by at least one grade level each year until we send the class of 2008 to college.

A GLIMPSE OF OUR SCHOOL

Take a peek into Mrs. Boykin's kindergarten class for a few minutes. She and the children are standing in a circle, holding imaginary baskets. "What do you want to get rid of this morning?" she asks. "Not being friendly," one child responds. With that, the class reaches into its "baskets" and together "hurls" the negative trait to the ground. Another child responds, "Disobeying the teacher," and so on. Next Mrs. Boykin asks, "Now what kind of good things do you want to put in the basket?" "Kindness," "respect," and "getting a good note" go into the basket. Finally, the good traits are removed from the basket and placed "deep in the heart." Now class can begin.[6]

God has given us a highly committed, well-trained, educated, and gifted staff who have molded a solid educational philosophy designed to address the unique challenges facing inner city children. Fear of physical harm and intimidation, poor self-esteem, deficient language background, and fine and gross motor skills that are below developmental norms, history of family alcohol or drug abuse, absence of parents, perfectionist parents, hunger, lack of appropriate role models, preoccupation with death—these are some of the unique challenges that face many children as they enter the doors of inner city schools today.

Inner city students often enter school with huge language and vocabulary skill deficits. Their social, emotional, and economic milieu has precluded exposure to the learning necessary to truly prepare them for a strong academic start. Their aptitude and potential are great, but the teaching methodology and curriculum selection must address the deficient skills of those who enter unprepared into a highly challenging academic setting. Many children who enter school in the inner city will be the first in their family to graduate from high school or perhaps the first to attend college. These hurdles are monumental and must be understood and addressed from the earliest grades. The necessary support systems must be put in place as these children enter the upper grades and prepare to accomplish what their families long for—successful completion of their education.

Does it work? More than a third of the student body at Circle-Rock are performing two full grades above their current grade level. Nearly all other students are at or above grade level. This strong performance is even more amazing when you consider that the public school system would consider many of our children "special needs." We consider them "special opportunities" because we know that God's gifts in them can be released through excellent teaching, patience, love, and prayer.

Circle-Rock Prep School (CRPS) has been specially designed to meet the individual needs of children who are predominantly from a low-income neighborhood. More than half of the families enrolled earn less than fifteen thousand dollars a year. CRPS is distinctive in at least the following three ways:

- *Affordability:* a sliding-scale tuition gives every family a chance.
- *Academic excellence:* through unwavering standards and proven methods of instruction.
- *A thoroughly Christian approach:* teaching biblical truth and absolutes, with strategies to help build Christian character.

The programmatic goal of CRPS is to prepare students who are

- *academically excellent* and thus competitive,
- *socially appropriate* in their behavior,
- able to *discriminate right from wrong,* and
- able to *apply their knowledge* of biblical thought in real-life situations.

Staff carry out these goals by using procedures that provide a reinforcing and consistent educational environment with clearly specified rules, consequences, and opportunities to experience success in every area of instruction. Faculty teach appropriate social skills and offer instruction from a Bible-based curriculum that is uniquely designed to build Christian character traits, which are derived from precepts, principles, and the person of God.

It is our dream that someday these very talented students will go on to college, receive professional training, and return to work in, invest in, and provide leadership for the Austin neighborhood. Their motivation will come from their love for God, a love nurtured through the school's emphasis on *responsibility, respect,* and *reconciliation*: three "Rs" of Circle-Rock Preparatory School.

- *Responsibility:* To embrace the ability to choose for oneself between right and wrong; to answer for one's conduct. We teach our students to own their choices; this will help them to overcome many of life's challenges and difficult circumstances. Marva Collins instructs children in her inner city schools that taking responsibility makes a "lifter" out of a "leaner."[7]
- *Respect:* To regard highly and to prize accordingly. We teach our students that they are of great value to Almighty God. This gives them the basis for true self-esteem and for valuing others with a joyful heart.

- *Reconciliation:* To be reconciled to God through Jesus Christ and to resolve conflict with each other through biblical concepts of reconciliation (restoration to harmony). We teach our students to value relationships, working out their differences and placing each other's needs ahead of their own needs, as Christ taught.[8]

When we provide Christian education with the highest of educational standards to low-income minorities, we put our concern for racial reconciliation and justice into action. We become God's instruments of redemption by bringing beauty out of ashes. We can nurture a new generation. Graduates from CRPS will be Christ's ambassadors of reconciliation (2 Cor. 5:20) and fully equipped community leaders.

WHAT CAN **YOU** DO?

When asked what would be worse than being blind, Helen Keller, who became blind in infancy, replied something like this, "To have eyesight but have no vision." Nobody wants to hear about problems that seem to have no solutions. To bring solutions requires vision. The issue of the education of inner city children is solvable—it takes a long-haul view and returns long-term benefits. Remember, it costs society heavily when the talents and potential of children remain undeveloped and left to the godless streets.

Consider these realities: Society is without answers to its urban and racial problems. African-American males who make up only 6 percent of the population fill more than 50 percent of our one million jail and prison cells. The annual cost of imprisonment in Illinois is about $25,000 per inmate, not counting the police and court system. The average stay in prison is four years at taxpayers' cost of $100,000. Repeat offender rates are as high as 70 percent. The cost to victims is beyond calculation. For many jailed minorities, prison is the only "secondary education" they will ever receive. Gangs rule nearly every jail and prison.

Contrast: The actual annual cost to educate a child at CRPS is $4,200. This is just over half the public school cost ($7,600) in a system where many schools' performance scores show fewer than 10 percent of their students at national norms. All CRPS families pay something for the education of their child. For most it is an extreme sacrifice, whether the monthly amount is $50 or $250. Subtracting the average family tuition obligation, the net contribution cost of an education at CRPS is $2,600. This means:

- CRPS could educate three children for the same amount of money spent by the public school system to educate one student.

- Preventing one imprisonment pays for the complete thirteen-year education of three children, or the annual education of more than thirty-eight children.

Simply stated, Christians have the opportunity to make a powerful impact on the future by investing deeply in the education of inner city children and youth today. We should be the ones who are standing up to address the anti-achievement ethic, the devaluing, and the subsequent disengagement of too many inner city schoolchildren today.

Christian schools in the inner cities of America have the awesome opportunity to address situations of despair and hopelessness with the profound, living, powerful Word of Almighty God. Educational doors for urban children can be opened by the people of God who understand the great value God places on each individual. Claude Steele wrote in *The Atlantic Monthly* that learning requires a strongly accepting relationship between teacher and student, a valuing and optimistic atmosphere in which the student "identifies" with learning. Students achieve when they possess confidence in their ability—and when their teachers share that confidence in them. You simply cannot encourage too much. Encouragement builds confidence, which motivates toward achievement.[9]

SOME HELPFUL HINTS

I would like to offer several practical steps for people who are interested in affecting the long-term educational outcome of inner city students. If you are a city dweller contemplating the option of starting or participating in a Christian school, some of the suggestions will be particularly helpful to you. If you live outside the city, some of the suggestions will have potential for you to be a person of influence to empower young minds with a God-centered, biblically based education.

Powerful, Positive Environments

Christians have the opportunity to create powerful and positive environments for learning. These are places where specific behavioral, academic, and moral objectives are upheld and where it is expected that every person will achieve those objectives. What will you see in a "powerful positive environment"?

- *Positive Expectations*—everyone will be encouraged to zealously strive for excellence in all dimensions.
- *Praise and Reward*—these are profusely given for achieving the set expectations. Just as encouragement builds confidence in the student, praise for meeting the set expectations gives students the view of themselves as successful and competent.

- *Parent Involvement*—parents need to understand and support the goals and values of the powerful environment. This may require very creative programs of parent enhancement.
- *Employee Engagement*—staff are student-centered; they refuse to accept failure in the student's education; they take personal responsibility for ensuring that each student succeeds to his or her highest potential.[10]

With the use of "I Can Problem Solve" (ICPS) Curriculum, students learn how to identify problems, how to plan and communicate, and how to resolve conflict.[11]

Distinctively Christian Teaching

I have heard it said that although we go through Christian motions daily, we may have stopped thinking as Christians. Tim Heaton, assistant professor of education at Cedarville College in Ohio, expressed my sentiment in regard to curriculum when he wrote in *Christian School Education*,

> *I'd choose a textbook and ancillary materials . . . [that] contain the truth of God whether or not the author labels it as such. It should be of high quality, extending learning beyond the classroom. It should support the curriculum, not define it. We as Christian educators need to remind ourselves continually that God's truth does not come from any single source other than the Bible and the Holy Spirit, who works out His truth daily in the lives of believers. Our goal should be to make sure that our students view the world, including what is taught in textbooks, through a biblical lens and have personal ownership of their belief system. Decide what truths you want your students to know, what character qualities you want them to exhibit, what skills they should have, what methods will serve their various learning styles and make them lifelong learners, and what materials and strategies will teach them to be discerning and to think biblically.[12]*

Regarding teacher selection, Heaton said:

> *I'd look for teachers who have a thorough understanding of biblical integration, can springboard off textbooks in creative ways, know children and how to meet their age-level needs, teach everything from a biblical world and life viewpoint, and have a good knowledge of the Word of God as well as of their subject matter. I'd look for teachers who can teach biblically apart from any textbook.[13]*

When Alondria was first enrolled at Circle-Rock Preparatory School, her mother was not really enthusiastic, and the mother was not regularly attending church. But Alondria started bringing home Scriptures and singing lots of Bible songs. Now she and her family are singing together at home. Her mother says, "If you want your children to be strong, productive adults, they not only need to be educated, but they also need to know the Lord. What better place to send your kids than a place that promotes good education and spiritual well-being? It's been a positive experience. I've even become a regular attender at the church."

Parent Enrichment

As education empowers students, it often also moves parents to a new level of hope and expectation for themselves. "In choosing either a private or public school, parents see their choice as an extension of parental responsibility. For many parents, the decision to send their children to a neighborhood non-public school is tantamount to taking the first step on a ladder out of poverty, for themselves and their children."[14] The decision by an undereducated or low-income parent to enroll a child at Circle-Rock has sometimes eventually led to the parent returning to school and improving his or her own living circumstances so that the whole family has benefited. That choice, made by parents who had just enough hope to walk through the door of Circle-Rock to ask about enrolling their children, was rewarded and reinforced when they saw that their children were really making educational progress. They have then tried even harder to move past their circumstances and to continue educating their children. In inner city America, private (Christian) schools are intervening early to break the cycle of poverty. At Circle-Rock we also offer parents a selection of topical classes to enhance and support their parenting and living skills. These classes are taught by professionals in each field and are announced in advance so that parents can arrange to attend.

Staff from the Neighborhood

Seeing that neighborhood residents make up a significant portion of the school's staff also lifts parents' self-esteem and gives them a sense of closeness not shared as readily when staff come from outside the school community. "At many neighborhood-based private schools, more of their faculty and board members are likely to live within walking distance of the school. Where this is the case, . . . such a school becomes an active partner in solidifying or revitalizing the neighborhood."[15]

Last summer Mrs. Boykin, a teacher at Circle-Rock, decided to tutor several of her students in reading for a couple of hours a day in her home. This daily contact outside the school building provided the opportunity and time for friendship right on her front porch. One of the children's mothers was expecting her second baby, and in late summer Mrs. Boykin received a phone call from the very excited father announcing that his wife had gone into labor and wanted to make sure Mrs. Boykin knew it was "that time"!

Partnering with Local Colleges and Universities

Colleges, universities, and other training institutions in the vicinity of a Christ-centered school may be called upon to partner with the school to the mutual benefit of students from both. At CRPS we have enjoyed the benefit of a community nursing training program whose director focused several of her students' field projects on our student body. These future community nurses came to understand the health needs of our community better, and the children discovered things like how many germs remain on their hands even after washing with soap (through the use of a special light).

Involving a team of doctoral students in psychology from another local college has led to the college funding an upper-level doctoral internship. This will be used, in part, to develop psychological services at CRPS as well as long-term parent training in many areas of mental health often not available in schools with a large low-income enrollment.

Christ-centered urban schools should be considered hotbeds of training for education majors in local colleges. This is particularly applicable for students who plan to teach in an urban environment or in a cross-cultural setting of any kind.

Parents and friends from a wide vaiety of occupations should be introduced to the students of a Christ-centered school from the earliest grades. Many children in urban areas are introduced to athletics, music performance, and government work, to the exclusion of most other professions. People from all walks of life can volunteer to introduce students to their profession, thereby opening up a world of options previously unknown to many urban inner city children.

Outside the Neighborhood

Clever and creative ideas often come from outside the needy communities, and we who receive the benefit of those ideas are very grateful. Each year Circle-Rock has been the recipient of some wonderful blessings cooked up in the minds of suburban dwellers who love the Lord and want to get to know us.

A homemaker who loves crafts came to our first-year kindergarten and did a craft with the students once a week. The next year a suburban businesswoman visited Rock Church and struck up a conversation with one of our teachers. She used her considerable talent to influence other women in her prayer group to make a youth bed sized "prayer quilt" for each first grader. When the quilts were completed, the women came to the school on a Saturday for "tea" with the students and their parents. During the tea, each child received his or her beautifully handmade, personalized prayer quilt and had a picture taken with the lady who made the quilt and who was praying for the student's family.

A home-schooling family comes one afternoon a week to tutor several of the oldest students in reading and math. The two home-schooled junior high boys have developed wonderful relationships with the students they tutor, and everyone is all smiles when they see the guys coming each week. A former dentist, living in a retirement village nearby, loves to knit and has contributed more than one hundred hand-knit stocking caps for the students to receive at our annual Christmas program, where many family members will hear the fantastic true meaning of Christmas for the first time ever.

A youth group from Minnesota has contributed folding tables, a television, and a VCR to the classrooms over the past two summers when they came on a work team. Vacation Bible schoolers from near and far have helped to stock the school supply cabinets each fall, as well as providing hundreds of books for the classroom libraries.

Conclusion: Where You Can Fit In

Many very deserving inner city Christian schools would relish the opportunity to introduce you to the life of their school. By watching them work with the children and praying for them, you will come to understand how you can assist in the very difficult but worthwhile task they are doing. Financial assistance is always necessary and appreciated because a truly affordable inner city school cannot exist on tuition income alone. But many other kinds of resources are also useful and necessary in these schools. What I find true with rare exception is that the "giver" becomes the "receiver" and God gets the glory.

Incumbent with any worthwhile venture, including the quality education of inner city children, is the tough, gritty, hard work—work whose payoff most often comes in the long run rather than the short run. This work pays off by the benefit it bestows on the next generation of American life rather than on our generation. This work will make "lifters" out of almost certain "leaners" (Marva Collins's phrase) because young students have internalized your enthusiasm for their success, thereby endowing them with enthusiasm for their own success. Why do we do it? Because the lost and untapped resources of undereducated children is a shame and a sin we cannot allow ourselves to accept. Because inner city children come to school with precious God-given ability that deserves our best effort to nurture and develop into all it is capable of imparting to the world.

Reflection Questions

1. Why should the education of inner city children be of concern to Christians who are not themselves living or working in the city? (Matt. 25:40, 45)

2. How might educational *philosophy* and educational *methodology* differ between a suburban Christian school and an urban inner city Christian school?

3. What would the desired outcomes be if a school were designed and operated as
   a. an evangelistic outreach for non-Christian families (or in combination with Christians)?
   b. a discipleship ministry for children and youth who become Christians through your church or parachurch ministry?

4. How would you demonstrate the importance of input from parents and community residents when determining *when, whether,* and *how* to start a school in a particular inner city neighborhood?

5. Considering the ethnic makeup of the community targeted for a new Christian school, how would the leadership and staffing of the school reflect the community?

For Further Reading

Collins, Marva, and Civia Tamarkin. *Marva Collins' Way: Returning to Excellence in Education.* New York: Putnam, 1982.

Collins, Marva. *"Ordinary" Children, Extraordinary Teachers.* Norfolk, Va.: Hampton Roads, 1992.

Hale-Benson, Janice E. *Black Children: Their Roots, Culture and Learning Styles.* Provo, Utah: Brigham Young Univ., 1982.

Hayre, Ruth Wright, and Alexis Moore. *Tell Them We Are Rising: A Memoir of Faith in Education.* New York: John Wiley & Sons, 1997.

Ladson-Billings, Gloria. *The Dreamkeepers: Successful Teachers of African American Children.* San Francisco, Calif.: Jossey-Bass, 1994.

chapter twenty-seven

REACHING YOUTH INVOLVED IN GANGS

TWO CONTRASTING APPROACHES

TOM LOCKE

Introduction:
The Old West Revisited

Westerns of the 1940s and '50s had many Americans mesmerized in front of radios and televisions listening to the adventures on the frontier. Westerns basically came in two types. One was of the sole warrior —the Lone Ranger, Marshal Dillon, Sheriff this or that—against one, two, or more bad guys. The bad guys were bank or train robbers or other marauders running wild in the land where the rules were often broken, and problems were only made right through violence and brute force. The other type of Western depicted the cavalry who, as a team, came to the rescue of someone to the blaring, triumphant call of the bugler. If it was a one-man show, the sheriff, marshal, or whoever needed unique skills: a quick draw (fastest in the West) or a rifle that could spin while chambering itself and loading the next shell in machine-gun-like performance. The hero wore white and the bad guys wore black, and we all knew who to cheer for. With the cavalry, though, we did not know who exactly got the credit. We just knew that, when we heard that bugle blow, help was on the way in the form of an invincible army that would surely vanquish the bad guys and that always seemed to be just over the hill.

We have a new kind of Wild West today—closer than we think,

and just as violent, though not quite as entertaining. If only it were a fictional tale—where the heroes were on the way on their white horses, guns a blazin', ready to clean up the town—would that not solve the problem we face with gangs? Instead, normal everyday folk must take up the challenge of gangs that market drugs to our cities and suburbs, take our children and enlist them in dangerous and illegal activities, and threaten the safety of our communities and families. The goal of this chapter is to explore the basic culture of gangs, their origins, their function, and their appeal to young people; to learn the methods for understanding and reaching youth involved in gangs; and to overview two styles of functioning gang ministries (the cavalry and the lone ranger) to determine the most effective method of outreach.

JUST WHAT IS A GANG?

What is a gang? The most popular images of gangs are either the 1950-ish leather-jacket-wearing, hotrod-driving bad boys or the 1990-ish colors-wearing, drive-by-shooting, drug-dealing, child-killing bad boys we still see on television occasionally. Both groups are urban; both are rebels—with or without causes—and both cause mortal fear in the hearts of those who encounter them.

In general, gangs are groups of people who, for various reasons, do not feel they fit into the majority culture and have found in a relationship with one another a basis for bonding into a separate society. A gang functions as a counterculture or subculture. A subculture is a group that lives by its own private rules when in its own group, but that functions as part of the larger society. Most people reading this book live in the subculture of evangelicalism. Evangelicalism is a subculture because it doesn't necessarily oppose the way the majority culture runs. We work, we pay taxes, we obey laws and raise our families to do the same, we vote, and we participate in society. In general, we do not believe the society at large is out to get us. We do believe, however, that we have a message to carry, and that there are certain things that are OK with society that are not OK with us. We fellowship with each other and, in our individual denominations, separate ourselves from those who do not seem to hold our particular point of view. We fellowship with like-minded people in order to keep our traditions strong. Many different factors can establish our membership in a subculture: race, ethnicity, age, religion, career choice, nationality, size, likes and dislikes. Subcultures are generally not seen as a threat.

A counterculture is similar to a subculture with a few major differences. Countercultures usually oppose the dominant culture by disregarding the laws that the dominant culture has set up to maintain order. Countercultures view themselves as the victims of the dominant culture in most regards. They see themselves as outcasts, unwelcome in society at large for any number of reasons. But instead of withdrawing to themselves and becoming reclusive, they band together to, in their own way, protest the dominant culture by not participating. There are a lot of psychological and emotional reasons for this behavior, but my point here is just that gangs are a counterculture, and as such, are not impressed with our laws or ways of life. In general, most do not want to be responsible citizens. Most enjoy the adrenaline rush their lives give them. They live like Billy the Kid in Wild West frontier towns, which they see as "up for grabs" to the strongest.

Why Do Gangs Form?

As with most organizations that gain any substantial membership, gangs form out of perceived necessity. In the metropolitan Chicago area, an estimated 100,000 young people are involved in gangs.[1] The largest of these gangs are the Disciples, with about ten thousand members; the Latin Kings, about seven thousand members; and the Vice Lords, which separate into various components but all told are about six to seven thousand members. There are about 120 different gangs in the Chicago area, which separate under two federations called People and Folks. (Please refer to the chart on the next page.) The two federations have "themes," or identifying statements, which they use to define themselves. The Folks' theme is "All Is One." The People's theme is "All Is Well." These statements are used in conversations as a general way of "representing" or showing affiliation to a particular group. The Folks use a six-point star (Star of David) to identify their territories. The People use a five-point star (Islamic star) to identify theirs. Each point of the stars has a principle. The six principles of Folks are love, life, loyalty, wisdom, knowledge, and understanding. The five principles of People are love, honor, obedience, sacrifice, and righteousness. Sound like nice groups to be a part of, huh? As the chart indicates, Folks wear their hats to the right and cross their arms left over right (so that their hand is to the right). People wear their hats to the left and cross their arms right over left, so their hand is to the left. The colors each gang uses to represent itself are listed next to the gang names.[2]

The stars do not represent any type of religious views in general. But some gangs affiliated with People use the Quran as a guiding text in setting some of their laws. These gangs include the El Rukns and some of the various sections of the Vice Lord organization. Some sections of Folks use the Bible to help set some of their laws—namely the Disciples.

CHICAGO STREET YOUTH
GANG & ORGANIZATIONS

FOLKS— "All Is One"

Love
Life
Loyalty
Wisdom
Knowledge
Understanding

Caps: right
Arms: left over right

Ambrose (black & blue)
Ashland Vikings (green)
Black Souls (black & blue)
Deuces (green & black)
Disciples (black & blue)
  Black Disciples
  Black Gansters,
  Gangster Disciples
  Del Vikings Maniac Latin D's
  Satan's D's (yellow & black)
Dragons (maroon & gray)
Guess Boys PP (pink, blue)
Harrison Gents (purple & black)
Imperial Gangsters (pink & black)
Insane Popes (black & white,
  blue & black)
LaRaza (red, white, green)
Latin Eagles (gray & black)
Latin Jivers (brown & black)
Latin Souls (black & maroon)
Latin Lovers (red & yellow)
Milwaukee Kings (orange & black)
Nasty Boys PP
O.A.'s (gold & brown)
Simon City Royals (black & blue)
Spanish Cobras (green & black)
Spanish Knights (maroon & black)
Two–Six Nation (beige & brown)
Two–Two Boys (beige & brown)
United Latino Org. (gray & blue)

Independent: Gaylords (black & blue)
    Ridgeway Party Boys
    Pachucos

PEOPLE— "All Is Well"

Love
Honor
Obedience
Sacrifice
Righteousness

Caps: left
Arms: right over left

Bishops (copper & black)
Black Pea Stone Nation (red & white)
Cobra Stones (red, green, & black)
Counts (red & black)
Coulter Kings (black & gold)
El Rukns Org. (black, green & red)
Fillmore Boys (black & gray)
Freaks
Ghetto Boys Org. (orange & green)
Insane Unknowns (white & black)
Kedzie Boys (red & white)
Laflin Lovers (orange & black)
Latin Brothers (purple & white)
Latin Kings Org. (gold & black)
Noble Knights (black & dark blue)
Party Gents (maroon & black)
Puerto Rican Stones (orange & black)
Saints (blue & black)
Spanish Lords (red & black)
Stone Kents (black & gray)
12th Street Player/Cicero (black & white)
Vice Lords Org. (black & gold)
    Conservative
    Four Corner Hustler
    Renegade
    Insane
    Revolutionary
    Travelling
    Undertaker
    Unknown
    Mafia Insane
    Cicero Insane, etc.
Warlords (gray & blue)
White Knights

As you can see, the level of organization of gangs in the Chicago area is considerable. The level of sophistication is also impressive. Because Chicago has such an established gang structure, the city's communities are not open to the influences of other national gangs like the Crips and Bloods. In Chicago, however, Crips generally align with Folks, and Bloods align with People. All four of these federations are nationally known and have members in various cities, suburbs, and small towns from coast to coast. But why?

Depending on whom you speak to about the issue of gangs, the answer you receive could vary greatly. Regardless of who answers, it must be concluded that gangs meet the perceived needs of their members in some way. Instead of discussing what people who affiliate with gangs might perceive as needs, let us instead simply discuss some facts about gangs and gang membership.

Everything You Always Wanted to Know About Gangs . . .

Most metropolitan areas have a huge illegal drug trade. Billions of dollars a year are waged in the war on drugs, but even more billions are made on the street selling drugs. The bulk of these drugs are imported into the country by large cartels or the Mafia (both of which are really just gangs with a lot of money) and distributed in a type of multilevel marketing. By the time the drugs have reached the streets, they have been mixed with other substances to stretch them, and the price has multiplied considerably.[3] Gangs, at least on the streets of poorer urban communities, control who gets to sell these drugs. Neighborhoods are divided up and fought over for the control of the drug traffic in those communities. Thus, the illegal drug business is big business for gangs of all types.

As a sidenote, the evangelical community, as I've dealt with it, tends to equate drugs and gangs with the inner city and race. This is no doubt due to the media coverage of these issues. However, it is important to realize that African-Americans account for only 12 percent of drug users in this country, while white Americans account for 70 percent, according to the National Institute on Drug Abuse.[4] I make this point only because we tend to dismiss that which we feel does not apply to ourselves. Drugs are a national problem, and so are gangs.

It is possible for young kids, only ten to thirteen years old, to make upwards of three hundred to four hundred dollars a week for being a lookout for drug dealers.[5] These children position themselves on street corners and watch out for police and suspicious characters and warn the dealers when they see them. With this early warning, dealers are able to hide drugs. One young man I know began in the gang because his father would not buy him a pair of Michael Jordan gym shoes. He found he could earn the money for himself on the street watching out for police. Smaller dealers often work twelve to sixteen hours a day selling drugs and can make hundreds of dollars a day. And larger dealers, further up the ladder in gang rank, can make thousands of dollars a day. Remember, this money is all tax-free.

So it is no surprise that in communities where the unemployment rate can be as high as 50 percent or more, gangs are a method of economic survival. In a culture that lauds the accumulation of money and material possessions, many young people see gangs as a way out of poverty and lack. But is that all? What about in suburban communities where gangs are on an upsurge?

People in the suburbs like money too. But there are other reasons gangs exist. *Power* is addictive. I remember one young man who was so impressed with the position he had gained in his gang that he put it to me like this, "When I say 'jump,' they jump. If I wanted that guy dead right there, he'd be dead." In communities where poverty and disenfranchisement leave victims and a victim mentality in their wake, a sense of power is a very appealing element of gangs. If a community is ruled by a gang, then the gang members have the same respect in that community that aldermen, policemen, or congressmen have in the dominant community. If a young person is being intimidated in school by the bigger kids, gang membership usually puts a quick stop to such harassment. In communities where gang membership is so rampant that every young person is assumed to be in a gang, it does not take many beatings to make a "neutron" (non-gang-affiliated youth) join a gang.[6]

One Big Happy Family?

Gangs also have an element of belonging. I have often heard young men refer to their gang as their family. Many young men would have no sense of who they were apart from their gang—no purpose in life. For many, the gang leader is like a father whom they can respect and honor for his power and wealth, perhaps much unlike their real fathers. Gangs are willing to recognize young people's gifts and contributions. Gangs will let a ten-year-old join, let a thirteen-year-old have rank and "call shots." A sixteen-year-old can run a whole community. While we are telling kids to shut up, gangs are making them leaders.

Gangs are relatively strict on their members. Although they play fast and loose with the dominant culture's laws, they do not deal in a leisurely manner with the laws of the gang. Members are often beaten for such trivial offenses as missing meetings or even being late, talking out of turn, or disobeying an order from a leader. Apart from the military, it is hard to find a career as exacting as gang membership.

Although gangs are mostly seen as a male phenomenon, plenty of young women join gangs affiliated with the male gangs, with names such as Lady Gangsters, Latin Queens, and Lady Lords. Some girls join the male gangs and even rise through the ranks to leadership positions by proving themselves and their loyalty on the streets.

Finally, in a world of bungee jumpers, sky surfers, and hockey players, the gang is a source of excitement rarely rivaled. Nothing quite feels like a bullet whizzing past your head as you run. At least that's what I understand from the stories I've been told—war stories of young men fighting for their own causes and barely escaping the jaws of death. These stories are told by young men so excited they are almost giddy. Adrenaline is a powerful hormone. In a community of workaday people often settling for mediocrity, the gang lifestyle is like living inside a video game.

Combining the economic, social, emotional, psychological, and hormonal factors, it should be easier to see what gangs are providing for young people across the country. Sure, there is a huge negative side of gang membership, but like an alcoholic getting drunk, the consequences aren't realized until one hits rock bottom.

HOW DO WE REACH GANG MEMBERS?

Understanding these realities is the first step in learning how to minister to youth involved in gangs. Most of us are not warriors. We do not tote guns and shoot bad guys dead in the streets at high noon. In fact, we've become quite appalled at the use of violence. It is OK to watch it on television westerns or in the movies, but we would never think about actually going toe-to-toe with the bad guy except in our dreams. We are happy to have policemen, marshals, and federal agents go into the fray against the evildoers. We watch comfortably, through our television sets at night, the news of the latest tragedy. In the world of high-noon shoot-outs, we are the people in the general store peeping through the crack in the wood wall, wondering who's going to bite the dust next. That's why the idea of gangs in our communities immobilizes us. We just do not understand it. It is a completely different world. Therefore, our general instinct is fear. Such a response, though wise in many regards, will not help us make effective change in the communities we wish to reach.

To understand how to reach young people involved in gangs, we must begin with the very needs they are looking to have met by the gangs and build from there. As we already discussed, the gang meets economic, social, emotional, and psychological needs of youth. These are the things for which young people turn to gangs. They are also often the same things for which young people turn to God. I am not saying anything new. Our world has many substitutes for the blessings God wants His children to possess. For the remainder of this chapter, I will discuss two different types of ministry currently going on with gang members and the pros and cons of each. Throughout the discussion I will outline the basic principles needed to gain a hearing from young gang members.

My experience with gangs began quite naively in 1988, when I was a freshman at Moody Bible Institute, assigned a ministry working in the Cook County Juvenile Detention center. Little did I know that the young people I spoke with on a weekly basis, as part of my Practical Christian Ministry,[7] were mostly gang members. Nor did I know I had been working the whole year with a man known to be a leader in street-gang ministry, Gordon McLean of Metro Chicago Youth for Christ (YFC). After my first year at the detention center, the former chaplain, Rick Gawenda, asked me to do an internship with him over the summer. This internship led to a better relationship with Gordon and a position later that summer with YFC. From there I was immersed into the world of gangs for the next eight years.

The Lone Ranger Rides Again!

During that eight years I found myself a lone ranger, riding into "Wild West Side" neighborhoods and bringing the gospel of Christ to one or two at a time. The nature of our ministry was simple. The idea was to reach the gangs through their individual members. We met young people incarcerated in the detention center or jail and began Bible studies and counseling sessions with them. As this relationship was strengthened, we then met their friends, and so on and so on. On the streets, our goal was to meet the leader of the gang, the chief. A relationship with him helped make our work on the streets that much easier. Once we knew the chief, everyone wanted to know us. My first contact was a young man named Kojo, who introduced me to his friend Dale, who in turn introduced me to his chief, Carl. After I met Carl, young men began coming up to me to introduce themselves.

The concept is excellent. It certainly is effective for becoming known and respected in a community and for having a relatively safe passage into and out of the neighborhood. But it takes a considerable amount of time and money. Often, in order to have any time to meet with these young people on the streets, we needed to go to a safe, relatively private meeting place. This usually meant McDonalds or Burger King. Two or three meetings a day with four or five young people, and you can see what I mean.

During our meetings on the streets, we did casually what we did more formally in the jails. We asked about issues they were facing, offered counsel and a listening ear, and challenged them to trust Christ and live their lives according to biblical principles. I call this method the lone-ranger style because it related to how I felt as a minister. I was there, by myself, in a community racked with every type of dysfunction and social ill. I rode in on my white horse with the remedy to ease their woes, if they would only listen. It required specialized training and gifts. I had been a counselor with inner city youth for five years and had already experienced my share of challenges. But in many ways, my work with YFC was unlike anything I had ever experienced.

Being a lone ranger meant I was able to spend as much time as needed with individual young people who needed more time, or who were more responsive to my message. The young people trusted me, and I could be an advocate for them with their schools and parents and even a mediator between them and rival gangs. In addition, I did not need to get the approval of a board or a group to move the ministry in different directions or to pursue different methods of outreach.

But the disadvantages eventually came to light. First of all, I did not come from a similar background. I had not grown up in gang-infested neighborhoods or in poverty. My world and my perspective were quite different from theirs, and that difference could not help but shine through. Spending time with one person meant I could not spend time with others. I also lacked accountability and support. But, mostly, what I came to realize over eight years of this type of ministry was how overall ineffective it truly was as a method of winning young people to Christ.

The type of outreach I was doing was set up to fill a gap back in the late 1940s and 1950s. Ministry organizations by the truckload set up to address the needs of youth, including college students, which they felt the churches were missing. Since that time, many churches have made great strides in improving their outreaches to youth. Many, in fact, have hired parachurch workers to be youth directors because of just such expertise. Many (though not all) youth programs that were formerly run by parachurch organizations were taken over by churches and run just as, if not more, effectively. This is what I refer to as a cavalry approach.

Unmasking the Lone Ranger

With young people involved in gangs, the needs that we are attempting to address are the same needs they found met in the gang. Besides the needs they are aware of—economic, social, emotional, psychological, and hormonal—we attempt to meet spiritual needs. The mere diversity of these needs militates against their being met by one person or one relationship. Therefore, the lone ranger going out to minister to these young people will find himself ultimately overwhelmed by the need. A gang member who truly commits himself to the Lord has a lot of issues to deal with. A lone ranger can help with counseling in general; help former gang members find a legitimate job, get back in school, or complete their GED; and hopefully point them to a church that will somehow understand how to deal with their uniquenesses. But what he cannot do is replace that family they lose when they choose this new faith, or be there for each step of growth and development.

It was my experience that converted gang members needed constant attention because they rarely had friends besides their gang buddies. They had often been kicked out of school. They did not fit in with the youth at church. They knew nothing of the customs of churches and felt awkward attending. Also, most church members felt awkward when gang kids attended. Getting a gang youth to return a second week to church was nearly impossible unless I accompanied him myself. And even that was extremely awkward to both him and my fellow church members. In fact, I know one church youth pastor who was fired for reaching out to gang youth in his community and bringing them to church. Parents did not want their daughters meeting gang members in the youth group or dating them. He was told his job was to minister solely to church members.

Another downside to the lone-ranger method is funding. How do you support an independent ministry? If you are working in a poorer community, you are unlikely to find money in that community to support your efforts, so you often have to raise funds, and likely attend church, in a suburban community. Thus, taking a gang youth with you to church could be an even more outrageous proposition. Fund-raising in ministry is likely to take up as much time as the actual ministry you do. Unfortunately, fund-raising often leads to the exploitation of the very people you are trying to help. More than one lone ranger has left the frontier because the support dropped out.

Most teenagers are highly social beings. Dating, hanging out, and going to parties are definitely on the agenda. But how will a lone ranger meet this need? How much accountability can be provided? How much can we really be there? It seems simple enough to win a young person to a relationship to Christ and send him to a church and hope things will be just fine, but my experience shows that things are far from that simple. Age gaps alone limit closeness to youth. They must have various positive peer relationships also.

Here Comes the Cavalry

A young man, who was initially led to the Lord in our ministry, fell away from the Lord and back into drug use, along with his wife. Members of a local church doing a community outreach brought him back into the fold. They were able to put him and his wife both into a church-sponsored drug-counseling program. The program did not work for his wife, and she ran off with another man, leaving their children without care. Other members of the church took the children in and cared for them while the young man was finishing his program. When he finished they used church connections to get him a job, an apartment, and legal representation to be able to gain custody of his children. Meanwhile he visited his children regularly and maintained attendance in church and Bible study and in meetings with his church-appointed mentor. After two years, he has finally been able to regain custody of his children and is working, attending church, and serving God. As I write this, he just walked out of my office.

These experiences are not uncommon for churches that band together to minister to those hurting in their communities. But these experiences are rare for lone rangers. Most often, the young people who truly grew in their relationship with God had found good churches with young people similar to themselves to fellowship with. Others realized they needed to get away from the gang in order to grow, or that they needed a new family, so they left town.

A Glimpse of the Cavalry in Action

The phenomenon of Salem Baptist Church on Chicago's South Side is a great example of cavalry ministry. Sensing generational differences between the youth and the adults, Salem initiated both a separate youth church and a children's church. With a youth-church membership of 1,100 and a weekly attendance of four hundred to five hundred, the church is meeting needs.[8] Amazingly, young people from as far away as Wisconsin come weekly to attend the youth church. Also, most of the youth travel to the church by themselves as opposed to coming with their parents. In other words, most of the members of the youth church are independent members, not the children of the church members. The music, worship, and all aspects of the ministry are run by and geared toward the youth. The church has been the site of many a young gang member's conversion to faith in Christ. Almost every month, according to Rev. Harvey Carey, youth pastor, someone "drops their flags" (quits the gang). How does he explain the church's appeal to gang youth?

> *Gang youth are like any other group. They feel they need belonging, to be part of a community, a family. We assume that churches offer this but not all do. Salem*

does. Gang youth are drawn to a church that is bold and definitive on certain is-sues. Gang guys are into confrontation. They don't like status quo. They like to deal with issues facing them such as drying up Roseland (the community of the church),[9] closing down liquor stores and crack houses, getting prostitutes off the streets, and shuttling crack users to detox. When gang members see this happen-ing, they are amazed because so many other churches are caught up in church stuff. We also do Evangelism Invasions on every first Saturday. We take hundreds of teens out to the malls, projects, the parks, parties—go to where the teens are—and have prayer rallies. Gang members see this and ask what we're doing. When the gang kids hit rock bottom they remember us. We have Saturday night JAM sessions "Jesus and Me". The focus is towards the unchurched teen modeled after Willow Creek's Seeker service. We use high school and gang basketball tourneys to invite them in—Vice Lord night, Gangster night. They come and check us out. Because of the relationship with the church we have no [rivalry] problems.[10]

The church, as a cavalry, comes to the rescue of young gang members, offering family, giving job training, and helping with education and basic overarching needs of the gang member. Each member of a sensitive church must see his or her role in the community to effect change in the lives of young people. Just as each one of us needs the church to truly grow in faith, so also the gang member needs the church to effect growth in his life. Many mothers, fathers, sisters, and brothers come around the gang youth to support him in unique ways, which no lone ranger could ever truly accomplish. This new family eases his conversion and strengthens his resolve to continue his walk with God as he finds a new family helping root him in righteousness.

What advice does Rev. Carey have for churches or individuals that are considering this type of ministry?

It can't just be an idea—like a Thanksgiving or Christmas basket give away. It must be a God-birthed idea. The heart of the church must be in this mission. Your effort must be genuine and consistent. When you break your promise, they don't need you. When they've stuck their necks out and trusted you and you've pulled back, they don't want anything to do with you. You need to be ready to put up with getting your car tires stabbed. . . . There's always a season of testing.[11]

Conclusion:
Mobilizing the Community

Consider for a moment your conversion to Christ. Most likely, the true growth occurred in your life once you became a member of a church. In that church, many people added to your development. Rarely is one person able to truly help a person grow in every area of life. The soil of the church is where Christians are most able to grow. Lone-ranger ministries serve a purpose in filling in where churches are lacking vision, but they are only temporary fixes, if that. The true role of lone-ranger ministries should be to train churches to do outreach. But to truly, effectively change our communities, we must mobilize the tremendous potential of the community church, think creatively, and move boldly. Can you hear the bugle blowing? Charge!

Reflection Questions

1. Can you imagine yourself joining a gang? Why or why not? Why do young people most often join gangs?

2. What is a counterculture or subculture? How does it affect our ministry approach?

3. What personal biases may hinder your own involvement in ministry to gang members?

4. What other evidence supports the conclusion that the cavalry method is more effective than the lone ranger? Is there any time when the lone-ranger approach is superior?

For Further Reading

Chideya, Farai. *Don't Believe the Hype—Fighting Cultural Misinformation About African-Americans.* New York: Plume Penguin, 1995. Helps us break down biases that may hinder cross-cultural ministry.

Mayers, Marvin K. *Christianity Confronts Culture.* Grand Rapid: Zondervan, 1987. Looks at taking the gospel cross-culturally, understanding cultural issues and people.

McLean, Gordon, et al. *Cities of Lonesome Fear.* Chicago: Moody, 1991. Good on getting into what life is like on the streets for young men involved in gangs. Explains the lone-ranger approach in detail.

Samenow, Stanton. *Inside the Criminal Mind.* New York: Random, 1984. Good insight on criminal thinking and behavior—what is going on in the mind of a gang kid.

chapter twenty-eight

KIDS . . .
WITH KIDS

NEW MOMS CARES FOR UNWED
TEENAGE MOTHERS AND THEIR CHILDREN

CONNIE MEAD

Introduction: A Glimpse into the World of Unwed Teen Mothers

My name is Lakeisha and I am sixteen. My mom [who is thirty-two] got a new boyfriend. When she found him forcing himself on me, she put me out. It was easier to think that it was my fault than to lose her new boyfriend. I knew a guy who would let me stay with him if I slept with him. Within a year, I was pregnant. Two years later, I was homeless with two children."

"My name is Tuesday. My mother took me to my friend's house to play when I was five. She never came back. I went from relative to friend to relative for three years until they finally put me in foster care. At age ten, my foster mother forced me to start sleeping with her son —or she'd put me out. At twelve, I became pregnant with my first child."

POOR TEENAGE MOTHERS—WHAT ARE THEY LIKE?

New Moms serves disadvantaged young mothers and their children in a poor community on the Northwest Side of Chicago.[1] The group of teenage mothers represented in this chapter are as individual, as unique, and as diverse as any group of youth. However, their similarities must be noted for you to understand the context of their lives and their community.

Our young mothers are thirteen to twenty-one years old. They are among the most vulnerable and at-risk of the community's adolescent parents. Most have no permanent home and move from one transient living situation to another. Often after a girl is kicked out of her mother's house, she will move in with a boyfriend or a relative or a friend—until that relationship deteriorates and she must move on. Typically, these teenage mothers and their children have moved between two and eight times in the previous year. They frequently live doubled- or tripled-up in extremely crowded apartments with numerous building code violations. Many are officially homeless, already living on the streets or in other places considered unfit for human occupancy.

Ninety-five percent are either Hispanic or African-American, and generally their children are five years old and younger. Most are survivors—or continuing victims—of abuse, neglect, abandonment, and domestic violence. When they come to New Moms, approximately 80 percent have dropped out of school. Almost all are on welfare or have no income at all. Only about 25 percent have ever held a job. More than 75 percent do not live with their immediate family.[2] Nearly all lack self-esteem and a family structure that positively reinforces their desire to improve their life situations.

Our moms generally come from two, three, or four generations of teenage mothers who have been single parents because the fathers do not live with the families. This lack of men in the household has been prevalent for decades, since public aid became available only to families who did not have an adult male as head of household. If the father stayed with the family, the family was ineligible for public assistance. This massive deterioration of the family has been passed down as a legacy to each new generation. Current public aid has changed this rule, but the legacy remains and is a big reason there are so few two-parent families in poor urban neighborhoods.

Walk (Literally) a Mile in My Shoes

I would like to take you for a quick tour of the living standards for our moms. Walking is the most frequently used mode of transportation. To deliver their babies and get other medical attention, moms take the bus to the hospital, *walk* to give birth (imagine that!), or take an ambulance.

The bus and the "el" train are the next most common means of transportation. Buses run on a regular schedule—in good weather. Service suffers whenever the transportation companies have difficulties (snow, cold, budget cuts, etc). If a family has a car, it is generally a one- to five-thousand-dollar vehicle that requires frequent maintenance. There are no taxi stands in our neighborhood. Taxi drivers prefer not to even come into our community.

Generally, our young mothers either ignore illness or visit a hospital emergency room. A routine well-baby visit can take four to eight hours due to very overcrowded doctors' offices and poor bus routes to the required clinic. Prescriptions have taken up to three days to get filled because of paperwork snafus. All of this results in physical health having a lower urgency than is common in more privileged communities.

Our clients do their grocery shopping at the high-priced corner convenience store or by a bus trip (with child in tow) to a more major grocery store. Purchases are limited to what a shopper can physically carry or get into a two-wheeled metal cart. Moms take laundry to a neighborhood laundry facility or wash it in the apartment sink. Often, they dry clothes by a room space heater or in front of an open oven door. Ironing boards are scarce. Clothes are ironed on the floor, the bed, or a table. Children are often accidentally burned by irons.

Personal hygiene and family health items are considered a luxury. People seldom use paper towels and napkins. Dish soap is too expensive, so mothers use bleach to wash dishes. Dishcloths, dish towels, hot pads, and proper cooking utensils are rare. Mothers don't change babies' diapers very frequently, to "stretch" the family budget. Diaper rash is thus quite common.

Blazing Summers, Freezing Winters . . .

During the heat of the summer, air conditioners are nonexistent. People hang out of their windows (often without screens that could protect the babies from falling) or sit on building stoops to get some breeze. Apartments are either very cold or very hot—both of which result in sick kids.

Low-cost apartments usually do not include major appliances. Frequently, refrigerators and ovens do not work. Styrofoam coolers are a weak attempt to keep food and the baby's milk cold. A hot plate or stove top is used for cooking. Microwaves are nonexistent. Properly vented and functioning hot-water heaters and room heaters are a challenge to find. Often, each room has only one electric outlet, with none in the bathroom. Doorbells, if they exist, usually do not work. Apartment mailboxes are not properly secured, so mail disappears on a regular basis. Most families do not have their own personal phones and must use pay phones or a neighbor's phone.

Generally, leases are rare, with a month-to-month arrangement being the most common landlord-tenant relationship. Rent is usually paid in cash, but most landlords do not give receipts, so our moms have no proof of rent payment. A "lockout" (which is illegal) is the most common way of losing the apartment. A "lockout" means part or all of one's possessions are thrown on the street, locks are changed immediately, and the person cannot reenter the apartment for anything left behind.

We are aware that many teenage mothers do not live in these life situations. This chapter is not *about them.* Teenagers who become parents in communities with good school systems, with numerous after-school and weekend activities, where cars are the normal means of transportation, etc., require different sensitivities than what we will talk about in this chapter.

"Didn't They Know They Would Get Pregnant?"

The question comes in many shapes and sizes, but the most common question from people outside the neighborhood is "Don't these girls realize what you do to get pregnant?" There is an unspoken air that these young women are ignorant, particularly about the facts of life and the results of sex at an early age. Nothing could be farther from the truth.

Most of the young women we serve have been sexually or physically mistreated since they were infants. In many cases, they feel they have no right to protect themselves. They do not think in terms of being abused or mistreated; rather, mistreatment is just considered a normal part of life, the way it is and always has been. The concept that our bodies are temples of the living God (1 Cor. 3:16) is in stark contrast to "my body belongs to my mother's boyfriend, my uncle, my brothers—anyone who sees fit to use me." It is a brand-new concept to most of our participants that God uniquely made them, that they are worthy of love that does not demand anything from them, and that they have incredible potential.

For a young girl who has only known physical touch as sexual, becoming pregnant is not a matter of not knowing it will happen but rather a question of "When will it happen?" Their understanding of sexual issues is far greater than others their age—it is their perspective of why it happens that is so vastly different. Physical intimacy is, in their view, about how to please a man so that you do not get beaten, thrown out of the house, or, even worse, told what a piece of trash you are. The harsh reality is that when young girls are subjected to sexual and physical abuse, they end up believing they are worthless, unlovable for any reason other than for sex, and incapable of a hope-filled future. We stand in the gap to proclaim the truth that each mom and each child are uniquely and wonderfully made (Ps. 139:14).

Family–the Key to Success

We all need a supportive family to thrive and grow into all that God has for us to be. So, what do we do for these young girls who do not have that family environment? The answer is simple—and yet so complex. We create it. We ask God to give us the grace and understanding of what it means to be a family, and then we begin to replicate that for those who do not have a supportive family.

New Moms acts as a family, with staff playing the parental role of loving and nurturing these teenagers through their "difficult years." Our teenagers talk back, argue, complain, and throw tantrums. Sound like any teenagers you know? But unlike most families, our family members have struggled to survive. They talk about "making it to sixteen," meaning they survived sixteen years of life (or whatever age they are).

We help them relax violent verbal and physical patterns and learn more acceptable ways to work out differences. This is true in their parenting practices, interpersonal relationships, and how they deal with authority figures (employers, landlords, teachers, etc.). But these kids also yearn for the structure and rules that come from loving parents who are trying to train their children up in the way they should go (Prov. 22:6).

The young moms play the sibling role to each other, which includes fighting with each other over big and small things, jealousy, and sibling rivalry. Surprisingly, we hear very little "Mom loves you more than me" because, for many, the love modeled by staff is the first unconditional love they have ever known. Once they are secure in believing that staff members truly care about them, they do not feel a need to fight for the staff's attention. Instead of wanting to hoard a staff person for themselves, they want that person involved with as many others as possible. Gradually, they learn to nurture and support each other— much as a healthy biological family does.

Isolated and Alone

Our moms are isolated and alone—living their adolescent years shouldering adult parenting responsibilities. We have kids pretending to be adults, but who have never been children. It is not surprising that they are confused and have believed the lies they have been told.

Poor inner city communities lack resources that are common elsewhere. In communities with more affluence, youth are encouraged through educational opportunities, sports teams, boys' and girls' clubs, after-school programs, and church youth groups. The young women we serve have dropped out of school, never had sports teams available to them, don't know of a girls' club they could join, never attended an after-school program, and do not attend church.

Declining Teenage Pregnancy Rates?

Surveys and research have recently touted a decline in the percentage and number of teenage girls getting pregnant and having babies—but we have not seen this occur among our clientele. Among the very poor and oppressed (those most marginalized by society), there has not been a decline in recent years. Inner city poor teenagers are dropping out of school, joining gangs, becoming pregnant, and parenting at an alarming rate.

The national annual statistics suggest that fewer than 1 percent (0.6 percent to be exact) of all babies are born to ten- to nineteen-year-old females.[3] In contrast, the city of Chicago has an average of 13 percent of all babies being born to teenagers.[4] However, our neighborhood of Humboldt Park, West Town, and Logan Square have annual birth rates of 29 percent, 20 percent, and 19 percent respectively to adolescent girls ages ten to nineteen.[5] Not only are these staggering percentages, but the actual number of births ranges between 1,200 and 1,700 babies each year. An overwhelming 84 percent of these births are to *unwed* teenage mothers.

HOW NEW MOMS SERVE KIDS . . . WITH KIDS

New Moms serves teenagers from multiple ethnic groups in one group—which we have been told has been unsuccessful for others. One observer noted, "Staff of different ethnicity truly believe they are equal, which has resulted in an interesting phenomenon—the moms act as if they are all equal too. I've never seen anything like it." New Moms does not pretend we are all the *same*—Puerto Rican, Mexican, African-American, African, Anglo—but we are all *equal*. There is a huge difference between those two statements. Working as one body in Christ, many members but one body, makes us behave differently (1 Cor. 12:21–31).

New Moms' MISSION is to enable, empower, and equip at-risk adolescent parents and their children through Christian-based services and mentoring.

We wholly believe in the value of life (Gen. 1:26–27) and the uniqueness and dignity of every individual (Ps. 139:13–16). We believe that God created all people and that He has a plan for each person's life (Ps. 139:16b; Jer. 29:11). We believe that through His love and power, Jesus Christ can change any of our lives (2 Cor. 5:17).

These prevailing beliefs drive how we treat participants, their children, and each other.

New Moms' VISION is to be a model Christian agency serving the disadvantaged through building God-centered, stable, self-sufficient families and supporting local community revitalization through strategic alliances.

New Moms' KEY BELIEFS are:

- *Jesus Christ is the source for new beginnings, new hope, and new life.*
- *Each individual can have a bright and hopeful future.*
- *Each person is greatly valued and gifted by God.*
- *Positive parent-child relationships provide a foundation for the self-esteem and dignity of each individual.*
- *Positive family relationships are the cornerstone of healthy communities.*
- *Being part of a supportive family is essential to healthy personal development.*
- *The local church is the primary vehicle for nurturing a growing relationship with God.*
- *Personal change occurs from the inside out.*
- *A personal relationship with Christ maximizes the results of New Moms' clinical services.*

New Moms' CORE VALUES are:

Servant leadership and accountability

Prudent financial management

Impeccable integrity

Relentless affirmation of each person's dignity

Initiative, creativity, and teamwork

Trust

The Good News (and the Bad News)—They Are Kids!

Teenagers are notorious for doing it their way, bucking the system, and trying to change the world. Poor teenage mothers are no different. Even though they have heard only negative things about themselves and their capabilities, they are just "teenager enough" to say, "I'm going to be the exception—I'm going to be different."

But, like most teenagers, they do not know how to make the changes in their lives that will give the results they want. That is where you and I have an incredible opportunity. We can turn that teenage energy and peer pressure to an advantage. We can form small groups that will encourage and enable teenage mothers to believe in God, find value in themselves as human beings, and begin to articulate a hope-filled plan for a better tomorrow.

Sound idealistic? Perhaps a little. But New Moms has been doing it for sixteen years and is known for our success in taking "highly marginalized youth" and helping them into a different life. We have an incredible opportunity to love these young ladies, their boyfriends, their extended families, and their young children. When we model God's love in all we do, they cannot help but want the structure and affirmation that comes from such a loving family. We have seen this proven true time and time again.

This does not mean that they become a part of the family of God at breakneck speed. They thirst after God and long for His peace, but pride and Satan are alive and well. Scriptures tell us to plant the seeds and water them, but God does the harvesting; only He can bring a soul into the kingdom (1 Cor. 3:6). But teenage mothers and their children are fertile soil for our planting! (Matt. 13:23).

It is a joy when we catch a glimpse of seeds we thought were planted on rocky ground. If anyone's heart was rocky ground, it was Darniece's. She broke rule after rule in our shelter program and we finally had to dismiss her. She threatened to kill staff, and we knew she meant it. We watched carefully as we came and went, trusting we would not be jumped by her gang-bangin' boyfriend. Two years later, Darniece came to our office to say she was sorry for the way she had acted and that she had found God. Darniece had completed her GED ("General Equivalency Diploma," a high school diploma equivalency) and was working as a security guard. She was engaged to be married, she and her fiancee were buying a house, and she was scheduled to begin a graphic arts program at a local college. Praise God!

You see, the other good news about them being kids is this: They have had fewer years for habits to form. They are fresh and moldable. They have tough skins, created by having to survive on the street, but they are hurting and crying inside. The toughest moms we serve are the ones hurting the most, crying out for someone to help them.

Four (or Is It Five?) Basic Principles

New Moms has had four basic philosophical principles driving all our programming:

1. Modeling Christian Principles and Practices (with each staff person's personal testimony and life needing to shine for Jesus in order to have this truly happen).
2. Comprehensive, Integrated Services (to the degree that it is really hard to separate the services from each other).
3. Starting from a Group Model and Focus That Exerts Positive Peer Pressure (most social service experts teach that you must work with the individual services first—we are dealing with young folks who lack a family support system, so we have made the group service the first element).
4. Relationship Building (this is the foundation for absolutely everything New Moms does, and our success is in direct proportion to our effectiveness in building relationships).

A fifth principle is evolving and will be implemented in the next few months as we move into the next level of vision implementation:

5. Strategic Alliances (we believe that strategic alliances with faith-based groups will enable us to exponentially increase the impact we have on individuals, families, and our community). This is particularly true if we as one greater church in Christ link arms and do everything possible to affect our community with the life-changing power of God.

New Moms programming includes seven service components with the following service categories:

1. nonresidential services
2. residential/shelter services
3. children's services
4. kin and near-kin outreach—*monthly family celebrations*
5. material aid that is earned through incentive programs
6. career readiness, work, and education services—*the Rising Star Career Readiness Program*
7. faith-based community development—*the local church alliance*

HOW WE CAN BEST SERVE KIDS . . . WITH KIDS

We believe the best way to serve poor teenage mothers and their children is to expect more of them than they expect of themselves, to believe in them, and to constantly encourage them through modeling Christ's love. We must hold them accountable and help them feel responsible for what they accomplish. We must show the right combination of grace and tough love. This is not easy. The only way to do this is to spend time on our knees before the throne of grace and to remember that there, but for the grace of God, go I. We must rely on God's Holy Spirit to help us discern the best answer to sticky situations.

In addition, we recommend training on setting and maintaining boundaries. One cannot do this work without personal times of re-energizing. A 24–7 (twenty-four hours a day, seven days a week) schedule leads to fast burnout and results in helping no one. New Moms staff do not attend participants' personal private events (birthday parties, social gatherings), but we do go to public events such as high school graduations and award ceremonies. We never give participants our home phone number or address. We do not take participants to our personal family gatherings or to church with us. This is really tough, but it is where the value of strategic alliances comes in; it is far better for someone else to encourage our participants in local church participation.

Actual services for these young families must be a combination of parent and child services, education and training, earned material aid, broad-based support, and individualized attention. This combination is necessary to prepare teen families to move from:

- isolation to having a support network
- dependence to independence
- being abusive parents to family nurturers
- crisis-driven responses to future planning
- welfare to career employment
- hopelessness to a life filled with eternal hope in Jesus Christ through individual choice

Helping Homeless Kids . . . with Kids

Teenagers and children living in unpredictable and often violent situations need to be helped into safe and stable situations. They may need material aid including housing, food, clothing, transportation, and child care; but we are careful to allow them the dignity of earning these items. Giving aid away should be done only once and only when it is a life-threatening situation. We are creative and give a high value for low investment to encourage the mom in her efforts to change her life situation.

Housing options, in order of preference, should be:

- resolve the conflict and continue living with immediate family
- move in with kin or near kin

- get one or two roommates who can pool resources to obtain quality housing and necessities
- shelter program (remembering very few accept parenting youth)

If your ministry believes it can place moms in church homes, you need to provide extensive training for the host families. Teenagers who have been homeless really push the limits of authority figures, and the hosts must be trained to handle the resulting issues.

Be sure the mom initiates the option she pursues. You can make calls on her behalf, advocate for her, and go with her, but do not do it for her. She must make the request herself for her dignity and also to increase her ability to succeed. Never decide for a mom that she must move out of a situation, no matter how intense you think it is. She may feel even more trapped if she leaves a situation, and she will usually return to it anyway. She must decide to leave a situation herself, or the decision can be made by legal entities that are in place to protect her.

Violence and Other Life–Threatening Situations

If a family is living in an environment that is life threatening to the mom and/or the child, you may need to report the situation to the Department of Children and Family Services (DCFS) or your state's equivalent agency. Check your state's laws. If the child is under the age mandated by law, you may be *required* to report any suspected abuse, neglect, or abandonment. The state considers children unable to protect themselves and has created these laws to intervene when family situations deteriorate. State-appointed authorities determine the validity of the suspicion and take what they consider to be appropriate action.

If at all possible, have the teenager make the call to the authorities herself or, at minimum, have her in the room when you make the call. If you give her the respect of including her in the process (even if she is the perpetrator), you have a high likelihood of continuing the relationship with her and helping her correct the problem. If she is not included in the process, she will most likely flee and you will never hear from her again, losing your opportunity to intervene in her family's life.

THE REWARDS OF SERVING

The best part of being called to serve others is that we get to see lives change. Here is a later chapter in the lives of the two girls we started with:

"My name is Lakeisha and I just graduated from the New Moms' Housing Program. During the year I was there, I got my GED, took a 'Discovery Process' at New Moms and found out I am a dominant personality who needs a leadership role. I'm getting my associate degree in political science and have a job as a conference scheduler. I was just promoted to manager. Someday, I plan to be a state senator."

"My name is Tuesday and I just made twenty-two. I have three wonderful kids. We moved around a lot—but I have my own place now. I finished high school and am working as a secretary. Thanks to New Moms, I found God and things will be different for my kids!"

Tuesday came to New Moms for seven years. We were her family. For six and a half years we worked with her and her family, cried with her, and petitioned God for her to give her life to Him. For six and a half *long* years! In the last few months she came here, she did a work internship and was constantly in close proximity to staff. Finally, one day she decided this God stuff was real and she wanted to have Him control her life too. Tuesday calls us every few weeks to update us on her family news—and to see if we have a New Moms job to offer her yet. With her, it was a long time before we saw spiritual results. For others, it is short. For some, we never know. But we must keep on sowing the seeds.

Conclusion:
Watching for God to Do a Miracle

God has been very gracious to New Moms. I could easily fill a book on all the "God-sightings" and miracles we have seen over the years. As I write this chapter, we are in the midst of another great adventure. Sometime back we recorded God's vision for New Moms as far into the future as we can see. For nearly two years we have been searching for a building to purchase for our shelter program, and every single door has closed along the way. We have prayed fervently for the past year. Three months ago, we sat down with the vision and figured out the square footage needed for each part of the vision, and we kept looking for a building.

One month ago, God brought a property to our attention that is perfect for future vision programming. One week later, we were talking with another building owner that has an ideal property for another part of the vision. A few days later, the third property (the one we were actually looking for) popped onto the scene. We currently barely have the money to buy one building, and we certainly do not have the funds for three buildings. But God does. And if this is truly His vision for New Moms for today, He will make it happen. We need to be completely obedient to God and listen carefully to the Holy Spirit's promptings.

I believe *there is no greater thrill, no greater pleasure, no greater life than to live in complete obedience to God.* Your heart will dance, you will have power you never knew possible, and the kids . . . with kids will notice. They will see, feel, and touch the power and love of our Almighty God, and that's what it is all about. To God be the glory!

Reflection Questions

1. Contrast the life of a teenage girl you know with the one described here. What similarities and differences do you see?

2. What are the similarities and differences between the living environment described here and what you understand a third-world country to be?

3. What would you tell a homeless young family about God's love for them? How could you show that love?

4. What positive activities are offered to the youth of your community? How frequent are those activities? Do the activities and the frequency match the level of activity desired by your youth?

5. What activities could your church offer to help create a more positive family structure in the community?

chapter twenty-nine

THE HOME
AS A MINISTRY BASE

THE HOMEWORK CLUB AND OTHER
WAYS TO MEET NEIGHBORHOOD NEEDS

RUSS KNIGHT

Introduction:
Old Verse, New Meaning

But ye shall receive power, after that the Holy Ghost is come upon you: and ye shall be witnesses unto me both in Jerusalem, and in all Judaea, and in Samaria, and unto the uttermost part of the earth." (Acts 1:8 KJV)

In this verse Christ gave His marching orders to His mighty army. He tells us to be witnesses first of all in the very place we live.

Urban ministry is greatly affected by the increased mobility of families and individuals. Joy G. Dryfoos pointed out that "Americans move a lot. During the past five years, two out of five 10–14-year-olds moved."[1] We should see our new mobile neighbors as a great opportunity, but many of us are retreating from the battle. When I was speaking in a suburban church recently, a gentleman told me that even though he had lived on the same block for ten years, he only knew one other family personally. God gives each of us our own personal Jerusalem, and He expects us to wage serious warfare in that spot. How can He trust us with Judaea, Samaria, and "the uttermost part of the earth" if we cannot even deal with *Jerusalem?*

Whether we live in a dorm room, in an apartment, in a house, or on a farm, we must conclude that God gave it to us. Our residence belongs to Him and He expects us to use it for His glory. It was not given to be hoarded or hidden, but to be used as a tool for evangelism and the overall glorification of God.

Unless you live on a block where everyone is already a Christian, God brings many evangelistic opportunities to your doorstep. Some things are the same whether you live in the city, the suburbs, or a rural area. Today's child is more alone than ever before and has fewer spiritual hooks than those of previous generations.

More children grow up in single-parent families and experience genuine poverty than ever before. The National Center for Children in Poverty reports, "Children born outside of marriage who grow up with single mothers are likely to be poor for most or all of their childhood."[2] Some of these problems were with us in the past, but they were not as intense as they are today. In urban communities, the density of population and the socioeconomic conditions tend to make the fall-out more noticeable.

Although much is justifiably made of the abortion problem, many urban teen girls who get pregnant carry their babies to term, give birth, and keep their babies. This has created the problem of "babies raising babies." Rebecca A. Maynard in her book *Kids Having Kids* pointed out, "Each year, about 1 million teenagers in the United States —approximately 10 percent of all 15–19-year-old-women—become pregnant. Of these pregnancies only 13 percent are intended." The author also noted that "teenagers living in single-parent households are one and a half to two times more likely to become teenager parents than those in two-parent families."[3]

NATIONAL STATISTICS AND TRENDS

"But Jesus said, Suffer little children, and forbid them not, to come unto me: for of such is the kingdom of heaven." (Matt. 19:14 KJV)

Children were a priority to Christ and should be the same to us. When no one appears to be watching our children, they are forced to grow up in the streets without supervision and completely vulnerable to all of the negative elements that prey on the young and unsuspecting.

It has become clear to many that while reaching children is a definite priority, reaching parents (especially young mothers) is even more strategic in changing the negative cycles and trends that now enslave many inner city residents. For example, of the 28 million children aged ten to seventeen living in the United States, 30 percent live in large cities. About one quarter of these children live with only one parent, and one in five are in poverty. Furthermore, about 25,000 juveniles are currently confined in long-term, state-operated juvenile institutions, and only one in four of these grew up with both parents.[4]

To further complicate this picture, Maynard reported, "Only 35 percent of teen mothers have graduated from high school, that is, have received a regular high school diploma, by age 30 compared with over 85 percent of women who delay motherhood."[5] When a young mother, still in her teens, is forced to raise a child either alone or with a mate who is also a high school dropout, those children are not normally going to be exposed to excellent parenting. Children of such parents will usually suffer from poor eating and nutritional habits, poor values training, too little or too much discipline, and an overall disrespect for authority. We have consistently observed these tendencies over more than twenty-five years of ministry in Chicago.

Meanwhile, teens without a high school education are likely to encounter a lifetime of economic stress. Young mothers who are living in poverty at the time of their infants' birth rarely escape the poverty cycle. This has also been noted in *Indicators of Children's Well-Being,* where the writers stated, "Parents' income and employment are indirect indicators of children's well-being. . . . Poor children fare worse than rich children on nearly every outcome that social scientists have studied. This led to the conclusion among many policy makers and child advocates that low parental income hurts children's outcome."[6]

The phenomenon of children having children often carries some predictable consequences. Most notably is the way this child-mother will feel once that sweet doll-like baby grows up. Many times the attachment wanes. The child-parent no longer finds joy in watching over the demands of a nearly helpless little person. The atmosphere at home is often filled with tension, anger, and confusion. Kids from these homes suffer as a result of what their parents were not exposed to and don't know or value.

That many young teen mothers are not working does not automatically mean that they will spend volumes of time with their baby, toddler, preschooler, kindergartner, or school-age child. All too often these inexperienced and frustrated mothers see their children as the source of all their problems. We have heard many blame their child for holding them back and keeping them from experiencing a "normal" life.

As the small child grows, the young mother often has a difficult time keeping him or her entertained. She is not nearly as imaginative as older mothers tend to be. Immature mothers are also unaware of how to create a "child-friendly" environment.

Sending their child out to play until it gets dark is how many of these young mothers get time with their friends or time alone. The child gets all of the "benefits" of not being supervised most of the day. The child on the streets is not taught proper manners, not told what the boundaries are in his world. His mother was not raised in a structured environment, and so she does not know how to give what she herself did not receive. In our neighborhood we observe that many families do not have set mealtimes, planned nutritious meals, times for study and homework, chores, or a set time to go to bed.

3)   A great percentage of the kids in my neighborhood must get themselves up for school in the morning without the benefit of anyone who is charged with fixing them a good breakfast. Five or six years ago, we actually fed breakfast to a group of eight children in the morning before walking them to school. The next year, the school's breakfast program picked up these children.

It is not unusual for children to ring our bell and practically "demand" the sports equipment we supply for those playing on our property. Sometimes instead of asking politely they will say, "Give me the volleyball," and rarely will they say, "Thank you." This has become one of the many ways in which we affect informal teaching—insisting that they ask properly before we grant their requests.

SOUTH CHICAGO—OUR NEIGHBORHOOD

"Then saith he unto his disciples, The harvest truly is plenteous, but the labourers are few; pray ye therefore the Lord of the harvest, that he will send forth labourers into his harvest." (Matt. 9:37–38 KJV)

Before moving to our current neighborhood, South Chicago, in 1985, we prayed that God would help us find a community where we could use our home for ministry. Both my wife Beth, who is European-American, and I, who am both African- and Native American, came from large families where our parents were not only birth parents to several children, but also "Mom" and "Dad" to most of the kids in the neighborhood. Our homes were always full of people. A climate of inclusion was established as a part of our mutual histories.

Having lived in apartments and a borrowed home for the first twelve years of our marriage, we had always exhausted all available space in trying to carry out the principles of hospitality that we inherited from our parents.

Although most folks view their homes as places of retreat and rest, we have been taught to operate on God's behalf "everywhere and all of the time." For many, home represents control, privacy, and disengagement. Home for the Knights also represents headquarters for ministry to our neighbors and those whom God sends our way.

The official 1990 census revealed more than 40,000 persons in the community of South Chicago, including more than 13,000 children up to the age of seventeen.[7] On our immediate block, there are about sixty-five households that altogether constitute a minimum of three hundred persons. By making an unofficial count at our most recent block party we determined that most of those living on our block are children.

In our move to South Chicago, God overwhelmingly answered our prayers for a ministry opportunity. Our new neighborhood was primarily divided between Mexican-Americans and African-Americans. Dozens of children were playing in the streets until well after dark. It didn't take long to figure out that we were located in or near the turf of six different gangs. The Latin Dragons, the Latin Counts, and the Latin Kings are mostly made up of Mexican youth. The Stones, the Bloods, and the Disciples are predominantly composed of African-American youth.

Through mere casual observation we noted that the kids playing on our block did so without any adult supervision and that younger kids were being recruited by older gang members, who use them in carrying weapons and drugs. Not being busy after school makes numbers of young children "available" to the gang recruiters. Younger kids receive little to no hard sentencing in the current juvenile justice system. Jeffrey A. Butts in an article in the *Juvenile Justice Bulletin* informed us, "Juvenile courts in the U.S. processed more than 1.5 million delinquency cases in 1994 . . . of all delinquency cases adjudicated in juvenile court in 1994, 29% resulted in out-of-home placement and 53% were placed on probation."[8] We also observed that children from our neighborhood didn't do homework with any regularity, and we felt we just might hold the key to helping make some of these young people less "available" to recruiters.

The Homework Club

"And Jesus, perceiving the thought of their heart, took a child, and set him by him, and said unto them, Whosoever shall receive this child in my name receiveth me." (Luke 9:47–48b KJV)

Most urban kids need a great start or they will never reach their true potential and we will never benefit from the many great things they might have accomplished. It has become clear to my wife and me that the lack of a great start too often leads to mediocrity, drug dependency, jail time, or premature death. From their first day at school, not much is expected of many of these kids. Even when a teacher suspects the high potential of a new student, she is rarely able to count on the

support and partnership from many young single mothers. Most are
unaware of how to help their children. The Parent-Teacher Association
lists the following ways:

1. Be involved.
2. Provide resources at home for learning.
3. Set a good example.
4. Encourage students to do their best in school.
5. Value education and seek a balance between schoolwork and
   outside activities.
6. Recognize factors that take a toll on students' classroom performance.
7. Support school rules and goals.
8. Use pressure positively.
9. Call teachers early if there is a problem so that there is still
   time to solve it.
10. Accept your responsibility as a parent.[9]

Shortly after we took possession of our home in this new neighborhood, some children rang our bell asking if our kids could come out and
play. My wife, Beth, informed them that our kids first had to do homework, and she invited them to come into the house and do theirs while
waiting. Thus began the ministry concept called "Homework Club."

Slowly the numbers grew that first year until we had almost twenty-
five children coming to our house after school for the express purpose of
doing homework. We discovered that most of these kids had not been in
the habit of doing homework. No one at home insisted or checked. Often, even if a parent was at home, that parent felt unempowered to assist
the child in doing his or her assignments. These parents were often
themselves dropouts or had a language problem. So, although they did
not come by and meet us, they were happy that we, as new neighbors,
were offering our home after school for their kids to do homework. Neither did they forbid their children from taking advantage of this new resource, which also served as a great baby-sitting service.

In time it became clear that without even "trying," we had a great
deal to offer these children. Computers, encyclopedias, dictionaries,
books to read, plenty of paper and pencils, flash cards, and poster
board are just a few of the materials and tools we naturally kept in
ready supply in our home. Once we began to view this as our ministry,
we made sure we had these items and more on hand each day.

Often Christians do not develop the many ministries that they
could, simply because they do not perceive that they have anything

special to offer to those around them. I believe that many of the things that we "know and do" naturally can be extremely valuable to many of our neighbors. I call these *bridges* to ministry. Such a list might include cooking, sewing, carpentry, mechanics, collecting, parenting, gardening, budgeting, reading, typing, photography, or arts and crafts.

At the "Homework Club," which meets in our home, we supply a caring adult (Beth) who has answers to lots of questions and is creative, resourceful, fun, a disciplinarian when needed, and the best baker in the neighborhood. In fact, many of these kids did not know that cookies did not just come from the shelves of grocery stores. Many have since learned to bake cookies themselves and see that there really is a connection between baking and math.

When we first arrived in this community, our kids attended the grade school closest to our home, and that is where most of the kids who live near us attend. We became familiar with their system of homework and with most of the teachers during those years. Homework gives the child an opportunity to "practice, practice, practice," and it also helps the good teachers know where each child is in his or her academic development. Answering the question as to why teachers give homework, the PTA lists the following:

- to help students understand and review the work that has been covered in class
- to see whether students understand the lesson
- to help students learn how to find and use more information on the subject

The PTA also points out that homework is the link between school and home that shows what children are studying.[10]

Currently, those elementary-age children from the neighborhood grade school who have signed up for "Homework Club" arrive at the Knight house after school and participate in the homework club until 5:00 P.M. each Monday, Tuesday, Wednesday, and Thursday. Since we follow the same schedule as the public school, we have no homework club on Fridays or holidays. A sample schedule for the club is on the following page.

While assisting club members in doing their homework, it often becomes apparent that some cannot read or need additional help in math. This is an ideal time to introduce a tutor or find ways to give more attention to those in need. This might also be an opportunity to point these problems out to the parents or teachers who are connected with the children and offer helpful suggestions.

HOMEWORK CLUB SCHEDULE

Time	Activity, Game, Craft	Comment/ Explanation
2:30 P.M.	Homework, Project, Reports	Everyone must work on "real" homework until 3:00 P.M. Those finishing early must read a book from the bookshelves. This is a great time for those in the "Pay-to-Read" program to get ahead. (This program encourages kids to read a book and write a summary for a $2.00 reward.)
		Help is given to those requesting it, and snacks are given to all (cookies, cake, brownies, or popcorn is served with milk or Kool-Aid).
3:30 P.M.	* Games include Memory, Sorry, Othello, Tribulation, Where in the World Is Carmen	Every half hour kids change partners to play a different game or activity. The sign-up board they used when entering
4:00 P.M.	Sandiego?, UNO, mini computer games. * Other activities include drawing,	will indicate who is with whom. Most games and activities have more educational value than the kids realize until it is ex-
4:30 P.M.	painting, baking cookies, arts & crafts.	plained. Two at a time and half-hour time periods allow us to keep peace while conforming to attention times.

5:00 P.M.   DISMISS

Over the years, our own biological children have gotten involved in helping the club members with reading or math. This has proven to be an ideal way of instilling a sense of mission within the entire family.

"But how and when do you present the claims of Christ to your neighbors?" some have asked. Our response is simply "all the time." We are always demonstrating who God is through our consistent, caring lifestyle. Then, on more occasions than we can count, some child or adult will ask, "Do you go to church?" or "Where do we go after we die?" or "Why do you do this—are you rich?" Questions are usually the window to our verbal witness. Some of the questions neighbors ask that might lead naturally to personal evangelism are: "Are you a Catholic?" or "Is there really a place called heaven?" or "Why do you let us come here?" These questions never fail to evoke a complete and evangelistic answer from our family. On one occasion one of the neighborhood boys asked if I was Katie's father and then asked if I was a "preacher." I not only had an opportunity to inform him that I really was a preacher, but also to explain to him that not everyone who claimed to be a "preacher" was a preacher of God. I went on to tell him how one becomes a preacher who represents the Lord.

One of the other ways we have managed to bring our neighbors face-to-face with the claims of Christ is to invite them to attend church with us. Periodically we have taken from one to three kids with us to church (that's all the additional people our small station wagon will hold).

Several times during the year, we invite some of the club members to have dinner with our family. Besides getting a chance to explore our house, this usually represents a special occasion for kids who do not often eat good, solid meals. There are usually no mealtimes in their homes. No one asks God's blessing for the food. The whole family does not sit around a table and eat together.

It is at these extended times, when we have invited neighbors into our home, that we not only demonstrate another model of family life, but we also find out what life is like in their homes. These times convince us that we are always "teachers." We teach both formally and informally, but we always teach.

Though there have been times during the school year when we have had the help of nearby Christian college students, we usually end up running the program ourselves because coordination has proven to be too difficult. When the school year ends, we reward the faithful either by hosting a party or by sponsoring a trip downtown to places none of them have ever been before.

THE NEIGHBORHOOD PARK

"Let your light so shine before men, that they might see your good works, and glorify your Father which is in heaven." (Matt. 5:16 KJV)

Whether we sit out on our porch or indoors, the sound of gunfire has become commonplace in our neighborhood. Many no longer even seek cover. Innocent bystanders have been known to actually run toward flying bullets instead of away from them. Gang drive-bys regularly take the lives of children. In my neighborhood, when we hear bullets, we quickly usher those playing nearby into our home, which is considered a "safe house" by everyone.

Less than a year after we were in our new home, the apartment house next door burned down completely. Once the land was cleared and leveled, it was placed up for sale but remained unsold for about three years.

During that time we dreamed about owning that property, but we did not have the money to buy it. Our late friend, national evangelist Tom Skinner, also challenged us to buy the property. So we intensified our prayers. God opened a door when the owner of the property suddenly approached us and asked, "Would you be interested in buying the property for one dollar if I offered it to you?" Naturally we quickly purchased the land.

All of the parks in our neighborhood were considered to be in a particular gang's turf. Not many parents would allow their children to travel into a different turf on the other side of the tracks. Realizing the problem and the need, we decided to create a safe place for all children.

Once our friends understood what we intended, they insisted on helping. So, with their financial support, we fenced the property, designed a basketball court, built a sand-volleyball court, put in a tetherball pole, and introduced something called box hockey. On an average day here at the park, we might easily have thirty children (from preschool through high school age) playing here at one time. They only have to knock on the door and ask for the equipment needed.

Up until recently, the basketball court was the centerpiece of the neighborhood park, often engaging individuals and teams until we had to close the park due to darkness. Several years ago our first summer basketball tournament attracted about eighty kids from throughout the community and was a tremendous success. Members from all six gangs played together peacefully.

The Sign Posted on the Knights' Property

Private Property
This park has been
provided as a place of peace.

Please respect yourself
and each other.

God Bless You.

Not one shooting or gang fight has ever taken place on our property. The rules we set up and posted were honored over the years by all who played at the park. However, last summer we decided to eliminate basketball from the park's activities and replace it with a playground for infants and those up to the age of ten.

One of our motivations for this radical action had to do with our confidence that God was moving us in the direction of trying to reach some of the young mothers in our community. More and more young girls were having babies at younger and younger ages, and once they gave birth, they often found the task of parenting to be more than they could handle. One young mother was heard to say, "I never thought this child would take so much time. I cannot even breathe. . . . I must get away."

YOUNG MOMS CLUB

"Train up a child in the way he should go: and when he is old, he will not depart from it." (Prov. 22:6 KJV)

For many years we have watched fourteen-year-old girls have children long before they had even completed childhood themselves. Most of these young mothers were following in the footsteps of their own mothers, grandmothers, aunts, older sisters, and other peers who had had children out of wedlock.

In the past, young mothers had the benefit of having their own mothers teach them how to care for their child. Each generation of mothers has had less and less time to prepare their daughters for the important task of motherhood, since the age of these young mothers continues to drop. Two generations of mothers, forced to begin raising a child before they finished high school, are justifiably lacking what we used to refer to as "mother wit." They usually suffer from having to raise their child alone and without the benefit of the extended family, which used to assist with this task. Unfortunately, what these girls don't know hurts not only them, but their children as well. As noted in *Indicators of Children's Well-Being,* "Recent years have brought increasing evidence that the failure to complete high school is associated with problems in employment, earnings, family formation and stability, civic participation, and health."[11]

Many children are raised in single-parent homes by young mothers who do not have much to pass on to their offspring. These girls have not completed childhood #101 or adolescence #202. They certainly have not yet learned how to treat a child who has suddenly become their sole responsibility. Some of the questions facing young mothers that will need to be answered are:

1. How am I going to take care of myself and my child financially?
2. Where are we going to live, and what will be the living expenses?
3. Should I breast-feed my baby? How often?
4. Should I hold my baby a lot?
5. How often will I need to take my baby to the doctor?
6. What does the baby's crying mean?
7. Do I need to eat special foods?

Usually someone (mother or grandmother) is available on a temporary basis to answer these and other questions. Unfortunately, those things all mothers should know about their kids from infancy to three years old are not always known by these young mothers, and this will most often handicap the child for life. Most young mothers are not aware of what kinds of things they need to teach their preschooler in order to ensure that he or she is school-ready when beginning the educational journey. We have observed from Homework Club that many kids from poor/single-parent homes start school well behind other kids. These young mothers do not understand that they are responsible for preparing their young for school. They often feel that it is solely the job of the schoolteacher to educate their children. Parental participation is not a model they are familiar with. They continue this process of disengagement throughout the time their child is in school.

Young Moms Club desires to teach young mothers how to be involved in their child's education starting in the preschool ages. My sons, Russell III and Aaron, both learned their colors by learning to play "UNO" with the many teens who were ever-present in our home. Our daughter, Katie, learned to count by listening to her mother count the time on our microwave oven while warming baby food. Here are a few of the things we suggest to mothers preparing their children for school:

A BEGINNING KINDERGARTEN STUDENT SHOULD KNOW

1. His or her "real" full name and how to spell it
2. His or her street address and telephone number
3. His or her mother/father's "real" full name
4. The full alphabet and the sounds the letters make
5. How to spell the words from a limited small-word bank
6. How to count up to at least twenty
7. The names of the colors

Our primary objective will be to teach the mothers how to help their children. Eventually, we hope to link each young mother, soon after her child is born, with an older mom from the neighborhood and local church when possible. The older mother can be a good older friend and can informally pass on some of her wisdom within the developing relationship.

The initial attraction for participation of young mothers might come from the new playground, since younger kids will not be allowed to play here without an adult to oversee their play. Others might get involved with us even before their child is born. Some will contact us directly, and some by referral. We have several mentors ready to get involved. One curriculum model might include:

LIFE SKILLS FOR YOUNG MOMS

YOU
* Self-development
* Communication Skills
* Relating to Others
* Practical Problem Solving
* Decisions & Options

YOUR BABY
* Prenatal Care & Wellness
* Fetal & Maternal Development
* Parental Cost
* Labor & Delivery
* Postnatal & Neonatal Care

YOUR ROLE
* What to Expect of the Newborn
* So Now I Am a Parent
* Child Care
* Child Development
* Child Neglect & Abuse

YOUR FUTURE
* Developing a Healthy, Safe Environment
* Looking into a Career
* Setting Goals
* Options on Child Care
* Searching & Applying for a Job
* Being a Working Parent
* Are You Employable?
* Economic Resources

* These skills will initially be communicated one-on-one from mentor to young mother out of their growing relationship. Later it will be decided whether or not an actual class is needed. We will attempt to demonstrate acceptance and love, while using the opportunity to share God's design for sexuality and His ability to grant forgiveness with a new start once we are in His eternal family.

HOSPITALITY HOUSE (THE KNIGHT INN)

"Be not forgetful to entertain strangers: for thereby some have entertained angels unawares." (Heb. 13:2 KJV)

Beth and I both come from large families and homes that always had plenty of guests. We began practicing the same concept early in our own marriage while we were living in apartments. In our first year of marriage, at various times, we had a college student living with us, and, later, a family of four for about four months.

These days it all might begin with a simple phone call or letter from someone who is a total stranger to us, asking to stay in our home and participate in life in the inner city.

Over the years we have entertained more individuals and groups than we can possibly count. While our guests usually speak of the vital service we render them, we can certainly testify that our lives have been richly blessed by everyone who stays here. Some stay for a few days, weeks, and even years.

When new or old friends arrive, we simply stay with the formula —we don't change anything. Our lives and ministry go on as usual. It is our goal to include our guests into our lives, not to "entertain" them. They are given a room so that they can relax, study, sleep, or simply join the family in whatever we might be doing at the moment.

Sometimes, we even get to show them our city—the good, the bad, and the ugly. We make sure that they take public transportation to and from their destinations if they are with us for more than three days. That is a great learning experience.

Not only do we share our blessings with our guests, but they also share some of their histories and customs with us. Hanna, from Norway, taught our daughter Katie a little of her language. John, Ron, and Robert from Wellington, New Zealand, left us a Maori doll and a few coins. Others have given me a spoon from their country for my collection. We have gained new friends from the places listed on the next page.

Having Christians from all over the world in our house allows our kids and the kids from the neighborhood a chance to dialogue with people from places they might not even be able to pronounce. Those who come to our home and neighborhood often leave with a more positive view of the city. Some have left sensing God's call to them for urban ministry. Others get to see our family up close and personal and see if we really do accurately represent who God is in our everyday lives.

VISITORS' LOG
* From the Knight Inn (1985 to 1998)

Place of Origin
Africa
Zaire
Monrovia, Liberia
Lagos, Nigeria

Islands
Nassau, Bahamas
St. George's Grenada
Jamaica, West Indies
San Juan, Trinidad

Australia
Ipswich
Mosley
Melbourne
Sydney

New Zealand
Auckland
Wellington

Great Britain
London, England

Scandinavia
Oslo, Norway
Stockholm, Sweden

Asia
Tokyo, Japan

Canada
Montreal
Ontario

U.S.A. (West)
Portland, Oregon
San Jose, California

Place of Origin
U.S.A. (East)
Brooklyn, New York
Bronx, New York
New York, New York
Saccasunna, New Jersey
Russell, Pennsylvania
Beaver Falls, Pennsylvania
McKeesport., Pennsylvania
Baltimore, Maryland

U.S.A. (Midwest)
Akron, Ohio
Chagrin Falls, Ohio
Dayton, Ohio
University Heights, Ohio
Logansport, Indiana
Whiting, Indiana
Indianapolis, Indiana
Huntington (College), Indiana
Detroit, Michigan
Lansing, Michigan
Fergus Falls, Minnesota

Deerfield, Illinois
   Trinity College

Chicago, Illinois
   Moody Bible Institute
   North Park College

Wheaton, Illinois
   Wheaton College
   Asbury College

Rockford, Illinois
Rockton, Illinois

* This is just a small sample of where people have come from over the past twelve years. Many of these individuals and groups were recommended by The Seminary Consortium for Urban Pastoral Education (SCUPE) based here in Chicago. For twenty-five years this agency has developed innovative approaches to urban theological education. Its mission is to develop leaders and provide educational resources to enhance the spiritual, social, and physical quality of life for those who live in the city.

Several years ago one of the nearby suburban churches converted our bland, empty attic into a very modern second floor complete with a bathroom and two extra bedrooms. They wanted us to be able to enlarge our capacity for service. It was just what we needed, but could not afford. This was a great statement concerning the unity of the body of Christ.

The city and suburban church can actually work together on kingdom business once we each realize that both can be givers and receivers. Now for our basement . . .

Conclusion: Whatever It Takes

As home missionaries for nearly thirty years, we are committed to using everything available to reach some with the gospel of Christ. Nothing is off limits. Not our house, car, property, friends, or even our privacy.

When kids get hurt in the neighborhood, they run to our home for a bandage. When several families lost everything to a terrible fire, we helped find food, clothes, and some cash through our own contacts. During drive-by shootings, our home has served as a safe house until all is quiet. A mother who was trying to find work received some financial help from our "Emergency Assistance" fund established so that we will have the ability to respond to genuine needs when they occur. A Mexican doctor who wanted his credentials recognized here in America needed some tutoring in English before he took his exam, and he came to our home for that help. A Polish woman who could not afford to put her husband in a nursing home received help three times a day for five years from our family. Three unsaved teens were given a scholarship from our family to go to a Christian youth conference. Two of them were saved at the conference, and the other received Christ a year later.

One of the overwhelming benefits of doing ministry out of our home is the marvelous way in which God continues to give us both our personal needs and the resources necessary to continue being givers. While not rich by this world's standards, we are extremely blessed.

Since God has so graciously invited us into His eternal family and stands ready to receive all who come to Him, we believe we can do nothing less than invite others to Him through our service and verbal witness each day right here in our home and community.

Reflection Questions

1. Why not start right where you are? Assess the unaddressed educational needs of your community. What are they? Do you have the resources needed to make a difference? Which of these do you possess: skills, aptitude, talents, gifts, facility, support team, a plan, or money? How can you use them?

2. How can you help meet the recreational needs of your community? Can something as simple as teaching kids to cook or play chess or hosting a Ping-Pong tournament provide an evangelistic or pre-evangelistic opportunity? Explain.

3. What do you have to offer a young mother or an emerging young father? How will you build a bridge in order to make a difference?

4. How open is your home to ministry? Is your personal property available? In what ways can it be more available?

For Further Reading

Community Area #46 Profile: The 1990 Census. *Demographics and Housing Characteristics of Chicago and Community Areas.* Chicago, 1994.

Decker, Scott H. and Barrik Van Winkle, eds. *Life in the Gang.* New York: Cambridge Univ., 1996.

Dryfoos, Joy G. *Adolescents at Risk: Prevalence and Prevention.* New York: Oxford Univ., 1990.

Hauser, Robert M., Brett V. Brown, and William R. Prosser (editors). *Indicators of Children's Well-Being.* New York: Russell Sage Foundation, 1997.

Klein, Malcolm W. *The American Street Gang.* New York: Oxford Univ., 1995.

Landre, Rick, Mike Miller, and Dee Porter. *Gangs: A Handbook For Community Awareness.* New York: Facts on File, 1997.

Maynard, Rebecca A. (editor). *Kids Having Kids: Economic Cost and Social Consequences of Teen Pregnancy.* Washington, D.C.: The Urban Institute, 1997.

McCord, Joan (editor). *Violence and Childhood in the Inner City.* New York: Cambridge Univ., 1997.

National Center for Children in Poverty. *Five Million Children: A Statistical Profile of Our Poorest Young Citizens.* New York: National Center for Children in Poverty, 1990.

Payne, James L. *Overcoming Welfare: Expecting More from the Poor and from Ourselves.* New York: Basic Books, 1998.

Scarpitti, Frank R., Margaret L. Andersen, and Laura L. O'Toole. *Social Problems.* New York: Addison-Wesley Educational Publishers, 1997 (3rd edition).

Yablopsky, Lewis. *Gangsters: Fifty Years of Madness, Drugs and Death on the Streets of America.* New York: University Press, 1997.

NOTES

Foreword

1. Michael T. Kaufman, "A Folklorist Finds the Melting Pot Brimming in Queens," *New York Times,* 26 July 1995, sec. B, p. 1, col. 2, Metropolitan Desk.

2. Winthrop S. Hudson, *The Great Tradition of the American Churches* (New York: Harper & Row, 1953), 141. Hudson quotes other advocates for city ministry on p. 110 (also see note 1 on p. 271): "We must save the city if we would save the nation." (Josiah Strong); "If religion fails in America, it will fail most colossally in the cities" (H. K. Rowe).

3. Ibid., 110.

4. I counted 1,090 uses of the words for city in the Hebrew Old Testament and 160 references in the Greek New Testament.

Chapter 1: Chicago's Place in World Evangelization
By Ray Bakke

1. Herbert Asbury, *Gem of the Prairie: An Informal History of the Chicago Underworld* (DeKalb, Ill.: Northern Illinois Univ., 1942), 1.

2. See especially the essay by Richard C. Wade, "Urban Life in Western America, 1790–1830," in *American Urban History: An Interpretive Reader with Commentaries,* 3d ed., ed. Alexander B. Callow (New York: Oxford Univ., 1982), 68–81.

3. Four excellent standard histories of Chicago that I recommend include: William Cronon, *Nature's Metropolis: Chicago and the Great West* (New York: Norton, 1991); Donald Miller, *City of the Century: The Epic of Chicago and the Making of America* (New York: Simon & Schuster, 1996); Dominic A. Pacyga and Ellen Skerrett, *Chicago: City of Neighborhoods* (Chicago: Loyola Univ., 1986); Harold M. Mayer and Richard C. Wade, *Chicago: Growth of a Metropolis* (Chicago: Univ. of Chicago, 1969).

4. For a delightful recent history of the University of Chicago set in the context of theological history, see Conrad Cherry, *Hurrying Toward Zion: Universities, Divinity Schools, and American Protestantism* (Bloomington, Ind.: Indiana Univ., 1995). A little classic on the famous urban sociologists of Chicago is Robert E. L. Faris's *Chicago Sociology, 1920–1932* (San Francisco: Chandler, 1967).

5. See Michael F. Funchion, "Irish Chicago: Church, Homeland, Politics and Class—The Shaping of an Ethnic Group, 1870–1900," in *Ethnic Chicago: A Multicultural Portrait,* 4th ed., ed. Melvin G. Holli and Peter D. Jones (Grand Rapids: Eerdmans, 1995). Though it is not a history per se, this collection of essays has evolved into the best single book to understand Chicago as we know it today.

6. New York, Boston, and Chicago have provided numerous scholarly case studies. For an understanding of Irish political behavior, I highly recommend *The City Boss in America: An Interpretive Reader,* ed. Alexander B. Callow (New York: Oxford Univ., 1976).

7. Melvin G. Holli, "German American Ethnic and Cultural Identity from 1890 Onward," in *Ethnic Chicago.* For marvelous essays on urban Czechs, Irish, Germans, Poles, Slovaks, Jews, and Armenians and the ways their religious traditions shaped (and were shaped by) their life in Chicago and other northern cities, see *Immigrants and Religion in Urban America,* ed. Randall M. Miller and Thomas D. Marzik (Philadelphia: Temple Univ., 1977).

8. Michael Novak, *The Rise of the Unmeltable Ethnics* (New York: Macmillan, 1971). The "melting pot" image first appeared in Israel Zangwill's play by that name in 1914. This violent image is drawn from the steel industry. Heat the slag (ore) in the pot, and the pure gold (WASP) goes to the bottom. Ethnic distinctives (language, culture, race, etc.) rise to the top to be discarded. Other books that have helped me better understand the concepts of ethnicity, race, and assimilation in Chicago include: Leonard Dinnerstein and David M. Reimers, *Ethnic Americans: A History of Immigration and Assimilation* (New York: Harper & Row, 1975); Andrew M. Greeley, *Why Can't They Be Like Us?* (New York: Institute of Human Relations, 1969); Studs Terkel, *Race: How Blacks and Whites Think and Feel About the American Obsession* (New York: New Press, 1992); Thomas F. Gossett, *Race: The History of an Idea in America* (Dallas: Southern Methodist Univ., 1963); John Higham, *Strangers in the Land: Patterns of American Nativism 1860–1925* (New York: Atheneum, 1978); William Petersen, Michael Novak, and Philip Gleason, *Concepts of Ethnicity* (Cambridge, Mass.: Belknap, 1980); Thomas Bentz, *New Immigrants: Portraits in Passage* (New York: Pilgrim, 1981).

9. Start with Carl W. Condit's *The Chicago School of Architecture: A History of Commercial and Public Building in the Chicago Area, 1875–1925* (Chicago: Univ. of Chicago, 1964), but, in my opinion, to understand Chicago one needs exposure to Thomas S. Hines's work, *Burnham of Chicago: Architect and Planner* (New York: Oxford Univ., 1974).

10. Holy Family Church and the Taylor Street communities have seen the ravages of time, but the church has been restored. This is the church that founded Loyola University and once named Mother Cabrini among its numbers. St. Frances Xavier Cabrini was the first American to be canonized by the Roman Catholic Church. Sent to the U.S. by Pope Leo XIII in 1889 to minister to Italian immigrants, she lived mainly in New York City and Chicago, directing the establishment of hospitals, orphanages, nurseries, and schools in the United States and in Latin America.

11. Edward Kantowicz, *Polish-American Politics in Chicago: 1888–1940* (Chicago: Univ. of Chicago, 1975).

12. In addition to reading the books already mentioned about the Polish in Chicago, I recommend visiting the 9:00 A.M. service at St. Hyacinth Polish Catholic Church on Wolfram and Central Park, just off Milwaukee Avenue, to see Polonia alive and well today.

13. Standard biographies of D. L. Moody include Richard K. Curtis, *They Called Him Mr. Moody* (Garden City, N.Y.: Doubleday, 1962), which highlights Moody as evangelistic communicator; and James Findley, *Dwight L. Moody: American Evangelist, 1837–1899* (Chicago: Chicago Univ., 1969), which sets Moody in the larger theological context of American Protestantism. The recent biography written by Lyle W. Dorsett, *A Passion for Souls: The Life of D. L. Moody* (Chicago: Moody, 1997) adds the much needed discussions of Moody's educational and sociological significance. James Gilbert's *Perfect Cities: Chicago's Utopias of 1893* (Chicago: Univ. of Chicago, 1991) adds a marvelously reflective piece on Moody's evolving view of cities and urban evangelism coming out of the World's Fair experience in 1893 in his chapter on "The Evangelical Metropolis," 169–208.

14. For an excellent introduction to the ministry climate of this period see the unpublished dissertation of Clinton E. Stockwell, "A Better Class of People: Protestants in the Shaping of Early Chicago, 1833–1873" (Univ. of Illinois at Chicago, 1992), especially chapters 12–15 on the city mission, YMCA, and the temperance and antislavery movements.

15. William Adelman, *Haymarket Revisited* (Chicago: Illinois Labor History Society, 1976). Adelman, a long-time scholar of Chicago's labor history, takes the reader on an engaging tour of the landmarks associated with the Haymarket riot, telling the stories along the way. The Illinois Labor History Society has also published other guides to Chicago's unique labor history.

16. James F. Findlay, Jr., *Dwight L. Moody*, 322–38. See also Dorsett, *A Passion for Souls*, 165–69, for a marvelous summary of the relationship and role of Emma Dryer in the development of what we know today as the Moody Bible Institute.

17. William Stead, *If Christ Came to Chicago* (Chicago: Laird & Lee, 1894), 463.

18. Personally I don't think we Protestant evangelicals can understand Chicago's spiritual history without reading Charles Shannabruch's marvelous study, *Chicago's Catholics: Evolution of an American Identity, 1830–1930* (Notre Dame, Ind.: Univ. of Notre Dame, 1981).

19. Students of urban migrations and their impact on Chicago should begin with the large picture portrayed by David Ward in *Cities and Immigrants: A Geography of Change in Nineteenth Century America* (New York: Oxford, 1975), then move toward specific studies, such as Nicholas Lemann, *The Promised Land: The Great Black Migration and How It Changed America* (New York: Knopf, 1991).

20. For the finest scholarly discussion of public housing for the poor in Chicago, see Devereux Bowly, *The Poor House: Subsidized Housing in Chicago, 1895–1976* (Carbondale, Ill.: Southern Illinois Univ., 1978).

21. For an excellent history of slum development, see Thomas Lee Philpott, *The Slum and the Ghetto: Neighborhood Deterioration and Middle-Class Reform, Chicago 1890–1930* (New York: Oxford Univ., 1978). A most readable history of how not to redevelop slums is found in Bernard J. Frieden and Lynne B. Sagalyn, *Downtown, Inc.: How America Rebuilds Cities* (Cambridge, Mass.: MIT, 1989).

A HEART FOR THE CITY

22. By now most urban pastors and mission leaders have learned not to define city neighborhoods as problems to be fixed, but rather as assets to be identified and built upon. This approach was made popular in the writings of Chicago scholars Ed Marciniak of Loyola University and John McKnight of Northwestern University. See Marciniak's *Reversing Urban Decline* (Washington, D.C.: National Center for Urban Ethnic Affairs, 1981); *Reclaiming the Inner City* (Washington, D.C.: National Center for Urban Ethnic Affairs, 1986); and McKnight's *The Careless Society: Community and Its Counterfeits* (New York: Basic, 1995).

Chapter 2: Called to Christ, Called to Compassion
By Joseph Stowell

1. Leo Tolstoy, *How Much Land Does a Man Need? And Other Stories* (New York: Penguin, 1993), 114–23.

Chapter 3: A Case for Wholistic Urban Ministry
By Glen Kehrein

1. Ray Bakke, *The Urban Christian* (Downers Grove, Ill: InterVarsity, 1987), 109.

2. Vance Packard, *Nation of Strangers* (New York: McKay, 1976), 106–7.

3. Nicholas Lehmann, *The Promised Land: The Great Black Migration and How It Changed America* (New York: Knopf, 1991), 81.

4. Howard Aldrich, "Ecological Succession in Racially Changing Neighborhoods," *Urban Affairs Quarterly* 10 (March 1975): 327–48.

5. The social and personal drama of racial transition is captured poignantly through the personal reflections honestly shared by Rosen in this excellent book. Although these voices all come from a community on Chicago's South Side, they speak the same feelings shared by millions of Americans with this common experience of racial clash. Louis Rosen, *The South Side: Racial Transformation of an American Neighborhood* (Chicago: Ivan R. Dee, 1998).

6. Lehmann, *The Promised Land,* 6.

7. Ibid., 72.

8. John Herbers, *The New Heartland: America's Flight Beyond the Suburbs and How It Is Changing Our Future* (New York: Random House, 1986), 18f.

9. Robert E. Webber, *The Church in the World: Opposition, Tension, or Transformation?* (Grand Rapids: Zondervan, 1986), 156.

10. Charles Howard Hopkins, *The Rise of the Social Gospel in American Protestantism, 1865–1895* (New Haven: Yale Univ., 1940), 130.

11. Webber, *The Church in the World,* 163.

12. Walter Rauschenbusch, *A Theology of the Social Gospel* (New York: Abingdon, 1945).

13. Harold Carl, "What Liberals Believed and Why Fundamentalists Made Such a Fuss," *Christian History* 16, no. 3 (1997): 20–22.

14. "The Press Weighs In: Condensed Editorials from the Summer of 1925 Show a Nation at Odds," *Christian History* 16, no. 3 (1997): 19.

15. David Knox, *Not by Bread Alone: God's Word on Present Issues* (Edinburgh: Banner of Truth, 1989), 41.

16. Dieter T. Hessel, *Social Ministry* (Philadelphia: Westminster, 1982), 20.

17. D. G. Hart, "Right Jabs and Left Hooks," *Christian History* 16, no. 3 (1997): 24.

18. Donald Dayton, *Discovering Our Evangelical Heritage* (New York: Harper, 1976).

19. Donald A. McGavran, *Ethnic Realities and the Church: Lessons from India* (Pasadena: William Carey Library, 1979).

20. C. Peter Wagner, *Our Kind of People: The Ethical Dimensions of Church Growth in America* (Atlanta: John Knox, 1979).

21. David Claerbaut, *Urban Ministry* (Grand Rapids: Zondervan, 1984), 132.

22. John Perkins, *Let Justice Roll Down: John Perkins Tells His Own Story* (Glendale, Calif.: Gospel Light, Regal, 1976); Stephen Berk, *A Time to Heal: John Perkins, Community Development and Racial Reconciliation* (Grand Rapids: Baker, 1997); Terry Whalin, John Perkins, *Today's Heroes Children's Series* (Grand Rapids: Zondervan, 1996).

23. Ronald Sider, *One Sided Christianity?* (Grand Rapids: Zondervan, 1995).

24. J. C. Pollock, *Moody: A Biographical Portrait of the Pacesetter in Modern Mass Evangelism* (New York: Macmillan, 1963), 34f.

25. Ibid., 52.

26. J. Wilbur Chapman, *The Life and Work of Dwight L. Moody* (Chicago: Winston, 1900), 100.

27. For a more comprehensive understanding about reconciliation, see Raleigh Washington and Glen Kehrein, *Breaking Down Walls: A Model of Reconciliation in an Age of Racial Strife* (Chicago: Moody, 1993).

28. Bob Lupton, "Relocation: Living in the Community," in *Restoring At-Risk Communities: Doing It Together and Doing It Right,* ed. John M. Perkins (Grand Rapids: Baker, 1995), 83.

Chapter 4: A Philosophy of Urban Ministry
By Wayne L. Gordon

1. John Perkins, *A Quiet Revolution: The Christian Response to Human Need: A Strategy for Today* (Waco, Tex.: Word, 1976); *Let Justice Roll Down: John Perkins Tells His Own Story* (Ventura, Calif.: Gospel Light, Regal, 1976).

2. John Perkins, ed. *Restoring At-Risk Communities: Doing It Together and Doing It Right* (Grand Rapids: Baker, 1995); John Perkins, *Resurrecting Hope* (Glendale Heights, Calif: Gospel Light, Regal, 1995).

3. John Perkins, *With Justice for All* (Ventura, Calif.: Gospel Light, Regal, 1982).

4. See Carey Casey, "Daddy, Are You Going to Be a Sermon Today?" in John Perkins, *Resurrecting Hope,* for further discussions of relocation in the Lawndale community.

5. Amy Sherman, *Restorers of Hope: Reaching the Poor in Your Community with Church-Based Ministries That Work* (Wheaton, Ill.: Crossway, 1997).

6. Glen Kehrein and Raleigh Washington, *Breaking Down Walls* (Chicago: Moody, 1993).

7. Spencer Perkins and Chris Rice, *More Than Equals: Racial Healing for the Sake of the Gospel* (Downers Grove, Ill.: InterVarsity, 1993).

8. "Helping the Poor Help Themselves," *Christianity Today,* 3 February 1997, 70–73.

9. See Wayne Gordon, "Indigenous Leadership Development" in Perkins, *Restoring At-Risk Communities,* for further discussion of leadership development in the Lawndale community.

10. See Keith Phillips, *No Quick Fix: Healing for Fractured Families* (Ventura, Calif.: Gospel Light, Regal, 1985); *Out of Ashes* (Los Angeles: World Impact, 1996); *They Dare to Love the Ghetto* (Ventura, Calif.: Gospel Light, Regal, 1975).

11. See Mary Nelson, "Redistribution: Empowering the Community," in Perkins, *Restoring At-Risk Communities* for details on Bethel New Life.

12. Wayne Gordon, *Real Hope in Chicago* (Grand Rapids: Zondervan, 1995).

13. See chapter 2 in Perkins, *Resurrecting Hope* for details on the Mendenhall Ministries.

14. See Robert Lupton, *Theirs Is the Kingdom* (New York: Harper & Row, 1989); *Return Flight* (FCS Urban Ministries, 1993).

15. See Glen Kehrein, "The Local Church and Christian Community Development," in *Restoring At-Risk Communities*, ed. John M. Perkins, for details on Circle Urban Ministries.

16. See Perkins, *Resurrecting Hope.*

17. See Perkins, appendix of *Restoring At-Risk Communities*, 239.

18. John Perkins, *Beyond Charity: The Call to Christian Community Development* (Grand Rapids: Baker, 1993), 35.

Chapter 5: Promoting Racial Reconciliation in the City
By Milton Massie and Marc Henkel

1. Spencer Perkins, "A Quest for Higher Ground," *Reconcilers* (Spring 1998): 25–26.

2. The Christian Community Development Association, 3827 W. Ogden, Chicago, IL 60623.

3. Tribune News Services, "Study: Chicago 3rd Most-Segregated City," *Chicago Tribune* (29 January 1997), 10.

4. Tom Brokaw, "Why Can't We Live Together?" *Dateline NBC Special,* videotape (27 June 1997).

5. "Race Relations Trends," *Metropolitan Chicago Information Center,* Internet: www.mcic.org/trend/race.html (1996), 1.

6. Ibid., 1.

7. Jim Wallis, "Evangelicals and Race," *Sojourners Online,* Internet: www.sojourners.com/soj9703/9703441a.html (April 1997), 1.

8. Ibid., 1.

9. Ibid., 2.

10. Alex Spencer-Byers, "Special Report: Race at Wheaton," *Racial Reconcilers Online,* Internet: www.netdoor.com/com/rronline/Reconcilers/resource_center/wheaton96.html, (April 1996), 1.

11. Staff of the *Chicago Tribune, Chicago Days: 150 Defining Moments in the Life of a Great City,* ed. Stevenson Swanson (Chicago: Cantigny First Division Foundation, 1997).

12. "Study: Chicago 3rd Most Segregated City," *Chicago Tribune,* 10.

13. Pierre de Vise, "'Most Segregated' Still Defines City," *Chicago Tribune,* 21 February 1997, 24.

14. Marie K. Rowlands, *Down an Indian Trail in 1847* (Palos Heights, Ill.: Dutch Heritage Center, Trinity Christian College, 1949), 1–256.

15. Spencer Perkins and Chris Rice, *More Than Equals: Racial Healing for the Sake of the Gospel* (Downers Grove, Ill.: InterVarsity, 1993), 208–15.

16. Raleigh Washington and Glen Kehrein, *Breaking Down Walls: A Model for Reconciliation in an Age of Racial Strife* (Chicago: Moody, 1993), 131–32.

17. Spencer Perkins and Chris Rice, "Reconciliation: Loving God and Loving People," in *Restoring At-Risk Communities: Doing It Together and Doing It Right,* ed. John M. Perkins (Grand Rapids: Baker, 1995), 132.

Chapter 6: Becoming an "Insider"
By John Fuder

1. Abdon M. Pallasch, "Amid Lower Wacker's Homeless, Love Blooms," *Chicago Tribune,* 19 June 1998, 7.

2. Mary Schmich, "Homeless Gizmo Won't Let Cold Take His Breath Away," *Chicago Tribune,* 19 January 1997, 4.

3. Cindy Richards and Diane Struzzi, "Lower Wacker to Shut Its Gates on Homeless," *Chicago Tribune,* 29 January 1999, 1.

4. Abdon M. Pallasch, "Both Sides in Homeless Suit Urged to Negotiate," *Chicago Tribune,* 17 June 1998, 4.

5. Matt O'Conner, "Homeless Sweeps Can Continue—Judge Refuses to Block Lower Wacker Cleanups," *Chicago Tribune,* 6 February 1998, 3.

6. "The Homeless, the City, and the Law," *Chicago Tribune,* 21 February 1998, 22.

7. Wade McHargue and Josh Withey, interview by John Fuder, 11 June 1998.

8. Ibid.

9. Keith Phillips, *They Dare to Love the Ghetto* (Ventura, Calif.: Regal, 1975), 178.

10. Billy, interview by John Fuder, 28 June 1998.

11. Pallasch, "Both Sides in Homeless Suit," 4.

12. David Southwell, "200 Protest Closing Wacker to Homeless," *Chicago Sun-Times,* 30 January 1999, 8.

13. A term used by anthropologists to connote one who guides, instructs, or informs another regarding a particular culture or subculture. The intent is to gain the "emic" (insider) vs. "etic" (outsider) perspective. James P. Spradley's writings are helpful in this area, specifically, *The Ethnographic Interview* (New York: Holt, Rinehart & Winston, 1979); *Participant Observation* (New York: Holt, Rinehart, & Winston, 1980), and, with David W. McCurdy, *Anthropology: The Cultural Perspective,* 2d ed. (Prospect Heights, Ill.: Waveland, 1989). A more recent text is by Elizabeth Chiseri-Strater and Bonnie Stone Sunstein, *Fieldworking: Reading and Writing Research* (New Jersey: PrenticeHall, 1997). For a Christian perspective, see Charles H. Kraft, *Anthropology for Christian Witness* (Maryknoll, N.Y.: Orbis, 1996), and Paul G. Hiebert, *Anthropological Insights for Missionaries* (Grand Rapids: Baker, 1985).

14. John E. Fuder, *Training Students for Urban Ministry: An Experiential Approach* (Ph.D. diss., Biola University, 1993).

15. *Los Angeles Times,* 30 June 1993.

16. Paul Koegel, Audrey M. Burnam, and R. K. Farr, "Subsistence Adaptation Among Homeless Adults in the Inner City of Los Angeles," *Journal of Social Issues* 45, no. 4: 83–107.

17. Fuder, *Training Students for Urban Ministry*, 32.

18. State of California Task Force on Gangs and Drugs, 1989.

19. Al Santoli, "What Can Be Done About Teen Gangs?" *Parade*, March 1991.

20. Leon Bing, *Do or Die* (New York: HarperCollins, 1991).

21. Richard Ropers, "The Rise of the New Urban Homeless," *Public Affairs Report* 26, no. 5, 6 (1986): 1–14.

22. Fuder, *Training Students for Urban Ministry*, 181.

23. Ibid., 245.

24. Rich Kris, Personal Ministry Journal, Fall 1998.

25. Noah Parsons, Personal Ministry Journal, Fall 1998.

26. Roger S. Greenway, *Apostles to the City* (Grand Rapids: Baker, 1978).

27. Roger S. Greenway and Timothy M. Monsma, *Cities: Mission's New Frontier* (Grand Rapids: Baker, 1989), 192.

28. D. P. McNeill, D. A. Morrison, and Henri J. M. Nouwen, *Compassion* (New York: Doubleday, 1982), 4.

29. Fuder, *Training Students for Urban Ministry*, 275.

30. Harvie M. Conn, "Theological Education for the City," *Urban Mission* 10, no. 2 (December 1991): 5.

31. From the hymn, "Where Cross the Crowded Ways of Life," by Franklin Mason North (1850–1935).

32. Fuder, *Training Students for Urban Ministry*, 259.

Chapter 7: Training College Students for Urban Ministry
By Robert C. Smith

1. Earle E. Cairns, *Christianity Through the Centuries* (Grand Rapids: Zondervan, 1954), 456, and Tim Dowley, *Eerdmans' Handbook of the History of Christianity* (Grand Rapids: Eerdmans, 1977), 553.

2. Walter A Elwell, *Evangelical Dictionary of Biblical Theology* [CD-ROM] (Grand Rapids: Baker, 1998).

3. Paul Enns, *The Moody Handbook of Theology* (Chicago: Moody, 1989), 147.

4. Ibid., 23.

5. Elwell, *Evangelical Dictionary*.

6. Douglas Groothuis, *The Soul in Cyberspace* [CD-ROM] (Grand Rapids: Baker 1997) .

7. James and Lillian Breckinridge, *What Color Is Your God? Multicultural Education in the Church* (Wheaton, Ill.: Victor, 1995), 55.

8. Michael S. Bassis, Richard J. Gelles, and Ann Levine, *Sociology: An Introduction* (Upper Saddle River, N.J.: McGraw-Hill, 1991), 2.

9. Raymond J. Bakke, *A Theology As Big As the City* (Downers Grove, Ill.: InterVarsity, 1997), 12–13.

10. Based on Bassis, *Sociology*, 8.

11. George Gmlech, "Introduction: Part Two: Urban Fieldwork: Anthropologists in Cities," in *Urban Life: Reading in Urban Anthropology*, 3d ed. (Prospect Heights, Ill.: Waveland, 1996), 139.

12. James P. Spradley and David W. McCurdy, *Anthropology: The Cultural Perspective*, 2nd ed. (Prospect Heights, Ill.: Waveland, 1996), 1, and Elizabeth Chiseri-Strater and Bonnie Stone Sunstein, *FieldWorking: Reading and Writing Research* (Upper Saddle River, N.J.: Prentice-Hall, 1997), 3.

13. Ibid.

14. Spradley and McCurdy, *Anthropology*, 355–69, provide a very useful thirteen-week fieldwork project appendix that can be adapted for the urban context.

15. *Participant-observer* refers to the stance of the researcher who becomes involved in the daily life of an observed culture.

16. Jaime S. Wurzel, *Towards Multiculturalism: A Reader in Multicultural Education* (Yarmouth, Maine: Intercultural, 1988), 1.

17. U.S. Bureau of Census, Current Population Reports, Series P25–1130, "Population Projections of the United States by Age, Sex, Race, and Hispanic Origin: 1995 to 2050." Population Division U.S. Bureau of the Census, Washington, DC 20233.

18. Ibid.

19. "How We're Changing: Demographic State of the Nation (1997)," U.S. Department of Commerce, Economics, and Statistic Administration, Bureau of the Census, Current Population Reports, Special Studies, Series 23-193, March 1997, 2.

20. William A. Henry III, "Beyond the Melting Pot," *Time* 135 (9 April 1990): 28.

21. Wurzel, *Towards Multiculturalism*, 1.

22. *Ethnocentrism* is the belief that one's culture is superior to that of other groups. It is the tendency to view the norms and values of one's own culture as absolutes and to use them as a standard against which to judge and measure all other cultures.

23. John Perkins, *A Quiet Revolution: The Christian Response to Human Need: A Strategy for Today* (Waco, Tex.: Word, 1976), 218.

24. Ibid.

25. Linda H. Lewis and Carol J. Williams, "Experiential Learning: Past and Present" in *Experiential Learning: A New Approach* 63 (Summer 1994): 6.

26. David A. Kolb, *Experiential Learning* (Englewood Cliffs, N.J.: Prentice-Hall, 1984), 5.

27. Stanley J. Grenz, *A Primer on Postmodernism* (Grand Rapids: Eerdmans, 1996), 8.

28. John M. Perkins's 3Rs of community development (relocation, reconciliation, and redistribution) can be seen throughout his writings, but especially in the following books: *The Quiet Revolution* (Waco, Tex.: Word, 1976), 218–20; *With Justice for All* (Ventura, Calif.: Regal, 1982); and *Resurrecting Hope* (Glendale Heights, Calif.: Gospel Light, Regal, 1995).

29. Allan M. Thomas, *Beyond Education: A New Perspective on Society's Management of Learning* (San Francisco, Calif.: Jossey-Bass, 1991), 128.

30. Ibid., 129.

31. Paul Stanley and J. Robert Clinton, *Connecting: The Mentoring Relationships You Need to Succeed in Life* (Colorado Springs: NavPress, 1991), 32.

32. See Paul Stanley and J. Robert Clinton, *Connecting: The Mentoring Relationships You Need to Succeed in Life*, chapter 13, pages 197–213, for a discussion of the process of selecting an individual to mentor.

Chapter 8: Ministerial Formation in the African-American Church
By Dwight Perry

1. Andrew Hacker, *Two Nations: Black and White, Separate, Hostile and Unequal* (New York: Scribner, 1992), 3.

2. Joseph Barndt, *Dismantling Racism* (Minneapolis: Augsburg, 1992), 11–12.

3. Ibid., 28.

4. J. O. McCloud, "Theological Education and Racial/Ethnic Leadership," *Journal of Theological Education* (Autumn 1992): 71.

5. Dwight Perry, "Institutional Racism Within Conservative Evangelical Settings: The Discongruence of Right Theology Yet Wrong Sociology," Trinity Evangelical Divinity School, 1992.

6. Carl A. Volz, "Seminaries: The Love of Learning or the Desire for God?" *Dialog* 28, no. 2:102.

7. Ibid., 105.

8. James F. Hopewell, "A Congregational Paradigm of Theological Education," *Journal of Theological Education* (Autumn 1984): 51.

9. Linda Cannell, "Theological Education: Retrospect and Prospect," Trinity Evangelical Divinity School, 1995, 2.

10. Ibid., 3.

11. W. Clark Gilpin, "The Seminary Ideal in American Protestant Ministerial Education," *Journal of Theological Education* (Spring 1984): 85.

12. Anthony T. Evans, *Are Blacks Spiritually Inferior to Whites?* (Wenonah, N.J.: Renaissance Productions, 1992).

13. Dwight Perry, "Educational Precedents for Valued Ministerial Attributes and Practices." Trinity Evangelical Divinity School, 1998.

14. Dwight Perry, 1987, 1995.

15. McCloud, "Theological Education and Racial/Ethnic Leadership," 71.

Chapter 9: The Role of Preaching in the African-American Church
By James Ford Jr.

1. Henry H. Mitchell, *Black Preaching* (San Francisco: Harper & Row, 1979), 17.

2. Frank A. Thomas, *They Like to Never Quit Praisin' God: The Role of Celebration in Preaching* (Cleveland, Ohio: Pilgrim, 1997), 31.

3. Paul Enns, *The Moody Handbook of Theology* (Chicago: Moody, 1989), 193.

4. Thomas, *They Like to Never Quit Praisin' God*, 37.

5. Anthony T. Evans, *Are Blacks Spiritually Inferior to Whites?* (Wenonah, N.J.: Renaissance Productions, 1992), 105.

6. Ibid., 57.

7. Ibid., 86.

8. Edward V. Hill, "The Resurrection," audiocassette.

9. Anthony T. Evans, "The Christian Coalition," audiocassette.

10. Warren Wiersbe, "Teaching the Parables," audiocassette.

11. William Thrasher, Hermeneutics class, the Moody Bible Institute of Chicago.

12. Thomas, *They Like to Never Quit Praisin' God,* 37.

13. Shadrach M. Lockridge, "The Lordship of Christ," audiocassette.

14. Gardner C. Taylor, "The Day Christ Died," audiocassette.

15. Richard Allen Farmer, personal conversation.

16. Anthony T. Evans, *Are Blacks Spiritually Inferior to Whites?* 18.

Chapter 10: Multiplying Churches to Take Cities for Christ
By Tom Maluga

1. Dr. Dale W. Cross, Executive Director of Heart of Atlanta Network, wrote in a guest editorial for *CMBA Life,* "Churches must be revived or replanted as an integral, redemptive force for community life."

2. Thanks to Phil Miglioratti, Prayer Coordinator for the Chicago Metropolitan Baptist Association, for this quote and his leadership.

3. Pastor Jim Cymbala's own account of their growth in and impact through prayer is given in his book *Fresh Wind, Fresh Fire: What Happens When God's Spirit Invades the Hearts of His People* (Grand Rapids, Zondervan, 1997).

4. Dr. Dale W. Cross, guest editoral, *CMBA Life.*

5. Thanks to Keith Draper, New Work Coordinator for the Metropolitan Baptist Association, for the seed idea regarding these two models of church starting in Acts.

6. A fuller explanation of this approach to church multiplication can be obtained from HOPE Ministries (P.O. Box 141312, Grand Rapids, MI 49514; or phone 800-217-5200).

7. Mitch Leman, the dynamic director of this ministry, wrote in his job description proposal: "It would be naive to think that our methods and work will accomplish anything unless it is Christ Himself doing the work through us. The apostle Paul's remarkable evangelism and church planting ministry was accomplished *through the power of the Holy Spirit* (Acts 13:2, 3). Thus, we will seek the power of God in all aspects of our lives and ministry by being devoted to prayer and fasting, even as the apostles were (Acts 6:4)."

8. Jim Queen, interview with the author, August 1998.

9. Pastor Spencer Jones, interview with the author, August 1998.

10. This strategy was taken from conference materials prepared by Jim in 1997.

11. Thanks to Garry Arkema and Brian Bakke from the Uptown Baptist Church for putting these principles into graphic form.

Chapter 11: The Use of Arts in Urban Evangelism and Discipleship
By Brian Bakke

1. Quotation from Martin Luther, printed on page 23 of *Art for Faith's Sake,* a catalogue of the prints from an art show by the same name at the Evangelical Lutheran Church of America Lutheran Center; Jerry A. Evenrude Music and the Arts, Division for Congregational Life, Evangelical Lutheran Church of America.

Chapter 12: Rethinking the Church to Reach the City
By Mark Jobe

1. Leadership Network, "Urban When It Wasn't Cool," *Net Fax,* no.77 (4 August 1997), 1.
2. George Barna, *The Second Coming of the Church* (Dallas: Word, 1997), 53.
3. Charles Leroux and Ron Grossman, "Chicago's Racial and Ethnic Evolution," *Chicago Tribune,* 10 February 1999, sec. 1, p. 17.
4. *The Princeton Religion Report,* January 1996.
5. George Barna, *American Society for Church Growth Journal,* Autumn 1996.
6. Ibid.
7. Ibid.
8. Cited by Bob Lehman at the "Growing a Healthy Church" conference, Sonlife Ministries.
9. Ibid.
10. I first heard Peter Wagner use this term at a conference in Chicago called "Breaking the 200 Barrier."
11. George Barna, *The Second Coming of the Church* (Nashville: Word, 1998), 198.
12. Henry Blackaby, *Experiencing God* (Nashville: Broadman & Holman, 1994).

Chapter 13: New Wineskin—Same Vintage Wine
By Michael N. Allen

1. A. Earl Parvin, *Missions in North America* (Sarasota, Fla.: Association of North American Missions, 1997), 42.
2. U.S. Bureau of the Census, telephone interview, March 1999.
3. Ibid.
4. Ray Bakke, *A Theology As Big As the City* (Downers Grove, Ill.: InterVarsity, 1997), 15.
5. Bill Hull, *The Disciple-Making Church* (Old Tappan, N.J.: Revell, 1990), 162.
6. D. James Kennedy, *Evangelism Explosion,* level 2 leader's kit (Wheaton, Ill.: Tyndale), 11.
7. Exodus International (1998 Conference).
8. Viv Grigg, *Companion to the Poor* (Monrovia, Calif.: MARC, 1990), 29.
9. Hull, *The Disciple-Making Church,* 156.
10. Joseph C. Aldrich, *Lifestyle Evangelism* (Portland, Ore.: Multnomah, 1981), 74, 76.
11. Howard Hendricks, *Say It with Love* (Wheaton, Ill.: Victor, 1972), 77.
12. Bill Hull, *The Disciple-Making Church,* 33.
13. Ibid., 9.

Chapter 14: The Church Behind Bars
By Len Maselli

1. U.S. Department of Justice, Bureau of Justice Statistics, *Prison and Jail Inmates at Midyear 1997* (Washington, D.C.: GPO, January 1998), chap. 30, p. 3.
2. U.S. Department of Justice, Bureau of Justice Statistics, *Sourcebook of Criminal Justice Statistics 1995* (Washington, D.C: GPO, 1995), 339.

3. Leon Pitt, "City Violent Crime Rate Down," *Chicago Sun-Times,* 18 April 1998, 13.

4. Department of Justice, *Sourcebook,* 362.

5. John L. DiIulio, "Moral Poverty," editorial, *Chicago Tribune,* 15 December 1995.

6. Ibid.

7. Ibid.

8. Department of Justice, *Sourcebook,* 128.

9. Dan Lungren, "Three Cheers for Three Strikes," *Policy Review: Journal of American Citizenship* 80 (Nov-Dec 1996) .

10. Justice Policy Institute, *Striking Out: The Crime Control Impact of "Three Strikes" Laws,* (Washington: 1997).

11. U.S. Department of Justice, Bureau of Justice Statistics, Press Release, 15 July 1998, www.oip.usdoj.gov/bjs/welcome.html.

12. "Robber Convicted in 2nd Holdup of Same Bank," *Chicago Tribune,* 3 July 1998.

13. Gallup Organization, "Two-Thirds of Americans Have No Doubts About God's Existence," *Emerging Trends,* September 1997.

14. George H. Gallup International Institute, "Religious Faith Is Widespread but Many Skip Church," Gallup Poll, March 1997 (Princeton, N.J.: Gallup, 1997).

15. DiIulio, "Moral Poverty."

16. Ibid.

17. Byron Johnson, "The Faith Factor," *Corrections Today* (June 1998): 107.

Chapter 15: Incarnational Ministry in the Latino Community
By Noel Castellanos

1. Manuel Ortiz, *The Hispanic Challenge* (Downers Grove, Ill.: InterVarsity, 1993).

2. Frank James, "Census: Cook County's White Population Falling," *Chicago Tribune,* 5 September 1998.

3. Gary Moore, "The Next Wave: A Burgeoning Group of Hispanic Newcomers Is Reshaping the Suburbs, from Houses of Worship to Workplaces and Beyond," *Chicago Tribune,* 15 March 1998.

4. The term *Anglo* is used to refer to the U.S.A. majority white population.

5. Geoffrey Fox, *Hispanic Nation* (New York: Carol, 1996).

6. Edward James Olmos, *Americanos* (Waltham, Mass.: Little, Brown & Co., 1999).

7. Earl Shorris, *Latinos: A Biography of the People* (New York: Norton, 1992).

8. Manuel Ortiz, *The Hispanic Challenge.*

9. Linda Chavez, *Out of the Barrio: Toward a New Politics of Hispanic Assimilation* (New York: HarperCollins, 1991).

10. Justo L. González, *Santa Biblia: The Bible Through Hispanic Eyes* (Nashville: Abingdon, 1996).

11. Manuel Ortiz, "The Primacy of Youth Mission in the City and Throughout the World," *Shout* 2, no. 3 (Fall 1998).

12. Julia Alvarez, *How the Garcia Girls Lost Their Accents* (New York: Penguin, 1991).

13. John Perkins, *With Justice for All* (Ventura, Calif.: Regal, 1982).

14. Wayne L. Gordon. *Real Hope in Chicago* (Grand Rapids: Zondervan, 1995).

15. Noel Castellanos and Mark R. Gornik, "How to Start a Christian Community Development Ministry," in *Restoring At-Risk Communities: Doing It Together and Doing It Right,* ed. John M. Perkins (Grand Rapids: Baker, 1995).

Chapter 16: Reaching the Chinese Community
By David Wu and Michael Tsang

1. U.S. Bureau of the Census, Press Release, 27 April 1998.

2. Susan Lee Moy, "The Chinese in Chicago," in *Ethnic Chicago,* ed. Melvin G. Holli and Peter D. Jones (Grand Rapids: Eerdmans, 1995).

3. William Droel and Ed Marciniak, "Historic Chinatown and Bridgeport: The New Synergism" (Chicago: Loyola Univ. Inst. of Urban Life, 1995).

4. U.S. Bureau of the Census, 1990.

5. Carol Stepanchuk and Charles Wong, *Mooncakes and Hungry Ghosts: Festivals of China* (San Francisco: China, 1991).

6. Gail Law, *Chinese Churches Handbook* (Hong Kong: Chinese Coordination Centre of World Evangelism, 1982).

7. 1998–1999 *Directory of Chinese Churches and Bible Study Groups in North America* (Paradise, Pa.: Ambassadors for Christ, 1998).

8. U.S. Bureau of the Census, 1990.

9. "Pictorial History in Brief," *Bor Yum* magazine, 75th anniversary edition (Christian Union Church), October 1990.

10. *Open Doors 1997/1998,* Institute of International Education.

11. Dorothy and Thomas Hoobler, *The Chinese American Family Album* (New York: Oxford Univ., 1994).

12. Illinois Department of Revenue, 1997 Annual Report.

Chapter 17: Outreach to the Jewish Community
By Michael Rydelnik

1. Michael Medved, "What Do American Jews Believe?" *Commentary,* August 1996.

2. Max Dimont, *The Jews in America* (New York: Simon & Schuster, 1980), 225–26. Although Dimont's statistics are somewhat dated, they reflect the continuing tendencies in the American Jewish community.

3. Medved, "What Do American Jews Believe?" 72.

4. F. D. Moule, *An Idiom Book of New Testament Greek,* 2d ed. (Cambridge: London Univ., 1959), 98; Friedrich Blass and Albert Debrunner, *A Greek Grammar of the New Testament and Other Early Christian Literature,* trans. and rev. W. Funk (Chicago: Univ. of Chicago, 1961), 34.

5. Walter Bauer, W. F. Arndt, and F. W. Gingrich, eds., *A Greek-English Lexicon of the New Testament and Other Early Christian Literature* (Chicago: Chicago Univ., 1979), 726.

6. John Murray, *The Epistle to the Romans,* vol. 1 (Grand Rapids: Eerdmans, 1973), 28.

7. God has many purposes in saving people, the most important to glorify Himself. However, the Greek syntax is clearly a purpose clause, showing that one of God's purposes is to provoke jealousy among the Jewish people.

8. TaNaK refers to the Hebrew Bible, what Christians call the Old Testament. The three Hebrew consonants comprising the word signify the Old Testament's three divisions: T for Torah (the Pentateuch); N for Neviim (Prophets); K for Ketuvim (Writings).

9. For a thorough discussion of Christian anti-Semitism, see Edward Flannery, *The Anguish of the Jews* (Mahwah, N.J.: Paulist, 1985), 28–155.

10. The false idea that all the Jewish people are solely and perpetually guilty for the death of Christ is the foundational idea behind all Christian anti-Semitism. For a refutation of this false argument, see Michael Rydelnik, "Who Are the Christ-Killers?" *Moody Monthly* 86, no. 2 (October 1985), 38–42.

11. John Chrysostom, *Homilies Against the Jews* 4.1; 6.1, 3–4.

12. See *Augustine Ennaratio* on Psalm 68:1, 22; 56:9; *Epistles* 137.16; *Reply to Faustus* 13.10.

13. Martin Luther, *Of the Jews and Their Lies.*

14. See endnote 11.

15. The best recent book on Messianic prophecy is Walter Kaiser, *The Messiah in the Old Testament* (Grand Rapids: Zondervan, 1995).

Chapter 18: Bridging the Gap to Islam
By Raouf Boulos

1. David Barrett, *Religion Today Online,* 21 January 1997.

2. Fareed H. Numan and the American Muslim Community, *AMC Online,* "The Muslim Population in the United States," December 1992.

3. Ibid., 2.

4. Walter Martin, *The Kingdom of the Cults* (Minneapolis: Bethany House, 1985), 364.

5. Abdul H. Siddiqui, *The Life of Muhammad* (Des Plaines, Ill.: Library of Islam, 1991), 41.

6. Muhammad H. Hayakal, *Life of Muhammad* (Indianapolis, Ind.: North American Trust, 1976), 55, 61.

7. Ibid., 62–63.

8. Ibid., 72.

9. William J. Saal, *Reaching Muslims for Christ* (Chicago: Moody, 1993), 30.

10. Ibid., 27–29.

11. Ibid., 30.

12. Ibid., 31.

13. Norman L. Geisler, *Answering Islam* (Grand Rapids: Baker, 1993), 293–94.

14. Ibid., 173–74.

15. Bruce H. Wilkinson, Walk Thru the Old Testament Seminar (Atlanta: WTBM, 1994).

Chapter 19: Missions in Reverse
By Sunday Bwanhot

1. Ralph D. Winter, "Editorial Comment on Standard Missions," *Mission Frontiers* 20, no. 3–4 (March–April 1998): 19.

2. EMS, "Challenges," *EMS Prayer and News Letter,* no. 1 (1996): 1.

3. SIM, " Nigerian Couple Serving as Missionaries to Chicago," *SIM Now,* no. 73 (1995): 3.

4. Winters, "Editorial Comment on Standard Missions," 19.

5. Wolfgang Eberhard Lowe, *The First American Foreign Missionaries: "The Students"* 1810–1820 (Ph.D. diss., Brown University), 74.

6. Navigators, "Mission Outposts Meet Challenges of Changing America," *One to One,* no. 24 (Spring 1998): 2.

7. EMS, *Introducing the Bwanhots* (Brochure, Jos, Nigeria).

8. Patrick Johnstone, *Operation World* (Grand Rapids: Zondervan, 1993), 563.

9. Ibid.

10. Terry Muck, *Alien Gods on American Turf* (Wheaton, Ill.: Victor, 1990), 14.

11. Kenneth B. Mulholland, "Partnering in an Era of Change" (paper presented at IFMA conference, 1995), 2.

12. Cited in ibid.

13. Johnstone, *Operation World,* 566.

14. SIM, *Reaching the World at Our Doorstep* (Brochure, Charlotte, N.C.).

15. Philip Barker, "The African in Chicagoland" (M.A. class paper, Moody), 30.

16. Ibid., 29.

17. Mulholland, "Partnering in an Era of Change," 4–5.

18. Ibid., 5.

19. Steve Hawthorne, "Laying a Firm Foundation for Mission in the Next Millennium," *Mission Frontiers* 20, no. 3–4 (March–April 1998): 11.

20. Ibid., 11.

21. "Mobilizing a Sleeping Giant," *Mission Frontiers* 18, no. 11–12 (Nov.–Dec. 1996): 29.

22. Glenn Schwartz, "It's Time to Get Serious about the Cycle of Dependency in Africa," *Mission Frontiers* 19, no. 1–2 (Jan.–Feb. 1997): 8.

Chapter 20: Restoring Dignity to the Homeless
By Arloa Sutter

1. Roger S. Greenway and Timothy M. Monsma, *Cities: Missions' New Frontier* (Grand Rapids: Baker, 1994), 183.

2. Chicago Coalition for the Homeless.

3. Greenway and Monsma, *Cities,* 183.

4. Laura Waxman and Sharon Hinderliter. "A Status Report on Hunger and Homelessness in America's Cities: 1996." U.S. Conference of Mayors, 1620 Eye St. NW, Suite 400, Washington, DC, 20006-4005.

5. Edward Lazare, "In Short Supply: The Growing Affordable Housing Gap," 1995. Center on Budget and Policy Priorities, 777 N. Capitol St., NE, Suite 705, Washington, DC 20002-4230.

6. Community Media Workshop lists this information, which comes from a 1995 study conducted by Northern Illinois University. A recent "Job Gap" study by the Chicago Urban League and the University of Wisconsin-Milwaukee found that 290,000 unemployed low-skill workers and welfare recipients compete for 69,000 entry-level job openings statewide, a four-to-one ratio. The Chicago gap is wider, with six unemployed per available job.

7. Marvin N. Olasky, message at College Church, Wheaton, 1996.

Chapter 21: An Old Lighthouse for a New World
By Phil Kwiatkowski

1. James R. Adair, *A New Look at the Old Lighthouse* (Chicago: PGM, 1996), 105.

2. Michael R. Sosin, Paul Colson, and Susan Grossman, *Homelessness in Chicago* (Chicago: Univ. of Chicago, 1988), 95.

3. Adair, *A New Look,* 108.

4. Pacific Garden Mission Annual Statistics, 1996.

5. Roger Greenway, "City Rescue Missions: Old Lighthouses Still Needed," *Urban Mission* (June 1998): 49.

6. Adair, *A New Look,* 24.

7. Ibid.

8. Greenway, "City Rescue Missions," 48.

9. Ibid., 53–54.

Chapter 22: Who Is My Neighbor?
By Chad Erlenborn

1. U.S. Committee for Refugees, *World Refugee Survey 1998,* Immigration Refugee Service of America, 1998.

2. Exodus World Service, *Journey to Freedom* (P.O. Box 7000, West Chicago, IL 60186).

3. Ibid.

4. Ibid.

5. InterAction: American Council for Voluntary International Action, *U.S. Refugee Admissions Program for Fiscal Year 1999: Recommendations of the Committee on Migration and Refugee Affairs,* April 1998 (1717 Massachusetts Avenue, Suite 801, Washington, D.C. 20036).

6. Jewish Federation of Metropolis Chicago, *Illinois Refugee Social Service Consortiume* (1 South Franklin, Chicago, Illinois).

7. Exodus World Service, *Seven Key Principles Describe God's Abiding Concern for Refugees* (P.O. Box 7000, West Chicago, IL 60185-7000).

8. World Relief, *U.S. Ministries . . . A Reason for Hope* (World Relief U.S. Ministries Headquarters, 201 Route 9W North, Congers, New York 10920).

9. Linda Keys, *Chicago, A World Relief City Briefing,* World Relief International Office, May 1997, 19.

10. Ibid.

11. Joseph Aldrich, *Lifestyle Evangelism: Crossing Traditional Boundaries to Reach the Unbelieving World* (Portland, Oreg.: Multnomah, 1981), 67.

12. Mark McCloskey, *Tell It Often . . . Tell It Well* (San Bernardino, Calif.: Here's Life, 1986), 53.

Chapter 23: Reaching the Homosexual Community
By Brad Grammer

1. Dr. Judith A. Reisman and Edward W. Eichel, *Kinsey, Sex and Fraud,* eds. Dr. J. Gordon Muir and Dr. John H. Court (Lafayette, La.: Huntington House, 1990), 17–55.

2. Marlin Maddoux and Christopher Corbett, *Answers to the Gay Deception* (Dallas: International Christian Media, 1994), 15–16.

3. Joe Dallas, "Responding to Pro-Gay Theology," *The Journal of Human Sexuality,* exec. ed. George A. Rekers (Carollton, Tex.: Lewis and Stanley, 1996), 79.

4. A 1990–91 British survey; a Canadian survey; a 1987 Norwegian survey; and a 1989 Danish survey (Maddoux and Corbett, *Answers*), 16.

5. Phone conversation with the Higleys of L.I.F.E., Inc., 20 July 1998.

6. Lesbian activist with ACT-UP, interviewed in "Gay Rights-Special Rights" video (quoted by Joe Dallas, "Responding to Pro-Gay Theology," *Journal of Human Sexuality,* 79).

7. Bob Davies and Lori Rentzel, *Coming Out of Homosexuality* (Downers Grove, Ill.: InterVarsity, 1993), 24.

8. Ibid., 24–25.

9. Cited in Joe Dallas, *Desires in Conflict* (Eugene, Oreg.: Harvest House, 1991), 116.

10. Cited in Davies and Rentzel, *Coming Out,* 24.

11. Dallas, *Desires,* 250–51.

12. Ibid., 260.

13. Anita Worthen and Bob Davies, *Someone I Love Is Gay* (Downers Grove, Ill.: InterVarsity, 1996), 161–62.

Chapter 24: Ministering in the Projects
By David C. Brown and Dana Thomas

1. The Endowment for Community Leadership Ten Year Plan.

2. Devereux Bowly, *The Poorhouse* (Carbondale, Ill.: Southern Illinois Univ., 1978), 12.

3. The Endowment for Community Leadership Ten Year Plan.

4. Bowly, *The Poorhouse,* 18.

5. "The Road to Hell," *Chicago Tribune Magazine,* 31 March 1985.

6. Chicago Housing Authority Statistics.

7. Chicago Housing Authority Fact Sheet, 1996.

8. Ibid.

9. Ibid.

10. Arnold R. Hirsch, *Making the Second Ghetto* (New York: Cambridge Univ., 1983).

11. Ibid.

12. Ibid.

13. Charles W. Colson, *Life Sentence* (Lincoln, Va.: Chosen, 1979), 149.

14. Donald S. Whitney, *Spiritual Disciplines for the Christian Life* (Colorado Springs: NavPress, 1994), 35.

Chapter 25: Reaching the Next Generation for Christ
By William Paul Dillon

1. Children's Defense Fund, 25 East E Street, Washington DC 20001, January 1999.

2. Child Evangelism Fellowship, P.O. Box 348, Warrenton MO 63383.

3. 1995 ACT scores, ACT research department.

4. Chicago Public Schools, 1995–96 school year.

5. *Chicago Tribune*.

6. U.S. Bureau of the Census, 1990.

7. Ibid.

8. Sonlife Ministries, 526 N. Main, Elburn, IL 60119.

Chapter 26: Children of Promise
By Lonni Kehrein

1. Chicago Board of Education 1997 Report Card.

2. Howard Lee, "Poverty: Fighting the Enemy Within," *Chicago Sun-Times,* Letters, 1 October 1996, 22.

3. Andrew Billingsley, *Climbing Jacob's Ladder: The Enduring Legacy of African-American Families* (New York: Simon & Schuster, 1992), 183.

4. Joseph Stoutzenberger, *The Christian Call to Justice and Peace* (Winona, Minn.: Saint Mary's, 1987), 74.

5. Marva Collins, *"Ordinary" Children, Extraordinary Teachers* (Norfolk, Va.: Hampton Roads, 1992), 43.

6. "The Reconciler," *Circle Urban Ministries Newsletter,* Winter 1998.

7. Collins, *"Ordinary" Children,* 72.

8. *Circle-Rock Preparatory School Parent-Student Handbook,* 1998, 7.

9. Claude M. Steele, "Race and the Schooling of Black Americans," *The Atlantic Monthly,* April 1992, 68–76.

10. Thomas E. Linton and Michael Forster, "Powerful Environments for Underclass Youth," *The Education Digest,* March 1990, 27–31.

11. Myrna Shure, "I Can Problem Solve": An Interpersonal Cognitive Problem Solving Program. Research Press, 1992.

12. Tim Heaton, "Finding God's Truth in the Secular Curriculum," *Christian School Education* 1, issue 3 (1997–98): 8, used by permission of ACSI, Colorado Springs, CO (1999).

13. Ibid.

14. Ed Marciniak, "Chicago's Private Elementary and Secondary Schools—Their Role in Neighborhood Revitalization," *A Report from the Institute of Urban Life* (Loyola Univ. Chicago, 1998), 1.

15. Ibid., 8.

Chapter 27: Reaching Youth Involved in Gangs
By Tom Locke

1. Commander Donald Hilbring, Chicago Police Department Gang Investigation Section says, "125 street gangs [operate] in [the] Chicagoland area. . . . There are between 30,000–50,000 hardcore gang members in the city and overall 100,000 gang members which include both hardcore and wanna-bees or marginal members." Quoted in Chicago Crime Commission Web article "Gangs, Public Enemy Number One": http://oicj.acsp.uic.edu/spearmint/public/pubs/cjfarrago/cccgangs.cfm.

2. Chicago Police Department reports.

3. Ibid.

4. Farai Chideya, *Don't Believe the Hype: Fighting Cultural Misinformation About African-Americans* (New York: Plume Penguin, 1995), 210–11.

5. Chicago Police Department reports.

6. In heavily gang-populated communities, youth are sometimes assumed to be members of the gangs in their communities, which leads to their being beaten up. Actually joining the neighborhood gang gives the opportunity for revenge.

7. Practical Christian Ministry is a program of the Moody Bible Institute, which gives students the opportunity to do hands-on ministry while enrolled at Moody. The program is required of all undergraduate students.

8. The Rev. Harvey Carey, youth pastor, Salem Baptist Church of Chicago, interview by the author.

9. "Drying up." The law of the City of Chicago states that communities may choose to vote themselves "dry"—meaning no liquor can be sold in that community. Salem Baptist Church spearheaded a drive to get this issue on the ballot and got it passed. In November of 1998 Roseland became a dry community, thus reducing the number of negative hangouts and improving the community's property values.

10. Carey interview.

11. Ibid.

Chapter 28: Kids . . . with Kids
By Connie Mead

1. Although New Moms serves only this one community, I have personally networked with other ministry leaders. The challenges that our moms face are common to many of the poor communities of Chicago and other urban areas.

2. New Moms' intake data.

3. National Center for Disease Control.

4. Illinois Department of Public Health.

5. Ibid.

Chapter 29: The Home as a Ministry Base
By Russ Knight

1. Joy G. Dryfoos, *Adolescents at Risk: Prevalence and Prevention* (New York: Oxford Univ., 1990), 18–19.

2. National Center for Children in Poverty, *Five Million Children: A Statistical Profile of Our Poorest Young Citizens* (New York: National Center for Children in Poverty, 1990), 29.

3. Rebecca A. Maynard, ed. *Kids Having Kids: Economic Cost and Social Consequences of Teen Pregnancy* (Washington, D.C.: Urban Institute, 1997), 1–2.

4. Dryfoos, *Adolescents at Risk,* 26, 41.

5. Maynard, *Kids Having Kids,* 59.

6. Robert M. Hauser, Brett V. Brown, and William R. Prosser, eds. *Indicators of Children's Well-Being* (New York: Russell Sage, 1997), 237.

7. The 1990 Census: Community Area #46 profile, *Demographics and Housing Characteristics of Chicago and Community Areas.* Chicago, Ill., 1994, 20–45.

8. Juvenile Justice Bulletin, Oct. 1997.

9. PTA: *How to Get the Best Education for Your Child,* 1989.

10. Ibid.

11. Hauser, et al., *Indicators of Children's Well-Being,* 153.

INDEX

Notes are designated by *n*. Where confusion could occur, notes are further defined with a chapter number (*ch.*)

SINCE 1894, Moody Publishers has been dedicated to equip and motivate people to advance the cause of Christ by publishing evangelical Christian literature and other media for all ages, around the world. Because we are a ministry of the Moody Bible Institute of Chicago, a portion of the proceeds from the sale of this book go to train the next generation of Christian leaders.

If we may serve you in any way in your spiritual journey toward understanding Christ and the Christian life, please contact us at www.moodypublishers.com.

"All Scripture is God-breathed and is useful for teaching, rebuking, correcting and training in righteousness, so that the man of God may be thoroughly equipped for every good work."
—*2 TIMOTHY 3:16, 17*

MOODY
PUBLISHERS
THE NAME YOU CAN TRUST®